POLITICAL THOUGHT IN AMERICA

CONVERSATIONS AND DEBATES

Second Edition

Philip Abbott
Wayne State University

WAVELAND
PRESS, INC.

Prospect Heights, Illinois

For information about this book, write or call:
    Waveland Press, Inc.
    P.O. Box 400
    Prospect Heights, Illinois 60070
    (847) 634-0081

To   Megan E. Abbott
          . . . like some green laurel
                      —W. B. Yeats

        Joshua D. Abbott
          Hosanna the Home Run!
                      —Gregory Corso

Contents

Preface to the Second Edition

In this second edition of *Political Thought in America*, I have retained the format of presenting American political thought through the examination of nine crises. When I wrote the first edition, however, the Cold War was just ending. This new edition gives more attention to the parameters of this extended crisis. Since the Depression, America has never existed without the Cold War as the central feature of its political thought, both in terms of international and domestic issues. On these terms, the collection of political thinkers that helped create what is often called the "Reagan revolution" is especially significant. These men and women, including Reagan himself, self-consciously attempted to not only rethink the Cold War abroad but also to re-evaluate the consensus on economic policy that had been forged by Franklin D. Roosevelt. Chapter 9 now includes a discussion of this "revolution" with special emphasis on the conversations and debates that Ronald Reagan and others led regarding Roosevelt and New Deal liberalism.

In the first edition, *Political Thought in America* ended with discrimination as a topic. Needless to say, this crisis has not been resolved. However, there have been significant attempts to reassess the strategy and goals of the civil rights and feminist movements. In this second edition, I review recent feminist and African-American political thought of writers who continue to struggle with the alternatives of assimilation and separatism.

Finally, scholarship which focuses on these crises has expanded considerably. Thus each bibliographic essay contains new material.

I am delighted to receive comments from both instructors and students. Please contact me via mail or e-mail with suggestions or queries.

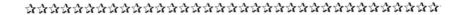

Preface

In *John Brown's Body* Stephen Vincent Benét offered this admonishment to those who would write about this nation:

American Muse, whose strong and diverse heart
So many men have tried to understand
But only made it smaller with their art,
Because you are as various as your land.

I have taken Benét's warning seriously. Rather than present any particular approach to American thought, I have attempted to place theorizing in the context of the conversations and debates of men and women who have struggled to extricate themselves and the nation from crisis. Frequently these American political theorists, too, have failed to grasp the complexity and greatness of the nation as they have engaged in those difficult tasks. There have been moments in these crises, however, when the American muse has been captured and political understanding has been enlarged. I have placed special emphasis upon those moments and those writers who have conveyed clarity and vision to the American political experience. This identification itself constitutes a conversation and a debate in which I hope the readers of this volume will engage.

I benefited greatly from the counsel of Leo Wiegman, a truly ideal editor. Acknowledgment is also due to William D. Richardson of Georgia State University and Richard C. Sinopoli of the University of California at Davis, who offered both spirited advice and thoughtful questions. Conversations with my wife, Patricia, were especially valuable since it is her generosity and patience which made this project possible.

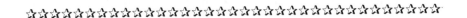

Chronological Listing of Major Political Speeches and Writing 1630–1989

The following is a chronologically arranged listing of major works in American political thought discussed in this book. It is certainly not a complete list, and it does not include theorists, such as John Locke and Alexis de Tocqueville, on whom Americans have heavily relied. The listing does include some writings of persons such as Harriet Beecher Stowe and Horatio Alger, who are not conventionally defined as political theorists but whose works function as exemplars of American political culture. The chronology is designed to illustrate the generational efforts of Americans to confront crises in our society and to illustrate how Americans have spoken to one another, often in urgent terms, through speeches, reports, sermons, treatises, trial testimony, novels, and autobiography. (An asterisk indicates a collaborative effort.)

John Winthrop (1588–1649)	"A Modell of Christian Charity" (1630)
Anne Hutchinson (1591–1643)	"Trial Testimony" (1637)
Roger Williams (1603–1683)	"The Bloody Tenet of Persecution for Cause of Conscience" (1644)
William Penn (1644–1718)	"Frame of Government of Pennsylvania" (1652)
Benjamin Franklin (1706–1790)	*Autobiography* (1791)
Peter Oliver (1713–1791)	*The Origin and Progress of the American Revolution* (1781)

Martin Luther King, Jr. (1929–1968) "Letter from Birmingham Jail" (1963)
"I Have a Dream Speech" (1963)

Daniel Bell (1939–) *The End of Ideology* (1960)
The Cultural Contradictions of Capitalism (1976)

Tom Hayden (1939–) *"The Port Huron Statement" (1962)

Shulamith Firestone (1945–) *The Dialectic of Sex* (1970)

Susan Faludi (1959–) *Backlash* (1991)

Derrick Bell (1930–) "The Space Traders" (1990)
"The Afrolantica Awakening" (1992)

Christopher Layne (1949–) "The Real Conservative Agenda"
(1986)

Francis Fukuyama (1952–) "The End of History?" (1989)

Introduction

THREE AMERICAN "LANGUAGES"

The central premise of this book is that the history of American political thought can be understood as a series of conversations and debates. Every American is a participant in this process. Every American can quote portions of the Declaration of Independence and the Constitution and, in varying degrees, apply the precepts of both documents to a problem in current public policy. In nearly every contemporary debate, whether it be over abortion, the causes of unemployment, or the nature and remedies for racial discrimination, arguments are anchored in these or other major expressions of American political thought.

What every American might not realize is that these debates are based upon the resolutions of fierce and often disorderly controversies of previous generations. The Declaration of Independence, for example, represents the culmination of many potentially discordant themes in early American political thought. The Constitution as well represents a second attempt to provide a grounding for American political practice. Thus the current American consensus can be seen as the result of a series of crises that have been thus far successfully resolved—that is, if one takes the preservation of an evolving national identity as a goal.

But the history of American political thought as a series of debates and crises overcome only begins to convey the character of our national experience. For success or failure, resolution or indeterminacy are evaluations derived in part from the language of political discourse that is employed. From one perspective, the Constitution of 1787 is a victory, from another perspective a defeat. To cite another instance, the political accommodations Americans made to the emergence of an industrial society might be regarded as a national success; from another perspective they might be regarded as a process of subjugation.

1

Biblical Thought

There have been three major "languages" or traditions of discourse that Americans have employed to interpret the national experience. One, which has its origins in the first settlements in the New World, comprehends America as *part of a divine experiment*. The Judeo-Christian tradition in American political thought explains political events in terms of an overarching plan, partly discernible by humans, which projects the nation at any point in time on a discernible path toward fulfillment or corruption. Most participants in this language acknowledge that America as a nation continually faces a choice. Will it continue to follow the path of righteousness and receive the favor of God, or will it reject biblical injunction and follow the path of so many nations in the course of human history—a path which enjoys a period of ascendance followed by decline?

The definition in the Judeo-Christian language of the nature of success and failure as a divinely appointed nation varies. From the conceptions of the early Puritans to the religious communities of our day, it includes a moral assessment of current political practice and attempts to connect personal experience to divine imperatives. The Judeo-Christian tradition in America has itself undergone its own series of crises. Various attempts to form a "city upon a hill," a community organized according to Christian precepts, have failed or required drastic reformation. But the scrutiny of public policy by those committed to a Judeo-Christian perspective has informed American debate over independence, slavery, industrialization, the Cold War, and discrimination.

Republicanism

A second language in American political thought is *republicanism*. Republican political thought has existed as an interpretation of politics since the origin of city-states in ancient Greece. Although it contains numerous versions, republicanism is best defined as a commitment to the principle that there is a *res publica* (public thing) that can only be legitimately interpreted by citizens at large. Republicans are distrustful of definitions of the public good as defined exclusively by monarchies or other elites, and are devoted to the project of developing political structures based upon the common participation of citizens at large. But republicans do not accept any form of political activity as legitimate. The central feature of their model is that political activity must be carried on in the spirit of *republican virtue*. Citizens must be willing, often heroically, to undertake political action on the basis of a commitment to the common good. Nations in which political activity is based upon class or individual self-interest are doomed to degenerate to tyranny. Republican political thought was the dominant ideology of the American Revolution. Many Americans, however, came to the conclusion that the tradition of republicanism was hopelessly utopian and needed major revision. The Constitution itself is a document that in fundamental ways represents an attempt to recognize the fact that virtue does not govern political activity. Despite this departure, the language of republicanism continues to be part of American political thought. It forms a significant part of the debate over slavery and industrialization. Whenever an American raises the question that current political practice must be evaluated not by self-interested compromise but by the patriotic reflections of committed citizens, he is speaking the language of republicanism.

Liberalism

The third major language of American political thought is *liberalism*. The fundamental premises of this tradition are sometimes difficult for students to understand since liberalism is also used as a partisan symbol of contemporary discourse. But the "L-word" is only one recent manifestation of American political ideology, and represents a more inclusive language than the latest political debate. In more general terms, a liberal perspective, at least as it has been articulated in the American context, takes the individual as the basic unit of politics and sees his development as the central criterion for the success or failure of any political system.

The dominant speaker of this liberal language is John Locke (1632–1704). Indeed, many scholars regard this English philosopher as the single most important figure in the history of American political thought. Louis Hartz, for example, contends that very few Americans have escaped completely what he calls the "tyranny" of Locke's ideas. In his *Two Treatises on Government* Locke challenged the politically dominant notion that authority was absolute, indivisible, and derived from patriarchal rule ordained by God and extending from Adam to the present. Locke insisted that authority was limited and divisible, arguing that others had failed to establish the differences among "the ruler of a commonwealth, a father of a family, and a captain of a galley." While Locke reserved a place for the divine in politics (he contended that all political disputes ultimately rested upon an "appeal to Heaven," and that parental authority was derived from an obligation imposed by God to "preserve, nourish and educate" children), he offered a justification of authority that rested primarily upon individual consent. He insisted that the nature of political authority could only be understood by positing a condition in which individuals find themselves without government. In a "state of nature"—which Locke defined as a "state of perfect freedom" in which individuals can "order their actions, and dispose of their possessions, and persons as they think fit . . . without depending upon the will of any other man"—there arise certain "inconveniences." Locke repeatedly contended that the state of nature was not a "state of war." Nevertheless, he noted that property is insecure in the state of nature, and that individuals who must punish those who violate others' rights must do so on an ad hoc and hence inefficient basis. (Locke also suggested that the absence of an "indifferent judge" in the state of nature leads to only a rough system of justice since individuals are often driven by revenge.) Thus governments are created by the individual consent of human beings to protect their natural rights of "life, liberty and property." Locke was careful to limit the scope and administration of government to the defense of these rights, arguing that "wherever law ends, tyranny begins."

Historically, liberals have defined the individual very differently. Indeed, in Locke's own writings it is sometimes unclear as to whether personhood is connected with the ownership of property (the world was made for the use of the "industrious and rational"), the capacity to reason, or a biblical injunction. Thus a major aspect of American political thought, as debate and conversation, has centered upon what constitutes the true nature of a person. Is an individual best understood (for better or worse) as one who maximizes his or her self-interest? Or is an individual an evolving entity that is capable of new heights of moral and creative expression? In liberal political thought the central problem rests upon the extent to which political structures advance (or at least do not inhibit) individual pursuits, and how political institutions can accommodate different conceptions of individualism.

From the perspective of a liberal language, American political thought can be seen as a series of debates that focus upon what appropriate political institutions and practices foster particular conceptions of individualism under new conditions. The Constitution can be supported, for example, as a framework under which people with very different individual perspectives can function. On the other hand, are some conceptions of individualism too narrowly conceived, or is it necessary to pass laws requiring some individuals to constrict their life plans in order to advance the individualism of others? These are questions which liberals have faced as they have attempted to define what it means to be an individual in the face of racial discrimination or economic change.

CONSERVATISM AND RADICALISM

These three languages—biblical thought, republicanism, and liberalism—do not exhaust the parameters of American political theory. At least two other languages have been spoken. One is the language of *conservatism*, the other the language of *radicalism*. The existence of these two traditions should not presuppose that the three primary traditions do not contain either conservative or radical elements. American conservatism has attempted to employ certain features of the basic languages of the American political tradition. But in its essence it has questioned the central tenets of a free society, however interpreted. Are men and women free to pursue their own objectives independent of social and political hierarchy? Is there not some underlying order in human relationships that cannot be challenged without risking anarchy? Those who dissented from the Revolution raised this question as did the southern critics on the eve of the Civil War.

The language of conservatism has often merged with the major traditions of American political discourse, but it has also set out on its own, often in what it regarded as splendid isolation, to critique the current consensus. Similarly, the Left has employed terms of political discourse that have often puzzled or even angered Americans. In attempting to translate the European categories of political thought to the American experience, radicals have sometimes highlighted inconsistencies in the biblical, republican, and liberal traditions that were incomprehensible to Americans. More often, however, radical political theorists have failed to appreciate the uniquely American character of political debate and thus have been forced to converse only with themselves. When radicals have found a national audience in a crisis, such as during the Great Depression, they have found that they must translate their own political theory into a national idiom.

If one then attempts to understand American political thought in terms of a series of debates and conversations, it is a troubling but important fact that these debates have been undertaken by people who have spoken different languages. Most persons realize how difficult is argumentation in itself. But imagine how problematic debate is when participants speak in different languages. For example, in a recent poll Americans preferred freedom over equality by a 72 to 20 percent margin. But what does freedom mean for those Americans who responded to the question? Is it the freedom of the biblically inclined American who measures time in millennial terms and defines liberty as freedom from sin? Or is it the freedom of the American committed to republican principles who explains liberty as devotion to the common good? Or is it the freedom of the liberal American who wishes to be left alone to make money or define himself or herself? These three basic interpretations leave aside those of the conservatives and radicals who define liberty even more differently.

COMMON MOORINGS

These cacophonous strains in American political thought should not obscure a basic and often unintentional consensus in the three basic languages. Each of these languages partakes of a common idiom and, as such, can be seen as dialects of the same language. Each sees America as a unique society in the course of world history as a chosen people or as the repository of republican hopes or an American Dream of material success or spiritual fulfillment. *American exceptionalism* as a political doctrine that asserts that America is a unique phenomenon in world history is rarely challenged in American political thought, except by some conservative and radical dissidents. Moreover, the economic system that gives meaning to the various conceptions of freedom is invariably one which might be called *capitalistic*. The belief that the struggle for existence is best undertaken individually is a fundamental tenet of American political culture. The biblical heritage in America is predominantly a Protestant one. While the connection between economic success and religious piety is a complicated historical phenomenon, the emphasis on personal salvation in a religious sense and on economic success has had a close psychological if not a logical connection. For republicans, a free-enterprise system is the exemplary manifestation of the independent citizen. How else can a person freely criticize the state except from a position of economic independence? The liberal commitment to free enterprise has been vulnerable to some critiques from the Left. Nevertheless, in the liberal ethos the answer to the question of what economic system best exemplifies personal autonomy has been almost invariably capitalism. Finally, the common philosophical thread that unites each of the three languages of American political thought is *individualism*. In the biblical tradition, individualism is interpreted in terms of salvation and grace; in the republican tradition in terms of the independent citizen; and in the liberal tradition in terms of a free-thinking person.

These three political traditions or languages of discourse have not been static. Nor should American political thought be conceived abstractly as an ongoing debating society. Voices are not equally heard and participants do not politely wait their turn to speak. Americans have been historically confronted by a series of crises that have threatened to make the interpretation of political life by one or more of these languages obsolete. The stakes can be high during these periods of crisis. Individual careers are placed in jeopardy, lives and livelihoods are threatened, and the future of the nation itself is in doubt. Many of these national emergencies are those which any political system eventually faces: revolution, founding, economic collapse, and civil war. Others reflect America's own particular history, such as the nation's origins in invented communities. In all cases the resolution of these crises can only be understood in terms of attempts by women and men to apply their understanding of the nature of politics, derived from their own experiences in their own lives and through the languages in which they have been accustomed to speak, to current problems.

AMERICAN CRISES

What are the major crises in American political thought? The newness of America still remains a central tenet of our political culture, although the exaltation of the origins of America as a nation has partially hidden the debates that reflected this early crisis. For the origins of America as nation lie in the belief that it is possible to "invent" new communities based upon common acceptance of a new way of life. The colonial political experience is complicated by the fact that there existed not a single crisis but multiple crises derived from the nature and purpose of settlements in the British Empire during the seventeenth century. In New England the idea of a homogeneous religious community, a city on a hill, came under challenge. In Pennsylvania the dominant religious community was faced with the question of how it could continue to govern in a pluralistic society and still remain true to its commitments. Virginians were confronted with, and persistently refused to recognize, the contradiction between their goals as a colony of country squires and the realities of slavery and tobacco economics. The debates among Roger Williams, Anne Hutchinson, John Winthrop, and John Cotton in New England and the Quaker oligarchy and its challengers in Pennsylvania were debates over the soul of the future of these newly invented communities. In Virginia debate took the form of a short-lived rebellion.

The resolution of these various colonial crises was barely complete when the question of independence emerged. In fact, one could argue that the struggle for independence represented an extension of the individual colonial crises. In any case the most intriguing aspect of the American Revolution as a crisis is that in the quest for a new society independent of British rule, America did not undergo the same sort of revolutionary process that most other nations have traversed. Most violent changes in political authority seem to initiate a process of increasing fragmentation and violence, followed by an extreme centralization of power and often a reign of terror. When a society appears to become exhausted from numerous attempts to create a new order, another form of dictatorship, often called by political scientists and historians a *Thermidor* (after the month in which Maximilien Robespierre was overthrown in the French Revolution), seems to arise. The Thermidorian revolutionary stage is a particularly tragic one since ideals of liberation are abandoned in favor of establishing order. While the generalization is disputable, there was no reign of terror or Thermidor in the American Revolution. One reason America escaped this tragedy may have been the application and reformulation of a particular kind of political thought by American revolutionaries. *Republicanism*, as redefined in the American context, served successfully as a cohesive anticolo-

nial ideology as well as a check upon the temptations to politically central-
ize and systematically use terror to subdue opponents of the Revolution.

Every revolution must effectively lead to the creation of a new order
to replace the old. Despite the ingenuity of American republicans, the
founding of a new regime was not a simple task. American revolutionaries,
while they escaped the carnage that characterized the English, French, and
Russian revolutionary efforts, could not establish a founding on their first
try. The period between the late 1770s and 1780s was a crisis manifested in
two foundings—the Articles of Confederation and the Constitution. Paralleling this national instability were numerous state crises in which various
state constitutions were formed and re-formed in attempts to found durable
institutions. The debates between supporters and critics of the first founding and supporters and critics of the second were framed primarily in the
language of republicanism. But now the debate centered upon different and
competing tenets of republican thought. Republicanism, which had been a
language of national solidarity, was now a language of contention and discord. The political theorists of the second founding, writing under the collective name of "Publius," did not totally abandon republicanism, but in
attempting to provide "republican remedies for republican defects," they
introduced a new kind of discourse, one which contained elements of liberalism. Thus Publius argued in support of the Constitution that no political
system could rely upon enlightened statesmen or patriotic motives to guide
the country and remain stable. Recognition of the power of individual
desire must be a central part of the system. Was the Constitution, the second
founding, the outcome of a theoretical refinement of republicanism or its
practical abandonment, a Thermidor (albeit a mild one)? This question is
still part of our national debate.

No sooner had the government of the second founding been set in
place than another crisis developed. The supporters of the Constitution had
insisted that by recognizing the contentious nature of human beings in
their new framework, political conflict could be contained and routinized.
But "factions" emerged in the new republic. Political issues were defined
and debated along the lines that had long existed in Great Britain. What in
essence was a "court party" led by Alexander Hamilton struggled with a
"country party" led by James Madison and Thomas Jefferson. The conflict
between these two factions reached such an intensity in Washington's second term that two opposing political parties, the Federalists and the Republicans, were formed to contest elections and win control of national and
state governments. Both parties regarded a victory by the other as paramount to the end of a free society. Republicans depicted Federalists as
"monocrats" who had designs to introduce aristocracy and monarchy to
America. Federalists regarded Republicans as part of an international conspiracy to extend the French Revolution to America and inaugurate a reign

of terror here. The conflict between these two parties led to the victory by Republicans, often called the *revolution of 1800*. Following a period of relative decline in factional competition, however, a new set of forces emerged. Led by Andrew Jackson, the Democratic party charged that the nation was again slipping into the grip of aristocracy and pledged itself to policies of national reform in the name of Jefferson. Democrats were challenged by the Whigs, who claimed that the Jacksonians had no idea of America as a single nation and were incapable of governing.

The conflicts of these two-party systems eventually produced a consensus that resolved the crisis over the existence of factions: organized opposition through party competition was an essential part of the preservation of a republic. In the course of this long crisis over the legitimacy of an organized opposition, the four political parties of the early period of the republic (the Federalists, Republicans, Democrats, and Whigs) also managed to present for debate four identifiable philosophies of government that were mixtures of the three languages of American political theory.

However routinized and relatively peaceful political debate became by the middle of the nineteenth century, political parties and their leaders could not contain and resolve one moral and political problem: the continued existence of slavery. Civil war, one of the most calamitous events that can befall a nation, was America's next crisis. The severe disintegration of consensus in the 1850s is reflected in two different responses to the slavery question. Abolitionists contended that the continued existence of the institution constituted a moral crisis for all Americans and argued over morally acceptable courses of political action. Southern political theorists such as George Fitzhugh searched through the history of Western political thought for defenses of slavery. In this atmosphere of division, Abraham Lincoln brilliantly fashioned a political theory combining elements of the biblical language that critics of slavery spoke with elements from the republican tradition. Lincoln's resolution, however, took on more problematic proportions once the war was won by the North. In the Reconstruction Era, issues of states' rights and the legitimate scope of government were again raised as Americans addressed the question of how far southern society should be changed in order to protect the rights of former slaves.

The industrialization of America created another crisis which posed complex challenges to American political thought. On the one hand, great concentrations of wealth and power were inconsistent with the tenets of both republicanism and liberalism. On the other hand, the promise of abundance had been part of the American ethos since the days of Benjamin Franklin, and Locke had argued that "different degrees of industry were apt to give men possessions in different forms." Social Darwinism, an elaborate ideology that claimed to address economic and political problems on a scientific basis, brought these contradictions in balance by redefining both republicanism and liberalism. Three significant alternate interpretations of industrialization attempted to compete with the new Darwinist language. Populism, probably America's only indigenous radicalism, presented an image of an agrarian republic imperiled by rapacious industrial "robber barons." Progressivism attempted to offer another version of scientific discourse by defining political and economic problems as capable of resolution through reform by professionals. Socialism offered its own remedies to industrialization based partly upon models derived from European theory and partly upon an interpretation of Judeo-Christian and republican traditions.

These ideologies of industrial protest produced some amelioration in the conditions of a new economic order. But in 1930 the American political system was descending toward economic collapse. Herbert Hoover produced what for many Americans was an impressive defense of liberalism under modern conditions. But the Depression shattered his synthesis and opened up a debate over the nature of the American economy, one in which the core political beliefs of the nation were questioned. For many American political theorists in the Depression not only was capitalism a failure but individualism was bankrupt as well. It was in this context of national crisis that Franklin D. Roosevelt, borrowing innovatively from Jeffersonian political theory, fashioned a "new social contract" for liberalism. But the New Deal synthesis was never fully accepted by all Americans. Roosevelt was forced to debate his reformulation with writers from both the Left and the Right.

America's involvement in world affairs had historically been intense but sporadic until the post-World War II period. Even before Allied victory was complete, a new war, the *cold war*, began. The Cold War significantly altered American society in that the republic was now committed to international intervention and a wartime economy without a foreseeable conclusion. Various American political theorists have attempted to justify this commitment and show how it was an unavoidable one. Others have argued that participation in the Cold War has led to the sacrifice of central American values.

The final crisis discussed in this book involves what has been called the *second reconstruction*—the crisis over the dismantlement of racial segregation and challenges to gender discrimination. In an important sense, black and feminist protest in the 1960s and 1970s represents the continuation of the struggles of previous generations of thinkers to engage in a debate over the justice of race- and gender-based limitations on equality of opportunity and the appropriate means for overcoming such practices. These protest theorists face a number of difficult problems in confronting discrimination, for they must make crucial decisions over what language to frame their challenge in. Martin Luther King, Jr., for example, left a legacy which based protest on an interpretation of biblical and republican traditions. Betty Friedan grounded her feminist critique in the liberal tradition. Other writers, however, have searched for new or other languages from which to build their arguments.

These nine crises (represented here as inventing communities, the Revolution, the founding, factions, the Civil War, industrialization, the Depression, the Cold War, and discrimination) are not a complete representation of American political thought. But these crises, including the conversations and debates of Americans who have addressed them, are illustrative of the political thought of what is in many ways a unique nation.

☆ *Bibliographic Essay*

In *Habits of the Heart: Individualism and Commitment in American Life* (Berkeley: University of California Press, 1985) Robert Bellah, Richard Madsen, William M. Sullivan, Ann Swidler, and Stephen M. Tipton have collaborated to present a study which employs the metaphor of languages as a model for the study of American political culture. The authors describe the existence of two languages, biblical and republican, which, they contend, have become "second" or partially lost languages, overwhelmed by the dominance of the first language of individualism. *Community in America*, Charles H. Reynolds and Ralph V. Norman, eds. (Berkeley: University of California, 1988), contains searching critiques of *Habits of the Heart* on both methodological and theoretical grounds.

Unarguably, the most influential study of American political thought, and one which emphasizes the dominance of the liberal idea, is Louis Hartz's *The Liberal Tradition in America* (New York: Harcourt Brace Jovanovich, 1955). Richard Hofstadter's *The American Political Tradition and the Men Who Made It* (New York: Alfred A. Knopf, 1948) employs a different focus and methodology as well as a slightly different definition of liberalism, but his conclusions are very similar to Hartz's. Also see Herbert McCloskey's and John Zaller's *The American Ethos* (Cambridge: Harvard University Press, 1984) for an examination of the significance of survey data for delineating the liberal tradition in America and Ann Norton's *The Republic of Signs* for a delightfully presented treatment of the interaction between liberalism and popular culture.

Part of the argument over the nature and importance of the "language of liberalism" in America extends to arguments over what John Locke himself said. Hartz emphasized the transformation of Locke's ideas as they were applied to a new culture. Nevertheless, a quest for the "real" Locke is still a central task for an understanding of American political thought. Peter Laslett's introduction to *John Locke: Two Treatises of Government* (New York: Mentor, 1965) is a valuable review of Locke's general theory and historical context. John Dunn's *The Political Thought of John Locke* (Cambridge: Cambridge University Press, 1969) emphasizes the theological base of his political theory. On the other hand, Richard Ashcraft in his *Revolutionary Politics and Locke's* Two Treatises of Government (Princeton: Princeton University Press, 1986) argues for an interpretation of Locke that places him within the republican tradition. Compare both to C. B. Macpherson's *The Political Theory of Possessive Individualism* (Oxford: Oxford University Press, 1962), which makes Locke the central figure in the development of liberalism and capitalism. For recent applications of Locke to the American context, see: Jerome Huyler, *Locke in America: The Moral Philosophy of the Founding* (Lawrence: University Press of Kansas, 1995); Thomas Pangle, *The Spirit of Modern Republicanism: The Moral Vision of the American Founders and the Philosophy of Locke* (Chicago: University of Chicago Press, 1988).

Wilson Carey McWilliams's *The Idea of Fraternity in America* (Berkeley: University of California Press, 1973) focuses upon what he calls American variants of "the ancient imperatives of fraternity" (both in biblical and republican forms) in the history of American political thought. Also see John H. Schaar's "The Case for Patriotism," *New American Review* (May 1973), for a similar approach. John Diggins in *The Lost Soul of American Politics* (Chicago: University of Chicago Press, 1984) criticizes interpretations which he regards as overemphasizing republican themes in American political thought. Although phrased in different terms from the contemporary debate over the nature and relative importance of different American languages, Vernon L. Parrington's classic three-volume *Main Currents in American Thought* (New York: Harcourt Brace Jovanovich, 1927, 1930) explores the conflict between what he calls an agrarian Jeffersonianism and capitalist Hamiltonianism in American history, concepts that roughly correspond to the languages of republicanism and liberalism.

Analyses of American political thought which inform us about the nature and importance of biblical language include William G. McLaughlin, "Pietism and the American Character," in Hennig Cohen, ed., *The American Experience* (Boston: Houghton Mifflin, 1968), pp. 39–63, which emphasizes the individualist elements in this American language, and his *Revival, Awakenings and Reform* (Chicago: University of Chicago Press, 1978), which discusses the communitarian potential of American religious movements; Winthrop Hudson, *Religion in America* (New York: Scribner's, 1981); Reinhold Niebuhr, *The Irony of American History* (New York: Scribner's, 1952), which attempts to show how religion can add a needed sense of the tragic to American culture; Barry Alan Shain, *The Myth of American Individualism: The Protestant Origins of American Political Thought* (Princeton: Princeton University Press, 1996) emphasizes the dominance of religious accounts of politics over republican and individualism in the revolutionary and founding periods. Richard John Neuhaus, *The Naked Public Square: Democracy and Religion in America* (Grand Rapids, MI: William B. Eerdmans, 1984) presents a strong case for the necessity of a religious language in American culture, while Robert Booth Fowler, "Religion and Liberalism in America," in Philip

Abbott and Michael B. Levy, eds., *The Liberal Future in America: Essays in Renewal* (Westport, CT: Greenwood Press, 1985), pp. 85–106, re-forms the argument on the relationship between religious and other languages by arguing that biblical languages represent a "challenge" and an "alternative." Sidney Mead's *The Lively Experiment* (New York: Harper & Row, 1963) contributes to the debate by arguing that nowhere in the history of Christendom have churches been more "completely identified . . . with their country's political and economic system" than in America while Mark Roelofs, *The Poverty of American Politics* (Philadelphia: Temple University Press, 1992), emphasizes the contradictions between religious understandings of America and "interest-seeking" Madisonian ones.

The tensions between the language of conservatism and America's dominant languages are explored in Clinton Rossiter's *Conservatism in America: The Thankless Persuasion* (New York: Alfred A. Knopf, rev. ed., 1962). Rossiter reaches his conclusion as a conservative. For a viewpoint that reaches some of his conclusions about American conservatism in a much less sympathetic manner, see Daniel Bell's collection, *The Radical Right* (Garden City, NY: Doubleday, 1963). William F. Buckley in his introductory essay ("Did You Ever See a Dream Walking?") to Buckley and Charles R. Kesler, eds., *Modern American Conservative Political Thought* (New York: Harper & Row, 1988) argues that conservative discourse in America is in a period of ascendance. Also see George H. Nash's thorough presentation of recent conservative theory, *The Conservative Movement in America* (New York: Basic Books, 1979), for a similar argument.

A classic statement on the political difficulties in translating European radicalism to the American experience is Leon Samson's *Toward a United Front* (New York: Farrar and Rinehart, 1935), Chap. 1. Norman Thomas attempts to find a place for socialism in the American tradition of dissent *(The Great Dissenters* [New York: W. W. Norton, 1961]). Also see John P. Diggins's *The American Left in the Twentieth Century* (New York: Harcourt Brace Jovanovich, 1973) for a historical review which places emphasis on this question.

Inventing New Communities

INTRODUCTION

It is certainly correct to say that America as a nation-state was created in the crisis of revolution. But American political culture and thought were formed over the course of the century before the open conflict with Great Britain. It is tempting to view this colonial period before 1760 in genetic terms. Revolution represented the "birth" of the American republic, and the formation of colonial settlements represented its gestation. There is a sense in which this creation narrative is correct for, as we shall see, the ideology of the American revolutionaries was very much dependent upon their colonial experience. But from another perspective, the history of colonial settlements is a story of separate crises and resolutions, a story, if you will, that lies beneath another story of the Revolution. Space does not permit us to examine all these stories, for there are thirteen of them. Instead, we will concentrate upon three stories that are relevant to the revolutionary crisis and continue to attract the contemporary imagination: the settlements in Massachusetts, Pennsylvania, and Virginia.

The first five generations of Americans are a narrative of the conscious attempt to invent new communities. This image of colonial settlements as utopian efforts is partially hidden by the projection of a conservative ethos filtered through the experiences of subsequent history. The Puritan settlements in Massachusetts evoke impressions of a dour and intolerant people; the eighteenth-century Quaker is immortalized as the archaic figure on a cereal box; and the Virginian plantation owner is remembered as an elegant Leslie Howard dancing to a Mozart minuet. Without a doubt these images in popular culture do capture elements of the traditional orthodoxy of the American colonial mind, but they also obscure

15

the novelty of colonial community building. A vision of an entirely new form of community defines each of these settlements. Two are religious (emphatically so in inspiration), and another secular but no less utopian.

Each of these invented communities owes its initial formulation to political, economic, and religious conflicts in England during the sixteenth, seventeenth, and eighteenth centuries. The Puritan settlements, which began with the first arrivals of dissidents at Plymouth in 1620, and then with the Great Migration to Massachusetts Bay from 1628 to 1640 that brought 50,000 new inhabitants to America, were the result of Reformation politics in England and Europe. The Quakers, who settled in West Jersey, Rhode Island, and Pennsylvania, were one of well over a hundred religious sects that emerged during the English Civil War. The Virginia colonists had a more checkered history, but the settlement finally became established as a result of land hunger on the part of British traders.

The origins of the Puritan settlements in Massachusetts can be traced to the almost accidental participation of England in the religious reform that swept Europe early in the sixteenth century. When Henry VIII formally severed the English church from Rome in 1534, he did so for reasons largely nationalistic and personal. Soon, however, Protestant sentiment began to have an impact on the island. The regents of Edward VI managed to solidify and codify England's own peculiar reformation with the promulgation of the Forty-Two Articles of faith and a Book of Common Prayer in 1553. But when Mary Tudor assumed the throne, she attempted to return the country to Catholicism. Upon Elizabeth's accession, Protestant doctrines were reintroduced and the new queen appointed bishops who supported her reformation of a national church.

Throughout these crises, a group of individuals was formed who challenged the Protestant content of Henry's and Elizabeth's reformation. According to these deeply religious supporters of the Crown's new policies, the new church was only "Popery without the Pope." The Acts of Supremacy passed in 1534 confiscated monasterial property but did not alter Catholic theology. Elizabethan reforms were equally cautious. Elizabeth, in fact, was not excommunicated by the pope until 1570. When the English Protestants left England for exile in Europe in Queen Mary's reign, their discontent with the progress of reformation in England was expanded and reinforced by the new theology and practice in Germany and Switzerland.

The foremost influence upon these reformist members of the Church of England (the Puritans) was John Calvin. Calvin experienced his own personal conversion in 1536, left the Catholic Church, and published at the age of twenty-seven *The Institutes of the Christian Religion*. Except for a brief period of exile, Calvin presided over a Protestant theocracy in the city of Geneva, Switzerland, until his death in 1564. Calvin's theology is a subtle and complex blend of Old and New Testament visions overlaid with a precise and demanding code of living. When Martin Luther challenged church doctrine in 1518, he substituted the Catholic belief that personal salvation could be attained through sacrament and works (obeying church rules and helping others) with "justification by faith." Only through a complete devotion to God could a person hope to achieve salvation. Like Luther, Calvin supported the Scripture as the individual's central contact with God. But unlike Luther, Calvin drew an even more onerous path to salvation for Christians. After the Fall, no human being can be said to deserve salvation, no matter how pious his or her life or beliefs may be. Salvation was the result of God's grace, which was independent of any individual effort.

Compounding this individual sense of hopelessness is Calvin's doctrine of predestination. God knows even before an individual's birth whether she or he shall receive his grace or be damned for eternity. "Predestination," wrote Calvin in *The Institutes*,

> we call the external decree of God, by which he has determined in himself, what would become of every individual of mankind. For they are not all created with a similar destiny; but eternal life is foredained for some, and eternal damnation for others.

Moreover, very few individuals are predestined to be touched by God's grace.

How can a church be organized that is consistent with this theology? Calvin borrowed from the early church doctrine of St. Augustine to distinguish between an invisible and a visible church. The former was a concept used to describe the unity of all Christians past and present, while the latter was meant to identify those in a particular congregation who had been saved. Church governance could only be managed by those "elect" who had received a clear sign of God's grace. For those who remained unregenerate, their only hope was to continue church attendance and pious living in the anticipation that they would some day experience a sign of grace, even if it was as late as the moment of their death.

In an unanticipated way, Calvinism had reintroduced a sense of hierarchy into Protestant theology. Gone, as in Lutheranism, was reliance upon the priest as an intermediary between the person and God. But this was somewhat replaced by the position of the elect, who now as "visible saints" interpreted an individual's conversion experience as genuine or as an act of deception. This return to community was also reflected in Calvin's attitude toward the state. Luther's theory focused almost entirely upon government as an engine of repression. In his effort to sharply divide religious from political authority, Luther, according to the twentieth-century Lutheran theologian Reinhold Niebuhr, promoted "a perfectionist private ethic in juxtaposition to a realistic, not to say cynical, official ethic." Rulers were "fools"; rare is there a "wise prince," was Luther's own assessment although he was forced to admit that the state was necessary for protecting Christians from the "unrighteous." Calvin accepted the Lutheran doctrine that government was the result of human corruption, but insisted that political authority could not only serve as a "defence of pure religion" but also "promote our concord with each other." In the sense that every person had two callings, a general one which signified God's grace and a particular one which signified an individual's own predestined vocation on earth, the magistrate must satisfy both. He must be a member of the elect, and he must be a devoted, just, and talented leader.

When the Puritans returned to England after spending time in Geneva and other Protestant municipalities, they confronted the Church of England with a new, radical resolve. As Michael Walzer writes in his study of the Puritans (*The Revolution of the Saints*), "[T]heir exile had taught them the style of free men; its first manifestation was the evasion of traditional authority and routine." The Puritans attacked traditional Anglican practices such as services in Latin, the use of prayer books, and the wearing of surplices. When these demands failed to produce change, they met secretly in their own conferences independent of the official church and began to develop their own services. When James I took the throne in 1603, the Puritans focused upon a new form of church organization, the presbytery, as one that could best promote their views. James correctly saw that a government without the ability to appoint its own bishops challenged his own authority ("No bishop, no king"). The Puritans in despair saw physical separation from England as the only opportunity to reform the church. One group (the Pilgrims) emigrated to Holland but, concerned that their children might be corrupted by Dutch culture, left for America in 1620. Ten years later another group obtained a royal charter and left for the colony of Massachusetts. The experiments in Massachusetts, while modeled in part on Calvin's Geneva and in part upon the semisecret congregational practices already in place in England, were thus part of an effort to create a new kind of society based exclusively on this new understanding of God and the person.

When the Puritans left for America, they emigrated in a spirit of desolation. Protestant gains had been pushed back in Germany; the Huguenots (French Protestants) had been massacred; and the appointment of a new archbishop in England had led to new repressive policies. John Winthrop, the leader of the Massachusetts experiment, wrote: "All other churches of Europe are brought to desolation, and our sins . . . do threaten evil times to be coming upon us." Neither Winthrop nor anyone one else anticipated the resurgence of Protestant forces that led to the Civil War in England in 1642. Until the restoration of Charles II in 1660, the breakdown of political and religious consensus produced an enormous variety of religious sects. Some, like the Fifth Monarchists, were founded on the presumption of an imminent Second Coming of Christ on earth. Others, like the Levelers, reinterpreted the Gospel in politically radical equalitarian terms.

Amidst this intensely charged millenarian atmosphere, the Quaker movement was born. George Fox, who was born in 1624 as the son of a weaver, after a deep conversion experience traveled throughout England during the English Civil War. Meeting with various congregations and sleeping in fields, he fought off alternate feelings of religious depression and exhilaration. "I . . . saw," he wrote in his journal, "that there was an ocean of darkness and death, but an infinite ocean of light and love, which flowed over the ocean of darkness." In the early 1650s he began to share his religious vision with groups of individuals who gathered to hear his preaching. Why, asked Fox, had God spoken directly to people in the Scriptures but was apparently silent today? Fox's answer was that the churches had failed to consult the "inner light" that resided in every human being. If individuals could just focus their sense of desperation as isolated mortal beings upon "the divine Light of Christ," they could literally speak to God since this relief from loneliness was available to every person.

The *Children of Light*, as this new religious group called themselves, refused to offer any specific doctrine. Their religious services, held in steepleless meetinghouses, were performed without ministers, sermons, or ceremony in an effort to reproduce the spirit of primitive Christianity. Individuals would report to the group their own accounts of the appearance of an inner light in their lives. But what created an antagonism between Quakers and the political authorities was a set of injunctions concerning external conduct. The Quakers' religious beliefs were mystical and defied categorization in terms of the contending Puritan, Anglican, and Catholic doctrines. But the Quakers also developed a series of commandments to define themselves as a group potentially threatening to the contending political authorities, both Anglican and Puritan; They refused to take oaths, which made them an object of suspicion to the Puritans who, after the Oath of Abjuration, demanded that citizens prove they were not Catholics. They refused to join the Puritan Army on the grounds that Jesus' teachings required pacifism. They developed a series of proscriptions that angered the upper classes, including refusal to remove their hats except in prayer, refusal to accept the new address of *you* as a sign of respect and deference, and refusal to refer to days of the week (Monday, Tuesday, etc.) except as "First Day," "Second Day," etc. Similarly the months were to be known as "First Month," "Second Month," etc.

In an attempt to impose the government's authority, the Conventicle Act was passed in 1664. It sought to destroy nonconforming churches by forbidding religious meetings of five or more people, except in an Anglican house of worship. As a result, many new sects met secretly. But not so the Quakers. They continued their meetings in public; when arrests depleted their numbers, the Quaker children continued to hold meetings until they, too, were arrested.

These acts of repression led some Quakers to seek propagation of their ideas in America. But the Puritans reacted resolutely and violently to these "invasions." The General Court of Massachusetts passed a statute that provided fines for any person who brought Quakers or Quaker literature into the colony. Any Quaker who managed to avoid these restrictions was arrested and legally enjoined from participating in any conversation with the inhabitants of Massachusetts. Some Quakers found refuge in the more tolerant Rhode Island colony. In 1681 William Penn, an aristocratic convert to Quakerism, obtained a proprietary charter from Charles II to form a colony that would receive the Society of Friends.

The Virginia settlement represented a very different kind of utopia from the Puritan and Quaker experiments. Early colonization was driven by a pure profit motive. The Virginia Company, a trading corporation capitalized at the sum of 100,000 pounds, obtained a royal charter in 1606 to develop commercial investments for its stockholders. The ventures were disastrous; there were no profits and no dividends to report to the stockholders. The colonists at Roanoke vanished, and the settlers at Jamestown were reduced to surviving on a diet of "Doggs, catts, ratts, and mice"—not to mention boiled shoe leather. Of the 500 men living at the settlement in 1609, only 60 were alive a year later. Virginia held the unenviable reputation in England of "a misery, a death, a hell." In an effort to attract colonists the company attempted to lure religious dissidents by hiring clergy to promote the venture. For a brief period Thomas Dale, a Puritan army officer, ran the colony. When investors were about to cut their losses and send the colonists home, John Rolfe reported that his experiments in growing West Indian tobacco were successful.

With the potential for a lucrative cash crop, the colony began to attract the attention of the English lower-middle class. Charles I is reported to have said that Virginia was "founded upon smoke." But tobacco represented only a portion of the Virginian experiment. As historian Daniel Boorstin has observed, the utopian dream of the prosperous seventeenth-century tradesman was to become a country gentleman:

> To retire from a place behind the shop-counter or from a seat at the clerk's desk to a spacious manor house in the midst of broad acres— this was the daydream of the rising middle class.

According to Boorstin, this utopia was the counterpart to the twentieth-century American's dream of a "costly suburban estate, membership in a country club, and winters in Florida." But as the author of *The Americans: The Colonial Experience* notes, this seventeenth-century aspiration was more grandiose than that of the average contemporary American:

Becoming a country gentleman in those days meant joining the governing class. To acquire a manor house meant also to become a justice of the peace, a power over the local pulpit, a patron and father-confessor to the local peasantry, an overseer of the poor, and perhaps sooner or later a member of Parliament, a knight, a baronet—even conceivably a member of the House of Lords.

Such aspirations were possible, although unlikely, in England. In Virginia, with the enticement of *headrights,* a system of granting fifty acres of land for every person transported to the colony, the ideal of the country gentleman seemed a real possibility.

Thus the Virginia utopia was born as an experiment in which a gentry class would be transplanted without the great families that forded over it and the urban masses that challenged it in England. The community that the settlers sought to invent was at once a conservative and a radical vision: conservative in the sense that it sought to imitate existing social patterns; radical in the sense that it assumed that institutions could be re-created instantly in another alien environment.

Prerevolutionary America is the story of these utopias: the dream of founding a society on Scripture, on the inner light, on the life of a country gentleman. How did these men and women construct these invented communities? How well did they work?

MASSACHUSETTS: THE "CITY UPON A HILL"

When Sumner Chilton Powell wrote his Pulitzer prize-winning history of colonial Sudbury, Massachusetts, *Puritan Village,* in 1964, he was awed by the dramatic changes the Puritans had instituted. "How many men today," Powell asked, "founding a 'godly plantation' on the moon or on any habitable planet, would make as many significant alterations in religion, in social organization, in local government, and in attitude and values generally?" Gone was the complex legal structure of the ancient English village (courts-baron, courts-leets, courts of investigation, and views of frankpledge). Even English common law was abandoned, although introduced later. Gone were the structures and practices of the medieval church (presentments, ecclesiastical courts, archdeacons, certificates of penance, and holy days). Gone, too, was the political and criminal justice system (justices of the peace, mayors, and knights of the shire).

What was substituted in their place? Puritan political structure and practice was disarmingly simple. Kenneth Lockridge, in his study of Dedham, Massachusetts (*A New England Town: The First Hundred Years*), uses the unwieldy but helpful term *Christian Utopian Closed Corporate Community* to describe the settlements in the Massachusetts Bay Colony.

The Puritan conception of Christianity envisioned a community governed by visible saints. They were decidedly unevangelistic (closer to today's Amish than to today's fundamentalist Christians) as well as unsympathetic to other religions. The utopian and corporate ideal of the experiment was never stated more clearly and eloquently than by John Winthrop in his speech delivered aboard the *Arbella:* "[W]e must delight in each other, make others' conditions our own, rejoice together, mourn together, labor, and suffer together, always having before our eyes our commission and community. . . ." Winthrop used a verse from the Sermon on the Mount (Matt. 5:14) to convey the exemplary purpose of the settlement: "[W]e shall be as a City upon a Hill, the eyes of all people are upon us. . . ."

In accord with this vision, the Puritans created a governor and assistants and a General Court to govern the settlement generally. Each town elected members of the Court and governed itself through the election of selectmen and a town meeting. Strictly speaking there was no "church" in the colony, for each town had its own church. Thus while the Puritans kept the fiction that they had adopted a presbytery, in fact their church government was congregational.

Perhaps the most puzzling aspect of the organization of the colony for the modern person is the relationship between church and government. Puritans, like Calvin himself, professed to advocate separation of church and state. But church membership was required to vote for members of the General Court and to hold office. Church attendance, as well as contributions, was mandatory and governmentally enforced. In the first generations, the ownership of land (which was provided, upon application, by the town) was limited to those who were "likely to be received members of the Congregation." Certainly these practices suggest the existence of a theocracy. But for the Puritans the two realms were separate in the sense that ministers did not hold office, nor did a reprimanded church member lose his political rights to attend the town meeting.

Puritans regarded the city upon a hill, however, as a single entity in which both sets of institutions, church and state, promoted a common purpose. There were tensions, nevertheless. The Bay Colony was not the static oligarchic society that many unsympathetic historians have described. In fact, the Christian Utopian Closed Corporate Community can be seen as a set of communities in nearly constant ideological motion, ever striving to maintain a consensus.

Unity was the value Puritans most frequently used to describe both their religious and political activity. They had jettisoned the elaborate feudal structure of the English town. They had decided as well to divide religious and political power. Each town church, according to the congregationalist principle, was given wide latitude. Puritan doctrine required an emphasis on belief rather than just attention to outward conduct. All of this meant that unity had to be largely achieved through persuasion and consensus. Two practices were employed to foster this effort.

One practice was the sermon. The Sunday sermon of today is but a tiny remnant of Puritan practice. There were actually two Sunday sermons, a lecture-sermon on Thursdays, election-day sermons, special sermons on fasting and thanksgiving days (there were fifty of these, for example, in 1675-76), and sermons for community events and tragedies (executions, Indian massacres, and epidemics). Failure to attend a sermon resulted in fines. The sermon as a form of ideological persuasion had already been developed in England. As Michael Walzer writes, the English Puritans "despite their isolation, their exclusiveness, and their introspective devotion . . . wrote and preached with an intense awareness of an audience. . . . [T]hey consciously aimed to shape other men to their own godly purpose, to proclaim the Word in such a way as would best arouse and mobilize all the potential saints for the 'exercises' of spiritual warfare and pilgrimage."

The sermon came to be a carefully prescribed form of discourse. It must be written in a "plain style." Latin references were largely eliminated. It had three parts: the proclamation of a doctrine based upon a citation from Scripture; the reasons for the doctrine; and the uses of the doctrine for the event or issue under study. The Puritan sermon, under these restrictions, was a highly patterned mode of expression. It was, in Perry Miller's words, "more like a lawyer's brief than a work of art."

An excellent example of the sermon as a means by which the clergy interpreted and defined events for a congregation is Increase Mather's "A Discourse Concerning the Uncertainty of the Times of Men," delivered in 1692. Two young ice skaters had drowned in a pond. An accident which results in death always challenges religious belief. Why do tragedies such as this happen? Why does God permit these untimely deaths? Mather chose as his doctrinal source two lines from Ecclesiastes 8:5,6 ("a wise man's heart discerneth both time and judgment"; "Because to every purpose there is time and judgment, therefore the misery of man is great upon him"). Mather asks why God should deny to human beings the knowledge of their death and offers three reasons: (1) "His children might live by faith"; (2) "obedience may be tried"; (3) with this knowledge, "there would be nothing but weeping in many families, weeping in many times, and in some whole countries." The minister's comfort to the bereaved families and a shocked community may not seem great, but Mather's point in the sermon was that the event was divinely rational in a twofold sense. Death and tragedy are hidden because otherwise human beings could not bear to live in this world. The parents of the young men could not have lived with the knowledge of these early deaths. These deaths are also a reminder to the living that their own moment may be near, and they should take this event as an opportunity to reflect upon their own "time and judgment."

Increase Mather's 1692 sermon was not a momentous one for the people of Boston, but it illustrates the effort of New England churchmen to use every possible instance to reinforce the common bonds of the community. Even when life went relatively smoothly, the clergy would demand that its congregation search in their hearts for inner hostility ("ill-temperedness" or a "quarrelsome disposition"), and confess and discuss their doubts and feelings. Punishment for failure to exemplify what Puritans called *religious discipline* could be mild (*censure*) or severe (*excommunication*), but the goal was always restoration into the community. In Watertown, for example, the congregation gave a recalcitrant parishioner a week to repent. He waited two, but he was welcomed back to the congregation.

The other major practice of consensus was the town meeting. The meeting was a secular institution. Only church members could vote or hold office at the General Court, but towns almost never applied the visible saint requirement. Once a year every male inhabitant of the town met to elect selectmen and other officers to run the community between the meetings as well as to set general policies. Scholars have experienced difficulty assessing the role of the town meeting. Kenneth Lockridge found that until well into the eighteenth century, the meetings at Dedham, Massachusetts, simply ratified the recommendations of the selectmen. But Michael Zuckerman in his study of the meetings (*Peaceable Kingdoms*) contends that patterns of "deferential voting" miss the point of the structures. The meetings, argues Zuckerman, were not destined to be "a school for democracy." He also denies that the meetings were simply an arena in which simple folk quietly deferred to local oligarchies, since in many towns the roughness of the economy meant that there were no oligarchies. The refrain "by common consent" and "sense of the meeting" by which towns unanimously reported the results of their deliberations were, for Zuckerman, the outcome of hard-won efforts, many of which were negotiated at taverns, churches, and across fence posts, to achieve consensus. "Unanimity," he writes, "was, indeed demanded, demanded almost as a matter of social decency, so that a simple majority commanded little authority at the local level and scarcely even certified decisions as legitimate." Many inhabitants would refuse to convene if attendance was too low and refuse to vote on an issue, preferring to adjourn to a specified date, if consensus was lacking.

All of these efforts to build consensus, however, did not prevent the emergence of factions in the churches and towns. John Winthrop, the first governor of the colony, reports in his journals of his peripatetic travels to this congregation or that town to mediate factional disputes between a minister and his congregation or warring cliques. According to Edmund S. Morgan, a modern biographer, Winthrop was obsessed with the nightmare that scores of New England towns would "splinter . . . into a hundred earnest little Utopias, each feeding on its own special type of holiness and each breeding new types, multiplying like earthworms, by division." Two such instances early in the colony's experiment illustrate very clearly the fragile nature of the Puritan utopia. One involves Roger Williams's challenge to Puritan orthodoxy in 1636; the other, Anne Hutchinson's shortly after.

In order to appreciate both of these conflicts, it is necessary to briefly review Puritan doctrine. John Cotton, the preeminent colonial minister and theologian of the first generation, expressed its delicate nature thus:

> There is . . . [a] combination of virtues strangely mixed in every lively, holy Christian: and that is, diligence in worldly businesses, and yet deadness to the world. Such a mystery as none can read but they that know it.

Cotton noted that the ideal Christian must be a loving spouse, raise children, excel at his calling whether it be farming or trade— "yet his heart is not set upon these things. . . ." Puritans called this particular attitude of usefulness to family and community *weaned affections*. Puritan poetry, especially that of Anne Bradstreet, as well as the innumerable journals that the colonists circulated among one another, often expressed these feelings exquisitely.

Many years later Max Weber in *The Protestant Ethic and the Spirit of Capitalism* (1905) argued that this combination of asceticism and religious reward for material success led to capitalism wherever the Puritan ideal established a cultural beachhead. But the political implications of the doctrine in the first generation of the American experiment involved less the secular transformation of the religious ideal through material success than interpretations of the doctrine that challenged Puritan conceptions of community. For the Puritans were well aware that their doctrine skirted two ancient Christian heresies. One, Arminianism, assumed that individuals could by their efforts direct the course of their salvation. The other, antinomianism, asserted the utter helplessness of an individual before God but, once saved, a responsibility only to divine command. Puritans were especially sensitive to the charge of Arminianism. This, after all, formed the basis of their critique of both Catholicism and the Anglican Church. On the other hand, they attempted to soften the antinomian implications of their doctrine, as Calvin too had done. Covenant or federal theology developed by the colonial Puritans contended that God operated through covenants (a covenant with Adam, with Abraham, with Christ) and that each Christian could hope for his or her own covenant with God in which salvation was the reward for grace. *Sanctification* was the term Puritans used to describe those who behaved piously. While they were careful to distinguish between sanctification and *justification* (salvation through grace), Puritans admitted that sanctification was a sign or consequence of justification. Puritan doctrine was then just a short theoretical distance from Arminianism and even, as Weber later argued, from the religious legitimization of material success. On the other hand, admittance of individual direction by the Holy Ghost implied a highly individualist conception of religion that would likely destroy the communitarian ideal of the city upon a hill. Most Puritans knew all about these tendencies in their hearts; hence Cotton's talk of the "mystery" of the devout Christian. But two militant Puritans, Williams and Hutchinson, relentlessly explored the question.

The engaging and thoughtful young man who arrived in Massachusetts in 1630 is often referred to as the American *apostle of religious freedom*. Such may have been the legacy of Roger Williams's writings and actions, but it certainly was not his intention. Shortly after his arrival Williams was asked to join the ministry of the Boston church. His response shocked the congregation: "I durst not officiate to an unseparated people." Throughout his brief stay in the Massachusetts Bay Colony, Williams attacked seriatim every political compromise the Puritans had made and challenged weak points in Puritan theology. He demanded that the Puritans openly announce their separation from the Anglican church; he demanded that Puritans who returned to visit England and attended Anglican services be excommunicated; he demanded that the colonists renegotiate their agreements with the Indians; and he demanded that the Puritans reject King Charles I's charter since he was a "hypocrite" and a "liar." Williams argued that regenerate men ought not to pray with those that were not yet saved, even with their own unregenerate spouses. He contended that the government had no authority in religious matters, and that no church could be justified.

Both Winthrop and Cotton replied to each of these critiques, but Williams seemed to be a moving target. He would drop one argument only to pick up another. When he assumed an informal post at the Salem church and began to gather a faction which supported his views, the General Court acted. The issue was a delicate one for the civil authorities, since practice demanded that wide leeway be given to town congregations. Winthrop urged Williams to reconsider his opinions, asking him to reflect upon how everyone else could be wrong but himself on these political and theological points. Williams's answer was sharp but in keeping with the Puritans' own style of argument in England. John Milton, for example, wrote, "Let them [the Anglicans] chant while they will of prerogatives, we shall tell them of Scripture; of custom, we of Scripture; of acts and statutes, still of Scripture." Williams enjoined Winthrop: "Abstract yourself with a holy violence from the dung heap of this earth." The confrontation between the two men illustrated a dilemma in the creation of any community. Should the rigorous examination of the central features of society at some point be placed aside in order to build a consensus? Williams did not think so; he loved living in "these wonderful, searching, disputing and dissenting times." Winthrop, who felt he was charged with preventing the city upon a hill from splintering into little utopias, thought otherwise. Williams was expelled from the colony and made his way south to Rhode Island to form his own utopia.

The debate that Williams had insisted upon pursuing reemerged less than a decade later when Massachusetts opposed Williams's effort to obtain a royal charter for the Rhode Island settlement. The series of polemical essays between John Cotton and Williams carried on the debate in a more systematic fashion. Cotton's writing has been lost but Williams's survived. In *The Bloody Tenet of Persecution for the Cause of Conscience*, he argued forcefully for religious freedom and a sharp separation of church and state. The essay is organized appropriately in the form of a dialogue between "peace" and "truth," with Williams taking the positions of the latter. Persecution of religious beliefs is always mistaken. Williams accepts the harm done by "evil doers," "seducing teachers," and "scandalous livers," but he insists that God permits these transgressions until he determines a time for retribution and repentance. To use the "sword" to promote beliefs can only make "a whole nation of hypocrites." Moreover, civil officers can easily mistake "true messengers" as seducing teachers. Elijah was regarded as a "troubler of the state"; Jesus was treated as a "traitor against Caesar." All of these individuals were "turners of the world upside down." Magistrates must, of course, proscribe religious practice that threatens the civil peace, such as "stealing, robbing, murdering, and perishing the poor." Thus presumably for Williams, Satanic belief, however abhorrent to Christian belief, must be tolerated until cults begin sacrificing individuals. The line between belief and action is not a firm one, and Williams seems at times to accept the principle of the "bad tendency" of a religious doctrine as a matter for magistrates. But his theoretical point was far from that of the Puritans.

There was as well an enormous theoretical gap between the Puritans' conception of a city upon a hill and Williams's model. For Williams, the goal, indeed the essence, of a good city is "well-being and peace"—a goal distinct from that of the church. For example, according to Williams, the nature of civil society in the ancient city of Ephesus remained the same even after Christians replaced the pagan worship of Diana with Christianity.

It is important to note, however, how Williams arrived at his position in *The Bloody Tenet*. For some time he had begun to doubt that a church in the Christian apostolic sense could be justified at all. Williams found no evidence (although Puritan ministers worked hard to instruct him on this point) that God had authorized the calling of any churches. Thus it was presumptuous of men and women to set up such "prudential inventions." Unlike his style on other issues, Williams never completely proposed the obvious conclusion to his position. He admitted that the New England

churches were good churches, perhaps the finest in the history of Christendom. But he reminded himself that they probably were not real churches.
No sovereign could ordain a minister of God (the Puritan position), but neither could a group of saints select a minister. Sometimes he seemed to favor
the limitation of Christian action to "prophets in sackcloth," that is, individual itinerant holy men and women. Williams's theological position was
essentially that of the Seekers in England, although he apparently never
had any contact with the sect that claimed that all churches were false.

It is from these religious convictions, then, that Williams came to
regard all Puritan theology and practice as inherently Arminian. Williams
did not celebrate the advent of a secular society. In fact, he eagerly awaited
the time when messengers from God would authorize the formation of a
true church. But his own convictions promoted a society in which religious
belief was a personal matter, and the community was thus based on principles other than religious ones.

Perhaps an even more important challenge to Puritan orthodoxy came
from Anne Hutchinson—if only because her conclusions were more optimistic and more attractive to the colonists. Hutchinson arrived in Massachusetts in September 1634. A strong and extremely talented woman, she
began to hold weekly meetings in her Boston home to discuss the sermons
delivered by John Cotton the previous Sunday. Since Hutchinson was held
in high regard for her activities as a midwife, undoubtedly many women
attended the gatherings. John Winthrop soon became suspicious that more
matters were under discussion than the summarization of the Boston minister's sermons. He was correct. On the pretext of elaborating upon Cotton's
words, Hutchinson launched an attack on Arminianism.

The Puritan vulnerability on this point is evidenced by John Cotton's
support of Hutchinson and her study group. Both Cotton and Winthrop
could agree (though they did not wish to dwell upon it) that those who were
communally recognized as "justified," even ministers, might not really be
saints. They may have willingly or unwillingly deceived examiners. Thus
the visible saints of the colony were undoubtedly polluted by impostors or,
more charitably, by those whose sanctification had been mistaken by the
community as justification. Winthrop worried when he heard members of
Hutchinson's group distinguish fellow inhabitants as persons of works
(those who only appear to be saved because of their outward conduct) and
persons of grace (those who were really saved).

At this point Hutchinson's critique widened. Persons of grace were so
imbued with the Holy Spirit that they could individually determine who
was justified. Hutchinson's supporters began to demand that persons of her
views be voted clerical offices in the church, and there were rumors of the
arrival in large numbers of like-minded people from England. Congregations in outlying towns were divided although they tended to support Win-

throp, whose popularity in Boston had dramatically ebbed. The governor acted in November 1637, summoning Hutchinson to appear before the General Court. Any objective reader of the transcripts cannot fail to be impressed with Hutchinson's intellect. On nearly every point she scored important points against Winthrop. Asked to justify her weekly meetings, she found two instances in Scripture that involved women teaching the Gospel, even to men (Titus 2:3-5 and Acts 18:26). On the verge of victory, however, she threw away her measured responses and reported personal revelations, including one that "God will ruin you and your posterity, and thus the whole State." Hutchinson was banished.

Why were Hutchinson's views regarded as so politically dangerous? Her antinomianism was a threat to her opponents for two reasons. To give individuals the authority to determine who had received signs of grace could break the church into thousands of shards, with each individual determining his or her own salvation. Second, the Puritans held steadfastly to Scripture as a guide to belief and conduct. If individuals talk to God independently without the anchor of scriptural authority, no Christian communion is possible. Thus the General Court concluded that Hutchinson "walked by such a rule as cannot stand with the peace of any State. . . ." For the Puritans, Hutchinson professed beliefs that, if practiced, would destroy the city upon a hill. To them, it was as if a large percentage of the population had become dedicated anarchists, electing themselves to government only to systematically destroy it.

The victories over Williams and Hutchinson were won at great cost. Congregations became extremely reluctant to admit any new applicants to their churches. John Winthrop wrote his son at Ipswich to "be very careful in admission of members." One observer in the 1640s noted that "here is required such confessions, and professions, both in private and public, both by men and women . . . that three parts of the country remain out of the Church." Darrett B. Ruttman, in his study, *Winthrop's Boston*, reported church membership at perhaps 40 percent of the population before 1637. After the Hutchinson battle it declined gradually but perceptibly to less than 20 percent. According to Edmund S. Morgan (*The Puritan Family*), the Puritan clergy withdrew to a kind of "tribalism" in which it abandoned its role in screening men for political society and instead strove to become a society complete in itself.

PENNSYLVANIA: THE "HOLY EXPERIMENT"

When William Penn received his charter for a colony in America he proclaimed the creation of a "holy experiment." "Mine eye," he wrote, "is to a blessed government, and a virtuous, ingenious and industrious government." Penn conceived of a city laid out in rectangular form with surrounding tracts of land parceled out like spokes of a wheel. The Quakers, a despised minority in England that was politically powerless and hence subject to arbitrary arrest and suppression, would create a utopia modeled upon the meetinghouse. Decisions would be reached by friendly consensus. All inhabitants who believed in God would be guaranteed freedom of worship, and all individuals who accepted Christ would be eligible for office. To the liberal European it was Penn's experiment, not the Puritans', which represented the practical fulfillment of an enlightened society.

From the beginning of the experiment, however, Pennsylvania was a colony seething with all modes of political conflict. Penn's supporters and opponents formed warring political parties; the Assembly was in almost constant conflict with the governor's Council; residents of lower counties fought upper counties; artisans in the city clashed with merchants; Quakers quarreled with members of other sects. The formal collective withdrawal of the Friends from elected political office in 1756 seems, from the perspective of these conflicts, an anticlimactic end to utopia.

Historians have focused upon a variety of factors to explain this discord. Penn, the founder of the colony, spent most of this time in London, delegating his authority to a local representative in the colony. Thus the experiment was lacking a "founding father" as a source of consensus. The policy of freedom of religion soon made the Quakers themselves a religious minority in their own colony. Pennsylvania attracted a large group of small-scale farmers and skilled artisans, non-Quaker in religious sentiment, who were often economically antagonistic to the Quaker merchant class. Unlike the Puritans, the Friends were an international movement, and their flexibility on doctrinal matters was limited by decisions made at the London Yearly Meeting. The Quakers themselves were transformed in this new environment. Barred from military, political, and religious careers in England, they gravitated toward business. Frederick Tolles describes the decline in religious commitment as the result of Quaker material success, a process he refers to as the journey from "meetinghouse to countinghouse." The mystical, antidoctrinaire theology of Quakers was also difficult to convey to the next generation. A portion of this group began to drift back to the Anglican Church by the second generation. Moreover, the accumulation of wealth often created the image among other colonists of the Quakers as a sect that used its religious and familial connections to further its members' business careers. The Friends placed a high value on equality. But, as Hugh Barbour has observed, to Quakers equality was conceived as "fundamentally... an assault on pride ... not as social reform." For example, John Whitehead, a Quaker, wrote: "We design to level nothing but sin."

But if the spirit of the meetinghouse was not effectively transferred to the political arena in the way Penn and other Friends anticipated, the colony nevertheless symbolized a different kind of experiment. The Quakers were a powerful minority whose political dominance was in part managed by their own religious organization. But as a vulnerable elite, they, as well as their opponents, were frequently forced to create coalitions with like-minded individuals and economic and religious factions. As these coalitions shifted across issues and time, the Quakers developed the subtle and complex talents necessary for coalition building. They carefully courted the new German sects in the outlying districts—the Dunkers, Mennonites, Amish, and others—who tended to vote for the Quakers out of respect for their piety. The Friends formed coalitions with leaders of the artisan class on certain issues. Men like Benjamin Franklin and Benjamin Rush aligned themselves with the Quakers in promoting various civic projects and in supporting the antiproprietary faction.

The county was the political unit for representation in the Assembly, and the provincial election process illustrates the impact of the Quakers. Since influential members of each community were aware that support was necessary for both Quaker and non-Quaker prospective candidates, organized informal meetings were initiated to draw up common slates. These gatherings were called *interest-making meetings*. Alan Tully, in his study of the colony (*William Penn's Legacy*), describes these as well-attended meetings of the upper- and middle-class in which specific questions and assessments were raised about possible candidates:

> Who on the basis of past performance deserved to be continued? Who because of illness or difficulties in personal affairs wanted to sit out a year? Who had support among Germans and Scotch-Irish as well as English Quakers? Other considerations were those that the voters were urged to weigh—a man's capacity, reputation, integrity, and his possession of those symbols which attracted respect.

Tully reports that while these interest-making meetings were often full of friction and debate with various factions pushing for advantage, the general process put a premium on compromise and persuasion. Meetinghouse values had so permeated the process that some non-Friends complained of officeholders who had become "Quakerized."

Friends also initiated a whole series of inventive civic projects, always in coalition with other groups, that were projections of their religious beliefs. For example, the Quakers were opposed to capital punishment, and the Assembly in 1682 banned the death penalty for all offenses except first-degree murder. This act opened up a public policy problem of significant proportions. Quakers were affronted by prison practices that required those incarcerated to pay the jailer for food and lodging. They were well aware that prisons were institutions in which prostitution, gambling, and consumption of alcohol were rampant. They also were opposed to what

Benjamin Rush called the "engines of public punishment"—whippings and stocks. Working from the principle that every single person was capable of reform through appreciation of the inner light, Quakers set out to create a new conception of the prison. They called their new invention the *penitentiary*. Prisoners would be isolated from other prisoners and given "indeterminate sentences." Only when the convict had an opportunity to reflect upon his transgressions and reported his revelations to the volunteers of the Philadelphia Society, a coalition of Friends and their sympathizers, would he be freed. Caleb Lownes, a Quaker, justified the new approach to criminal justice as the only approach which recognized individuals as "rational beings." In similar fashion the Quakers promoted the creation of the Pennsylvania Hospital, which was designed for "gentler" treatment of the mentally ill. The "cures" of both criminal offenders and those that George Fox once called the "distempered" are controversial to this day. Is the demand that both criminals and those mentally disturbed be subjected to "treatment" rather than punishment a form of political control or a misguided attempt at reforming the unreformable? In any case the Quaker experiments are still carried on today.

These and other practices of consensus and cooperation within an arena of competition and conflict represented the unanticipated achievement of colonial Quaker political culture. But the Friends faced another problem with which religious sects are frequently confronted in a pluralistic society: How many sacrifices in belief are acceptable for members to undertake in the service of the public good? Is it proper, to put the question from another angle, to uphold one's own religious beliefs as an officeholder in a society that is composed of many different religions?

Two Quaker prohibitions upon conduct limited their effectiveness as representatives of the community despite their attempts at coalition building. One involved the Friends' refusal to give any oath, secular or religious. Since oath giving was, and still is, an essential element of the criminal justice system, Quakers were unable to offer their considerable talents as judges (since officers of the court administer oaths) or participate in jury trials or appear as witnesses. The withdrawal from such an important part of a political system led many non-Quakers to question whether the Friends could function as productive citizens. Complex negotiations with Parliament and the participants of the yearly meetings resulted in an act which permitted, to the satisfaction of both Quakers and other religious groups, an "affirmation" rather than an oath in 1722.

More troublesome, however, was the Quaker opposition to the use of force to resolve disputes between individuals or nations. Assemblymen who were Friends strove mightily to avoid this confrontation between their pacifism and demands for protection from Indians and the French. Compromises were reached in which the Quakers permitted the deputy governor, who was purposely selected as a non-Quaker, to spend money for the "Crown's use" or for unspecified "charitable" purposes that everyone knew was appropriated for defense. The issue came to a head with the French and Indian War (1756–63), when revenue proposals for defense could no longer be hidden. Moreover, the brunt of French-instigated Indian massacres was being met by Scotch-Irish settlers on the periphery of the city. Benjamin Franklin attempted to resolve the problem by proposing in a pamphlet, *Plain Truth*, that a voluntary militia supported by private funds should not affront Quaker pacifist sensibilities. Many Friends actively encouraged the formation of such a military force, but other Quakers with "tender consciences" objected to what they saw as hypocritical behavior. En masse the Friends concluded that, in order to preserve their religious principles, they must in conscience resign their elective offices.

VIRGINIA: A "PIOUS AND CHRISTIAN PLANTATION"

The Virginia colony was settled by people with the same complex motives of material gain and religious advancement as the colonists in Massachusetts and Pennsylvania. It is true that the early settlements in Virginia were driven almost exclusively by a profit motive. In fact, Perry Miller concluded that "the glorious mission of Virginia came down to growing a weed." However, John Rolfe himself, the man most responsible for introducing Virginia to the tobacco crop, described land purchases from the Indians as the exchange of earthly pearls for "the pearls of heaven." Colonial Virginians were devout, but in a very different way from their northern counterparts. The Virginians' apparent casualness toward certain forms of impiety (gambling, horse racing, and cockfighting were de rigeur pursuits of upper-class Virginians) should not convey a lack of religiosity among the settlers. The difference between these settlements and the Puritan and Quaker experiences stems in large part from the fact that the religion of the Virginians was a heritage rather than a personal choice. Richard H. Niebuhr, in his analysis of American religion (*The Social Sources of Denominationism*), argues that it is this distinction that separates the sect from the church in a traditional sense of the concept. The church, according to Niebuhr, places importance upon sacrament and doctrine as a means by which we exercise rights we have inherited. The sect, on the other hand, as a newly invented institution, places its highest value on the religious experience itself, prior to fellowship in the newfound group. Very shortly, as we have seen, the sect must make a transition to a church and find means by which new generations can assume their inherited religion. As Anglicans, the Virginia colonists avoided this problem. Their religion was received as a given.

There were other factors that functioned to make the colony an exper- iment less religious in character. The plantation economy that emerged by the second generation never gave birth to towns or urban centers. Because the four major rivers that laced the tidewater provided convenient avenues of export from the plantation, towns and cities were unnecessary. Williams- burg was a political center that briefly swelled in population when the House of Burgesses met late in the year, just before the planting of tobacco. There were no watchful ministers to guide the conduct of the yeoman farm- ers or plantation owners. These men and women were largely on their own religiously, attending church weekly as part of their heritage as English sub- jects.

The inventive character of Virginia then came from the secular visions of its immigrants. The English background of the subsequently prominent Virginia families reveals their class origins—many were origi- nally drapers, goldsmiths, or soldiers. Many were the second and third sons of the landed gentry who, by the feudal laws of primogeniture, were unable to inherit the family estates. But economic factors quickly dissipated the dream of a society of relatively equal yeomen. By the beginning of the eigh- teenth century, the yeoman class had vanished. The major portion of tide- water land was in the possession of 5 to 10 percent of the population.

Two major factors account for this transition. One involved the pecu- liarities of tobacco cultivation. Tobacco is ecologically a voracious crop that robs the soil of nutrients; thus the land on which it is grown must be left fallow by the fourth harvest. Large tracts of land are necessary for people to be planters, and the search for ever-new plantations was incessant. Only those with access to venture capital could hope to compete. Second, the shortage of labor led to an almost exclusive reliance upon slavery. The early importations of slaves in the colony seem to suggest that servitude was lim- ited to the first generation. Hence, slaves were not theoretically different from indentured servants. But quite early, laws were passed guaranteeing slavery for succeeding generations. The plantation owners thus developed access to their own labor source which, given the expense in terms of initial capital outlay, was largely unavailable to small farmers.

The turning point in this transition from a utopia of yeoman farmers to one of a benevolent aristocracy was the aborted Bacon's Rebellion of 1676. Nathaniel Bacon, a plantation owner, largely through historical acci- dent became the spokesman of the downtrodden white farmer. At the time tillers on the periphery of all the colonies faced death from Indian attacks and, like most settlers, blamed the government inland for lack of concern. Bacon concentrated upon these concerns as well as those of the outlying small farmers who resisted the new aristocratic pretensions of the tidewater planters. Bacon and his volunteer band defeated the Indians and then turned their attention toward the political elite in the colonial capital.

When the governor's forces withdrew, a revolutionary government was instituted. An election was held—the first in fifteen years—and the new Assembly set out to dismantle the incipient landed aristocracy. A short time later Bacon died of natural causes, and the rebellion of small farmers, without leadership, collapsed. Bacon's Rebellion was the last instance in which white yeomen explicitly challenged the hegemony of the plantation aristocracy. The rebellion left no faction or party machinery in its wake.

Thereafter, the new tidewater aristocracy carefully cultivated the support of their lesser brethren. The dominance of the tobacco farmers in the economy and politics of colonial Virginia has been the subject of much discussion. Nearly every historian is astounded by the sober assumption of political responsibility by this parvenu ruling class. Bernard Bailyn describes the colonial aristocracy as a "remarkable ruling group." Daniel Boorstin writes, "Never did a governing class take its duties more seriously. . . ." Tidewater farmers shamelessly imitated their gentry counterparts in England. They read and reread Richard Brathwait's *English Gentleman* (1630), cultivated London accents, and imported British silver and furniture. The utopian aspirations of the tidewater farmers significantly expanded by the end of the seventeenth century; they no longer wished to be country gentlemen but fancied themselves to be aristocrats. But this ostentation, which nearly bankrupted some families, did not affect their solemn regard for what they regarded as their political duties.

If the tidewater planters saw themselves as aristocrats, they also saw themselves as *elected* aristocrats. Through a myriad of personal rituals the newly created great families of Virginia sought the support of the small farmers. Campaigning for election was regarded as beneath the sensibilities of an aristocrat, but the provision of a picnic by a candidate, replete with roasted pig or beef and ale, was an acceptable practice. Daniel Boorstin reports that George Washington's campaign expenses for the House of Burgesses never were less than 25 pounds. Most candidates for office were present on election day to personally thank each yeoman for his vote. (The secret ballot was an invention that was developed much later.) The conventional response went something like this: "Mr. Buchanan, I shall treasure that vote in my memory. It will be regarded as a feather in my cap forever."

Those who were elected to the House of Burgesses took their responsibilities quite seriously. It is important to note that the yearly convening of this body occurred just before the planting season and also inaugurated the Williamsburg social cycle. But to these "aristocrats" the cultivation of social graces was also part of their responsibilities. Attendance of elected representatives was mandatory. Fines of 300 pounds of tobacco per day were levied against absentees. Occasionally the sergeant at arms was ordered to arrest an absent member. Thomas Jefferson himself was once ordered to appear. Public apologies were required even after negligent members returned. The House discouraged the formation of factions and parties. "Principled" speeches were the norm. Representatives were honored for their general learning and oratorical presentation. As a group of individuals who were elected through complex mechanisms of personal deference, the House itself encouraged the careful personal political development of its members. The early careers of "founding fathers"—Washington, Jefferson, and James Madison—were formed through this careful process of tutelage.

The Virginia aristocracy had been firmly in place only a few generations before the revolutionary ferment began. But the imitation of the country aristocracy had been so fervently pursued that members of the ruling class saw themselves as purer judges of society than their English counterparts ever were. In fact, the diligent cultivation of the yeoman farmers ironically tended to make the tidewater aristocrats more sympathetic to democratic sensibilities than their northern counterparts. For example, John Adams always worried about the explosive potential of urban crowds, and Alexander Hamilton, whose early career was formed by his experiences in New York politics, referred to the people as a "great beast." On the other hand, Virginians were so accustomed to the cultivated deference of the yeoman farmer that these fears never seemed operational. The journal entry of a farmer's son illustrates the exalted status of the tidewater aristocrat. Devereux Jarratt had always been taught by his father that the freeholder was a person of exceptional independence. Jarratt "neither sought nor expected any titles" from this world and was proud that he lived "in credit among [his] neighbors." Nevertheless, young Jarratt reports that viewing a periwigged gentleman approaching his path on horseback created such a panic that he felt the impulse to run for shelter. He concludes, "Such ideas of difference between gentle and simple folk were, I believe, universal among all of my age and rank."

SUMMARY AND COMMENT

It is easy to conclude that these three experiments were failures. The city upon a hill, at least in its original formulation, collapsed within a generation. The holy experiment self-destructed. The pious and Christian plantation of yeoman farmers was transformed into a parvenu aristocracy whose economic and political dominance was based upon the production of tobacco and slave labor and the racist fears of white farmers.

But these utopias produced their own unexpected harvests of invention. The Massachusetts colonists created the town meeting, an invention of direct democratic rule whose potential as a form of governance still remains to be explored. The Pennsylvania colonists managed to create institutions of cooperation in the context of a religiously diverse society. The

Virginians produced a model of society based upon a politically dutiful elite.

Moreover, the idea of the invented community survived the crises of these experiments. In 1643 William Bradford, the governor of the Plymouth colony, compared his settlement to an "ancient mother" who had "grown old, and forsaken by her children." But what Bradford omitted in his complaint is that the Americans who left set out to invent ever-new communities. New towns, indeed new religions as well, were invented as settlers moved westward in search of both economic well-being and new forms of community. One pioneer remarked in her journal:

> If you accost a farmer in these parts, before he returns your civilities he draws from his pocket a lithographic city, and asks you to take a few building lots at one-half their value. . . .

This faith in the invention of new covenanted communities has been both a source of vitality in American culture and a source of instability. The sense of patience and endurance necessary to sustain communities over time has on many occasions led to the creation of "disposable" communities that are discarded shortly after the inevitable initial crises are confronted. America is strewn with ghost towns, abandoned communities, and communal experiments. They range from many of the early colonial experiments, the religious communes of the nineteenth century, and the prairie junctions in the West to the Woodstocks and suburban exodus in our own generation. On the other hand, the American understanding of community as an invented structure of new neighbors that is based upon newfound religious, economic, or political similarities has functioned as a source of cultural renewal. Most of our cities and towns are composed of new communities built upon the remains of abandoned efforts. Labor unions, religious organization, groups of citizens with common concerns from abolitionists to feminists, from environmentalists to tax protesters, carry on the national ongoing experiment that like-minded individuals can form their own cities upon a hill.

☆ *Bibliographic Essay*

On inventing communities and institutions in general see: Robert Nisbet, *The Twilight of Authority* (New York: Oxford University Press, 1965); George Kateb, *Utopia and Its Enemies* (New York: Free Press, 1963); Barbara Goodwin and Keith Taylor, *The Politics of Utopia: A Study of Theory and Practice* (New York: St. Martin's Press, 1982). Two recent studies in comparative perspective are: Benedict Anderson, *Imagined Communities* (London: Verso, 1983) and Eric Hobsbawn and Terrence Ranger, eds., *The Invention of Tradition* (Cambridge: Cambridge University Press,

1983). Hannah Arendt uses the concept of invention to describe the revolutionary process in *On Revolution* (New York: Viking Press, 1965). Also see Daniel Boorstin, *The Americans: The Colonial Experience* (New York: Vintage, 1958) for application of the concept to the political culture and institutions of early American settlements, and Philip Abbott, *Seeking New Inventions: The Idea of Community in America* (Nashville: University of Tennessee Press, 1987) for its use in characterizing the formation of American communities in general.

The radical implications of Puritan political thought are examined by Michael Walzer, *The Revolution of the Saints: A Study in the Origins of Radical Politics* (New York: Atheneum Publishers, 1968), and William Haller, *The Rise of Puritanism* (New York: Macmillan, 1939). Paul Seaver's *Wallington's World* (Stanford: Stanford University Press, 1985) is helpful in appreciating the worldview of a seventeenth-century English puritan artisan. Both Thomas Wertenbaker, *The Puritan Oligarchy* (New York: Scribner's, 1947), and Alan Simpson, *Puritanism in Old and New England* (Chicago: University of Chicago Press, 1955), are valuable for the connections made between Puritanism in England and America. The political impact of the Great Migration is discussed by Bernard Bailyn in a summary of his work, *The Peopling of America* (New York: Vintage, 1988). David Hackett Fischer argues in *Albion's Seed* (New York: Oxford University Press, 1989) that the political and social culture of Puritan, Quaker, Virginian, and Scotch-Irish settlements can all be traced to British folkways. Perry Miller's studies of American Puritanism are still unmatched for their subtlety and insight. See his *The New England Mind* (New York: Macmillan, 1939), as well as the reprints of his essays in *Errand into the Wilderness* (Cambridge: Harvard University Press, 1956), particularly chap. 3, "The Marrow of Puritan Divinity," which was the first exploration of Puritan covenant theology, and chaps. 1 and 10, which examine the theoretical implications of the idea of culture as an "errand." Also see Herbert W. Schneider, *The Puritan Mind* (Ann Arbor: University of Michigan Press, 1958), and Larzer Ziff, *Puritanism in America* (New York: Viking, 1973), for analyses of American Puritan culture; T. H. Breen, *The Character of the Good Ruler: Puritan Political Ideas in New England, 1630–1730* (New York: W.W. Norton, 1970).

Puritans themselves eschewed biographies as efforts that glorified individuals rather than God, but several modern studies are especially helpful as illuminations of Puritan thought and practice. See Edmund Morgan, *The Puritan Dilemma: The Story of John Winthrop* (Boston: Little, Brown, 1958), and *Roger Williams: The Church and the State* (New York: Harcourt Brace Jovanovich, 1967); Michael G. Hall, *The Last American Puritan: The Life of Increase Mather* (Middletown, CT: Wesleyan University Press, 1988). For biographies of Anne Hutchinson, see *Anne Hutchinson: Unsung Heroine of History*, by Bianca A. Leonardo and Winnifred K. Rugg (Tree of Life Publications, 1996), and *Anne Hutchinson and the Puritans: An Early American Tragedy*, by William Dunlea (Doriance Publishing, 1993). A convenient and valuable one-volume collection of Puritan political thought is Edmund S. Morgan, ed., *Puritan Political Ideas* (Indianapolis: Bobbs-Merrill, 1965).

An appreciation of the problems of the invented community can be attained through analyses of the ways Puritans struggled with theology and practice in the New World. Various studies of various New England towns or institutions are especially helpful here. See Sumner Chilton Powell, *Puritan Village* (Middletown, CT: Wesleyan University Press, 1963); Kenneth A. Lockridge, *A New England Town: The First Hundred Years* (New York: W.W. Norton, 1970); Darret B. Ruttman, *Winthrop's Boston* (New York: W.W. Norton, 1972); Richard L. Bushman, *From Puritan to Yankee* (New York: W.W. Norton, 1967); Michael Zuckerman, *Peaceable Kingdoms* (New York: Vintage, 1970); Edmund S. Morgan, *The Puritan Family* (New York: Harper & Row, 1966). The theoretical possibilities of the town meeting are explored in Jane J. Mansbridge, *Beyond Adversary Democracy* (Chicago: University of Chicago Press, 1980), and Benjamin Barber, *Strong Democracy* (Berkeley: University of California Press, 1984).

There are innumerable analyses of the impact of Puritan ideas generally upon subsequent American history. The classic and much disputed interpretation of Puritanism as a cultural stalking-horse of capitalism is Max Weber, *The Protestant Ethic and the Spirit of Capitalism*, trans. Talcott Parsons (New York: Scribner's, 1958). Much of American scholarship has been devoted to an overthrow of the "Puritan mind" as an oligarchic precursor to capitalist rule. See especially Vernon Parrington, *Main Currents in American Thought*, vol. I (New York: Harcourt Brace Jovanovich, 1930), as well as Wertenbaker (cited above) for this view. More recently interpreters have tended to see the Puritans as upholders of communitarian values over the appetitive aspects of the capitalist ethos. See especially Wilson Carey McWilliams, *The Idea of Fraternity in America* (Berkeley: University of California Press, 1973), chap. 5. The legacy of the Puritan ethos is complex on this point. John Kennedy, Mario Cuomo, and Jesse Jackson have all appealed to Winthrop's city upon a hill as an exemplar of political reform, but Ronald Reagan has also employed the metaphor as a symbol of individualism. For the student who wishes to explore the cultural distinctions here, Robert Bellah et al., eds., *Individualism and Commitment in American Life* (New York: Harper & Row, 1987), Parts 2 and 10, will be helpful.

The political environment of early Quakerism in England, as well as other sectarian geneses, such as those of the Ranters, Seekers, and others, is explored by Christopher Hill, *The World Turned Upside Down: Radical Ideas during the English Revolution* (New York: Viking, 1972). Daniel Shea examines the politically significant interior aspects of Quaker thought in *Spiritual Autobiography in Early America* (Princeton: Princeton University Press, 1980). Gary B. Nash, *Quakers and Politics* (Princeton: Princeton University Press, 1968) emphasizes the discordant strains of the political thought of the Friends, while Alan Dully, *William Penn's Legacy* (Baltimore: Johns Hopkins University Press, 1977), focuses upon the institutions of cooperation. It was Frederick Tolles's early work that emphasized the conflict between Quaker ascetism and the opportunities for material advancement in America. See his *Meeting House to Counting House: The Quaker Merchants of Colonial Philadelphia* (Chapel Hill: North Carolina University Press, 1948). For a view which emphasizes the continuities in Quaker thought, see Margaret Hope Bacon, *The Quiet Rebels* (Philadelphia: New Society Publishers, 1985); Louis B. Wright, *The Atlantic Frontier* (Ithaca, NY: Cornell University Press, 1959), chap. 5; Hugh Barbour and J. William Frost, *The Quakers* (Westport, CT: Greenwood Press, 1988). Essays on Penn as a political theorist as well as interpretations of the "affirmation controversy" can be found in Richard S. Dunn and Mary Maples Dunn, eds., *The World of William Penn* (Philadelphia: University of Pennsylvania Press, 1986).

The Virginia experiment has been surveyed by Bernard Bailyn, "Politics and Social Structure in Virginia," in James M. Smith, ed., *Seventeenth Century Virginia* (Chapel Hill: University of North Carolina Press, 1959), pp. 90–115; Clifford Dowdey, *The Golden Age* (Boston: Little, Brown, 1970); Perry Miller, *Errand into the Wilderness* (Cambridge: Harvard University Press, 1956), chap. 4; Charles S. Sydnor, *Gentleman Freeholders: Political Practices in Washington's Virginia* (Chapel Hill: North Carolina University Press, 1952). T. H. Breen raises the intriguing question, informed by anthropological theory, that the political personalities of the Virginia planters were derived from the maxim, "You are what you eat (smoke)." See *Tobacco Culture* (Princeton: Princeton University Press, 1985). Equally intriguing as theoretically informed history is Rhys Isaac's *The Transformation of Virginia, 1740–1790* (Chapel Hill: University of North Carolina Press, 1982). Isaac uses insights from symbolic anthropology to examine cultural relationships that are part "oral-dramatic" and part "script-typographic." In terms of primary resources, Jefferson's own account of his home state, *Notes on the State of Virginia*, William Peden, ed. (New York: Norton, 1954) must also be consulted.

☆ *Major Works*

1630	"A Modell of Christian Charity," John Winthrop
1644	"The Bloody Tenet of Persecution for Cause of Conscience," Roger Williams
1637	"Trial Testimony," Anne Hutchinson
1652	"Frame of Government of Pennsylvannia," William Penn
1791	*Autobiography*, Benjamin Franklin

Revolution

INTRODUCTION

Revolution is one of the most complex events in politics. It is nearly impossible to predict. Even Lenin, the great revolutionary strategist in exile in Zurich, was unprepared for the collapse of the Russian government and the abdication of the czar in 1917. Revolutions themselves occur from a variety of causes. Economic dislocations caused by modernization, a tax crisis, governmental inefficiency, military defeat, often in some combination, contribute to conditions susceptible to revolution. Many observers also place emphasis on what is called *failure of nerve* on the part of the government in power. Officials in the existing government seem unable to envision policy alternatives that will stabilize society.

In Russia efforts at land reform failed, and as the country was drawn into the war in Europe, economic conditions deteriorated rapidly. When this immobilization becomes widespread, many important segments of society can withdraw their loyalty to the regime; this affords opportunities for individuals to create new institutions that capture the allegiance of portions of the population and compete with the state. New political parties may form and grow, and even paramilitary organizations can be created. Sometimes existing institutions are transformed. In France a tax crisis forced Louis XVI to call the Estates General into existence. The body had not met since 1614. Soon its members reorganized themselves as the National Assembly and challenged the monarchy.

A revolution itself, at least in terms of the overthrow of an existing regime, can be quite brief or last for years. It can be the result of a coup d'état (the swift military capture of the reins of political power by an organized force), or it can produce civil war or a lengthy guerrilla war. In Russia the czarist regime collapsed quickly when troops refused to disperse rioters in Petrograd, the wartime name of St. Petersburg. In Cuba, China, and Nicaragua, the overthrow of the government was the result of years of guerrilla warfare.

In America the precipitating factors and early stages correspond to revolutions in other countries. In 1763 Britain emerged victorious from its war with France, but the conflict was expensive and governmental officials studied ways to raise revenue. One solution focused upon its colonies as a source of new tax revenue. A previous ministry under Sir Robert Walpole had refused to broach the issue, but George Grenville, upon surveying revenues in America, concluded that the expense of maintaining customs officials in the American colonies was greater than the revenues produced. He proposed to Parliament an increase on the tax on molasses (which was used to make rum). When American merchants complained, he lowered the increase but also recommended to Parliament an overhaul of the customs enforcement structure designed to prevent smuggling. Grenville also announced that he would propose further tax legislation in the form of stamps, which were to be purchased by the colonists at various levels of economic exchanges such as lawsuits, newspapers, advertisements, and diplomas.

The Sugar Act (1764) and the impending Stamp Act created a constitutional crisis for the colonies. In a flurry of pamphleteering, arguments were made suggesting that Parliament had no authority to tax commerce internal to the colonies, that Parliament could impose taxes as a means of regulating trade but not for revenue, and that Parliament had legislative supremacy but not a taxing power over the colonies. A central theme in all of these debates involved the right of Parliament to legislate in the absence of representation. Englishmen, so the colonists argued, had fought great historic battles extending back to the Magna Carta that had established the principle of no taxation without consent. The colonists used John Locke's defense of the Glorious Revolution of 1688 in his *Two Treatises on Civil Government* (1690) to furnish support for their position. Grenville responded to this charge through a subordinate, Thomas Whately. Whately contended that the Sugar Act and any other exercise of parliamentary taxing power were indeed based upon consent. Many Englishmen residing in the home country could not vote because of property restrictions or because they lived in boroughs that sent no member to the House of Commons. But these Englishmen, as well as Englishmen in the colonies, were *virtually* represented since every member of Parliament represented every person in the empire. Not only did this argument prove unconvincing to the colonists, but pamphleteers began to extend their critique of parliamentary authority. Daniel Dulaney, a Maryland lawyer, published an essay, "Considerations on the Propriety of Imposing Taxes in the British Colonies," which contended that even if virtual representation was a valid interpretation of consent, it assumed a commonality of interests between Britain and the colonies that did not exist.

It was in the context of these debates that colonial legislatures began to take formal action protesting the acts. Nine colonies sent representatives to New York in 1865. This "Stamp Act Congress" accepted "all due subordination" to Parliament but made a distinction between legislation and taxation. There were also varieties of extralegal activity. The British ministry decided that it would be politically advantageous to appoint colonials to administer the tax. Mobs of angry Bostonians arrived one evening to demand that a newly appointed agent, Andrew Oliver, resign his tax commission. He agreed, but his home was still pillaged. Shortly afterward, rioters burned the residence of Thomas Hutchinson, who was later to become the royal governor of Massachusetts. Organizations called the *Sons of Liberty* were formed which promised to resist the Stamp Act of 1765 "to the last extremity."

The Stamp Act was repealed by Parliament in February 1766, partly because Benjamin Franklin assured members of Parliament that Americans were only protesting internal and not external taxation. Franklin's position was a shrewd one. It defused the Stamp Act crisis, even though Franklin knew that public opinion in the colonies had already rejected that distinction. In fact, James Otis, a member of the Massachusetts Assembly, had written a pamphlet dismissing the difference two years earlier. Parliament too was apparently unconvinced, because it passed the Declaratory Act (1766), which asserted its legislative supremacy "in all cases whatsoever."

The crisis passed, but other questions immediately emerged. One involved the issue of British troops in the colonies. A billeting act was passed requiring colonial legislatures to finance the cost of these troops. When the New York legislature refused to appropriate funds, the ministry in London ordered the royal governor to veto every piece of legislation until the assembly succumbed. There were now 10,000 British troops in Boston. Political leaders expressed concern over these regiments. Colonists had fought off the Indians for over a hundred years without appreciable aid. Since the war with France was over, why was an army needed at all? Relations between colonists and troops deteriorated, and the inevitable occurred in March 1770. Harassed by snowballs and other projectiles thrown by Boston youth, the 29th Regiment fired on the crowd. Five people were killed in what became known as the *Boston Massacre.*

The tax question emerged again just a year after the repeal of the Stamp Act. A new ministry under Charles Townshend recommended a new set of taxes on imports on a large number of items, including glass, paper, tea, and paint. While Townshend never personally accepted the distinction between internal and external taxation, he used the argument to justify the legitimacy of his undertaking. The Townshend Revenue Acts (1767) produced a wave of nationalism as colonial legislatures and pamphleteers urged citizens to boycott British goods. The acts were repealed in 1770, except for a duty on tea. Colonial autonomy was soon again challenged when Governor Hutchinson of Massachusetts informed the assembly that neither he nor local judges would be paid by the legislature but by the king through custom revenues. This loss of legislative control of the executive branch so angered the colonists that the Boston town meeting created a new organization, Committees of Correspondence, to disseminate its own protests to other towns for discussion and adoption.

Tea became an issue again in 1773 when Parliament, in an effort to help the British East India Company, gave the corporation a monopoly on tea imports to the colonies. Prices would be lower, but local merchants would be frozen out of the tea business. Crowds of colonists appeared at the wharves when the first shipments of tea arrived. Ship captains agreed to leave without delivering their cargo, but Governor Hutchinson ordered them to remain. Crowds returned after dark and dumped the tea overboard.

The reaction of Parliament to the Boston Tea Party was the most drastic of the decade-long conflict. The Coercive Acts (called in the colonies the Intolerable Acts) closed the port of Boston to all commerce, placed the city under martial law, forbade town meetings, required royal officials accused of capital offenses to be tried in London, and withdrew the right of the assembly to appoint the governor's Council. Representatives from each of the colonies met at the First Continental Congress in Philadelphia in 1774 to respond to these actions. Without explicitly declaring rebellion, the Congress, after rejecting a conciliatory proposal, adopted a plan for nonimportation, nonconsumption, and nonexportation of British goods. In order to enforce the boycott, the new legislative body authorized each colonial town to form committees of safety to enforce the boycott and expose violators as "enemies to the rights of British America."

The following spring local militia, organized as minutemen, engaged a British expeditionary force searching for weapons caches at Lexington, a small Massachusetts village. Colonials continued their attack on the king's troops at Concord as the forces attempted to return to Boston. A month later the Second Continental Congress met to raise an army. The colonists were at war with the British Empire. The following year Patrick Henry, on instructions from the Virginia House of Burgesses, moved a resolution of formal independence. Thomas Jefferson provided the draft of the declaration itself two days later. In 1777 the Congress approved a constitution for all the former colonies. After more than five years of warfare, General Charles Cornwallis's surrender of his troops at Yorktown (1781) convinced the British Parliament to negotiate a peace treaty.

Up to this point the American Revolution bears remarkable similarities to other modern revolutions. For example, in France the Estates General transformed itself into an independent legislature rather than simply ratifying the king's revenue proposals. It then abolished the old representative system of estates (nobility, clergy, and commons). Independent political organizations called *communes* emerged in the cities. Crowds also engaged in independent actions, such as storming the Bastille (1789) and violent attacks on aristocrats. A Declaration of the Rights of Man was passed by the new National Assembly, which asserted new theoretical premises for the organization of government and society, much as the Declaration of Independence had done for Americans. A constitutional monarchy was formed in 1789, which withdrew from the king the right to dissolve the legislature.

In Russia during World War I economic deterioration as a result of war with Germany brought protest to the streets in Petrograd. Neighborhood-based groups of workers called *soviets* formed to organize demonstrations. When the troops refused to disperse the demonstrators, the czar abdicated. The new Russian legislature, the Duma, which had been created as a concession by the czar after the failed revolt of 1905, set up a provisional government to manage affairs until elections could be scheduled.

At about this point, in both France and Russia the revolutions began to depart significantly from the American case. In France the constitutional monarchy collapsed in September 1792 and was replaced by a revolutionary government. The new government abolished the monarchy and dramatically extended the suffrage to include all adult males. But the new revolutionary government was confronted with a counterrevolution in the province of Vendée as well as by international opposition. As a result, the government began to use imprisonment and execution to purge the country of those in the army and general population it felt were threatening the revolution. Factions emerged in the new legislature between one group, the Girondins, and a more radical group, the Jacobins. In May 1793 the Paris commune surrounded the assembly and arrested the Girondins. In September the *Great Terror* was inaugurated by the Jacobin lawyer, Maximilien Robespierre. Committees of public safety arrested and executed thousands of people whom the revolutionaries deemed a threat to the revolution. Robespierre justified this violence on the grounds that only terror could steel the virtue of the revolutionaries. Under his leadership the goals of the revolution expanded enormously. France was to initiate an entirely new civilization. Christianity was abolished, and even the calendar was changed to symbolize the break with the past. After more than a year of this violence and turmoil, Robespierre was overthrown in July (Thermidor in the new French calendar). A new government called the Directory reintroduced property qualifications for voting. Napoleon came to power in 1799;

it was to be nearly a century before France was able to create a democratic regime.

In Russia the elections planned by the provisional government were never implemented. V. I. Lenin, the leader of the radical wing (Bolsheviks) of the Russian Marxist party, returned to the country from exile in Switzerland with the aid of the German secret service. He immediately began a policy of opposition to the provisional government, calling for a new regime under the leadership of the soviets. Although the Bolsheviks represented a minority of the membership of the soviets, Lenin initiated a coup on November 7, 1917 that successfully overthrew the provisional government. Before the end of the year, the Bolsheviks outlawed the Cadets, a party of moderate reformers. Shortly afterward, the Social Revolutionaries, a large peasant party, was declared illegal. The Bolshevik program involved the nationalization of all property. Under the conditions of civil war, which began in 1918 when opposition to the Bolsheviks became organized, Lenin initiated a policy of *war communism*. This policy involved requisitioning all labor for the state. After a group of sailors at the Kronstadt naval base protested in 1921 against the absence of democracy in the new regime as well as the rise of a secret police force, the Cheka, Lenin relented somewhat and permitted some forms of capitalism under his New Economic Policy (NEP).

After Lenin's death in 1924, Joseph Stalin emerged after a power struggle. Consolidating his position, Stalin abandoned the NEP and initiated a program of collectivization of all agriculture in the country. Opposition was violent and fierce; some farmers burned their crops rather than hand them over to the government. A famine of major proportions was a result. In 1934 Stalin also began a purge of the Bolshevik party itself. Millions of people were arrested and forced to confess treason at show trials. Some were simply summarily shot or sent to labor camps. Stalin's policies were repudiated in 1956 by Nikita S. Khrushchev, but democratic reform did not follow. In 1985, Mikhail Gorbachev has attempted to initiate some democratic reforms which led to a cascade of changes that ended communist rule and the Soviet Union itself.

Why did the French and Russian revolutions proceed upon a different course than the American? Or, if the French and Russian cases are models, was the American experience a revolution at all? Crane Brinton, in his classic study of revolution (*Anatomy of Revolution*), argues that there is a "natural history" of national insurrection. Revolutions, despite important national variations, appear to undergo significant stages. Brinton contends that nearly all revolutions begin with a brief honeymoon period in which the population is so flushed with its success that nearly any change seems possible. The first revolutionary regime, however, experiences great difficulties in creating new, stable political structures and economic conditions.

These "revolutionary moderates" are challenged by radicals who argue that the new rulers are too timid to initiate the necessary revolutionary changes. When the radicals assume power, usually violently, they too are beset by difficulties. Their goals are much more ambitious and their support in the general population less extensive. Consequently, a period of terror follows in which the revolutionary moderates are purged and the population is submitted to organized violence. Brinton argues that no society can undergo this terror forever. Eventually the radicals are overthrown by groups in society committed to end the terror and revolutionary experimentation. Brinton calls this stage of revolution a *Thermidor*, after the French experience. Usually, in a Thermidor, the democratic reforms that appeared early in the revolution are wiped out along with many of the radical policies.

Brinton's model revolutionary stages (honeymoon, rule of the revolutionary moderates, accession of the radicals, terror, and Thermidor) are of significant predictive value in terms of the French and Russian revolutions and many others as well. But it appears as if in America the revolution never progressed beyond the stage of the revolutionary moderates. Why was America an exception to the natural history of modern revolution?

THE AMERICANIZATION OF REPUBLICANISM

There have been many explanations for the unique character of the American Revolution. To account for its peculiar course, some writers have emphasized the fact that the American Revolution was a colonial revolt. The Americans were faced with the task of liberating themselves from external rule rather than overthrowing their own rulers. But this interpretation overlooks the problems faced in dealing with the loyalists, those who wished to continue colonial status, as well as the fact that the issue of "home rule" quickly became merged with the question of "who shall rule at home." Moreover, colonial revolutions frequently proceed along the stages outlined by Brinton.

Louis Hartz, in *The Liberal Tradition in America*, has identified the primary cause for the character of the American Revolution as the absence of feudalism in the colonies. While in New England there was common agreement that society was composed of various "orders," and in New York, Maryland, and Virginia there were structures resembling feudalism, the complex European system of lords, vassals, and peasants was largely absent in America. According to Hartz, these "feudal relics" were easily removed during the revolution. Thus America was spared the trial of replacing a whole economic system with another, as was the case in France and Russia (and indeed in most modern revolutions).

Most revolutionaries discover that the church poses a major obstacle to radical change. The clergy is frequently politically allied with those in political power and holds a powerful influence over its congregations. In France church property was confiscated under the constitutional monarchy, and priests were forced to sign oaths of loyalty under the revolutionary government. Later the Jacobins attempted to create their own state religion. In America there was no single church but a variety of sects, which for the most part supported the revolution. The congregational structure of many of the American churches may have produced a receptivity to the American doctrines of consent. For example, the loyalist Peter Oliver somewhat cynically complained that the Boston clergy, "being dependent on the people for . . . daily bread [and] having frequent intercourse with the people, imbibed their principles." Moreover, the character of religious support may have influenced the direction of the Revolution.

Samuel Langdon's 1775 sermon, "Government Corrupted by Vice, and Recovered by Righteousness," illustrates the sober character of revolutionary endorsement from the pulpit. In the sermon Langdon reviews recent events in Massachusetts. He notes with sadness that Massachusetts has been "made a garrison of mercenary troops" and reports that the violence at Lexington and Concord was the result of self-defense ("he that arms himself to commit a robbery . . . is the first aggressor"). Langdon places the turmoil in a theocentric context:

> We must keep our eyes fixed on the supreme government of the Eternal King, as directing all events, setting up or pulling down the kings of the earth at his pleasure, suffering the best forms of human government to degenerate and go to ruin by corruption, or restoring the decayed constitutions of kingdoms and states by reviving public virtue and religion. . . .

After reviewing the troubled history of Israel in the Old Testament, he then applies his model of divine direction to current political events. The "excellency of the constitution" of England was once "the envy of neighboring nations." But the British nation is now

> a mere shadow of its ancient political system—in titles of dignity without virtue—in vast public treasures continually lavished in corruption until everything is exhausted, notwithstanding the mighty streams perpetually flowing in. . . .

England had become a corrupt empire past its prime when the "public good engages the attention of the whole" and, as such, Americans should feel no religious obligation to submit to its demands for taxes. In fact, the implication of Langdon's argument is that Americans have a religious duty to separate from the empire before they too become corrupted.

But here Langdon added a final point to his sermon. How certain could Americans be that they too were not on their own road to corruption?

> Have we not lost much of the spirit of genuine Christianity which so remarkably appeared to our ancestors, for which God distinguished them. . . . Have we not departed from their virtues?

Langdon hoped that much of our "true religion" remained, but his warning to his congregation that a just government is a gift from God that must be treasured gave a sense of restraint and pessimism to the American Revolution.

The existence of representative institutions in America is another commonly cited reason for the relative moderation of the American Revolution. The Virginia legislature was formed in 1619, and every other colony enjoyed representative government shortly after its establishment. This century of experience in representative politics made the colonial legislatures natural foci for revolutionary action. The French Estates General, on the other hand, had been moribund for 300 years, and the Russian Duma had never fully operated as a legislature. The new political structures that always emerge in a revolutionary situation were in America creatures of these legislative bodies. Institutions invented during the revolutionary moment have very fluid or nonexistent representative structures; hence, they offer easy access for the accession of radicals. This, no doubt, was part of the reason that Lenin introduced the slogan, "All Power to the Soviets." Even with this difference in America, however, the more informal structures sometimes threatened to overtake the legislatures as centers of revolutionary action. In Pennsylvania in the 1770s, for example, the twenty-five-member Committee of Public Safety grew independent and far more radical than the Assembly.

There are other additional factors as well that help explain the special case of the American Revolution. Revolutionary America was not faced with a threat from hostile neighboring countries, as were France and Russia. In fact, the first American foreign policy crisis did not come until 1800, and this was precipitated in part by the French Revolution. In her study of the American Revolution, Hannah Arendt notes the absence of extreme poverty in American cities as a reason the revolutionaries were not faced directly by the "social questions" of the French and Russian revolutions.

Certainly all these factors are important in accounting for the nature of the American Revolution. But an extremely important element concerns the political thought of the revolutionaries themselves. Robespierre justified the Great Terror from his interpretation of Jean Jacques Rousseau; Lenin cited Karl Marx as his guide. Certainly both revolutionary leaders are responsible for adapting and even willfully misinterpreting these theorists for their own ends. Yet both Rousseau and Marx did offer philosophies that justified the centralization of power. The American revolutionaries, on the other hand, looked to another tradition to guide and justify their revolt.

In fact, on one reading the American revolutionary pamphleteers fail to reveal any broad ideology. Most of the American revolutionaries wrote in a careful, legalistic style that Clinton Rossiter once described as "an informed, hardheaded appeal to the facts." But beneath the complex legal argumentation over the authority of the Parliament to tax and legislate and the locus of sovereignty in the British Empire lay an acceptance of a political theory that has a long, if irregular, history in Western thought: republicanism.

Americans found the sources of republican theory in their interpretations of both Sparta and Athens, in republican Rome, in Calvin's Geneva, in the early Saxon migration to England, in republican Florence, in the Commonwealth experience during the English Civil War, and in the behavior of Parliament in the Glorious Revolution of 1689. They cited the model of Lycurgus, the leader of Sparta; they cited Thucydides, the chronicler of Athenian history, and Aristotle; they cited Polybius and Cicero; they cited Richard Hooker, John Milton, James Harrington, Algernon Sidney, and John Locke. They also borrowed from the French philosopher, the Baron de Montesquieu; from John Trenchard's Whig commentaries on early seventeenth-century British politics; from the Dutch and German natural-law theorists, Hugo Grotius and Samuel Pufendorf.

What were the main features of an approach to politics that appears intermittently through the history of Western political thought? There are obviously great differences, both among these writers and in their historical periods, but the Americans emphasized three common elements: a commitment to republican government, a cyclical theory of corruption, and a belief in "republican virtue."

The American revolutionaries identified a form of government that they believed was the only structure capable of ensuring justice for the whole population. There were great differences of opinion about the precise institutions needed to constitute a republic. The colonists agreed, however, that the only legitimate government was one devoted to maximizing the general good of the entire community. Furthermore, they agreed that a republic was the only political form that would pass this test. Other forms, such as monarchies and aristocracies, might incidentally promote the public good, but they were by nature designed to promote the welfare of only part of the population. Because republics rested upon the consent of the whole population, they were free. Americans thus defined liberty less in the modern sense of the term as personal, individual absence of constraint than as the collective freedom of citizens from governmental tyranny.

As enthusiastic as American republicans might be for this form of government, all were aware that republics seemed to have a short history.

Both Athens and Sparta lost their republican forms; Rome degenerated into "Caesarism"; politics in Florence were turbulent and brought forth both demagogues and despots. Indeed, England itself, despite centuries of struggle to limit monarchy, was felt to be in transition. Most of the writers that the Americans drew upon had observed this process of seemingly inevitable decline. Thucydides described the transformation of Athens after it became an empire. Polybius and Cicero, as well as Machiavelli, wrote of republics in decline. The seventeenth-century Whig tradition was for the most part a history of lost battles. Thomas Dawes summarized the perception of these histories of republics when he wrote that "half our learning is their epitaph." Republicanism then had a premodern cast; history was a cyclical process of growth and then of decay and corruption rather than a linear development of liberation and progress. Gordon Wood, in his study of this period in America, concludes that the

> republicanism as Americans expressed it in 1776 possessed a decidedly reactionary tone. It embodied the ideal of the good society as it had been set forth from antiquity through the eighteenth century.

The only feature of republics that could delay this process of corruption was what would be called today a behavioral disposition toward public regardedness on the part of citizens. Americans called this set of attitudes *republican virtue*, and until the writing of *The Federalist*, no critic of the English policy could conceive of a viable republic with it. Republican virtue had a counterpart in Puritan thought. Winthrop spoke of the need for settlers to "entertain each other in brotherly affection" and to "abridge ourselves of our superfluidities, for the supply of others' necessities. . . ." There is no doubt that many Americans understood republican virtue in precisely these terms. Others, however, looked to the classics for their definition. Virtue was love, unconditional love, for one's country. Many of these Americans formulated the concept in military terms. Richard Henry Lee spoke of "honor, property and military glories." Benjamin Rush took Spartan virtue as his model: "Every man in a republic is public property. His time and talents—his youth—his manhood—his old age—any more, life, all belong to his country." Sometimes discussion of the attitudes antithetical to virtue help define the concept. Republics in decline were composed of citizens who were "effeminate," "steeped in luxury," "fawning," "submissive," or "timid."

How did these sentiments called republican virtue arise? How could they be maintained across generations? American republicans were more certain about the first question than about the second. Republics seemed to emerge as the result of fortuitous foundings. When Montesquieu said that democracy originated "in the woods," he was referring to the institutions of the Germanic tribes that overpowered imperial Rome. Americans focused on other foundings as well. They particularly noted the Saxon settlements in sixth-century Britain as well as the formation of the Lycurgan constitution of Sparta, the birth of republican Rome, and, of course, the resettlement of Judea after the Babylonian exile. There was clearly an element of colonial self-assertion in this approach to republican history, for the Americans could say that their apparent cultural primitivism was an asset.

More difficult, however, was the question of how this virtue could be maintained. Answers here varied and, as we shall discuss in a moment, were dependent upon a writer's own colonial experience. But there was agreement that republican virtue could continue to exist only where citizens were independent. Citizens who relied upon the government for means of support or who were in a subservient position to another could not be relied upon to exercise their liberty. Colonists frequently focused upon property ownership as a definition of personal independence. In a sense, the property qualification was a reaffirmation of British practice. In England, the voting requirement of an estate with an annual income of forty shillings was based on a 1430 statute that said in part that the land holding must be such that would "furnish all the necessities of life, and render the freeholder, if he pleased, an independent man." Property requirements for standing for elective office were much higher (600 pounds to be a member of the House of Commons from a shire). But Americans were very much aware that the availability of land in the colonies had exploded the British oligarchical practice of political participation. In 1656 James Harrington, the seventeenth-century English republican theorist, described a utopia (*Oceana*) in which private property was widely dispersed in relatively equal holdings. To the colonists, Harrington's utopia had been realized in America. Estimates of those who met the property qualifications for voting in the colonies before the Revolution range as high as 80 percent.

But there were stress points in the republican position. As Forrest McDonald notes, republican theory was

> at once individualistic and communal: individualistic in that no member of the public could be dependent upon any other and still be reckoned a member of the public; communal in that every man gave himself totally to the good of the public as a whole.

An overreliance upon the communal would erode the independence necessary for virtue; an overreliance upon the individual would erode the attention to public life that was essential to maintaining a republic. This theoretical stress in some ways seems to have acted as a moderating force in the Revolution, but it did produce different versions of American republicanism.

VARIETIES OF AMERICAN REPUBLICANISM

Despite a common agreement on republicanism and its major tenets (republican government, the inevitability of corruption, virtue, and independence), it should be noted that America was a culturally complex entity in the middle of the eighteenth century. Each colony had its own history, and participants in the revolutionary struggle interpreted republicanism differently. Urban centers developed their own version of republicanism—one quite different from that fashioned by agricultural republicans. Religious affiliation and tradition accounted for important variations as well. Ethnic background too influenced republican attitudes. Scholars have just begun to appreciate the various strains of prorevolutionary thought and develop various taxonomies to account for them. Let us focus our attention on protest in three colonies—Massachusetts, Pennsylvania, and Virginia—and suggest three varieties of republicanism: *moralist, radical,* and *aristocratic.*

Boston was the center of colonial revolt in the 1760s and 1770s. Indeed, it was the closing of the port and the imposition of martial law that precipitated the Revolution. At the hub of this protest was Samuel Adams, the son of a brewer. Both revolutionaries and loyalists have credited Adams with a major role in the struggle for independence. He led a caucus of the Boston town meeting that saved it from attempts to narrow its authority on the part of conservatives; he was instrumental in creating the Sons of Liberty and the Committees of Correspondence; he was a delegate to the Continental Congress and a signer of the Declaration of Independence. Men in his own generation expressed awe of Adams's organizational abilities. Thomas Jefferson called him "truly the man of the Revolution." A mark of approval in the 1760s was to introduce a local patriot as the "Samuel Adams of North Carolina" or the "Samuel Adams of Philadelphia." Thomas Hutchinson, the royal governor, described him as "our grand incendiary." A British captain wrote his father from Boston in 1775: "Would you believe it . . . that this immense continent . . . is moved and directed by one man!— a man of ordinary birth and desperate fortune, who, by his abilities and talent for factious intrigue, has made himself of some consequence."

Adams was the epitome of the proverb that "all politics is local." His affection for the local Puritan tradition was complete. An early biographer wrote that he was a "strict Calvinist," and "probably, no individual of his day had so much the feelings of the ancient puritans." One of the pressing political problems of the colonial protesters was how to involve larger numbers of citizens in organized opposition to the Crown. Adams had direct and close relationships with both the local merchants and artisans of the city through his visits to taverns and his duties as a tax collector. He seemed to know when to flood town meetings with participants so as to organize

street protests, and when to rely upon more conventional methods of political influence. He defended the expansion of the base of political protest by
contending the people "can judge, as well as their betters, when there is a
danger to liberty."

If Adams modified his Puritan heritage in a democratic direction, he
also accepted a central tenet of the New England tradition. Adams was
nearly oblivious to the propertied interpretations of republican virtue. "The
cottager may beget a wise son; the noble a fool," he wrote, "the one is capable of great improvement; the other, not." He inherited his father's shop but
was indifferent to enterprise. Adams was a public man. The characterization of him by a contemporary as a man who "ate little, drank little and
thought much" captures Adams's own vision of an independent America as
a "Christian Sparta." For Adams the future of the republic was dependent
upon the exhibition of this combination of Christian and Spartan virtues.
He believed in austerity, a "sobriety of manners . . . temperance, frugality,
fortitude." The British promoted "luxury and extravagance" in the colonies
because tyrants knew that they could not govern a country "where virtue
and knowledge prevail." Only detachment from worldly goods could free
oneself to the cause of the public good. Adams gloried in his own relative
poverty. He continued to wear the tricornered hat and cape long after they
went out of fashion. His friends bought him a new suit of clothes lest he
embarrass the Massachusetts delegation to the Continental Congress in
Philadelphia.[1]

Not all moralistic republicans accepted all the implications of Samuel
Adams's emphasis on private virtue. Adams's cousin, John Adams,
searched for institutional constraints to ensure the life of republics and
placed more emphasis on property as a basis for virtue. If Samuel represented an equalitarian moralistic republicanism, John Adams advocated a
more hierarchical version. But still, John Adams was in important ways a
moralistic republican. He wrote his wife, Abigail, that his children "shall
live upon a thin diet, wear mean clothes, and work hard, with cheerful
hearts and free spirits." His offspring must "revere nothing but religion,
morality and liberty." Adams recommended sumptuary laws (that is, taxes
on the consumption of luxuries), although he did not hold much hope for
their passage. He considered such laws a means of promoting frugal life-
styles in the public at large.

Philadelphia was in many respects economically similar to Boston. A
commercial center, it produced many products used by the colonies. But
Pennsylvania was less religiously and ethnically homogeneous than Massachusetts. As a result, the kind of artisans that Adams helped organize in
Boston held different viewpoints and ambitions than those in Philadelphia.
The wealthy merchants in the city tended to come from English Quaker
backgrounds, while the artisans were frequently Scotch-Irish Presbyterians

or German farmers. The two classes had their share of antagonisms, which were blunted by a common antipathy toward Britain as well as by frequent social and economic interaction between the two groups. The merchants' complaints centered around trade and banking policies, while the artisans were fed by religious animosities. Most troubling to members of the merchant class—even to those in alliance with the artisans—was the artisans' radical republicanism. According to American historian Robert Kelley, loyalists as well as many well-to-do Quakers looked upon the Scotch-Irish as "barbarians, whiskey drinkers, disloyal and violent men, republicans by instinct, whose ancestors had beheaded Charles I."

The radicalism of the artisans derived from both their cultural and economic position in Pennsylvania society. The status of an artisan in the house- or ship-building trades or in tailoring, the metal craft, or food processing was hard won, often involving years of apprenticeship as a journeyman. These men owned their own tools and frequently determined their own hours of work in their homes. They depended upon the merchants for contracts but were fiercely assertive of their status as independent men. Benjamin Franklin, whose personal success made him a hero of the artisans, claimed in his *Poor Richard's Almanack* that "he that hath a Trade, hath an Estate"; herein lay the radical republicans' interpretation of virtue. As historian Eric Foner notes in his biography of Tom Paine:

> The property of the artisan included his skill, his tools, perhaps his shop and his trade or customers, while the merchant's comprised liquid assets, his warehouse and ships, extensive holdings in real estate and commercial investments, an elegant residence and personal possessions. There was more than a simple difference in wealth here, there was a fundamental difference in attitude. To the artisan, property was legitimate and natural only if it were the product of visible labor.

The radical republicans quickly merged the questions of home rule and who should rule at home. If independence was necessary to prevent the "producing classes" from being forced into economic slavery by British aristocrats, then "great and over-grown rich men" ought to be prevented from controlling local politics as well. Working on the principle of all power to the producing classes, the first Pennsylvania constitutional convention rejected the Whig principle of balanced government and instituted a single legislative body and a vetoless executive council in place of a governor. It eliminated all property qualifications for suffrage save for the payment of taxes. The state constitution itself, in addition to a bill of rights, contained a series of republican admonitions. One urged citizens to only vote for candidates who had "a firm adherence to justice, moderation, temperance, industry and frugality." Introduced but defeated was an attempt to legally prevent the emergence of any extreme of wealth. The clause read:

> [A]n enormous proportion of property vested in a few individuals is dangerous to the rights, and destructive of the happiness of mankind; and therefore every state hath a right by its laws to discourage the possession of such property.

The political culture of prerevolutionary Virginia could not have been further removed from Massachusetts and Pennsylvania. In 1776 one Pennsylvania pamphleteer warned local voters to "let no men represent you . . . who would be disposed to form any rank above that of freeman." In Virginia it was accepted practice, enforced by multiple and complex informal mechanisms of deference, for the tidewater gentry to govern the colony. Nicholas Cresswell, a loyalist, wrote in his journal in 1777 that George Washington, "the American hero, was second son of a creditable Virginia tobacco planter (which I suppose may, in point of rank, be equal to the better sort of yeomanry in England)." But Washington and his tidewater brethren regarded themselves as aristocrats, beleaguered as they might be by British control of the tobacco market and the threat of social disgrace by bankruptcies. Aristocracy may seem antithetical to republican theory, as indeed it was to Samuel Adams and Franklin. But there was a tradition in republican thought (which included Aristotle, Cicero, and Montesquieu) that gave an aristocracy an important role in the maintenance of republics. Freed from the demands of everyday work, aristocrats could devote themselves to the public good and act as a buffer between the government and the people as a whole. Moreover, these were, after all, elected "natural" aristocrats, the most able men in the colony. Richard Henry Lee saw himself as such a man. Lee carried himself with a hauteur one biographer described as a demeanor that "seemed to the Lees only self-respect." Like all tidewater Virginians, Lee took his politics seriously. He assumed his seat in the House of Burgesses at the age of twenty-six, was a presiding officer of the Continental Congress, and after independence served in the U.S. Senate. Lee regarded himself as well as his colleagues as "tribunes" for the yeoman farmers he represented. "To what purpose," he asked John Dickenson in 1778, do people labor "if arbitrary will, uninfluenced by reason, and urged by interest, shall reap the harvest of their diligence and industry?"

For the aristocratic republicans, virtue rested in the protection of property and sound constitutional arrangements that assured a balance of power among the classes in society. They were less certain about the private virtue of the New Englanders and nearly apoplectic in regard to urban republican radicalism since, in Lee's words, "the spirit of commerce is the spirit of service."

THE AMERICAN REPUBLICAN SYNTHESIS

Two documents successfully wove together the basic symbols of these strands of republicanism that helped provide a republican consensus at a crucial moment in the revolution. One was Thomas Paine's pamphlet *Common Sense* (1775); the other was the Declaration of Independence (1776) drafted by Thomas Jefferson. Both tracts are themselves the result of efforts by extraordinary men who had absorbed the tenets of several cultures. Both knew intimately the republicanism of their region. Paine was an artisan (a staymaker and shopkeeper); Jefferson was a tidewater farmer and lawyer. But both men were also international figures. Paine had only arrived in Philadelphia in 1774; *Common Sense* expressed some of the hopes of the artisan classes in London as well as in America. In 1776 Jefferson had yet to become the habitué of Parisian salons but was the protege of the intellectual circle at Williamsburg.

Common Sense advances many of the tenets of radical republicanism. Paine rejected the balanced constitution favored by many moralist and aristocratic republicans in favor of a unicameral legislature. As a result, John Adams was less than pleased with aspects of the pamphlet. But the major thrust of the essay involved a codification of all the republican arguments. In fact, the novelty of *Common Sense* lay in the forthrightness with which Paine took the partially concealed republicanism of a tradition of legalistic pamphlets and brought the ideology to the forefront of his analysis. In Paine's argument it seemed as if a commitment to republicanism, once publicly recognized, required independence. Benjamin Rush warned Paine to avoid direct mention of republicanism and independence, but Paine ignored the advice, claiming that other writers sheltered themselves "in quotations from other authors."

The central stylistic and substantive theme of *Common Sense* was simplicity. This concept formed both the justification of republican government and the font of the essay itself. The pamphlet assumed no knowledge of Latin or Greek and translated any foreign expressions. Paine explained:

> As it is my design to make those that can scarcely read understand, I shall therefore avoid every literary ornament and put it in language as plain as the alphabet.

But if the "rudeness" of the language offended some Americans, there could be little room for disagreement about Paine's use of simplicity as a republican motif. All republicans celebrated virtue as a natural and plain quality.

Paine begins his essay by asserting a distinction between government and society. The latter is produced by our "wants" and the former by our "wickedness." Both promote happiness, but society does so positively by "uniting our affections," and government does so negatively by "restraining our vices." Paine illustrates his point by describing the origins of society and government itself, a favorite theme of the republican theorists. Society emerges through "a thousand motives." People need to cooperate to raise a building in the wilderness; humans are "unfitted for perpetual solitude." As the number and complexity of relationships increase, rules need to be made, for "nothing but Heaven is impregnable to vice." Early governments are simply occasions to make a few rules beneath some "convenient tree," and in this "first parliament every man will have a seat." As a colony of people increases in numbers, representation is a practical alternative.

For republicans who preferred to take their theory from the classics, this account of the origins of government had Aristotelian aspects with its assertion that people were naturally social beings. For those who took their republicanism from the seventeenth-century Whig tradition in England, Paine's account mirrored Locke's state of nature. But most of all the description of the origins of government and society corresponded to the American experience. Admittedly theoretically rarefied and somewhat idealized, Paine's account corresponded with the origins of the American coastal settlements in the seventeenth century. He described the existing arrangements of backwoods communities at his writing.

Having established that government was instituted for the "freedom and security" of its people, Paine proceeded to attack the British constitution itself. Protest writing in the 1760s and 1770s largely accepted the English political system as the culmination of centuries of struggle. Each interest had representation in the system; as a result, the political structure reflected the balance of forces in society. But for Paine the British constitution was a failure. First, it violated simplicity—"a principle in nature which no art can overturn." In fact, absolute governments, "though the disgrace of human nature," at least permit the people to "know the head from which their suffering springs." The British constitution is so complex that "the nation may suffer for years together without being able to discover in which part the fault lies. . . ." Second, it did not reflect a balance of forces but represented the "remains of two ancient tyrannies, compounded with some new republican materials." The monarchy represented the remains of "tyranny in the form of the king"; the House of Lords was an "aristocratical tyranny." Only the House of Commons contained "new Republican materials." These three sources of power do not reciprocally check one another, although one part may temporarily "clog" or "check the rapidity of its motion." Power still resides in the Crown. While Paine admits that monarchical control is not absolute, the English had, in effect, locked the door to absolute monarchy only to give the key to the Crown.

American pamphleteers, in their effort to avoid acceptance of parliamentary sovereignty, attempted to define some kind of commonwealth status with England by proclaiming their general allegiance to the king as a symbol of common nationhood. Paine directed his most pointed attacks at this argument. Here he used the biblical foundations of moralistic republican thought. Borrowing from the Exodus narrative, he described King George as a "pharaoh." Paine confronted directly the existence of kings in ancient Israel by employing some of Locke's arguments, according to which the early monarchical leaders were military men who never claimed hereditary succession. Locke further contended that the Israeli penchant for monarchs was the result of pagan influences. He concluded that "the will of the Almighty . . . expressly disapproves of government by kings." Paine's use of biblical interpretation was clearly tactical. According to John Adams, when he complained about the validity of this biblical interpretation, Paine "expressed a contempt of the Old Testament" and promised to write at a later date his own analysis of religion.

Political disagreements aside, many Americans felt a cultural identification with England that blocked open consideration of independence. Jefferson had carefully challenged this attitude in his 1774 essay, "A Summary View of the Rights of America." In it he contended that just as the Saxons left their "native wilds and woods" in northern Europe to form a new culture, so had the Americans established new societies conducive to their own public happiness. Paine went further. How could one rationally have allegiance to a monarchy that was traced to a "French bastard landing with an armed banditti" (William the Conqueror)? Appealing to anti-Catholicism, Paine described the parent-country argument as one of "low papistical design." Appealing to the Scots and Irish as well as to religious groups that had been treated as outsiders by the English when they resided in their homeland, Paine questioned the validity of the common-parentage position. He asked how this argument had any force when "this new world hath been an asylum for the persecuted lovers of civil and religious liberty from every part of Europe?"

Common Sense concluded with an appeal for a manifesto "setting forth the miseries we have endured" and declaring independence. Six months later the Continental Congress authorized a committee to draft just such a resolution. The Declaration of Independence, largely the work of Thomas Jefferson, has become a world historical document. But Jefferson's purpose in 1776 was less ambitious. As he wrote Lee in 1825, the Declaration was intended as a summary of republican theory as a foundation for revolution:

> [I]t was intended to be an expression of the American mind. . . . All its authority rests then on the harmonizing sentiments of the day, whether expressed in conversation, in letters, printed essays, or in the elementary books of public right, as Aristotle, Cicero, Locke, Sidney, etc.

As such, it is a magnificent summary. It includes all the dualistic symbols of republican thought, the description of tyranny as manifested in a "long train of abuses and usurpations" designed to reduce a free people to "absolute Despotism," and the outline of free government based upon the "consent of the governed." It neatly resolves the American discomfort in attacking Parliament by laying all the blame upon the king.

Yet for all its eloquence the Declaration does achieve its success as a consensus document by raising crucial republican concepts to a high level of abstraction. There is no greater subsequent source of contention in the Declaration than in the assertion of the self-evidence that "all men are created equal." The most glaring contradiction in the statement of equality was, of course, the institution of slavery. By 1776 colonial legislation had established black slavery as a hereditary condition, and complex sets of enabling laws guaranteed that status. Of the nearly 4 million inhabitants of the colonies at the time of the Declaration, almost 700,000 were slaves. Jefferson's attempt to make the slave trade part of the particulars of complaints against the Crown was removed upon southern objection. How did the republican revolutionaries reconcile slavery with equality? Some colonists exempted black Americans from the status of personhood. Most owners of slaves, however, appreciated the contradiction. Jefferson's own description of the institution is placed in the republican model:

> The whole commerce between master and slave is a perpetual exercise of the most boisterous passions, the most unremitting despotism on the one part, and degrading submissions on the other.

In other words, the master-slave relationship was a perfect negation of republicanism. George Mason's assessment mirrored Jefferson's. He anticipates Lincoln's assessment made almost 100 years later: "Every master of slaves is a petty tyrant. They [sic] bring the judgment of Heaven on a country . . . providence punishes national sins, by national calamities."

Despite these admissions, slave owners rarely implemented their own vague plans for manumission. A few felt that the further immigration of white labor would make slavery superfluous. Some northern colonies had already abolished the institution. Some historians argue that the practice of indentured servitude, although limited in duration, softened the discrepancy. Simply put, however, the primary explanation for the existence of the contradiction was the almost universal acceptance of racist patterns of thought. Jefferson's *Notes on Virginia*, for example, contains numerous observations on distinctions which "nature has made" among red, black, and white races in his region.

Perhaps no other American writer in the period reflected more upon the question of race than the author of the Declaration. Jefferson seems to have struggled with the question of the extent to which racial differences were the result of environmental influences (the drastically limited opportunities for black slaves) and some innate, although unexplained, deficiency. Unhappily for a man of such intellect, Jefferson concluded that although slavery explained many of the differences among the races, "it is not their condition, then but nature, which has produced the distinction."

The one area, however, in which Jefferson refused to accept racist explanation was in the realm of morality. Gary Wills, in *Inventing America*, argues that Jefferson relied upon the theorists of the "Scottish Enlightenment" (David Hume, Adam Smith, and Francis Hutcheson) for his approach to equality. This *commonsense school*, as it was called, asserted that moral knowledge was as innate as the traditional senses. Although individuals could be blinded, or born blind, most people were given by God the sense of sight. Similarly, argued the commonsense theorists, conscience (or a "moral sense") was universally a part of human character. In this respect, Francis Hutcheson concluded that "all men are created equal." Jefferson seems to have accepted this concept of an innate moral sense, for he wrote that "moral sense, or conscience" was "as much a part of man as his leg or arm." Thus in regard to black Americans, he was much more willing to attribute alleged moral differences among races to environmental factors:

> That disposition to theft with which [black slaves] have been branded, must be ascribed to their situation. The man, in whose favor no laws of property exist, probably feels himself less bound to respect those made in favor of others.

Jefferson concluded with a question: Might not the slave "justifiably take a little from one, who has taken all from him?"

Winthrop Jordon, in his classic study of racism in America, *The White Man's Burden*, argues that Jefferson's distinction between innate racial intellectual differences and innate moral racial equality was a self-serving one; it resolved the blatant contradiction between slavery and equality while still justifying the institution. Whatever the intent and impact of Jefferson's writing on this point, the moral sense interpretation of the self-evidence of equality is a major part of any interpretation of the document. It could satisfy all but the most obdurate slaveholders and fit well with both the deism of many of the radical republicans and the pietism of their New England brethren. Moreover, other definitions of equality, such as equality before the law, equality of political participation, or economic equality, could be derived independently from the phrase "all men are created equal" by each of the various kinds of republicans.

Another crucial phrase in the Declaration is that all men are "endowed by their Creator with certain unalienable rights, that among these are Life, Liberty and the pursuit of Happiness." The position of rights held collectively by the people against government is a central feature of

republican thought. Especially intriguing, however, was Jefferson's substi-
tution of the more common phrase of "property" or "estate," which was
employed by Locke, for "happiness." There was less novelty in Jefferson's
replacement than one might initially expect. The pseudonymous Cato,
whom Americans were fond of quoting, had said that to "live, securely, happily, and independently is the End and Effect of Liberty. . . ." But "happiness" implied a broader meaning than estate or property, however widely
the last two terms were interpreted. Two meanings are possible; together
they reveal all the tensions inherent in republican political theory. One,
which we can call *happiness-private*, is the more modern definition,
although it certainly was available to the American revolutionaries. It contends that the purpose of government is to facilitate, or at least not be an
obstacle to, each individual's efforts to satisfy private desires. Desires may
vary. Some persons may seek economic advancement; others may search
for intellectual or religious fulfillment. There is, then, a noticeable element
of liberal language in this crucial concept in the Declaration. Jefferson himself expressed his own interpretation of happiness-private once' when he
wrote that he yearned for a life away from public concerns "in the lap and
love of my family, in the society of neighbors and my books, in the whole-
some occupations of my farms and my affairs."

The other meaning, more consistent with the general thrust of republican theory, is *happiness-public*. Here happiness is a right to live in a
well-ordered society. Citizens by this definition have a right to participate
in a society in which they order their own institutions for their collective
benefit. For republicans such a circumstance was a rare and precious
opportunity in human history. As Charles Lee exclaimed to Patrick Henry,
he "used to regret not being thrown into the world in the glorious third or
fourth century of the Romans," but now his hopes "at length bid fair for
being realized."

The one meaning of happiness is individualistic; the other, collectivist. In the context of eighteenth-century America, the republicans embraced
both meanings. The tidewater Virginia aristocrat took his public duties
quite seriously, but so too did he devote time to expanding his own lands
for tobacco harvesting. The Philadelphia artisans were adamantly committed to extending democratic rights (public happiness), but they were also as
committed to individual material advancement (private happiness). As Eric
Foner notes in his study of urban republicanism:

> Culturally, there was a recurrent tension between the sense of mutu-
> ality and community, whether confined to a specific craft or extended
> to all artisans, and the strong tendency toward individualism and
> self-improvement.

Hannah Arendt, who in her analysis of the American Revolution places great weight upon the genius of the idea of public happiness, admits that "the historical fact is that the Declaration of Independence speaks of the 'pursuit of happiness,' not public happiness," and "chances are that Jefferson himself was not very sure in his own mind what happiness meant." Although the Declaration leaves the question of the definition of happiness itself in happy abstract repose, the two meanings (although not completely exclusive) left open the kind of society America might aspire to be after independence: a society in which Americans individually defined for themselves their goals and satisfactions, or a society in which Americans, to use Samuel Adams's phrase, collectively devoted themselves to the maintenance of a "Christian Sparta."

LOYALIST CRITIQUE

Every revolution has its dissenters. There are those who support the old regime as well as those who, while initially supporting revolution, withdraw their endorsement. Indeed, as revolutions seem to proceed upon the course of their natural history, the number of dissenters grows, and revolutionaries take more and more desperate steps to silence them. Even Thomas Paine, the quintessential eighteenth-century revolutionary, was jailed by Robespierre for opposition to the killing of the king and to the violence of the new revolutionary government. Only a bureaucratic error and the intercession of James Madison saved his life.

In America opposition to the Revolution was widespread but largely unorganized. As American revolutionaries intimated, loyalists tended to come from the more advantaged economic classes in society and were more likely to be British-born. But in Virginia Anglicans tended to be republicans while in New England they tended toward support for the Crown. William Nelson in his study *The American Tory* found that the Dutch and German populations assimilated culturally with the English-born colonists supported the Revolution, while those who weren't did not. How many loyalists were there? Phineas Bond, a Pennsylvania loyalist, contended that about 7 to 18 percent of the colonial population opposed the Revolution. Estimates of the number of loyalists who left the country during or after the Revolution range from 60,000 to 100,000.

It is a common error to assume that all loyalists were Tories, that is, supporters of the British majority in Parliament and conservative in outlook. Even such revolutionaries as Benjamin Rush, in assessing loyalist strength during the conflict, admitted that many Whigs were loyalists. Joseph Galloway, for example, was actually a member of the First Continental Congress before he abandoned the cause. Most loyalist Whigs were not willing to withdraw their support for what we would call today some sort of Commonwealth status with England.

But in terms of political theory, some of the most innovative analyses of the Revolution did come from the American Tories. Here were men who saw in the drive for independence what Bernard Bailyn, in *The Ideological Origins of the American Revolution*, calls "the threat to the traditional ordering of human relations implicit in Revolutionary thought." The question of home rule had already turned into a question of who should rule at home, and these men predicted that an inadequate, and indeed dangerously fragile, social order was implicit in republican thought. Let us briefly review two of these republican critics: Peter Oliver and Jonathan Boucher.

Oliver fits well the model of the classic American Tory. He graduated from Harvard in 1730. Using his contacts as a relative of powerful New England families, he amassed great personal wealth in the fledgling iron industry and in banking and commerce. In addition, he held major administrative and judicial positions in the Massachusetts Bay Colony. In the minds of the Boston republicans, Oliver represented the kind of new wealth and power being created by Crown policy. In the early 1770s Oliver became a central figure in the controversies of the day. He willingly assumed the position of stamp distributor and was a recipient of the new Crown policy of paying salaries from revenues of new tax legislation. The Massachusetts General Court, which was in the control of the republicans, drew up articles of impeachment to remove him as an officer of the court. When Oliver insisted on continuing on the bench, grand juries refused to participate in his judicial proceedings; at one point crowds forcibly dragged him from the courtroom. After serving briefly on General Thomas Gage's royally appointed council, Oliver left the colonies when the British evacuated Boston in 1776.

In London Oliver wrote *The Origin and Progress of the American Revolution*. If one searched for a work of political theory about the American Revolution close to the insightful and intense critique of Edmund Burke's *Reflections on the French Revolution*, Oliver's account would be the most likely candidate. Like Burke and perhaps like conservatives in general, Oliver was most successful when he exposed the inner structure of a historical narrative. Oliver's essay is based exclusively on an analysis of the political turmoil in Boston in the 1770s. Robert McCluer Calhoon, a student of loyalist political theory, concludes that Oliver, who was "intimately involved with the events he was describing ... seized upon pictorial description as a means of making his indictment persuasive. Pen sketches, figures of speech, and little dramatizations were his hypotheses—imaginative windows to the interior of tumultuous events."

The central metaphor that Oliver uses to describe the Stamp Act crisis and colonial reaction to the Townshend Acts is witchcraft. Oliver may not have literally accepted this characterization, but it permitted him to make his theoretical point. "Rebellion is as the sin of witchcraft," he once wrote before he left America for exile:

> [I]t is so, my countrymen! in a double sense; for in the first place, no person but one who was bewitched would run the risk of engaging in a rebellion; and in the next place . . . as witchcraft is renouncing the authority of God Almighty and applying to the Devil, so rebellion is withdrawing allegiance from the lawful sovereign, overturning his government and laws, and joining a power inimical to him.

Who were the necromancers? For Oliver, Samuel Adams is the bête noire of his account of the American Revolution. Adams seems to be everywhere; he attaches adherents to his "hindermost part . . . as rattles are affixed to the tail of a rattlesnake." Then there is James Otis, who in Oliver's account is a drunken although brilliant organizer, mobilizing the Boston clergy in support of his own personal ambitions. Oliver calls the ministers Otis's "black regiment," and describes them as basically timid individuals who "acquired a sense of self importance which was too apparent from their manners." "Tinctured with republicanism" by Otis and others, they fed upon the fears of the people rather than providing moral values.

And what role did the people at large play in the revolt? For Oliver, a man who had himself been jostled by crowds, the Boston population was totally bewitched by revolutionary elites. They were indeed, devilish— "dressed up by their seditious leaders with horns, tails, cloven feet." "[A]s for the people in general, they are like . . . [those]. . . Nobility in all countries, perfect machines, wound up by any hand who might first take the winch." Republican ideology was no more than another tool of bewitchment. "Liberty" was a word with a "magic sound" that

> echoed through the interior parts of the country, and the deluded vulgar were charmed with it; like the poor harmless squirrel that runs into the mouth of the rattlesnake the fascination in the word liberty threw the people into the harpy claws of their destroyers. . . .

Like Burke in his analysis of the role of the National Assembly in the French Revolution, Oliver committed the error of exclusively blaming revolutionary discontent on the machinations of political elites. Also like Burke, Oliver treated political issues as only manufactured constructs for advancing personal ambition. In America, so argued Oliver, all this turmoil was created to "gratify the artful smugglers in carrying their contraband tea trade to the Dutch." Also like Burke, Oliver could not imagine that men of middle-class and artisan backgrounds could possibly govern rationally and responsibly. But again like Burke, Oliver still managed to hit upon a truth concerning the kind of political order that was emerging from the political struggles in Boston in the 1770s. He discerned a society being born in which stability and social control were achieved less by structures of social deference and tradition than by the conscious, and perhaps permanent, mobilization of men and women through ideological goals. Here was a different interpretation of the consequence of relying upon republican virtue than that conceived by the revolutionaries. Oliver's own reactionary politics blinded him from seeing many of the advantages of an expanded political arena. It also enabled him, however, to catch a glimpse of a political order that would have horrified the republicans themselves—a world in which public policy is largely determined by mass manipulation through political symbols.

Jonathan Boucher became a loyalist through a different route than Peter Oliver. The son of an English tavern owner and sometime schoolmaster, Boucher arrived in Virginia in 1759. He first served as a tutor to a wealthy merchant and then as an Anglican parson for congregations in Virginia and Maryland. He sharply criticized the Stamp Act as "oppressive, impolitic, and illegal" and praised the opposition of Virginia's House of Burgesses to the Townshend Acts as "the most warrantable, generous, and manly [opposition] that history can produce." But throughout the prerevolutionary period Boucher never wavered in denunciation of independence. Thirteen of his sermons between 1759 and 1775 were collected and revised as *A View of the Causes and Consequences of the American Revolution.*

Boucher's forte lay in his talent for analyzing (and deconstructing) concepts. In one of his sermons he challenges the republican ideas of liberty, consent, and equality. The speech begins with a biblical quotation from Galatians 5:1 often used by the revolutionary clergy: "Stand fast, therefore, in the Liberty Wherewith Christ hath made us free." Boucher argues that St. Paul's injunction has no politically libertarian implications. The freedom of which Paul speaks is freedom from sin. Boucher admits that the acceptance of Christ permits an individual to become "more free in the inner man" by "being endowed with greater firmness of mind in the cause of truth, against the terrors and allurements of the world." He also admits that "in the infancy of Christianity" the "rumor was spread" that "the gospel was designed to undermine kingdoms and commonwealths." But Christian freedom is a far different value from political freedom. If the form of government God placed us under is "mild and free," it is "our duty to enjoy it with gratitude and with thankfulness"; "if it be less indulgent and less liberal than in reason it ought to be, still it is our duty not to disturb and destroy the peace of the community. . . ." Boucher also dismisses equality as inconsistent with the maintenance of any form of society:

> A musical instrument composed of chords, keys, or pipes, all perfectly equal in size and power, might as well be expected to produce harmony, as a society composed of members all perfectly equal to be productive of order and peace.

The deconstructive focus of the sermon, however, is upon the concept of consent. Boucher correctly sees consent as a theoretical construct designed to accommodate the values of liberty and equality to the need for political order. Locke used the concept of a state of nature to explore the consequences of a society of "perfect" freedom and equality, and concluded that certain "inconveniences" led individuals to consent to the creation of government to protect their life, liberty, and property. Individuals are no longer perfectly free or equal but have willed their own subordination. According to Locke, if the purposes for which government is instituted are abandoned, individuals have a right to withdraw their consent and form another polity. Boucher argues that the concept of consent simply cannot carry the theoretical weight Locke assigned to it.

Boucher targets the individualistic implications of Locke's theory. What counts for consent? Acquiescence cannot substitute for consent. Neither, on the principle of equality, can parents consent for their children. No act of compulsion, however "rightfully" conceived, justifies consent. Locke would have in principle agreed with all these points and even with Boucher's conclusion:

> The same principle of equality that exempts him from being governed without his own consent clearly entitles him to recall and resume that consent whenever he sees fit; and he alone has a right to judge when and for what reasons it may be resumed.

But while there is a sense in Locke according to which rebellion as withdrawal of consent is an individual determination, Boucher notes that those who exercise it when tyranny reaches "no farther than some private Mens cases" are "sure to perish." Revolution in practice is thus a majority right. Boucher seizes upon this transition in Locke's argument as evidence of the inevitable inconsistency of consent theory. Even if, Boucher asks, withdrawal of consent is a majority right, what kind of social life is possible, given that majorities fluctuate?

> Governments, though always forming, would never be completely formed: for, the majority today, might be the minority tomorrow; and, of course, that which is now fixed might and would be unfixed.

People would be "trained to make and unmake governments." "Such a system, therefore, can produce only perpetual dissensions and contests, and bring back mankind to a state of nature; arming every man's hand, like Ishmael's, against every man, and rendering the world . . . [a] field of blood."

Locke had insisted (and the signers of the Declaration of Independence had reiterated) that, given human nature, the right to withdraw consent would be exercised very rarely. Boucher disagreed. The doctrines of liberty, equality, and consent formed for him a "fantastic system." If implemented, such a system would make the world "wearisome," "confused," and violent. Shortly before he emigrated from America in 1776, Boucher wrote that his position was a lost cause. In fact, he already spoke as a person from another country:

> Early prejudices, fostered by education, and confirmed by religion, all conspire to cherish republicanism. Their schools, academies, or colleges seem . . . to have been instituted for that end. . . . The multitude will ever be wrought on by public speaking; in America, literally and truly, all power flows from the people.

Boucher was one of the 60,000 to 100,000 people who left America during or just after the Revolution. Unlike the French emigres, very few returned. Robert Palmer concludes in *The Age of Democratic Revolution* that "an important nucleus of conservatism was permanently lost to the United States."

SUMMARY AND COMMENT

The American interpretation of republicanism served to modify and restrain the revolutionaries. The republican suspicion of the state, the belief that all political systems (even republican ones) are subject to corruption, the insistence that virtue was already a feature of American life rather than an attribute that must be politically created—all these convictions served to moderate the natural history of the Revolution. This generalization should not obscure the fact that the differences among American republicans were not so negligible that under different conditions (the internationalization of the conflict, failure of colonial legislatures to respond to revolutionary demands from the populace, erosion of the measured support of the clergy, or an economic depression) a radical faction which abandoned republican restraint might not have emerged. Indeed, it was this fear of the expansion of revolutionary activity that drove many Americans to replace the first constitution with another when the republican consensus fashioned by Paine and Jefferson seemed to be disintegrating. Yet the accession of the radicals never occurred, and America was spared the ordeal of a Reign of Terror.

There are several consequences for subsequent political theory as a result of the special character of the American Revolution. In countries that suffer through the natural history of revolution, the conflict becomes culturally what might be called a *contested memory.* Radicals point to the revolution as a symbol of resolve and sacrifice. Conservatives point with horror to the errors and tragic costs of radical change. For Americans the Revolution serves more as an artifact of political consensus. In France the mention of Robespierre is itself a political act of some controversy. In America Jefferson is more of an icon, who is cited by modern conservatives as well as by liberals. The American contest that spared our nation tragic consequences may have also limited later political debate.

While the nearly universal acceptance of our Revolution amply served to promote the legitimacy of a new nation, it also creates difficulties for Americans when they confront the problems of other nations. Alexis de Tocqueville was one of the first writers to explore the consequences of a society like America in which people were "born equal." Tocqueville was, of course, acutely aware of the institution of slavery and restriction of the suffrage to males as well as economic inequality when he wrote his analysis of this country in the early nineteenth century. He meant to emphasize, however, that in America political rights and freedom from the bonds of feudalism had been achieved without a long, violent revolution. The absence of this perspective has led Louis Hartz to ask: "Can a people 'born equal' ever understand peoples elsewhere that have to become so?" Hartz's question explains in part why so many Americans initially eagerly support new revolutions around the globe only to be shocked and angered when they almost inevitably proceed upon the natural course that America averted.

Note

1 Although Adams asserted that "a citizen owes everything to the Commonwealth," he opposed what he called "utopian schemes of leveling, and a community of goods." Any law that threatened private property was "subversive of the end for which men prefer society to the state of nature."

☆ *Bibliographic Essay*

The Anatomy of Revolution (New York: Vintage, 1938) contains Crane Brinton's theory of the natural history of revolution based upon his analyses of the English, American, French, and Russian revolutions. For competing theories of the origin of revolutions and the revolutionary process, see Chalmers Johnson, *Revolutionary Change* (Boston: Little, Brown, 1966); John Dunn, *Modern Revolutions* (Cambridge: Cambridge University Press, 1972); Ted Gurr, *Why Men Rebel* (Princeton: Princeton University Press, 1970); Charles Tilly, "Revolutions and Collective Violence," in Fred Greenstein and Nelson Polsby, eds., *Handbook of Political Science*, vol. 3 (Reading, MA: Addison-Wesley, 1975); Theda Skopol, *States and Social Revolutions* (Cambridge: Cambridge University Press, 1979). A. F. C. Wallace's "Revitalization Movements," in *American Anthropologist* 58 (April 1956) is also important as a provocative anthropological interpretation of revolution. For useful reviews of these and other perspectives, see Issac Kraminick, "Reflections on Revolution: Definition and Explanation in Recent Scholarship," *History and Theory* 11 (1972); John Dunn, *Rethinking Modern Political Theory* (Cambridge: Cambridge University Press, 1985), chap. 4. For two recent accounts of revolutions that focus upon the difficulties involved in rebuilding new societies, see Simon Schama, *Citizens: A Chronicle of the French Revolution* (New York: Alfred A. Knopf, 1989), and Mikhail Heller and Aleksander M. Nekrich, *Utopia in Power: The History of the Soviet Revolution from 1917 to the Present* (New York: Summit Books, 1986).

Narratives of the American Revolution that emphasize ideological factors are Edmund S. Morgan, *The Birth of the Republic* (Chicago: University of Chicago Press, rev. ed., 1977); Clinton Rossiter, *The First American Revolution* (New York: Harcourt Brace Jovanovich, 1953); Edward Countryman, *The American Revolution* (New York: Hill & Wang, 1985). Bernard Bailyn was one of the first writers to recover the sense of republicanism in American political thought. See his *The Ideological Origins of the American Revolution* (Cambridge: Harvard University Press, 1967), and his collection of revolutionary pamphlets, *Pamphlet of the American Revolution*, 2 vols. (Cambridge: Harvard University Press, 1965). Also see Gordon Wood's *The Creation of the American Republic* (New York: W.W. Norton, 1972). Wood emphasizes the republican concepts of corruption and its premodern sense of history more than Bailyn, who focuses upon the republican interpretations of *liberty* and *power*. In his *The Radicalism of the American Revolution* (New York: Knopf, 1992) Wood argues that the changes brought about by the conflict were far reaching and just as radical as those of the French revolution. For influential analyses of republicanism in a European perspective, see J. G. A. Pocock, *The Machiavellian Moment* (Princeton: Princeton University Press, 1975) and Caroline Robbins, *The Eighteenth Century Commonwealthmen* (New York: Atheneum Publishers, 1968). Useful reviews of recent historical and theoretical studies that have relied upon republicanism to interpret early American history are Robert E. Shalhope, "Toward a Republican Synthesis: The Emergence of an Understanding of Republicanism in American Historiography," *William and Mary Quarterly* 29 (January 1972), and "Republicanism and Early American Historiography, *William and Mary Quarterly* 39 (April 1982); Linda Kerber, "The Revolutionary Ideology of the Revolutionary Generation," *American Quarterly* (Fall 1985). Jean Bethke Elshtain offers an important critique of the martial aspects of republican thought in *Women and War* (New York: Basic Books, 1987), chap. 2.

Differences among American republican ideologues are ably explored in Forrest McDonald's *Nocus Ordo Seculorum* (Lawrence: University of Kansas Press, 1985), chap. 3, and Robert Kelley, "Ideology and Political Culture from Jefferson to Nixon," *American Historical Review* (1977). Pauline Maier in *The Old Revolutionaries* (New York: Alfred A. Knopf, 1980) examines the political theories of both Samuel Adams and Richard Henry Lee as well as other activist-theorists. Eric Foner's *Tom Paine and Revolutionary America* (New York: Oxford University Press,

1976) is unparalleled in its careful examination of the climate of Paine's radical republicanism. It also contains a close reading of *Common Sense* and other works by Paine. Alfred F. Young's collection of essays, *The American Revolution: Explorations in the History of American Radicalism* (De Kalb: Northern Illinois University Press, 1976), is an important source for the student interested in the interpretation of republicanism by masses rather than elites.

Loyalist political thought, in general, is still a neglected topic of political theorists. G. N. D. Davis, *Allegiance in America: The Case for the Loyalists* (Reading, MA: Addison-Wesley, 1969), contains many useful excerpts of loyalist tracts as well as reactions from revolutionaries. Jonathan Boucher has received some attention, perhaps because of his apparent severe ideological rejection of republicanism. See Bailyn's analysis in *The Ideological Origins of the American Revolution*, pp. 314–19. Alfred Kelly and Anne Zimmer argue that Boucher was less a Tory than a Whig in "Jonathan Boucher: Constitutional Conservative," *Journal of American History* 58 (March 1972). Oliver's work has been finally reprinted in Douglas Adair and John A. Schutz, eds., *Peter Oliver's* "Origin and Progress of the American Rebellion": *A Tory View* (Stanford: Stanford University Press, 1961). Robert McCluer Calhoon's *The Loyalists in Revolutionary America, 1770–1781* (New York: Harcourt Brace Jovanovich, 1965) contains insightful sketches of loyalist theorists.

☆ *Major Works*

1776   *Common Sense*, Thomas Paine

1776   *"Declaration of Independence," Thomas Jefferson

1787   *Notes on the State of Virginia*, Thomas Jefferson

1781   *The Origin and Progress of the American Revolution*, Peter Oliver

1797   *A View of the Causes and Consequences of the American Revolution*, Jonathan Boucher

*A collaborative effort

Founding

INTRODUCTION

However complex the revolutionary process may be, the establishment of new political, economic, and social institutions is often even more elusive than the preconditions for rebellion itself. Despite the execution of Charles I in 1649, the English revolutionaries were unable to establish a stable new regime in the 1650s. The monarchy was restored in 1660. The Jacobin regime in France, despite its Reign of Terror, could not construct a new society. Indeed, the Directorate that followed was also an unstable political structure. The Soviet revolution did not seem capable of establishing new, permanent institutional structures, despite the efforts of Lenin, until Stalin consolidated power in the 1920s. This difficulty in creating new institutions after destroying the old is a major force in propelling revolutions across the stages described by Crane Brinton. In fact, the common resort to dictatorship as a solution to revolutionaries' inability to found a new regime is the central indictment that conservatives make against revolution in general. Thus Edmund Burke, who knew well the brutalities and injustices that existing governments can foster, still concluded in his critique of the French Revolution that to "rudely" tear apart the fabric of society involved a deadly risk of generations of chaos.

The founding—that is, the successful establishment of new institutional structures (economic and social as well as political) after revolution—is a precious moment in human history. Niccoló Machiavelli, the sixteenth-century Italian political theorist admired by the American revolutionaries, declared in his *Discourses* (1531) that those who possess the talent and will to found new republics are among the most admired people in history (and those who found tyrannies among the most despised). The American patriots, steeped as they were in the history of the failures of republican governments, were well aware of the delicacy of foundings.

Blessed as it was by the conditions described in the last chapter, America still had difficulty in creating a successful founding. In fact, there were two foundings as a result of the American Revolution. When the Continental Congress adopted the Declaration of Independence in 1776, it also resolved that each new state draw up a constitution, and that a constitution be created for a new national government. Both charges were executed. Some states simply deleted colonial references in their current constitutions, while others experimented with a variety of new constitutional structures. Whether state officials attempted to simply modify an existing document or to create an entirely new constitution, the process of constitution making went rather smoothly. Only Massachusetts submitted its new governing document to the voters at large; the other state constitutions were adopted by the existing legislatures.

The process was anything but effortless in regard to a national constitution. An entirely new constitution was offered to each of the states in 1777. Many of the new states, despite the pressures of engaging in a revolutionary struggle, responded cautiously. There were complaints about details as well as concerns about the method of disposition of new lands. Each state seemed to have claims against another. By 1779 Maryland still refused to accept the new constitution and was only persuaded to join when Virginia made a concession which left the land question open to the decisions of the new legislature. By February 1781 the new nation had a national constitution, although for over three years it fought a revolution without one.

The first founding would only last eight years. The nation had to struggle with such problems as the war debt, economic dislocations created by the revolution, admitting new states, adopting a procedure for incorporating new settlements, and efforts to find a new role as a trading partner with European countries now that America was outside the British Empire. Many former revolutionaries began to lose faith in the founding itself. Several efforts to amend the constitution were defeated. Despite these problems, Forrest McDonald, in his assessment of the period, declared the first decade in the history of the United States a "whopping success." Independence was achieved; a peace treaty with Britain was successfully negotiated; and despite important economic problems, the country as a whole was prospering. "The vast majority of people," he reports, "would probably have agreed they had no need for a stronger union. To be sure, there were assorted complaints, but not enough to shake most people from the conviction that the states were adequate to perform all the necessary functions of government. . . ."

But the group of influential leaders that included exponents of varieties of republicanism—Washington, Madison, Franklin, Hamilton, and John Adams—wondered whether the Articles of Confederation was an adequate national constitution. They also wondered whether the various state constitutions were capable of meeting important challenges. Washington wrote that "there are combustibles in every State which a spark might set fire to. . . . Good God! Who besides a Tory, could have foreseen, or a Briton predicted them?" Hamilton worried about the ultimate ability of America to function as a nation:

> There is something . . . diminutive and contemptible in the prospect of a number of petty States, with the appearance only of union, jarring, jealous and perverse, without any determined direction, fluctuating and unhappy at home, weak and insignificant by their dissensions in the eyes of other nations.

Adams concluded that Americans, in their propensity for faction and self-interest, "were like all other people, and shall do like other nations." In other words, a founding crisis emerged during the 1780s. Some leaders regarded the new constitution (and the state constitutions) as incapable of preserving the principles of the revolution, while others insisted that both were adequate.

The Articles of Confederation might have survived these doubts (unquestionably with major amendments) had not a tax revolt in Massachusetts created the specter of armed insurrection in 1786. The newly created Massachusetts legislature, unlike those in other states, had adopted a strict pay-as-you-go budget policy after the Revolution. This sense of fiscal responsibility was financed in large part by a regressive poll tax. Dislocations in agricultural markets as a result of the Revolution left farmers without outlets for their produce. Mortgage foreclosures and imprisonment for debts were results. The farmers themselves began to interpret these policies as a plot on the part of eastern merchants to buy up the land and make the free farmers peasants. Many of the tactics formerly employed by the revolutionaries, such as committees of correspondence and the forcible prevention of court proceedings, were now being used by the farmers. Hoping for a more sympathetic legislature, the protesters insisted in the fall of 1786 that no courts should meet until after new elections, which were scheduled for the spring. When the governor issued a proclamation forbidding unlawful assembly, Daniel Shay, a former captain in the revolutionary army, formed two or three thousand men into a militia. A volunteer force that was collected then routed Shay's contingent. The Massachusetts legislature treated the defeated insurgents leniently, pardoning or reducing sentences and permitting hard-pressed farmers to meet tax bills from unpaid soldiers' receipts. But *Shay's Rebellion*, as it became known, was regarded as proof of doubts felt about the viability of the existing founding. Jefferson, who was in Paris at the time, attempted to allay these fears by contending that "a little rebellion now and then is a good thing." In late February 1787, however, Congress authorized a meeting in Philadelphia to "render the federal constitution adequate to the exigencies of government, and the preservation of the Union."

The delegates to the Constitutional Convention in Philadelphia immediately decided not to amend the Articles of Confederation but to write an entirely new document. After a spirited ratification controversy in which supporters of the second founding took the name *Federalists*, the old Confederation Congress declared the new Constitution in effect and arranged for elections; March 4, 1789, was set as the date for the inauguration of the first American president. This second founding was much more successful than the first. The new Constitution did not degenerate into demands for another. With the great exception of the Civil War, this document has generally provided an arena for the peaceful settlement of our political disputes.

Was Shay's Rebellion possibly the beginning of a revolutionary stage in which radicals would capture power from the revolutionary moderates, thus tumbling the nation into civil war and a reign of terror? Or was the Constitutional Convention, our second founding, a bloodless Thermidorean coup in which the course of the Revolution was halted? Neither of these scenarios quite fit the American case. The goals of the Massachusetts farmers were limited, and no other state experienced anything like a Shay's Rebellion. Nor did the farmers of the second founding, with some exceptions, fully repudiate the republican theory of the revolution. Madison was careful to insist repeatedly that the new Constitution was designed to remedy republican defects with republican solutions. Still, there was an important ideological shift in America in the 1780s, one which reexamined the viability of republican political theory. This debate, which raged throughout the decade and reached its acme in the ratification of the new Constitution, produced the most significant political thought in the history of the republic.

THE FIRST FOUNDING AND ITS CRITICS

Often overlooked in the history of American political thought are the vitality and experimentation in constitutional theory in the period before the adoption of the Constitution. Thomas Jefferson tried to convey this mood of excitement when he wrote in 1776 that the work ahead was of such "an interesting nature" that "every individual would wish to have his voice" in the proceedings. But as Donald Lutz concludes in his study of early revolutionary constitution making (*Popular Consent and Popular Control*), these innovators have been "consigned to distant wings, trotted out only occasionally to play the role of short-sighted, obstructionist opposition to the Federalists." In failing to examine these innovations, Lutz remarks:

> [W]e have not only lost the earlier tradition of American political theory. . . . we have also lost the roots of federalist thinking, and thus ironically, the full measure of Federalist brilliance and originality.

The best way to attempt to correct this failing is to briefly examine representative models of state constitutions as well as to review the basic principles implicit in the Articles of Confederation.

In basic terms, the states created three types of constitutions after 1776: the Virginia model of legislative supremacy; the Pennsylvania experiment with a unicameral legislature; and the "mixed" approach of Massachusetts. In a broad sense, each of these types of constitution represented the application of republican principles prominent in the political cultures of each state.

The Virginia constitution retained the colonial two-house legislature but replaced the royal governor with an executive with redefined, and much more limited, powers. The new governor was selected by a vote of both legislative houses and was further constrained by a required reliance upon a council of advisers, who themselves were also elected in a joint ballot of the legislature. For Virginians, the legislature managed by the public-spirited tidewater aristocracy and standing for election every one or two years would provide the fulcrum for republican government. (A freehold was the condition of eligibility for office.) Most of the states copied the Virginia model, which also included a bill of rights in the constitution.

This fear of executive authority reflected colonial legislative experience with royal governors and their privy councils as well as republican theory in general. The fear was carried to its logical conclusion by the coalition of Philadelphia artisans and Scotch-Irish and German farmers who were instrumental in framing the Pennsylvania constitution. The Pennsylvanians abolished both an upper-legislative house and the governorship. In place of a chief executive, the constitution provided for an elected executive council with rotation in office to "prevent the danger of establishing an inconvenient aristocracy." Seats in the assembly were apportioned by population, and all male taxpayers and their adult sons were given the right to vote. Contemporaries were either fascinated or repelled by the Pennsylvania experiment. French economist Robert Turgot praised the Pennsylvania founders for creating a genuinely new polity. Jefferson derisively referred to that constitution as one run by a "set of workingmen without any weight of character." A twentieth-century historian, Samuel Eliot Morison, in *The Oxford History of the American People* (1965), has called that constitution "the nearest thing to a dictatorship of the proletariat that we have had in North America."

Morison's characterization, however, is misleading in the sense that while there was a centralization of political power in a single body, the Pennsylvania founders were scrupulous in limiting that power in terms of personnel and in reliance upon popular authority. Terms were for a single year, and no legislation could be enacted until it had been submitted to the population in the next election through representatives and then passed again in the next session. No representative could serve for more than four years in any seven. Moreover, the constitution created a unique institution, the *Council of Censors*, which was authorized to meet every seven years. The Council of Censors was derived from the Pennsylvania republicans' interpretation of ancient republicanism in which the Spartan ephors and Roman censors functioned as formal bodies charged with protecting the people's rights. Section 47 of the Pennsylvania constitution charged the council, which was to be elected and to remain in session no longer than one year, "to enquire whether the constitution has been preserved inviolate in every part; and whether the legislative and executive branches of government have performed their duty as guardians of the people . . . to enquire whether the public taxes have been justly laid. . . ."

The Council of Censors was designed to be a grand jury, a legislative investigating committee, and a blue-ribbon study commission all in one. It could pass public censures and order impeachments, and with a two-thirds vote it could also call a convention to amend the constitution if there was an "absolute necessity." Ironically, this is what the second session of the council did when it met in 1790. A new constitution was created with an upper house and governor and without a Council of Censors.

The Massachusetts constitution, which was not approved until 1780, is an important model for the development of state constitutional changes in the next decade. Although America had no hereditary titled aristocracy, the constitution relied heavily upon the republican theory of a *mixed government*, as developed in classical thought by Aristotle and Polybius and accepted by British Whig theorists. According to this theory, representation by various economic interests in society assured stability and liberty. Massachusetts kept a bicameral legislature but significantly altered revolutionary republican theory by dramatically increasing the powers of the governor. The new state chief executive was elected by the people at large rather than by the legislature. He was also eligible for reelection indefinitely and was given a veto power over legislative acts. The property qualification for voting (100 pounds) was the same in the senate as in the lower house, but eligibility for office in the senate was higher (300 pounds or an estate taxed at 60 pounds).

Compared to the excitement and experimentation in founding these various state constitutions, the attention paid to our national document was almost an afterthought. In fact, at one point during the revolution the business of the Continental Congress was delayed because so many delegates were in their home states participating in the drafting of their own state constitutions. There is a similarity between the Articles of Confederation and the Pennsylvania constitution. The Articles authorized a single legislature and an executive on the principle of rotation in office. (No congressional member could serve for more than three out of six years, and no president for more than one year in three.) A committee consisting of one representative from each state met when the legislature was not in session, and its powers were carefully limited. But the principle of legislative supremacy was part of a national model that conceived of the states as participants in a limited union. The new Congress was given the power of war and peace, monetary coinage, and authority in Indian affairs, but not the power of taxation. Even the authority to conclude treaties was limited by its inability to limit a state's right to collect custom duties. As John Adams summarized, the purpose of the first constitution was not to be one of "consolidating this vast continent under one national government," but "after the example of the Greeks, the Dutch and the Swiss. . . a confederacy of States, each of which must have a separate government." The preamble of the Articles reflects Adams's interpretation: the 'states hereby separately enter into a firm league of friendship with each other for their common defence, security of their liberties and general welfare. . . ."

The dissatisfaction with the performance of both the state constitutions and the national one can be illustrated by discussing two important documents of the 1780s: John Adams's *Defence of the Constitutions of the United States* and James Madison's "Vices of the Political System of the United States." Adams focused upon what he regarded as the deficiencies of state constitutional arrangements, and Madison concentrated on the Articles of Confederation. Both works are important theoretical precursors to the political thought of the Federalists in their justification for a second founding.

Adams's *Defence* was written in response to Turgot's criticism that most of the American state constitutional founders had missed a historical opportunity by imitating British constitutional arrangements. Adams's three-volume rejoinder was hardly at all a defense of most of the American constitutions but rather an indictment of most states who had abandoned the British model in favor of the Virginia and Pennsylvania versions of legislative supremacy; it was also a defense of the Massachusetts constitution, of which he was a major author.

The principle theoretical alteration in Adams's previous thought that animates the *Defence* is his dramatic loss of faith in the tenets of moralistic republicanism. Early in the revolutionary struggle Adams had expressed personal doubts about the viability of a society based upon republican virtue. "Even in New England" there was so much "rascality, so much venality and corruption, so much avarice and ambition," he wrote his wife Abigail, that perhaps republicanism was a doomed experiment. To contemporary historian Gordon Wood, "it was as if Adams was carrying in his own mind all of the promise and all of the anxiety engendered by the Revolution." By the 1780s Adams had lost all his faith in virtue as a source of restraint against individual and class self-interest. Elections were not a school for republican virtue since voters' opinions shifted according to demagogic appeals. There were "millions" of people whose "sentiments derived from education" were still no restraint "from trampling on the laws." The hope of an austere and simple American culture was a delusion. "The love of gold grows faster than the heap of acquisition"; "a free people are the most addicted to luxury of any."

Adams then arrived at the conclusion that there was no providential basis for America as an exception to the fate of other republics in history. Adams, however, had not become a Tory. He dearly believed in the existence of the "rich, the well-born and the able" but did not deny that an aristocracy represented a danger to society. If any theory of human nature approximates Adams's, it is probably that of Thomas Hobbes. The great English philosopher, whose masterpiece *Leviathan* was in part a reaction to the English Civil War, argued that the "natural condition" of humanity was one of competition, fear, and aggression. Hobbes concluded his famous description of the features of a "state of nature" (life without government) by remarking that if there are those who think his description is too harsh, why do they lock their doors at night and hide their valuables when they undertake a journey?

Adams did not propose Hobbes's solution—the absolute concentration of power in a single person or body. But Adams's observations on human nature are remarkably similar to those of the English theorist. All human life is a struggle for power, wealth, and deference, Adams concluded. "We may call this desire of distinction childish and silly but we cannot alter the nature of men." The desire for praise is so intense that "every man is miserable every moment when he does not snuff the incense." Ambition "takes the whole soul so absolutely, that a man sees nothing in the world of importance to others, but in his object." People are, for Adams, extremely unequal in their ability and talents even as they pursue distinction. This inequality "no human behavior can eradicate." But like Hobbes, Adams recognizes that this inequality is rarely accepted by other individuals who possess the same desires although not the same means to fulfill them. In a society without formal titles that attempt to justify inequality, each person who sees his neighbor "whom he holds his equal" with a new house or clothing "cannot bear it; he must and will be upon a level with him."

Given these assumptions, how can republics possibly survive, especially when in these regimes there are more opportunities for people to act upon their "constant desires"? Here Adams argues that the republican theorists of mixed government are as important to America as they are to polities with formal aristocracies. And here Adams relies upon Polybius, a crafty ancient Greek theorist in exile at Rome. Clearly writing after Rome was in decline as a republic, Polybius explains Roman imperial success as the result of Rome's mixed constitution. The people through their tribunes were able to exert influence on public policy; the aristocracy residing in the Senate represented the landowning classes; and the Roman consuls acted as mediators between both factions.

Adams took this lesson and those offered by other theorists to imply that some institutional structure is necessary in any society to mediate between the people as a whole and those who have excelled through talent or the advantages of birth. To Adams a bicameral legislature represented both wings of the results of "constant desire." For those human beings who aspired to greatness, there would be the lower chamber of the legislature. The Senate would be reserved for the already successful. The executive functioned as the balancer, the third part of a trinity of stability whose function was to balance the other two forces in society. For without an independent executive, the people would overcome the aristocracy of talent out of resentment. And without full representation the aristocracy would repress those less successful in the race for power and distinction. Thus Adams reintroduced executive authority to American republican political thought. According to him, states that failed in their foundings to respect this triumvirate solution to the problems of republics were courting disaster.

James Madison's essay, "Vices of the Political System of the United States," was completed in April 1787. A year earlier Madison had begun an exhaustive examination of the history of the confederate form of republics. Thomas Jefferson, on diplomatic assignment in Europe, sent Madison over 200 volumes from Paris to aid him in his study. From these and other sources Madison drew up a set of complex notes on the operation of past confederacies, ranging from comments on the ancient Greek Lycian Confederacy to the Belgic Confederacy established in 1679. The result of this effort was published in the spring of 1786 as "Of Ancient and Modern Confederacies." Many portions of these digests made their way into *The Federalist* when Madison, writing as Publius, concluded that past confederations provide "no other light than that of beacons, which give warning of the course to be shunned. . . ."

The negative historical lessons of previous confederacies were clear to Madison. But in "Vices of the Political System of the United States," he undertook the bold step of applying this history of failure to the brief life of the American Articles of Confederation. "Vices" is a brief work, more like a grocery list of indictments against the confederate form than a complete essay. But it is a major document—not only because of its immediate impact on the second founders and because of its insights into Madison's later thought but also because Madison provided an important focus for critics of the first founding. The troubles of the past years were the result, in major part, of the political structures that republicans had historically relied on. Confederacies, rather than protecting the republican governments of their constituent units, exacerbated the problems that all republican theorists admitted existed: the division of republics into warring factions, the decline of public virtue, and the inability to resolve conflicts peacefully. Past republican theorists from the Greeks to Montesquieu had insisted that republics could only function in political units small enough to enable representatives to be in direct contact with the people. The confederacy, then, was a concession to the need to resolve problems such as defense and cooperation that seemed to require larger political structures. To Madison the confederate model had never achieved these goals and, in fact, had contributed to the decline of individual republics.

In "Vices" he shows how confederacy in America is repeating these failures. To Madison the evils to which republics are prone are projected and magnified by confederate arrangements. States trespass upon the rights of one another. (For example, Maryland passes legislation favoring the ships of her own citizens.) States encroach upon national authority. (For example, Georgia negotiates its own treaties with the Indians.) States act independently with regard to foreign powers. (For example, the Treaty of Utrecht has been violated by several states.) States are unable or unwilling to come to the aid of their neighbors threatened by internal violence (for example, Shay's Rebellion). The indictment given the lengthiest treatment by Madison involves the "injustice of the laws of the state." The causes of legislative evils, according to Madison, can be traced to two sources: the representatives and the people themselves. The former may be driven by a sense of the public good, but unfortunately ambition and personal interest are the most prevalent motivations of legislators. The people, too, can be motivated by a desire to promote the "permanent good of the community," but they, too, often act upon baser desires. The failure of virtue to act as the prime motive for actions on the part of both representative and citizen is that

> all civilized societies are divided into interests and factions, as they happen to be creditors or debtors—rich or poor—husbandmen, merchants or manufacturers—members of different religious sects—fol-

lowers of different leaders—inhabitants of different districts—owners of different kinds of property &c and &c.

Madison's solution to the inability of republics to form just majorities would be fully presented in *The Federalist,* but in "vices" he states the central premise of his revisionist republicanism. We need to enlarge the sphere of conflict by abandoning the confederacy form for a more centralized government since "the inconveniences of popular States, contrary to prevailing Theory, are in proportion not to the extent, but to the narrowness of their limits." "Common passions" will be more difficult to form if political conflicts are to be decided at the national level. It is difficult to overstate the brilliance of Madison's contribution to republicanism. One of the most intractable problems in the history of political thought, in general, involves conceptualizing a level of government conducive to the values one seeks to maximize. For the Greeks, political organization was inconceivable other than through the city-state. Americans had largely accepted their own beloved states as the epitome of republican political organization. Nation-states and empires were structures appropriate only to monarchies and dictatorships. The idea of an *empire of liberty* implicit in Madison's theory became a model as exhilarating to the second founders as republicanism was to the revolutionary generation.

THE SECOND FOUNDING AND ITS CRITICS

When the Constitutional Convention completed its work in the summer of 1787, the document was not an institutional implementation of Madison's theory. The Virginian fought hard for, and lost, a provision for a national veto of state legislation that would seem to be a prerequisite for avoiding the kinds of problems he had raised in his critique of confederacies. He supported the Virginia Plan as essential to the formation of a truly national government; like the other delegates, he was forced to accept a compromise. In light of these and other concessions as well as the general political climate that led to the rejection of the first founding, how should the efforts of the second founders be judged?

There are three major interpretations of the convention as a new founding. Before we review the arguments of the Federalists themselves as well as their critics, it will be helpful to briefly discuss these assessments. One view, offered by John P. Roche, emphasizes the contingent elements of the constitution: the Great Compromise itself as a resolution between delegates of large and small states; the episodic history at the convention of the invention of the presidency; and the three-fifths compromise that permitted slaves to be counted for national legislative apportionment. For Roche, the Constitution was not "a triumph of architectonic genius." It was the result of effective but hurried committee action not unlike the activities of any modern legislative reform caucus. The Constitution was "a patch-work sewn together under the pressure of both time and events by a group of extremely talented democratic politicians."

Years earlier Charles Beard presented a much harsher assessment of the Constitution and the convention when he wrote *An Economic Interpretation of the Constitution* (1913). Examining the arguments of *The Federalist*, especially No. 10, as well as the economic backgrounds of the delegates to the convention, he concluded that

> the Constitution was essentially an economic document based upon the concept that the fundamental private rights of property are anterior to government and morally beyond the reach of popular majorities.

As to the ratification procedure itself, which stipulated the acceptance of the document by nine of the conventions rather than by state legislatures (the Articles had required unanimous consent for amendments), Beard said that if such revolutionary processes had been performed by Caesar or Napoleon, "they would have been pronounced coups d'état." Beard's insistence that the second founders economically benefited from the Constitution led to severe and damaging criticism of his method and findings. But other scholars, while rejecting the literalness of Beard's approach, still support his basic contention. Gordon Wood, for example, argues that despite the democratic rhetoric of *The Federalist*, the second founding represented a fundamental "repudiation of 1776" and the ratification debates represented a contest between "aristocracy and democracy."

Martin Diamond's assessment is considerably more charitable to the delegates at the convention. His focus rests upon the delicacy and momentousness of a founding in itself. For Diamond, the Federalists appreciated this moment in the history of regimes. Therefore, they designed a regime based upon reason that would guide the passions of its citizens in peaceful directions. Their "harsh realism" concerning the inability of human beings to engage in public regarding conduct necessarily required that "they be free of these shortcomings in order to have had a disinterested and true knowledge of political things." The men who came after them "need be only legislators who are but interested advocates and parties to the causes they determine" since the Constitution was designed to be "durable and self perpetuating." But for those who actually construct the system, a great measure of intellect and greatness was required. Diamond is careful to note that not all the delegates deserve the title *philosopher kings*, but enough of them were to deserve the title *founding fathers*.

Each of these interpretations of the second founding raises troubling questions. Beard's indictment is obvious in that it suggests that the Constitution itself is responsible for the grave political problems that have troubled America throughout its history. Roche's assessment is designed to illustrate how innovative and ingenious democratic politicians can be when confronted with an immense problem that demands resolution in a brief time. But he admits that his analysis means that the American Constitution may thus not be appropriate for export since its origins are considerably less than "semi-Divine." Diamond presents a view that suggests that all Americans owe an unredeemable debt of gratitude to the second founders, since it was they who saved America from the fate that had beset the republics of the past. But Diamond closes his essay with the observation that the kind of politicians and citizens that the Constitution is designed to produce and restrain may not be adequate. He asks:

> But does not the intensity and kind of our modern problems seem to require of us a greater degree of reflection and public-spiritedness than the Founders thought sufficient for the men who came after them?

An ideal place to begin to answer the questions raised by these interpretations is *The Federalist* itself. It is important to remember, especially since *The Federalist* has assumed such an exalted role in American political and constitutional theory, that the essays were written as partisan political documents. No writer of the papers was personally satisfied with the new Constitution. They wrote as political persons defending provisions and offering arguments that they themselves might not have adopted as their first choice. Forrest McDonald reports that of the seventy-one specific proposals Madison moved, seconded, or spoke unequivocally for at the convention, he was on the losing side forty times. Madison desperately wanted a congressional veto of state legislation; he opposed the listing of congressional powers and a vice presidency; and he favored the establishment of a national university and property qualifications for voting. None of these features appeared in the final document. Hamilton shocked the convention when he proposed that the new Constitution should include a president elected for life with an absolute veto over legislation. He left the meetings in June—only to return later to sign the document.

The essays themselves were written in great haste. Hamilton gathered together two other writers to provide ideological support for the ratification struggle in New York. The three contributors (Hamilton, Madison, and John Jay) assumed the pseudonym of *Publius*, a noble Roman who helped depose the Tarquin monarchy and found the Roman Republic. The identity of the authors was kept secret in order to permit the authors to advance opinions to which they might not wish to be personally committed. Moreover, the pressure of time was extremely intense. Madison later reported that "whilst the printer was putting into type the parts of a number, the following parts are under the pen, and to be furnished in time for the press." This secret collaboration has also led scholars to question whether *The Federalist* has a "split personality" (especially with the hindsight derived from the struggles between Hamilton and Madison in the 1790s). Are the Publius essays written by Hamilton more nationalistic and less democratic than those authored by Madison?

All of these circumstances seem to support Roche's thesis that the Constitution was a compromise document best understood in terms of the factional struggles of the late 1780s. Keeping these circumstances firmly in mind (the multiple authorship of the essays, the immediate political objective, and the writers' haste in composition), *The Federalist* still represents an attempt to bring into focus the application of republican theory to the founding of a new republic in America. There are eighty-five essays, many dealing with overlapping topics and extremely complicated constitutional questions. But it is possible to present a summary of their contents by focusing upon four concerns of Publius: the critique of the confederacy model of republics based upon general experience and the brief history of the American first founding; a philosophical diagnosis of the "diseases" of republican polities; a general set of remedies for these defects; and a defense of specific features of the new Constitution as the appropriate remedy.

A third of the essays are devoted to establishing the severe deficiencies of the current founding. Hamilton writing as Publius introduces the planned series by attacking the Confederation and warning that the Federalists' desire for "the energy and efficiency of government will be stigmatized as the offspring of a temper fond of despotic power." *The Federalist* contains numerous arguments against the confederate model of republics, many of which are derived from Madison's study written a year earlier. Confederations are politically unstable, with participant governments tending to encroach upon central authority (Nos. 17–20), and central authority is unable to perform basic tasks such as promotion of commerce and establishment of national defense (Nos. 4, 21, and 22).

These critiques are especially effective criticisms because of two tactical thrusts made by Publius. First, the authors, by focusing upon the confederacy model of republics, are able to direct their criticism to the historical structures of republicanism rather than against the theory of republicanism itself. While Publius contains many attacks on republican theory in general (as we shall review), the attention to the confederate arrangement in the essays places much of the blame upon the historical reliance on a loose collection of republics as the only permissible means of meeting the needs of coordination and common defense. In *Federalist* No. 9 Hamilton declares that traditional republican theory has already been made obsolete, since the constituent republics of the American Confederation are already much larger than most classical republican theorists envisioned. Focusing upon Montesquieu's assertion that republics must be small enough to permit active interaction between citizens and leaders, Hamilton concludes:

> [I]f we therefore take his ideas on this point as the criterion of truth, we shall be driven to the alternative either of taking refuge in monarchy, or of splitting ourselves into an infinity of little, jealous, clashing, tumultuous commonwealths, the wretched nurseries of unceasing discord and the miserable objects of universal pity and contempt.

In No. 14 Madison urges Americans to "shut your ears against . . . the unhallowed language" of classical republicanism and boldly accept novelty. "Is it not the glory of the people of America," he writes, "that, whilst they have paid a decent regard to the opinions of former times and nations, they have not suffered a blind veneration of antiquity, for custom, or for names, to overrule the suggestions of their own good sense, the knowledge of their own situation, and the lessons of their own experience?"

This position that the initial founding was unsuccessful because it was too conservative is a significant rhetorical advance over Adams's revision of republicanism. Adams, in his *Discourses*, argued that America was not an exception to the greed and self-interest that had plagued previous republican forms. Publius would certainly not disagree, but his critique is based upon the assertion that America is indeed exceptional in that it is capable of revising republican theory in entirely new directions. This combination of conservatism with nationalism and republican rhetoric pervades *The Federalist*. It is one explanation for the political success of the second founders.

The other major attack on the Confederation is especially brilliant because it focuses less on the immediate failures of the founding than upon the likely structure of government in America, given the assumptions of classical republican theory. There is, of course, mention of Shay's Rebellion and the Confederation's tax problems, but Publius directs his attention to the fact that since confederations always fail, we must look at America either as a collection of confederations or as a set of independent small republics. In other words, the authors of *The Federalist* offer criticisms of the Articles of Confederation based on the assumption that the Confederation has already been transformed into several confederative units or a collection of independent republics. For example, John Jay in No. 5 compares America to Great Britain. The latter has experienced great quarrels and tragedies because the "island should be one nation." He continues:

> Should the people of America divide themselves into three or four na-
> tions, would not the same thing happen? Would not similar jealousies
> arise, and be in like manner cherished?

The remainder of the essay is an account of the animosities that are certain
to occur if America becomes three republics. The northern confederacy
would certainly be the most formidable. And what would be the consequences should the southern confederacy be at war with a European
power with which the northern confederacy had established an alliance?

What might be called *disaster scenarios* appear in many of the essays.
In No. 8 Hamilton addresses an issue much on the mind of the opponents
of the Constitution—the absence of a prohibition of standing armies in the
proposed document. Here he assumes that America consists of thirteen or
more independent republics. In Europe the presence of innumerable forti-
fications makes military expeditions very costly and leads to cautious foreign policies despite the large number of troops in the field. But in America,
where there are no castles and no moats, circumstances would be radically
different. Populous states could easily overrun small ones. With this knowledge small states would rationally devote a good portion of their energies to
the formation of large disciplined armies. We know from history, concludes
Hamilton, that disciplined armies have triumphed over larger territories
with greater natural resources. The picture presented is one of a militarized
America in which large, roving armies in the service of the separate states
would be in nearly constant movement in order to gain the advantage from
preemptive strikes.

Of course, America was not in 1787 a territory of independent republics. Nor was it one in which there were any standing armies. The choice
offered the state convention delegates was a new constitution without a
prohibition against a standing army, which was a central tenet of republicanism and the Articles of Confederation. Still Hamilton insists that "these
are not vague inferences drawn from supposed or speculative defects in a
constitution . . . but they are solid conclusions, drawn from the natural and
necessary progress of human affairs."

The second motif of *The Federalist* is a philosophical analysis of the
weakness of republican governments. All Americans were especially vulnerable on this point since republican theory emphasized the fragility of
republican regimes and their propensity, along with other kinds of political
systems, to degenerate into corrupt forms. The core of the argument of Publius on this point is contained in No. 10. This essay written by Madison is
rightly regarded as a classic (perhaps *the* classic) statement of American
political thought. Indeed, if one were forced to present a single document
other than the Declaration of Independence that described the philosophi-

cal dimensions of the American political system after 1787, it would be this brief essay.

Madison begins his discussion by asserting that every "friend of popular governments" has been disturbed by the existence of the "violence of faction" in republican governments throughout history. And thus every republican will look sympathetically upon "any plan which, without violating the principles to which he is attached, provides a proper cure for it." He continues by recounting the complaints made by "our most considerate and virtuous citizens" that America is itself cursed by these republican defects. "Our governments are too unstable"; "the public good is disregarded in the conflicts of rival parties"; decisions are made not by the "rules of justice" but by the power of "the superior force of an interested and over-bearing majority."

Madison, writing as Publius, defines *faction* as

> a number of citizens, whether amounting to a majority or minority of the whole, who are united and actuated by some common impulse of passion, or of interest, adverse to the rights of other citizens, or to the permanent and aggregate interests of the community.

He contends that the causes of faction are myriad. They may result from religious differences, from differences in wealth, and from attachment to different political theories or to different political leaders. Even when there are circumstances in which there is no objective reason for factions to form, the "most frivolous and fanciful distinctions" will give rise to factions. Factions, then, are "sown in the nature of man."

Classical republican theorists as well as American revolutionaries could scarcely disagree with these comments. The novelty of Madison's argument rests with his assertion that neither enlightened statesmen nor religious commitment nor virtuous citizens can prevent the emergence of faction. "Enlightened statesmen will not always be at the helm" is one of Madison's retorts to republican theory. A more serious objection on Madison's part involves his estimation of the capacity of human beings to ascertain the public good. There is for Madison an unbreakable connection between "reason and self love" with the latter as the ruling force in human relationships.

In a single paragraph he rips away a centuries-old set of beliefs from republican theory. How can a republic survive if citizens will naturally form factions and ignore the public good? Are the proponents of monarchy and dictatorship, men like Hobbes in England and Oliver and Boucher in America, right after all about the futility of self-governance? In this essay Madison comes quite close—in a theoretical sense dangerously close—to the conclusion that the experiment in a free society is a mistake. But he skirts this inference by contending that while "liberty is to faction, what fire is to air," it would be folly to abolish liberty because it leads to discord as it would be an error to "wish the annihilation of air" because without it fire would not exist. Whatever criticisms subsequent generations might level against the second founders, they should be thankful for Madison's refusal to take the final step toward an obvious Thermidor. In this sense Diamond's admiration for the founders is well stated. Perhaps Publius stepped back before the abyss because he saw the possibility of civil war with a more frank appraisal of the effects of liberty. Perhaps Publius took Machiavelli's advice that those who squander the historical opportunity before them to establish republics deserve the contempt of later generations. Perhaps Publius was a committed republican who was simply working his way through a set of new challenges and was unwilling to rely upon previous theory. In any case, this single commitment to republicanism is the philosophical basis for the second founding and the American Constitution. Once Madison insists that the solution of dictatorship is worse than the problem of faction, he is driven to explore republican remedies for republican defects.

Publius outlines several general solutions to the "disease" of faction that so afflicts republican regimes. The first is the concept of the extended republic, which Madison himself identified in "Vices." The solution is first raised by Hamilton in No. 9. After establishing the point that American republics are already larger than Montesquieu envisioned as the requisite size for the maintenance of a free society, Hamilton still proceeds to examine the French political theorist's solution. Montesquieu, in *The Spirit of the Laws* (1748), argued that a "confederate republic" resolved the problem of combining the "internal advantages" of republican government with the "external force" of a monarchical one. Thus far Montesquieu's conclusion seems to support the defenders of the Articles of Confederation. But here Hamilton raises another point. The distinction between a confederation and the complete consolidation of constituent governments in a single regime is not a theoretical but a practical ("arbitrary" is Publius's expression) question. Hamilton argues that the division of power between local governments and a national one is not a result of a great dividing line in republican theory but a matter of "discretion." All sorts of different possible relationships are available and largely unexplored in the history of republican confederations. "The proposed constitution, so far from implying an abolition of the State governments, makes them constituent parts of the national sovereignty. . . ." The states are assured direct representation in the Senate and are guaranteed "certain exclusive and very important portions of sovereign power."

Madison directly proposes the concept of an extended republic as a solution to the problem of republican diseases in No. 51. In traditional republican regimes factions clustered around a limited set of interests. The divisions usually, as Madison observes in No. 10, originate over the unequal distribution of property, which is "the most common and durable source of faction." In such situations political life was no better than a "state of nature" with the stronger faction poised to "unite and oppress the weaker." But in a large republic in which centers of authority are dispersed between a national government and state governments, a "multiplicity of interests" are likely to emerge. For Madison "the degree of security . . . will depend on the number of interests and sects; and this may be presumed to depend on the extent of the country and number of people comprehended under the same government."

One of the primary structural devices proposed by Publius to create the extended republic is federalism. The term is derived from ancient usage which means *treaty* and described, in fact, the sort of system the first founders thought they had instituted. As Garry Wills notes in his analysis of *The Federalist (Explaining America)*, "by some kind of pre-emptive verbal strike, the centralizers seized the word and cast the original federalists in the role of antifederalists." Publius's description of the new Constitution as "federal" reflects the ambiguities resulting from this rhetorical theft. Often Publius undertakes to assure his readers that the federal union is not a threat to the states because history shows that states are more likely to encroach upon the prerogatives of the national government than vice versa (No. 17). Hamilton assures his readers that states have "co-equal authority" with the national government in matters of taxation. In No. 39 Madison reminds his readers that national powers are limited to "certain enumerated objects only." But if all these reassurances are to be taken at face value, then the Federalist argument for the serious deficiencies in the Confederation loses its plausibility.

Wills calls these comments "sweet talk," and suggests that Publius must be held accountable for those strict constructionist arguments that were later used in defense of states' rights policies that the Federalists certainly would have opposed. Madison eventually states the Federalist position when he points out near the close of No. 39 that the proposed Constitution is "neither wholly national nor wholly federal." Federal features are included in the Senate (two for each state elected by state legislators) and in the ratification process itself. National features exist in the apportionment of seats to the House of Representatives and the authority of Congress in general over individual citizens. Many portions of the Constitution are neither national nor federal but a "compound," such as the election of a president. Publius concludes by dismissing the focus upon the entire question. He defines republican government as one which derives its powers from the people through election.

Clearly what the Federalists did was to redefine the concept of federalism to include a government that did not totally abandon constituent units but that also departed from the republican method of a limited league of states. When Publius criticizes the Articles of Confederation, he speaks as a nationalist, assuming that the old definition of federalism as a treaty among states is untenable because the confederacy is bound to disintegrate at least into several confederacies. But when Publius speaks in defense of the new Constitution, he praises federalism (the new version) as a solution to the problem of faction in republican governments and as a method to extend the size of republican governments. Thus in No. 10 Madison praises federalism as a structure that limits the ability of factions to extend their reach to other states:

> A rage for paper money, for an abolition of debts, for an equal division of property, or for any other improper or wicked project, will be less apt to pervade the whole body of the Union. . . .

Both Madison and Hamilton would have preferred the Constitution to be more national and less federal than it was, and their defense was complicated by the fact that both emphasized its federal features in an effort to secure ratification. On the other hand, both men believed that the Constitution represented a close enough combination to deserve support. Their position on this question and on related issues can be illuminated by what Robert Dahl, a contemporary political theorist, has called the *Goldilocks problem* in democratic political philosophy. Dahl, in *After The Revolution* (1971), describes the search for political solutions to problems of size in terms of the fairy-tale character's quest for resolution of her needs that were not too big, not too small, but "just right." Publius regards the basic unit of republican government, the city-state in the classical age and the state in the American experience, as too small. A wide-ranging empire might be too large to maintain a republican government, but the thirteen states, given the right form of political organization, are just right. The extended republic is big enough to create a multiplicity of interests but not too big to prevent their eventual formation into a majority, should the need arise. Similarly, the abolition of the states would be a solution too drastic for resolving Goldilocks' dilemma. The country might be too large to govern directly. On the other hand, the limited conception of federalism in the Articles of Confederation was not strong enough to prevent disintegration and the successful control by factions in the states. The constitutional solution of a regime part national and part federal was "just right."

This Goldilocks approach also emerges in Madison's discussion of representation. *The Federalist* bristles with attacks on ancient republics for failing to protect their citizens from the effects of faction. In Nos. 10, 14, 49, and 55 Madison is sharply critical of direct democracy as well as of legislatures of too short a duration or too large a size. In fact, direct democracies are not, properly speaking, republics at all, despite the pronouncements of "some celebrated authors" (No. 14). In No. 49 he concedes that in a nation

of philosophers, a direct reliance upon opinion may permit stable government, but quickly reminds his readers that "a nation of philosophers is as
little to be expected as the philosophical race of kings wished for by Plato."
In No. 55 he concludes that in "very numerous assemblies . . . passion never
fails to wrest the scepter from reason. Had every Athenian citizen been a
Socrates, every Athenian assembly would still have been a mob."

Direct democracy then gives too much opportunity for factious activity that caused the turbulence of the ancient Greek polities and the Italian
city-states. So too do representative bodies that are too large since, for Madison, they approach the danger point of a factious society in microcosm. On
the other hand, too small a representative body must be avoided to "guard
against the cabals of a few." "Sixty or seventy men may be more properly
trusted with a given degree of power than six or seven. But it does not follow that six or seven hundred would be proportionally a better depository."
The size of the House of Representatives is thus vigorously defended on the
principle that it fits the Goldilocks test.

But the size of representative bodies is not the only concern of Publius. Representation, properly proportioned, is defended as a more general
solution to faction. Recall that Publius in No. 10 in effect rejected republican virtue as a barrier against faction. But now Publius is able to conclude
that in an extended republic with appropriately sized legislative bodies, the
opinions of the people can undergo a process which permits politicians to
"refine and enlarge the public view." Elected representatives under these
conditions are indeed capable of discovering "the true interests of their
country, and whose patriotism and love of justice, will be least likely to sacrifice it to temporary or partial considerations." This was Madison's assessment in No. 10. Hamilton repeated this conclusion when he defended the
electoral college as an institution designed to be "filled by characters preeminent for ability and virtue."

The creation of a *virtuous representative* out of the factious activity
that all republics can never completely avoid was still not enough in the
way of guarantee for the second founders. "Checks and balances"—the ability of each branch of government to defend itself against another—were
also discussed as a remedy for republican diseases. Although Publius
reminds his readers that the new Constitution is republican in the sense
that the national legislature is the predominant institution, in No. 48 Madison still insists that, even with the right size, the legislature cannot be
relied upon not to encroach upon the other branches of government. Both
republican Venice and the state of Pennsylvania are singled out as negative
examples of legislative tyranny. Jefferson's criticism of the powers of the
legislature in his state's constitution in *Notes on Virginia* is also cited. But
Publius rejects the idea of an absolute executive veto over legislation for the
same reason he uses in attacking legislative supremacy (although we know

that Hamilton supported this power at the convention). For Madison, writing as Publius, it is rejected because it might be "perfidiously abused." In this manner the powers of each branch of government (veto and override, selection of justices, senatorial confirmation, and other powers) are defended as part of a "just right" solution to the danger of concentration of power in a single department of government.

Despite the brilliance of Publius's arguments, not everyone in America accepted this defense of the new Constitution. Five states ratified the document quite quickly. Pennsylvania also accepted the new Constitution in part because of local political controversies. Massachusetts narrowly supported the proposal, but offered nine "recommendations" for revision. In New Hampshire the vote was delayed because the Federalists realized they lacked a margin for victory. The state ratified in the spring with suggested amendments, just as Massachusetts had done. North Carolina turned down the Constitution in July by a wide margin. The battles in Virginia and New York, two large states, were thus crucial and closely contested. *The Federalist* itself was written as part of the effort to promote adoption in New York; copies were rushed to Virginia as well in hopes that they might influence the outcome there.

Given the success of the second founding, the question naturally arises, "What did the Anti-Federalists want?" It is certainly a mistake to conclude that the Anti-Federalists were persons unable to see the problems in the Articles of Confederation, or at a broader level unwilling to revise republican theory. Nearly all the opponents of the Constitution accepted the need for major amendments to the Confederation, most of which implied a stronger central government. The various essays of the Anti-Federalists suggest support for a bicameral legislature at the national level as well as for some kind of executive authority. Thus the designation *men of little faith* as a description of the Anti-Federalists—that is, people unwilling to explore the structural possibilities of republicanism—is overdrawn.

Yet there was a difference in political philosophy between the supporters of the second founding and their critics. Since there is no equivalent text to *The Federalist,* a synopsis of the debate is difficult. Richard Henry Lee's *Letters from a Federal Farmer* (1787–88) will provide the focus for our review of Anti-Federalist political thought. The Virginia tidewater aristocrat we discussed in chapter 2 who supported the American Revolution was, along with Patrick Henry, a leader of the Anti-Federalist forces in Virginia. Lee epitomized the kind of objections that emerged from one form of revolutionary republicanism. *The Letters* went through four editions in three months. Although Lee produced another set, he failed to rally his fellow planters in rejection. The vote was 89–79 in favor of the Constitution.

Like all Anti-Federalists, Lee objected to the convention's complete abandonment of the Articles as well as the method of ratification. While the

Articles had required unanimous consent to amendments, the second founders boldly asserted that the new Constitution would be implemented by the assent of nine states. Moreover, the method of ratification recommended avoided state legislatures and called for constitutional conventions. This creation of a new political arena confounded the Anti-Federalists, who were late in organizing delegates. In Pennsylvania Anti-Federalists resorted to running Benjamin Franklin on their ticket, even though he was a participant and signer of the Constitution.

Lee knew that these objections were moot. The conventions were taking place, and implicitly the nine-vote minimum was being accepted as the standard for ratification. Nevertheless, Lee began his essays with the assertion that the political problems that had emerged with the Articles were not as theoretically significant as the Federalists asserted. "If we remain cool and temperate, we are in no immediate danger," he reminded his readers in No. 1.

> We are in a state of perfect peace, and in no danger of invasions; the state governments are in full exercise of their powers; our governments answer all the present exigencies. . . .

Lee was careful to note that "regulation of trade" and "securing credit" were not being successfully addressed by the Congress. He reminded his readers, however, that the nation had been "hardly removed from a long and distressing war." The "farmers, fishermen, etc. have not yet fully repaired the waste made by it." Lee concludes: "Industry and frugality are again assuming their proper station." He regards the arguments of those who claim that a crisis is at hand as a "custom of tyrants and their dependents in all ages."

At a theoretical level, Lee attacked Publius's description of the new Constitution as neither national nor federal by asserting that the so-called compound "only proves . . . that we cannot form one central government on equal and just principles." In other words he argues that the Goldilocks solution is not a rational resolution to the problems of size and faction, as Publius contended, but proof of the irrational compromises which must be met in attempting to create an extended republic from large and small states.

The concept of the extended republic is also subjected to criticism in Lee's assessment of the House of Representatives. The Anti-Federalist criticism of the House was so sharp that Publius devoted several essays to the subject. *The Federal Farmer* provides evidence of doubts about the virtuous representative. The so-called democratic branch permits representation of one in 30,000 inhabitants. Since thirty-three representatives constitute a quorum, Lee doubts that "the interests, feelings, and opinions" of the people can be served. Only "men of the elevated classes" will have the resources to be elected. To Lee the "licentiousness of the multitude" was but "small evils" compared to "the factions of the few." The new Constitution failed to provide an institution large enough to "sympathize" and "communicate" with the people. *The Federal Farmer* fears that the House will be influenced more by the "expectations of appointments and offices" of the executive than by the needs of the people at large.

The Anti-Federalists looked with suspicion upon the other arguments of Publius in support of the extended republic. Perhaps the single most frequent objection to the proposed constitution—aside from the demand that it include a "bill of rights"—was the absence in the new document of a prohibition against "standing armies." The belief that a permanent and professional military force was antithetical to republicanism was reinforced by British imperial policy during the Revolution. In brief, republicans argued that a large and heterogeneous state required by nature a large army to police its perimeters and to ensure safety at the center. Was this not the exact policy that had led to the stationing of British troops in the colonies? Was this not the exact policy that all imperial regimes resorted to? Publius rejected the prohibition against a standing army in *The Federalist* No. 8. To Lee the size of the proposed extended republic seemed to require a militia to "execute the laws of the union; suppress insurrections, and repel invasions." He was shocked to see "so many men in America fond of a standing army," and he expected the pressure upon the new legislature for provision of funds to be irresistible. Not only does an extended republic require a large military force to keep the peace, but "an army is a very agreeable place of employment for the young gentlemen of many families."

The Federal Farmer, reflecting the views of most Anti-Federalists, was extremely concerned about the powers of the Senate. A bicameral legislature was accepted as an appropriate remedy for republican defects (indicating how far American republicans had already departed from the Pennsylvania model). But the mixture of executive and judicial functions (treaty ratification, advice and consent of executive appointments, and impeachment) in the second house disturbed critics. They smelled aristocracy. Samuel Bryan of Pennsylvania, in his *Letter of Centennial,* argued that the powers of the Senate demonstrated that the Constitution was not fostering "balanced government" but "a permanent aristocracy." Thus what the Federalists regarded as a concession to the states was perceived by the Anti-Federalists as "the fetus of aristocratic domination." Striking in this regard was the Anti-Federalist reaction to the presidency. While some still insisted upon a plural executive, many in the opposition, like Lee, supported the presidency as well as the electoral college. Lee, in fact, like many Anti-Federalists, thought the president insufficiently powerful vis-à-vis the Senate.

In summary, the Anti-Federalists, despite variations in their assessment of the new Constitution, simply did not accept the idea of an extended republic. Republics, to be viable, must primarily be local. They were willing to extend the scope of national powers but not willing to conceive of a republic in which citizen loyalty was not chiefly directed toward a state. The "just right" solutions of a system part national and part federal, the complex system of national checks and balances, the concept of the virtuous representative who emerged from a multiplicity of interests—these arguments, and more—they saw as a movement of America away from republicanism and toward empire. As Herbert Storing concludes in his assessment of the opposition, where Publius saw "a finely wrought clock, the anti-Federalists saw darkness and danger." Patrick Henry, Lee's Virginia compatriot in opposition, complained that governments ought to be "like a beacon" clear and understandable to every citizen, "but this government is of such an intricate and complicated nature, that no man on this earth can know its real operation." To the Anti-Federalists, complexity was a sign of decadence, not of balance.

SUMMARY AND COMMENT

Both American foundings—the Articles of Confederation and the Constitution—represent the last time in American history that the fundamental principles of the regime would be examined by leaders in a position to alter its basic premises. With no disrespect to the first founders, the Articles were in important ways an afterthought since the core of the new political system was meant to function at the state level. It is only with the second founding that a truly national regime was conceived. Whatever the motives of the second founders, it is in the belief that an *extended republic* was possible that America was born as a nation.

Certainly the formation of the second founding was the result of a good deal of political compromise, as Roche suggests. But it is true, as the Anti-Federalists insisted and as Beard and other interpreters discovered, that an extended republic involved an exploration of a regime even newer than Madison intimated in *Federalist* No. 14. For good or for ill Publius modified republicanism, even of the American variety, so as to establish a new ideology for the United States. There are clear republican remnants in the Constitution—in the idea of the virtuous representative and even in the American version of the balanced Constitution. But the novelty of the Constitution lies in its philosophical assumptions, which might not have been fully appreciated even by Madison himself when he wrote *Federalist* No. 10. For the second founding was premised upon the assumption of a pluralist society in which different conceptions of the good life contest with one another, and the Constitution was designed as a structure in which these conflicts would compete. Republicanism, on the other hand, had always assumed a homogeneity of belief.

Once Madison had abandoned republican virtue as the central tenet in maintaining the American regime while still remaining committed to a free society, he opened the door to a regime that deserves the description *liberal* rather than republican. Publius's Constitution is not liberal in the sense that FDR created in the 1930s (as significant as that definition is). Instead, Publius's Constitution is liberal in the sense that politics is regarded as an arena in which many different interests are entitled to compete. *The Federalist* came to this conclusion as a result of its fear of majorities. Like Jefferson and Hamilton—two divergent figures who would compete for the soul of the republic in the next generation—Madison himself was in important respects a transitional figure; he was both republican and liberal. Madison, Jefferson, and Hamilton were liberal in their conception of politics as a theater in which every interest deserves to play its part; they were republican in their belief that there is a considered judgment of the community at large that ultimately must be discerned and followed.

Republicanism lost in 1787. But America won in its ability to secure a founding, albeit a second one, that evaded so many other revolutions. As Mercy Warren, an Anti-Federalist, observed ten years after the ratification debate, Americans were "too proud for monarchy, yet too poor for nobility, and . . . too selfish and avaricious for a virtuous republic."

☆ Bibliographic Essay

The importance of the founding is stressed by nearly all the classical republican theorists. See especially Montesquieu's *The Spirit of the Laws* and Machiavelli's *Discourses*. J. G. A. Pocock emphasizes this aspect of republicanism in his *Politics, Language and Time* (New York: Atheneum Publishers, 1971). Foundings in cross-national and historical perspectives have been explored from a variety of perspectives. Aaron Wildavsky in *The Nursing Father: Moses as a Political Leader* (University: University of Alabama Press, 1984) treats Moses as a paradigmatic case of a leader who confronted the paradox of employing his own talents for wider purposes. His leadership, according to Wildavsky, was directed toward constructing a regime designed to function without his own personal abilities. Along the way, Moses faced agonizing choices between freedom and order. Louis Hartz, in collaboration with several specialists, compares the American founding experience to that of four other cultures (Latin America, South Africa, Canada, and Australia) in *The Founding of New Societies* (New York: Harcourt Brace Jovanovich, 1964). Seymour Lipset compares the American case with that of Canada in *Revolution and Counterrevolu-*

tion (Garden City, NY: Doubleday, 1970), chap. 2. Also see the analysis of Karl Deutsch and associates, who examine the efforts of confederations, including the United States, to form new political units in *Political Community and the North Atlantic Area* (Princeton: Princeton University Press, 1957).

Two sympathetic examinations of the operation of state constitutions under the Confederation are Gordon Wood, *The Creation of the American Republic, 1776–1787* (New York: W.W. Norton, 1972), and Donald S. Lutz, *Popular Consent and Popular Control* (Baton Rouge: Louisiana State University Press, 1980). Wood is especially useful here for his assessment of John Adams's revision of republicanism, chap. 14. Lutz's synthesis of scholarship and his own research on this era is unexcelled. For an analysis of the brief-lived Pennsylvania state constitution, see J. Paul Selam, *The Pennsylvania Constitution of 1776* (New York: Octagon Books, 1971). For a more critical view, see Allan Nevins, *The American States during and after the Revolution* (Fairfield, NJ: Augustus M. Kelley, 1969). The Confederation is implicitly defended in the research of Merrill Jensen. See his *The Articles of Confederation* (Madison: University of Wisconsin Press, 1940) and *The New Nation* (New York: Alfred A. Knopf, 1950).

The second founding naturally has been the focus of many students of American political thought. Assessments have varied from awe of the achievement of the founding fathers to measured criticism to repudiation. Michael Kammens's *A Machine that Would Go of Itself: The Constitution in American Culture* (New York: Alfred A. Knopf, 1986) emphasizes the slow growth in the prestige of the founders, but his focus on the acceptance of an aspect of American constitutionalism, judicial review, must be considered as a major factor in his assessment. Martin Diamond's appraisal is more positive. See his "Democracy and the Federalists: A Reconsideration of the Farmers' Intent," *American Political Science Review* 53 (March 1959) as well as his extended treatment in *The Founding of the Democratic Republic* (Itasca, IL: F. E. Peacock, 1981). Beard's attack on the founders must be considered in the context of progressive reform (see chap. 8), but his *An Economic Interpretation of the Constitution of the United States* (New York: Macmillan, 1913) clearly opened old wounds in American political culture. Beard's analysis has been meticulously critiqued by Robert E. Brown, *Charles Beard and the Constitution* (Princeton: Princeton University Press, 1956) and Forrest McDonald, *We the People* (Chicago: University of Chicago Press, 1958). Neo-Beardians emphasize less the immediate class interests of the farmers than the change in ideological emphasis that marks the language of the farmers. See Gordon Wood, *The Creation of the American Republic,* Part 5, and Sheldon Wolin, *Politics and Vision* (Boston: Little, Brown, 1960), pp. 388–93. John Roche's view is a challenge to both complimentary and critical assessments of the founders: "The Founding Fathers: A Reform Caucus in Action," *American Political Science Review* (December 1961).

Despite the haste of their composition, the essays of *The Federalist* deserve to be read very closely. There are many editions of the papers available. Clinton Rossiter's collection is useful in that it includes the Constitution itself with annotated references to remarks in the essays by Jay, Hamilton, and Madison, *The Federalist Papers* (New York: New American Library, 1961). The debates at the Constitutional Convention are also available in a collection edited by Max Farrand, *The Records of the Constitutional Convention 1787*, 3 vols. (New Haven: Yale University Press, 1911). Douglass Adair's close reading of the essays with a view toward establishing the "schizoid" Publius interpretation are contained in *Fame and the Founding Fathers* (New York: W.W. Norton, 1974). Garry Wills extends Adair's thesis by arguing that both Madison and Hamilton were directly influenced by David Hume's concept of the commercial republic. See Wills's *Explaining America* (Garden City, NY: Doubleday, 1981). Most of Robert Dahl's theoretical work can be seen as a commentary on *The Federalist*. See his *A Preface to Democratic Theory* (Chicago: University of Chicago Press, 1956) for his interpretation and revision of Madison. Dahl's *Goldilocks problem* is presented in *After the Revolution* (New Haven: Yale University Press, 1970). Neal Reimer offers an able review of Madison as a political theorist in *James Madison: Creating the American Constitution* (Washington, DC: Congressional Quarterly Press, 1986), and Marvin Meyer provides primary material on the development of Madison's political thought along with incisive commentary in *The Mind of the Founders* (Hanover, NH: University Press of New England, 1981).

The Anti-Federalists are assessed by Cecilia Kenyon in "Men of Little Faith: The Antifederalists on the Nature of Representative Government," *William and Mary Quarterly*, 3rd series, 12 (1955). Jackson Turner Main provides a sympathetic review in *The Antifederalists* (New York: W.W. Norton, 1961). Christopher Duncan's *The Anti-Federalists and Early American Political Thought* (De Kalb: Northern Illinois University Press, 1995) is also positive in its assessment and a tour de force in terms of its interpretative range, since it connects the antifederalists to contemporary political thought. Herbert Storing offers a balanced account in *What the Anti-federalists Were For* (Chicago: University of Chicago Press, 1981), excerpted and published separately from his collection of Anti-Federalist writings, *The Complete Antifederalist* (Chicago: University of Chicago Press, 1981). The latter includes a reprint of Lee's *The Federal Farmer*.

☆ *Major Works*

1776   *Defense of the Constitutions of the United States*, John Adams
1787–88 *The Federalist*, James Madison, Alexander Hamilton, John Jay
1787   "Vices of the Political System of the United States," James Madison
1787–88 *Letters of a Federal Farmer*, Richard Henry Lee
* A collaborative effort

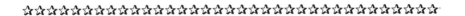

Faction

INTRODUCTION

America in 1789 seemed to have successfully managed a founding. Most of the new leaders held major positions in the reconstituted national government. George Washington was elected president and began his term with a degree of confidence and prestige rare for a leader of a new nation. The authors of *The Federalist* also assumed major positions in the new government. Jay became chief justice of the Supreme Court; Hamilton, the secretary of treasury. Anti-Federalists prevented Madison from assuming a Senate seat, but he managed to be elected to the House of Representatives. Jefferson, who stood somewhat aloof from the ratification controversy, was offered the cabinet post of secretary of state. Everywhere the Anti-Federalists were in retreat. Patrick Henry epitomized the attitude of resignation when he announced after Virginia voted for the new Constitution that he would "be a peaceable citizen." Only eight to thirteen Anti-Federalists managed to be elected to the House, and only in Virginia were Anti-Federalists elected as senators. Samuel Adams lost an opportunity for a seat in Congress because he was late in coming to the Federalist cause. Newspapers were invariably Federalist. Nearly all the varieties of republicans who became revolutionaries in the 1770s now supported the second founding. John Adams, the leader of the moralistic republicans, was vice president; the Philadelphia artisans rallied in support of the new document. The South had been a locus of antifederalism, but the leaders of the new nation were predominantly Virginian.

Despite this consensus, the idea of a nation was still largely incipient. The preamble of the new Constitution began with the phrase "We the people. . ." but the population of about 4 million people (including 700,000 slaves) was tied together by little more than a idea. Nearly all transportation was by water. The country had only seventy-five post offices. Ninety-five percent of the population lived on farms and in villages. There were no cities of over 50,000 people, and only twenty-four of over 2,500 persons. When Madison used the word *national* in proposing the second amendment to the Constitution, he was severely criticized by a Federalist-dominated House.

The Constitution, despite the propaganda of the Federalists that it was "a new order of the ages," was little more than a set of basic institutions and guidelines for future government. But the Federalists still felt they had solved a major defect in republican theory. Madison, in *Federalist* No. 10, argued that factions were endemic to republican government. The task of the new republican political scientist was only to limit their effects. But none of the authors of *The Federalist* had assumed that factions would emerge at the national level. Indeed, the purpose of a national administration was to create an arena in which party conflicts would be resolved by virtuous representatives. Madison described the task of national leadership as one which united "the minds of men accustomed to think and act differently." Contemporary political scientists might describe the second founders' vision as a one-party state. But for the second founders, America was conceived as a no-party state, at least at the national level.

Nearly immediately, however, the new national administration began to be perceived by some as a *court party.* Throughout the eighteenth century in Great Britain, political conflict revolved around those individuals who had political access to the Crown and used its offices to promote their own political careers and their economic projects, and those who felt alienated and disadvantaged from these arrangements. Court theorists argued that they possessed a national vision and accused the country opposition of being less talented and provincial in outlook. The country party, however, developed an ideology that portrayed the dominance of the court as the result of an elaborate structure of corruption.

American revolutionary republicans relied heavily upon this country political theory in devising their arguments against Crown policies. Conventional political wisdom after the Revolution assumed that court forces were functionally irrelevant in America. But the new national government renewed these old fears. Washington personally cultivated all the symbols of simple republicanism. He wore Connecticut broadcloth and proceeded very cautiously in assuming his constitutional mandate, particularly with the Senate. Yet Congress spent the first month of its session debating whether the title for the president should be "His Elective Majesty," and the new capital soon became the center for grand balls and new office seekers. A French aristocrat reported that "the splendor of the rooms, and the variety and richness of the dresses did not suffer in comparison to Europe." Madison himself complained about "the satellites and sycophants" who surrounded the new president.

None of these new practices would have in themselves given rise to an organized opposition at the national level had not the reigning Federalists themselves initiated a series of policies that frightened many of the new nationalists themselves and led them to form what in essence was an American *country party*. Alexander Hamilton as secretary of treasury offered a series of proposals recommending the assumption of the revolutionary debt by the national government and the redemption of notes used to finance the revolution at par by their holders. Later he proposed the creation of a national bank and policies designed to encourage industry in the new nation. James Madison, a fervent nationalist, almost immediately began to organize congressional forces to oppose Hamilton's policies. In fact, William C. Rives, a historian and the first biographer of Madison, concluded in 1859 that "the friends of union . . . had barely set down to the feast before the specter of dissension appeared."

In the early years of the republic, Madison's opposition functioned chiefly as a congressional faction within Federalist hegemony. But in the executive branch dissension too appeared. Thomas Jefferson was regarded by most Federalists with some suspicion but was welcomed into the administration on the assumption that he could be co-opted. The conflict between Hamilton and Jefferson assumed organized proportions by the early 1790s. The nationalists had a newspaper, the *Gazette of the United States*, that was subsidized by the government. The paper, edited by John Fenno, consistently supported Hamilton's policies. Jefferson, angered by the dominance of a "paper of pure Toryism, disseminating doctrines of monarchy, aristocracy and the exclusion of the influence of the people," set up a competing paper, the *National Gazette*, edited by Philip Freneau, who was given a sinecure in the Department of State.

From Madison's leadership in the House, Jefferson's and Hamilton's attempts to gain the support of Washington, and the coverage from these two papers, the first American party system was born. Federalists organized themselves as a partisan structure by 1794. Their opponents adopted the name *Republicans*.[1] This emergence of faction at the national level expanded rapidly. Representatives began to correspond with voters on the basis of partisan views and openly campaign for offices; local organizations emerged; legislative action began to be structured along the lines of voting blocs.

This emergence of faction at the national level was an unanticipated consequence of the new Constitution. As party organization mounted and rhetoric intensified, both sides insisted that the ascendance of faction was temporary and initiated by antirepublican forces. The Federalists were most adept at portraying themselves as an "anti-party" party. The speeches of Federalists emphasized the need for national unity and blamed the existence of political conflict upon a resurgence of antifederalism. Hamilton, writing under a pseudonym in the *Gazette of the United States*, described Jefferson as a misguided republican who had fallen victim to the "French disease" of assuming that the people as a mass can rule. Behind the "affectation of pure republicanism, primitive simplicity, and extraordinary zeal for the common good" lay the "most intriguing man in the United States," a potential demagogue and a "cautious and sly" supporter of faction. A New York Federalist devoted his own election address to the rise of faction, declaring that "party is a monster who devours the common good, whose destructive jaws are dangerous to the felicity of nations." To Jefferson and the nascent Republican party, Hamilton was a usurper who had converted Washington's executive authority into a *roi fainéant*. Party organization was necessary to rid the "infestation" of society by monarchists and aristocrats; when successful, party organization would disappear.

Politics in the 1790s was an era of more than rhetorical violence. A rebellion of farmers in western Pennsylvania was met by the forceful opposition of national forces. The Alien and Sedition Acts (1798) led to nullification resolutions by the Virginia and Kentucky legislatures. Republicans and some Federalists regarded the legislation as part of an attempt to repress opposition once and for all. The Virginia militia drilled in anticipation of an invasion by national forces; armies were formed in several states to repel what was perceived as an imminent attack from a newly recruited Federalist army. The French Revolution dramatically divided the two new parties. To the Federalists the Republicans represented a "fifth column" of the French Revolution; to the Republicans the support of Great Britain represented a turn to neocolonialism.

A truce of sorts was declared by Jefferson himself after he won the presidency. Both sides referred to the election as the *revolution of 1800*. Jefferson, in his first inaugural, affirmed that "we all are all federalists, we are all republicans." This assertion suggested that opposition, principled and emphatic though it might be, was legitimate. Jefferson himself was not free from opposition in his own presidency. His purchase of the Louisiana Territory led to defections from his party, and his neutrality and embargo policies in the wars between France and Great Britain created another secession movement among New England Federalists and repudiation from his own party. His efforts to rid his administration of Federalists who, in his own words, had retreated to the judiciary in order to engage in guerrilla attacks against the Republican majority, were a failure. Justice John Marshall used the controversy over Federalist appointments to assert judicial review over acts of Congress, and the impeachment of a Federalist justice failed.

The Republicans, triumphant in 1800, ruled at the national level for a generation. Factions, as the Republicans predicted, dissipated once "monocrats" were defeated. But in 1824 the one-party system began again to divide into factions and polarized into "Adams's men" and "Jackson's men." In the following election a new party system emerged, the Whigs and the Democrats, that mirrored in some respects the old Federalist-Republican battles but had personalities and agendas of its own. This second party system was more competitive and more organized than the first. The competition for political power at the national level produced what historian Richard McCormick has called a *hidden revolution.* In an effort to defend their policy positions and expand their political bases, both parties began to resort more and more to electoral support. The number of voters rose dramatically between 1788 and 1800 and again between 1824 and 1840, as presidential electors were chosen by the population at large; presidential conventions replaced congressional caucuses; and property qualifications were eliminated at state constitutional conventions.

Faction had become institutionalized in the form of party organization. Less and less was the rhetoric of opposition regarded as a threat to the nation; more and more was party competition seen as an essential part of national constitutional arrangements. The emergence of Federalists and Republicans in the 1790s and of Whigs and Democrats from the 1820s through the 1850s established the principle that factions could exist permanently at the national level, and that the republic could still remain intact over time. Sometime, perhaps as late as the 1840s, America had adjusted to the crisis of faction and accepted the idea of a permanent and organized opposition.

Out of this factional competition (Federalists versus Republicans, and Democrats versus Whigs), which was nearly fifty years in the making, there emerged four clear philosophies of government and four philosophically informed approaches to public policy. Although the issues debated in these years were complex and the ideological foci of the two competing party systems were not always directly comparable, the factional conflicts represent arguments over which value—freedom or order—should be predominant in this new nation. Both Federalists and Whigs emphasized the need for order; both Republicans and Democrats emphasized the importance of freedom.

FEDERALISTS

The political theory of the Federalists, at least if considered as a coherent whole, is now extinct. Certainly important remnants are still to be found, but the ascendant political position that emerged in the 1780s and was briefly triumphant in the 1790s has disappeared from American politics. Nationalism—a preeminent Federalist concept—of course, still exists as a value in American political thought as does a commitment to America as a strong, independent industrial empire. What died in 1800 or shortly thereafter was the explicit presentation of the idea of hierarchy in American political and social life. John C. Miller, in his study of the Federalists (*The Federalist Era*, 1960), describes the members of this early party as "surely the frankest politicians who ever graced the American scene. . . ." The Federalists, according to Miller, "made no pretence of being other than what they were: upper-class Americans who had a natural-born right to rule their inferiors in the social and economic scale."

Both Federalists and Republicans were parties that suffered from internal factional strife. Defections and antagonisms from within the ranks of politicians uncertain about the formation of the parties were, to say the least, disconcerting. But what few Federalists and Republicans realized was that their efforts represented attempts to form a broad-based national organization that necessarily required theoretical and policy accommodations. The Federalists, who were for a time quite successful in presenting themselves as a nonparty, began to succumb to factional disputes as competition with the Republicans became more acute. A split emerged between "high Federalists," those individuals most antagonistic to reform and compromise, and others who were moderate in their views. The Republicans too suffered from this same experience, particularly after their electoral success in 1800.

No individual represents the high Federalist position more distinctly than Fisher Ames. He was elected to the first session of the House of Representatives by defeating a hero of the Revolution, Samuel Adams. Ames at age thirty represented the rising new generation of Federalists. His speeches before the House in opposition to the newly formed Madisonian party are masterpieces of political rhetoric. His address in support of Jay's Treaty in a speech delivered in 1796 awed even the Republicans. Ames contended that for the House to oppose the Senate ratification of the treaty would be to tatter the honor of a new nation. Ignoring criticisms that commercial concessions would place America in the position of a neocolonial vassal to British interests, Ames called upon members of the House and all Americans to show their patriotism by supporting the administration. He asks in the middle of the speech:

What is patriotism? Is it a narrow affection for the spot where a man
is born? Are the very clods where we tread entitled to ardent preference, because they are greener? No sir, this is not the character of virtue, and it soars higher for its object.

Suppose, continued Ames, it was Great Britain who failed to honor the
treaty; ". . . wherever an Englishman might travel, shame would stick to
him; he would disown his own country." A citizen of "such a nation might
truly say to corruption, thou art my father, and to the worm, thou art my
mother and sister."

As Republicans gained ascendancy, however, Ames's rhetoric became
more vehement. He began to write more as an outsider in his own beloved
country. Plagued by a consumptive disorder, Ames almost seemed to regard
the fate of the second founding as parallel to that of his own cadaverous
body. Writing in many Federalist newspapers under Roman republican
pseudonyms, he passionately defended the Federalist faith: preference for
the British constitution as opposed to the American; a defense of property
as the basis for political participation; and an attack on the emergence of
faction as evidence of the failure of the American experiment. Ames was
deeply respected and even loved by New England Federalists. He was
offered the presidency of Harvard (which he declined for reasons of ill
health). To Federalist sympathizers he was one of the last guardians of *res
publica*—a kind of Cicero whose unfortunate political burden was to chronicle the descent of America from a republic to a democracy.

Contemporary analysts offer a different portrait of Fisher Ames. To
Vernon Parrington (*The Romantic Revolution in America*), Ames was what
he called a "tie whig" Federalist whose political thought was no different
from the Tories of an earlier generation. Some moralistic Republicans
became skittish after Shay's Rebellion and the economic dislocations of the
postwar period. According to Parrington, Ames, who generationally represented the ideology of theological stewardship in New England, "professed
republicanism, but . . . was instinctively aristocratic."

Even American conservatives have reached cautious assessments
about Ames. For example, Albert Beveridge, an early biographer of John
Marshall, described Ames as "that delightful reactionary." Russell Kirk
attempts to offer a balanced conservative assessment of Ames in *The Conservative Mind*. While he might not have had the political talents of John
Adams and Hamilton, who actively attempted to frame a political system to
conservative ends despite personal doubts about the long-term viability of
their efforts, Ames was "the most eloquent of the Federalists." Because of
his own pessimism, Ames focused his considerable theoretical abilities
upon an assessment of the American system "expressed with an irony and
penetration worthy of Voltaire."

The political work that best expresses the disappointment, fatalism, and anger of the high Federalists toward the second founding after the rise of the Republicans is Ames's "The Dangers of American Liberty." This essay was written in 1805 but not published until after his death in 1808. Just after Jefferson's election to a second term, Ames writes what is essentially a eulogy to the Federalist party. The essay is dedicated to the "persecuted federalists" who were now a "fallen party," never again destined to run the nation. But the theoretical focus of Ames is faction. The word *faction* is repeated nearly 100 times throughout the essay. It is the organizing concept for Ames's assessment of the reasons for the imminent end of the republic. "We are devoted to the successive struggles of factions, who rule by turns, the worst of whom will rule last, and triumph by the sword." "We are now visibly drawn with the revolutionary suction of Niagara," Ames tells his readers, "and everything that is liberty will be dashed to pieces in its descent."

Many of Ames's descriptions of faction had already been made by Madison himself, the leader of the current Republican faction, in *The Federalist* No. 10. But for Ames, the solutions offered by *The Federalist* involved too great a concession to democratic ideology. Americans had been too critical of the English constitution, regarding its success as accidental and the devotion of its citizens the result of historical "prejudice." Ames admits that no other constitution could have been ratified in America in 1787. "[N]o plan of government, without a large and preponderating commixture of democracy, can for a moment possess our confidence." Thus, the Constitution was "as good . . . as our country could bear," but it was not good enough. Federalists had hoped that the judiciary and the Senate would prove strong enough to prevent the rise of factional conflict. They were wrong.

Ames traces the rise of faction to two sources that have become so intertwined that in his mind the republic is living through its last days. The democratic institutions in the new Constitution, principally the House of Representatives, provided a haven for ambitious leaders, and the selfish designs of strong states in the Union, principally Virginia, provided a focus for dissension. Ames sees in the policies of Virginia Republicans nothing other than the pursuit of immediate political advantage. How can her citizens be so devoted to "abstract theories" of democracy when her leaders are aristocrats? Clearly, men like Jefferson and Madison have "fomented a licentious spirit" among their citizens and their neighbors in order to advance their own political ambitions. America was peopled by "demagogues" who led "lives like Clodius, and with the maxims of Cato in their mouths, cherishing principles like Cataline," acted "steadily on a plan of usurpation like Caesar." Ames recounts the fate of past republics that were destroyed by the machinations of designing politicians from strong states. "Is Virginia to be our Rome?" was Ames's ominous rhetorical prediction.

Republican virtue was no restraint against faction. Describing the country in even more deleterious terms than Adams did in his *Discourses*, Ames concluded that the very idea of a republic in America was a fiction: "[T]he republicanism of a great mass of people is nothing more than a blind trust in certain favorites. . . ." He dismissed the argument that debate was a substitute for violence. The belief that "Let only ink enough be shed, and let democracy rage [and] there will be no blood" was a delusion. At the close of "The Dangers of American Liberty" there is a small and faint expression of hope for the future of the American republic. American cities were much smaller than London or Paris; the absence of a standing army placed a restraint on demagogic ambition; the absence of famine in this country meant that the "political electricity" that strikes European nations was thus far lacking. Still Ames concludes that tyranny and revolution will come, "but not with so rapid a pace, as that of France."

Ames's assessment of the American regime at the height of Republican power illustrates more than Federalist despair. Ames, an important proponent of the second founding, may himself have been in his own way a "man of little faith." Since he was unwilling to graft party conflict and democratization onto his New England moralistic republicanism, his considerable theoretical talents were limited to replicating secular versions of the Puritan jeremiads delivered by his ancestors in the previous century. In this respect Louis Hartz concludes that high Federalists such as Ames lived in a "phantom world," seeing Robespierres and Bonapartes everywhere. The rights to property were never under threat by the Republicans nor under siege by an allegedly licentious people. Nor by any stretch of the theoretical imagination were Madison and Jefferson Jacobin centralizers of power. On the other hand, Ames's own alienation from power after the Washington administration provided him with an insight into the dynamics of a republic based upon party competition. The Republic may not have been in danger of the imminent collapse that Ames so sorrowfully and confidently predicted. But a republic based permanently upon party competition is not one based upon "sober reason," "legal restraint," and "public reason." It is an affair in which politicians push for immediate advantage, and the issues of the day are often discussed in terms that appeal to the "worst" rather than the best in us. The only alternative to this "vortex" of faction, however, that Ames was able to propose was governance by the elite from which he was himself born. Ames was correct in concluding that the Constitution was not a barrier against rejection of this kind of rule.

Alexander Hamilton's own aristocratic predispositions were not much different from Ames's. Hamilton, however, without possessing much faith in the Constitution, worked imaginatively to shape it according to the major tenets of federalism. In most important respects he was successful. Despite the revolution of 1800 and the centrality of Jeffersonianism in American political thought, important aspects of American constitutional practice are largely Hamiltonian. America as a nation in political and economic terms has in a fundamental sense followed the Hamiltonian path. Hamilton's two great contributions to American political thought rest upon his vision of the presidency as the center of national government, and upon his vision of America as a great industrial world power.

After Jefferson retired, he wrote an old friend about an encounter with Hamilton. We do not know Hamilton's version of the incident, but Jefferson's letter to Benjamin Rush reveals much about the antagonism between the two men as well as the different perspectives of the leaders of the first party system in America. According to Jefferson, Washington had asked the secretary of state to call together the heads of other executive departments to discuss some policy problems. During dinner Hamilton asked who were the portraits on the wall. Jefferson replied that these were pictures of the greatest men humanity had ever produced—Bacon, Newton, and Locke. Hamilton hesitated and then responded that "the greatest man that ever lived was Julius Caesar." The remark horrified Jefferson and served as proof to him that Hamilton was a potential usurper. Sympathetic interpreters of Hamilton regard the statement as a retort that attempted to convey that statesmanship represented the highest value for an individual, not the pursuits of philosophers. If the story is basically accurate, Caesar was certainly an unfortunate choice to make, even in a conversational gambit. Hamilton was as well versed in republican exemplars as was Jefferson, and he could just as easily have selected a less inflammatory example. Nevertheless, the exchange reveals a great deal about the differing visions of Hamilton and Jefferson. To Hamilton the "energy" of the executive branch was essential to the revision of American revolutionary republicanism.

In *The Federalist* Hamilton accepted the responsibility for defending the newly invented presidency against those who described it as "the fetus of monarchy." In No. 69 he dismissed the comparison between the president and a monarch by reviewing the powers of the president in relation to those of the Crown and the governor of New York. Hamilton's analogy was carefully chosen here, since he ignored the gubernatorial powers of the Virginia executive and those states that imitated the Virginia model. He also excluded from direct discussion the implications of a chief executive at the national level who possessed the powers of a strong state governor. Nevertheless, Hamilton was ideologically very adept in his choices. He declared that in nearly all cases the governorship was a more powerful office than the presidency. There was, he concluded, "no diadem sparkling" on the proposed president's brow, no "imperial purple flowing in his train."

In No. 70 Hamilton-Publius criticized republicans for relying upon temporary dictators to save republics in danger from without or within. Patrick Henry, speaking in opposition to the second founding, questioned whether a national executive was necessary since Washington had served the revolutionary cause so well as an ad hoc military leader. The reliance among republicans upon temporary dictatorships was certainly a paradoxical and weak point in their theory, and Hamilton seized upon the inconsistency. How many times, he asked, had the Roman republic sought refuge in the "absolute power of a single man, under the formidable title of Dictator? " As to the alternative of plural executives (which had been proposed at the convention and was, in effect, the practice in the Pennsylvania constitution), Hamilton argued that "republican jealousy" (fear of government) logically required a single authority. A plural executive deprives the people of the "two greatest securities" against the abuse of executive power: accountability and easy discovery of misconduct.

Hamilton's ideological ingenuity is at its optimum in his defense of the absence of a reeligibility requirement in the Constitution. *Rotation in office* was a principle dear to revolutionary republicans. Jefferson, in fact, listed its omission as a major defect in the proposed Constitution. Hamilton defends the document both on the general grounds of suspicion of executive power as well as for providing space for the emergence of the republican hero. "The love of fame, the ruling passion of the noblest minds" can prompt "a man to plan and undertake extensive and arduous enterprises for the public benefit." A wise republican will allow these great men to complete these undertakings lest "the most that can be expected from the generality of men . . . is the negative merit of not doing harm, instead of the positive merit of doing good." A reeligibility restriction would unintentionally create an environment in which a dozen men "who had credit enough to raise themselves to the seat of the supreme magistry" would wander "among the people like discontented ghosts."

The American presidency was but a pale copy of Hamilton's own vision of the office as he conveyed it to members in the early sessions of the Constitutional Convention in the summer of 1787. The president was not to be elected for life (thus Hamilton used his arguments against reeligibility as a substitute), and the president was not to be given an absolute veto (thus Hamilton defended the more limited exercise of executive power as a necessary protection against inevitable legislative encroachment in No. 73). Republicans came to believe that Hamilton's defense of the presidency was thus a theoretical precursor to a defense of monarchy. A more charitable interpretation of Hamilton on this point involves an appreciation of an attempt on his part to "tame" tyranny for the republican cause. For if, in Hamilton's mind, active executive authority was indispensable to good government, it must be somehow preserved although tempered in a republican

regime. Perhaps the Constitution erred because it tamed executive authority too much, even while recognizing its importance. Nevertheless, for
Hamilton the task of the statesman in a new republican regime was to take
every opportunity to assert executive authority in order to create constitutional precedents.

The rise of faction leading to party competition obscured Hamilton's
achievements in creating an executive-centered republican regime. Washington, despite the complaints of Hamilton (and Jefferson as well), did
much to operationalize Hamilton's model. Through Washington's actions
against Indians and rebellious western farmers at home and his policies
toward foreign conflict, he developed a conception of executive privilege,
personal diplomacy, and executive action independent of congressional initiative. When he left office in 1797, Washington had created a Federalist
model of the presidency very close to Hamilton's vision. As one scholar has
interpreted the period (Michael Riccards, *A Republic if You Can Keep It,*
1987), the presidency became an institution based upon

> mass appeal, often regardless of policy positions; strong assertion of
> executive authority, especially in foreign affairs; general disregard of
> political parties; preoccupation with official pomp and protocol as a
> way of protecting and buttressing the incumbent; a conservative eco-
> nomic and social organization; and aloofness toward legislative con-
> troversies except where they might infringe on the executive.

If Hamilton's vision, however, had only been limited to the support of
the presidency, the emergence of faction might not have occurred. Republicans were, after all, deeply ambivalent about executive authority. In a
series of reports to Congress, Hamilton attempted to create the foundation
of America as a major industrial world power. In his first "Report on Public
Credit" presented in early 1790, Hamilton attempted to align the forces of
capital in America to the new Constitution by proposing the national
assumption of revolutionary debts as they stood in 1783. Hamilton knew
full well that many revolutionary soldiers sold their bonds to speculators
during the conflict with Britain for a pittance. He also knew that some states
had very little war debt and others a major portion. His strategy was to align
capital to the second founding by removing the states from significant
financial decisions and making the federal government the guarantor of
debt. Despite organized opposition from Madison, Hamilton was successful.

Hamilton's next task, at least as he apparently saw it, was to create an
international medium of economic exchange in America and a central
source for investment capital. Late in 1790 he proposed the creation of a
national bank. In a study ("Report on the National Bank"), he carefully
noted the principal objections to his idea. He reviewed arguments suggest-

ing that the bank might establish excessive rates of interest, that it might provide loans to "unsound persons" and to areas not in the national interest, and that it might stimulate "overtrading" of commodities. Hamilton nevertheless rejected all these arguments by pointing to the success of national banks in Italy, Germany, Holland, Britain, and France. The national bank was necessary in his mind for the "augmentation of active capital," for aid to the federal government in emergencies, and for facilitation in the payment of taxes.

When Jefferson objected that a national bank exceeded federal authority, Hamilton wrote a letter to President Washington that has become a major source for those who would assert national authority. Hamilton, in his "Opinion on the Constitutionality of an Act to Establish a National Bank" (1791), contended that the Tenth Amendment was no restriction upon the federal government, and that the national government was authorized by the Constitution to undertake any project that was "an instrument or mean" for the execution of any of its "specified powers." Washington signed the bill, and the Bank of the United States became a major source of capital investment until it came under attack by the Jacksonian Democrats a generation later.

Hamilton's most ambitious project was never formally approved by Congress, although America gradually accepted his position. America in 1790 was an agricultural nation with important pockets of trading activity. Hamilton felt that the future of the country lay in the development of manufacturing. His "Report on Manufactures" (1791) was years in the making and carefully phrased so as not to directly upset farming interests. He admitted that "the cultivation of the earth, as the immediate and chief source of subsistence to a man, . . . has intrinsically a strong claim to preeminence over every other kind of industry." Nevertheless, wrote Hamilton in a discriminating bureaucratic language, the argument that agriculture is "not only the most productive, but the only productive, species of industry" is unproven. Farm labor was "periodical and occasional," and it ignored the advantages of the division of labor and employed less machinery. Is a piece of land, Hamilton asked, really likely to produce a greater surplus devoted to industry rather than to agriculture? Manufacturing offered opportunities for invention, useful employment for women and children, and attraction to potential immigrants who would "transplant themselves" in order to better their lives.

The report was debated largely in terms of the question of tariffs for American industry and their advantages for the northeastern portion of the country. But Hamilton's essay implicitly raised other extremely important questions about the future of the American polity. A central feature of republican thought (which we shall review shortly in our discussion of John Taylor and Jefferson) involved the assumption that the independent agricultural producer was essential to the maintenance of a republic. This model might be fictional, since American farmers were more dependent upon banks than they cared to admit. Still, the idea of a citizen whose income was independent from government and who was in a position to act as a sovereign participator in political affairs was a powerful theory. Hamilton in his report ignored this position. Although his own vision is only implicit, he outlined a different future for America. Individual effort in a collective enterprise benefited the upwardly mobile person and contributed to the economic power of the nation at large. Industrial collectivism, from this viewpoint, was a more rational alternative for the posterity of the nation than a collection of independent villagers. Federalists were slow to appreciate the full implications of Hamilton's vision. Many were landowners themselves. Many, like Fisher Ames as well as Hamilton himself, were unable to explore the popular attraction of this model.

REPUBLICANS

The basic policy predispositions of the Federalists—nationalism and a willingness to use government in support of economic objectives and cultural and political elitism—produced an unusual democratic moment in America. In this country the first mass movement championed localism and agrarianism. A major theorist of the new Republican party was John Taylor of Caroline. Taylor is primarily recognized today for his critique of John Adams's *Defence of the Constitutions*. But Taylor's work, *An Inquiry into the Principles and Policy of the Government of the United States* (1814); has always puzzled students of American political thought. Written (and rewritten) as a response to a work published nearly thirty years earlier, *An Inquiry* greatly suffers from different generational focuses. Adams's work was part of a movement attacking the "democratic" character of the revolutionary state constitutions. The constitutional issues he raised were settled by 1790. State constitutions had largely adopted the Massachusetts model and abandoned the weak executive Virginia approach as well as the antiexecutive unicameral legislature adopted initially by Pennsylvania. *An Inquiry*, then, had the air of a lost cause about it, even at its publication when Republicans had wiped out the Federalist opposition. Its regional reputation is also accentuated by Taylor's other comments defending slavery.

Since Taylor came to represent a troublesome wing of the Republican party itself (he opposed many of Jefferson's presidential policies), the Virginian has been relegated to the status of an early southern reactionary. There are clearly elements in Taylor's thought that prefigure the southern reactionary Enlightenment (see chapter 5), yet his work as a whole contains many other important theoretical features. Taylor represents a vision of southern aristocratic republicanism that supported the Revolution, opposed or acquiesced to the second founding, and attempted through its support of the Republican party to present an American future quite different from that of the Federalists. Thus to Taylor, Adams's *Defence* was crucial to an appreciation of current political divisions. Here one could discover the origins of the American departure from true republicanism. For Adams, according to Taylor, had committed the error of attempting to provide republican stability by giving each interest in society a permanent voice and a defense against the other, with the executive acting as a balancing force between the forces of aristocracy and the people. The second founders compounded this error by attempting to imitate the Massachusetts solution at the federal level.

John Taylor's critique, nearly hidden by his tardy response to Adams's *Defence* and obscured by the focus on practical aspects of rural life in his masterpiece, *Arator,* is that both Adams's and Madison's discussions of faction are theories that are standing on their heads and need to be turned right side up. Faction, in Taylor's view, is not endemic to republics. It is, in fact, a feature of politics noticeably lacking in true republican government. Taylor did not deny that both good and evil were part of human nature, but he argued that both tendencies need to be assessed in terms of the governmental systems that provide incentives or opportunities to each disposition.

In *An Inquiry* Taylor outlines the sources and origins of political power throughout history. Ancient authority rested upon superstition; medieval authority, upon conquest. In each case political authority was based upon the possession of certain talents wrested by one generation from others and imposed upon subsequent generations through the restriction of access to their sources of power, whether that be religious secrets, military knowledge, property, or general education. Thus while Taylor never denied that a "natural aristocracy" (as men and women of talent) could emerge in any single generation, he refused to accept Adams's constitutional solution since it solidified the advantages one elite enjoyed in a particular period of time for the ages. Such aristocracies may have been functional in the past, but

> knowledge and commerce, by a division of virtue, of talents, and of
> wealth among multitudes, have annihilated that order of men, who
> in past ages constituted "a natural aristocracy," (as Mr. Adams thinks)
> by exclusive virtue, talents and wealth.

The Massachusetts constitution and the second founding were justified on the grounds that they controlled faction, especially the propensity of those who are without property to covet the property of others. But in fact both arrangements accentuated and actually created factions that might never emerge in a different governmental system. The chief executive and judiciary are the focus of Taylor's analysis. The presidency was an institution "with far greater powers than sufficed to Caesar for enslaving his country." To Taylor, the elective basis of the president's authority magnifies rather than limits the power of the executive. "Marius, Sylla, Pompey, Caesar, Cromwell and Bonaparte were elected," he reminds the readers in *An Inquiry*. The presidency was for him a magnet around which people schemed for personal advancement and used the office of the executive to promote their interests. The president, for Taylor, "makes judges and generals" and men rich.

The bête noire of Taylor's later writings is the Marshall Supreme Court. In Taylor's cosmos, judicial and executive power were inextricably intertwined, however they may be divided by the second Constitution. In any three-party dispute the weakest agent will align with the strongest and, according to Taylor, "the judicial power has seized upon a quality peculiar to the American policy, to transform itself into a political department, and to extend its claims far beyond precedent." Jefferson complained that the Federalists had "retired into the judiciary" in order to make guerrilla attacks against the party that had the support of the people. Taylor offered a broader argument. He contended that, sooner or later and across time, the judiciary had to be regarded as an agent of the executive branch. Taken over the long haul, Taylor seemed to be saying that the Supreme Court would become a major force in the nationalization of American politics. For him this placed the judiciary in the service of "political law" or the service of factions centered around the presidency. Sometimes the Court would advance the cause of factions that had already lost control of the executive branch. But for Taylor this was not "balance," as both Adams and Madison claimed, but executive-dominated government.

Here in essence was the basis of Taylor's analysis. Faction was the result of a political system that put too much power in the hands of the executive branch of government. Presidential authority under the new Constitution created opportunities for a new form of aristocracy, an aristocracy of capital based upon "paper money" and advantages received from access to presidential initiatives in policy making. There is a great deal of novelty in Taylor's argument, for he is arguing that it is the governmental structure that creates economic structure.

As a political economist, Taylor regarded the rise of an industrial capitalist economy as the natural consequence of the new Constitution. The executive branch would provide—indeed it already was providing—opportunities for profit for the few through a national bank and currency system, and the Court was ratifying these policies. "The complete panoply of fleets, armies, banks, funding systems, pensions, bounties, corporations, [and] exclusive privileges" were replacing a government based upon popular right. The spirited attacks on the new "capitalist aristocracy," "alien stock-jobbers," "idle" capitalists as well as the division of society into producers and nonproducers led progressives in the next century to rediscover and celebrate Taylor's work.

But Taylor was not a proponent of national industrial regulation, since for him more government would only feed the growth of capital. Taylor was an agrarian, perhaps the most principled agrarian in American political thought. *Arator* extols the virtues of rural and agricultural life as good in themselves. But like Jefferson, Taylor offered a defense of agriculture that was decidedly modernist. Working the soil was the highest form of human happiness because it consisted of "fitting ideas to substances, and substances to ideas; and of a constant rotation of hope and fruition." Taylor spoke excitedly of the variation and change as well as the balance and stability of agricultural life:

> The novelty, frequency, and exactness of accommodations between our ideas and operations, constitute the most exquisite source of mental pleasure. Agriculture feeds it with endless supplies in the natures of soils, plants, climates, manures, instruments of culture and domestic animals. Their combinations are inexhaustible, the novelty of results is endless.

His vision, in short, is not one which describes or glorifies the poor, struggling dirt farmer but rather a vision that describes the gentleman planter. For Taylor it was only in a society completely devoted to these pursuits that agriculture could survive. A mixed economy of industry and farming would lead inevitably to the oppression of the latter by the former. While he hated political parties and saw their rise as a result of divisions created by the new artificial sources of wealth, he urged the organization of all farmers (also carefully adding "mechanics" as members of the producing class) into a mass movement that would dismantle the new powers recently asserted by the executive branch and the courts at the federal level. "We farmers and mechanics," he wrote in *Arator*,

> have been political slaves in all countries, because we are political fools. We know how to convert a wilderness into a paradise, and a forest into palaces and elegant furniture; but we have been taught by those whose object it is to monopolize the sweets of life, which we sweat for, that politics are without our province, and in us a ridiculous affectation. . . .

Despite Taylor's attempts to include groups other than farmers among the producing class, his writings remained very much a focus for regional protest. Madison, with his usual adeptness, had organized a party in Congress. It was Thomas Jefferson who created a national party. It is difficult to focus on this single achievement on Jefferson's part since his talents as a revolutionary theorist, Enlightenment intellectual, and politician are so manifold. But in many ways his role in the formation of a mass political party provides us with an opportunity to discuss the Sage of Monticello's general contribution to American political thought.

Early in 1799 Jefferson, in a letter to Elbridge Gerry, discussed a set of principles of belief that came to be treated as the Republican party platform in the election of 1800. Of course, the Republicans had no platform in the modern sense of the term, but Jefferson's comments were circulated by party activists and printed along with other speeches delivered by Jefferson for distribution. These brief comments are an exceptional statement not only of Jefferson's own political philosophy and that of the nascent Republican party but also of an ideology that in subsequent history came to be known as *Jeffersonianism*.

Although Jefferson did not arrange his platform as a list, let us now do so in order to appreciate Jeffersonianism as a set of principles:

> I am for preserving to the States the powers not yielded by them to the Union, and to the legislature of the Union its constitutional share in the division of powers. . . .

> I am for a government rigorously frugal and simple, applying all the possible savings of the public revenue to the discharge of the national debt; and not for a multiplication of officers and salaries merely to make partisans. . . .

> I am for relying, for internal defence, on our militia only, till actual invasion . . . and not for a standing army in time of peace, which may overawe the public sentiment. . . .

> I am for free commerce with all nations; political connection with none; and little or no diplomatic establishment.

> I am for freedom of religion, and against all maneuvers to bring about a legal ascendancy of one sect over another: for the freedom of the press, and against all violations of the Constitution to silence by force and not by reason the complaints or criticisms, just or unjust, of our citizens against the conduct of their agents.

> And I am for encouraging the progress of science in all its branches; and not for raising a hue and cry against the sacred name of philosophy. . . .

To these points Jefferson added that while he was "a sincere well-wisher to the success of the French revolution, and still wish it may end in the establishment of a free and well-ordered republic," he was not "insensible under the atrocious depredations they have committed on our commerce." To Jefferson, "the first object of my heart is my own country." It was in America that he "embarked my family, my fortune, and my own existence [and] I have not a farthing interest, nor one fibre of attachment" to any other countries but "in proportion as they are more or less friendly to us."

One can see important elements of republican thought in general and country ideology in particular in Jefferson's platform. There is his general fear of government; his opposition to standing armies; and his suspicion of executive power. In 1799 Jefferson, while supporting the second founding, asserted that he was "opposed to the monarchising of its features by the forms of its administration." The executive-dominated coalition of the Federalists was portrayed as a "first transition to a President and Senate for life, and from that to an hereditary tenure of these offices, and thus to worm out the elective principle." In other words, Jefferson had employed the concept of corruption so central to republican thought and depicted the Constitution in drift toward monarchy. (Federalists, of course, pursued this same theme with the transition toward one of democracy.)

But there are other ideological strands in the platform. Jefferson was never a traditionalist. He spent a good deal of time, particularly in his later years, contemplating theological questions. He read and reread the New Testament, but was largely uninterested in the mysteries of the Resurrection—let alone finer theological points. To him Jesus was a proponent of a "sublime morality," and only to this extent did Jefferson regard himself as a Christian. For ritual, a sense of the sacred, and even organized religion in general, Jefferson had little sympathy. Churches were products of ignorance and political props for monarchies.

Much closer to Jefferson's heart was his belief in the liberating effects of education. He wrote John Adams in 1816 that "education and free discussion" would eventually solve the problem of religious conflict, which was "a disease of ignorance." Jefferson often complained in his letters about Virginia's failure to adopt his proposal for public schooling. In correspondence with Peter Carr in 1814, he outlined a dual curriculum both for the "laboring and the learned" classes. The former would receive instruction in reading, writing, arithmetic, and geography; the latter (which included those entering "the learned professions as means of livelihood" and the wealthy, who, "possessing independent fortunes, . . . might aspire to share in the affairs of the nation") would be educated in higher mathematics, languages, and philosophy. He founded William and Mary as a college with a "plan so broad and liberal and modern" as to attract public support and "be a temptation to the youth of other States to come and drink of the cup of knowledge and fraternize with us."

Jefferson was, then, ideologically both a republican and a liberal. He accepted the republican interpretation of constitutional arrangements (limited power, legislative dominance, opposition to standing armies), and used the republican corruption theory to explain the early constitutional initiatives of the Federalists. In this respect Jefferson is the traditional republican while Madison (at least until the early 1790s) is the modernist, with his willingness to innovate and adapt the principles of British constitutional theory. But in his opposition to organized religion, his belief in education as an emancipating tool, and his general faith in science, Jefferson is very much a modernist and a liberal.

One can argue that these two ideological traditions that Jefferson embraced account for the innovative character of his thought. Jefferson's support of the yeoman farmer is central to his political philosophy. In his *Notes on Virginia,* farmers are described as "the chosen people of God" for classical republican reasons. Farmers are independent, and commerce creates dependence and "dependence begets subservience and venality, suffocates the germ of virtue, and prepares fit tools for the designs of ambition." But Jefferson's yeoman, even more than Taylor's, is also a scientist and a philosopher. The bountifulness of land in America permits "more freedom, more ease and less misery." Jefferson at Monticello is constantly tinkering with possible inventions, relandscaping in order to capture an aesthetics of a pastoral environment as well as reading the latest scientific or philosophical pamphlets. To Richard K. Matthews (*The Radical Politics of Thomas Jefferson,* 1984), Jefferson wanted the best of both worlds, "all the benefits of science, technology, and agriculture without any of the costs of industrialization." Later in his life he began to relent in his opposition to industry. He envisioned a nation of farms interspersed with cottage industry, and he began to explore the possibility of technology as a basis for providing the artisan with the same leisure as the farmer. Jefferson's political economy may have been utopian, but his perspective on agriculture and even on the relationship between work and leisure contains an intriguing combination of republicanism and liberalism.

Perhaps no idea of Jefferson's has stimulated the imagination of later American political theorists more than his proposal for a ward system. Jefferson led the formation of a political party despite his republican beliefs concerning the danger of organized faction. Even if we take into account the personal and mixed character of his own motivations (his rivalry with Hamilton, his tepid support of the second founding, his own ambitions), it is clear that Jefferson believed that the Constitution's limited provisions for political participation placed the republic in jeopardy. In his 1799 platform he complained that the "elective principle" was in danger of being "wormed out" of the federal Constitution. In a letter to John Taylor (1816), he defined a republic in terms of its provisions for political participation: "The further the departure from direct and constant control by the citizens, the less has the government of the ingredient of republicanism." The House of Representatives exemplified the "purest republican feature" in our Constitution. The Senate was less so and the executive still less. The judiciary was "seriously anti-republican." One of the purposes of the formation of the

Republican party was to arrest the formation of any more antirepublican practices. Jefferson did not seem to have appreciated party activity itself as more than a temporary remedy for participation. Nor did he generally look to the democratization of the federal Constitution (the direct election of senators and the obsolescence of the electoral college) as a solution.

Late in his life, however, Jefferson seemed to have become more and more convinced that some new structure needed to be invented in order to promote direct political participation. In letters to friends he recommended the formation of wards through a subdivision of counties. Each ward would have its own school, justice of the peace, constable, and militia captain. Most significant, however, the citizens of each ward or "hundred" would meet regularly. Jefferson felt that the attachment to republican government would be much stronger among citizens who regularly directly participated in their own affairs. The citizen of a "ward-republic" will "let his heart be torn out of his body sooner than his power be wrested from him by a Caesar or a Bonaparte." Jefferson notes in a self-effacing substantiation of his point that he felt the "foundations of government shaken under my feet" when the participators of the New England town meetings rose in opposition to his embargo policy during his presidency.

Critics of Jefferson, such as Herbert Croly (see chapter 6), regard the proposal as further evidence of Jefferson's unwillingness to conceive of democratization in other than local terms. Other writers, most notably Hannah Arendt (*On Revolution*), praise the idea as an attempt to reintroduce into the American Constitution a feature of direct participation ignored by the second founders. To Arendt, the American Revolution had escaped the nearly inevitable Thermidor, but it was Jefferson who "knew, however dimly, that the Revolution, while it had given freedom to the people, had failed to provide space where this freedom is exercised." Whatever the feasibility or merits of the ward system, the proposal illustrates the remarkable fertility of Jefferson's intellect. At a time when the second founding was in the process of veneration in popular culture, he was willing to reexamine its deepest philosophical structure. Louis Hartz, who was an ardent critic of American political thought, once concluded that America's secret of survival has been its ability (often expressed unsystematically) to unite different traditions of thought, combining "rock-ribbed tradition with high inventiveness, ancestor worship with ardent opportunism." Such, perhaps, was Jefferson's own genius. Possibly this aspect of Jefferson explains why we are all "Jeffersonians." In fact, the Sage of Monticello has been claimed as an exemplar by states' rights advocates, New Dealers, anti- and pro-war movements, liberals, radicals and conservatives, business leaders and farmers.

DEMOCRATS

The revolution of 1800 turned out to be a hyperbole in regard to the Jefferson administration. The Republicans did not initiate a late-blooming Jacobinism in America as the Federalists had predicted. Nor was Jefferson able or even willing to appreciably redirect the second founding, although it is difficult to predict the course of American constitutional development had the Federalists remained in power. His purchase of Louisiana from Napoleon shocked some members of his party. The acquittal of Justice Samuel Chase of impeachment charges and of Aaron Burr of treason were regarded as evidence of the limitations of majority rule under the new Constitution. In his second administration Jefferson seemed to have succumbed to the national idea of the Federalists by recommending a panoply of federal programs for roads and other internal improvements. His decision to embargo imported goods from both France and Great Britain led to a revolt within his own party. Jefferson left office under a cloud of disappointment. Although his early biographers and other historians harbored noticeable Federalist sympathies, Henry Adams's description in his history of the Jefferson administration is not exaggerated: The presidency

> which had made peace a passion could lead to no better result than had been reached by the barbarous system which made war a duty. . . . Jefferson's popularity vanished, and the labored fabric of his reputation fell in sudden and general ruin.

Nevertheless, the Republican party electoral coalition was so massive that it survived Jefferson's presidency. A second war with Great Britain was a severe jolt to the party, but Madison even endured the indignities of a brief and limited foreign occupation of the capital. In 1821 James Monroe received every electoral vote save one.

But by 1824 the Republican party was breaking up into factions. John Quincy Adams, who was secretary of state and had contributed thirty years to public service, was the heir apparent. But William Crawford, secretary of the treasury, obtained the nomination of the congressional caucus. "Favorite sons," including Henry Clay (speaker of the House) of Kentucky, Andrew Jackson (senator) of Tennessee, and John C. Calhoun (senator) of South Carolina, were nominated by their state legislatures. Calhoun later withdrew and accepted a position on the Jackson ticket. The election outcome followed along general lines the pattern anticipated by the second founders. With no candidate possessing a majority, the selection of a president was made by the House of Representatives. But this was not a choice to be made on traditional republican principles. The eminence of the candidates was not the issue; instead, factional considerations, attachment to individuals, and sectional interests governed the choice of the House. Jackson, who had probably received a plurality of the popular vote, was passed over, and Adams was elected president. Thus began the Jacksonian movement, the creation of the Democratic party, and arguably the most extended period of reform consciousness in American history. Jackson was elected president in 1828 and reelected in 1832. The Whigs were organized in opposition to the new Jacksonian forces. Thus was formed the most competitive party system in American history. Richard McCormick describes this *second party system* thus: "Voters everywhere thought of themselves as either Whigs or Democrats."

Who were the Jacksonians, and what was the essence of their political ideology? Scholars have presented numerous assessments of the significance of this second party system which, in effect, permanently institutionalized faction in the American political system. Alexis de Tocqueville, a French aristocrat who attempted to come to terms with what he regarded as a *new order* in the world emerging in America, interpreted the Jacksonian movement as part of an inevitable process of democratization in a society without an aristocracy. For Tocqueville, America was the first modern country, and a fortunate one at that, since Americans were creating an entirely new society without the violent revolutionary turmoil from which his own country had suffered. The author of *Democracy in America* (1835, 1840) portrayed Jacksonian America as a society of the future: "The nations of our day cannot prevent conditions of equality from spreading in their midst." Arthur Schlesinger, Jr., a contemporary analyst, accepts much of Tocqueville's assessment in *The Age of Jackson* (1945). To Schlesinger the agenda of the Jacksonian Democrats represented an extension of the Republicans: "Jacksonian democracy can be properly regarded as a somewhat more hard-headed and determined version of Jeffersonian democracy." There were as well, according to Schlesinger, striking similarities between Jacksonian Democracy and the New Deal. The newly reformed party was led by a charismatic and controversial leader—a factor that dramatically increased political participation by activating both urban workers and farmers.

Other scholars, however, have challenged the interpretation of the Jacksonians as egalitarians. Herbert Croly, in *The Promise of American Life* (1909), written two generations before Schlesinger's account, appreciated the democratic ethos of the new westerners. He even thought the campaign against the National Bank revealed "a latent socialism." But Croly concluded that the Democrats were at base committed to "rampant individualism": " . . . what they mean by individuality is an unusual amount of individual energy successfully spent in popular and remunerative occupations." Croly's assessment was broadened by the so-called entrepreneurial school of historians who, in critical response to *The Age of Jackson*, argued that the Jacksonians were not radicals or even liberal reformers at all but advocates of capitalism. Jackson's opposition to federal programs for internal improvements (roads, bridges, canals) and his attacks on paper currency and the Bank of the United States were, according to this interpretation, efforts on the part of small-scale capitalists and would-be business leaders to reform the political system so as to give themselves as much chance to make money as the eastern financiers and industrialists had.

An interpretation attempting to synthesize many of these views was advanced with great subtlety in Marvin Meyers's study of the Jacksonians. In *The Jacksonian Persuasion*, Meyers argues that the supporters of the Democrats were "venturesome conservatives." Extrapolating from Tocqueville's analysis, Meyers contends that the environment of relative equality that many Americans saw within their grasp in the early nineteenth century created a new "masterless man" who, "free to invent a fresh world," can see the opportunities for his own advancement but also craves stability. Jackson himself fitted this mood perfectly, since his policies were framed in terms of both preserving the values of republicanism and extending opportunity. As we examine various political theorists of this era, including Jackson himself, we can discern a nostalgic urge as well as an urgent desire to "start over."

Andrew Jackson and his party activists consciously appropriated the symbol of Jefferson. They told voters that they were committed to a return to the basic principles of the republic as understood by Jefferson. Jackson especially emphasized Jefferson's majoritarianism and his commitment to limited government. Merrill Peterson (*The Jeffersonian Image in the American Mind*) concludes that "so tight" were the Jacksonian symbols of Jefferson, democracy, and the Democratic party, that "one scarcely existed in the public mind apart from the others and attempts to disengage them met with fleeting success." Whigs complained about the highly developed tactic of Democratic debaters who answered opponents "by squirting Jefferson's opinions in their eyes."

In his second term Jackson initiated a long and bitter battle to dismantle the jewel of the Hamiltonian system, the Bank of the United States. The antibank campaign neatly combined dispositions of nostalgia for simpler republican times and individual desires for economic advancement. Jackson used country ideology to portray the bank as a "monster" that had created a new-moneyed aristocracy with the help of "designing politicians." He claimed the bank was undermining "those habits of economy and simplicity which are so congenial to the character of republicans." He also suggested that the time was not too late to begin again. The bank may have "already struck [its] roots deep in the soil," but its abolition would enable "the planter, the farmer, the mechanic, and the laborer" to realize that "their success depends upon their own industry and economy."

In addition to their deft use of Jefferson, the Democrats also added to the exemplar in three major ways. Republicans had made a distinction between a producing class and one preying upon the achievements of the producers. Both John Taylor end Jefferson grafted artisans to their theory, but the Democrats dramatically added other groups as well to what Jackson called the *real people*. Jackson reached both up and down the economic ladder in his reformulation. He included urban laborers as well as entrepreneurs. All those, in short, who depended upon their own "industry and economy" for their success were, for Jackson, "the bone and sinew of this country."

The shift from the republican paradigm on this point is subtle but very important. The republican model gave independence a central role in its conception of citizenship. The farmer's ownership of his own land, however modest, permitted him to speak and act independently since his livelihood was not contingent upon the goodwill of others. Jackson's expansion of the producing class to other groups meant effectively that new citizens were defined in terms of their ability to compete in a society of "equal rights and equal laws." The Democrats made willingness to work the criterion for the ideal citizen. Those who hope "to grow rich without labor" by manipulating the financial system to their benefit, by creating monopolies with the acquiescence of politicians, or by currying favors from the government to build projects for their private profit are the nonproducing classes.

Not only did Jackson's reformulation of citizenship broaden and redefine the electorate, it also altered it in other ways. Republicans had spoken often of a "natural" aristocracy; Democrats abandoned this formulation completely. The agrarian base of the Republican party as well as its reliance on classical republicanism and court ideology led men like Jefferson and Taylor to oppose industrialization. Jackson and the Democrats gave up the agrarian myth. In fact, the Jacksonian movement can be seen in part as an attempt to create an industrial capitalist society without the Hamiltonian idea through which it had been conceived by the Federalists. Adam Smith's *The Wealth of Nations* became the economic bible of the Jacksonians. Newspaper editorialists such as William Leggett and William Cullen Bryant argued that Smith had demonstrated that a capitalist society could be an equalitarian society once the mercantile restrictions were removed. Martin Van Buren wrote that a reformed capitalism would always guarantee to the laboring classes "a full employment of the fruits of their industry":

> Left to itself and free from the blighting influence of partial legislation, monopolies, congregated wealth, and interested combinations, the compensation of labor will always preserve this salutary relation. It is only when the natural order of society is disturbed by one or other of these causes, that the wages of labor become inadequate.

As Jacksonian Democrats abandoned the emphasis on agrarianism they also searched for new theoretical bases for their view of a competitive, industrial, but equalitarian society. Property ownership had been a common philosophical premise of many Federalists and Republicans. Fisher Ames and Jefferson would agree that owning property was an essential ingredient of any stable order, although the former believed that participation should be limited to men of wealth. When the Jacksonians expanded their conception of citizenship, property ownership by itself was too narrow a description of the real people. What philosophical concept then could encompass a society of the "working classes" (farmers, laborers, artisans, and small capitalists)? The eventual answer to this query was that *human rights* were the theoretical definition uniting all these kinds of industry. Orestes A. Brownson wrote in the *Boston Quarterly Review* in 1840, "We believe property should be held subordinate to man, and not man to property." As early as 1821, David Buel, Jr., wrote in defense of the extension of the franchise in New York that, while property was an "important object in every free government," our "community is an association of persons—of human beings—not a partnership founded on property."

The judicial application of the concept of human rights and economic opportunity is vividly illustrated in the Charles River Bridge case. A bridge had been constructed in the 1780s by Harvard College under a state charter. Stock in the bridge had risen dramatically over the years, and many wealthy Bostonians were the beneficiaries. But the bridge now needed so many repairs that the state legislature chartered the construction of another. Arguing that the new structure would lower the value of their investment, the Charles River Bridge stockholders asked for judicial relief to prevent the construction of a new bridge on the ground that the competition would constitute a breach of contract. Chief Justice Roger B. Taney, a Jackson appointee, delivered the majority opinion. He sided against the stockholders by contending that while the rights of property should be "sacredly guarded," we "must not forget that the community also have rights, and that the happiness and well being of every citizen depends upon their healthy preservation." Besides, continued Chief Justice Taney, "in a country like ours, free, active, and enterprising, continually advancing in numbers and wealth," new forms of transportation are essential and investment should not be impeded by old monopolistic charters.

A second alteration in the Jeffersonian republican platform involved a change in the attitude of the Democrats to the presidency. Indeed, Jackson and his party transformed the institution. It was, as we saw, the Republicans who had expressed distrust of the presidency as a Federalist institution. Although a series of Republican presidents had served to partially diminish this fear of executive power, the presidency before Jackson was still an institution modified by the Republicans. To the Democrats and to

Jackson himself, however, the presidency was the tribune of the producing classes. In a message to the Senate in 1834, Jackson declared that "the President is the direct representative of the people." Jackson as president was empowered to defend the people against "the rich and powerful" who would "bend the acts of government to their selfish interests." Where, continued Jackson, would the "humble members of society—the farmers, mechanics, laborers" turn without the "right to complain of the injustice of their government" to the president? Whigs, too, responded to the ascendancy of the presidency under Jackson by inverting their Federalist predecessors' arguments. The presidency, instead of an institution to protect the republic against the licentiousness of Congress, as Hamilton and Ames argued, was an "elective despotism." "King Andrew" needed to be (electorally) overthrown. But Jackson did not simply assert presidential power. He did so in a particular way. The republican leader epitomized by Washington was a nonpartisan figure. Jefferson defended party organization as a temporary expedient. Jackson and the Democrats created the idea of an intensely partisan president.

A third revision of Jefferson thus involved the recognition of faction in the form of political parties as a permanent and even desirable feature of the American polity. Jackson defended the extension of party loyalty to the bureaucracy in republican terms. Patronage or the *spoils system*—the replacement of government personnel with individuals loyal to the winning candidate—was an implementation of the republican principle of rotation in office. Bureaucrats can come to think of their positions as their own exclusive "species of property." Replacement would "destroy the idea of property so generally connected with official station." Besides, argued Jackson, "the duties of all public officers are . . . so plain and simple that men of intelligence may readily qualify themselves for their performance; and I cannot believe that more is lost by the long continuance of men in office than is generally gained by their experience."

Martin Van Buren, Jackson's successor to the presidency, may have been the first American politician to openly and systematically advocate the organization of factions into parties as a permanently desirable practice. Van Buren offered several reasons for his defense of parties. First, he contended that nonpartisanship could be a mask for the continuation of an elite in power. Free government requires a party opposition as "the vigilant watchman over the conduct of the people, and to compel their servants to act on principle." He even criticized the hope expressed in Monroe's second inaugural address that party organization might become extinct in America. Second, Van Buren defended parties as good in themselves. Party activity taught the values of discipline, loyalty, and devotion to a common cause. As one of Van Buren's friends concluded, "political consistency" is "as indispensable as any other moral qualification." Third, Van Buren asserted that party activity encouraged and assured mass political participation. Party competition serves to "rouse the sluggish to exertion, give increased energy to the most active intellect . . . [and] prevent that apathy which has proved the ruin of Republics."

No reform movement as massive as the one led by the Jacksonian Democrats can be confined within the borders of party organization. Many Americans found the central aspects of Democratic ideology inconsistent, too limited, or too timid. Edward Pessen, in his analysis of the Workingman's party, one of many local third parties in New York during this period, refers to those on the radical edge of the reform movement as "uncommon Jacksonians."

Extending Pessen's term to other patterns of thought in the period, let us look at various uncommon Jacksonians. One major group was the abolitionists, whom we shall discuss in the following chapter. However much the Democrats spoke of human rights and their precedence over property rights, party regulars were positively antagonistic toward the reform of slavery. (The *Dred Scott* decision of 1854 was delivered by the Taney Court.)

Another grouping, the one that Pessen studied, was composed largely of urban artisan and workers' clubs and parties that believed that the Democrats had not moved far enough or fast enough in creating an equalitarian society. A central figure in this movement was Thomas Skidmore, a leader of the Workingman's party who lost a seat in a campaign for the New York state legislature in a very close election. Skidmore's only book, *The Rights of Man to Property!*, owes much to Thomas Paine's later political thought. In fact, Skidmore's approach to political problems in general reflects the viewpoint of radical republicans two generations removed from the Revolution. The theoretical basis of the essay appears to predate Marx. The world, declares Skidmore, is "divided into two distinct classes: proprietors and nonproprietors; those who own the world, and those who own no part of it." The distinction between producing and nonproducing classes is clearly Jacksonian, but Skidmore anticipates Marx's theory of primitive accumulation in his account of the origins of private property. What moral principle, asks Skidmore, justifies the holdings of William Penn, whose property is valued in the millions, "merely because of a few beads having been given to some Indians some two hundred years ago?" Skidmore concludes that the authority of all governments has been tainted since the "first appropriation" made over a domain and transmitted to posterity has formed the basis for the justification of private property. But Skidmore's corrective is hardly Marxian. If a European model must be pursued, it is that of Pierre Joseph Proudhon, the French political theorist who attempted to find ways to confine the ownership of private property to producers.

Skidmore's plan was to hold a new constitutional convention that would absolve all debts, take a census of the population, and make an inventory of all existing property. A dividend would be declared to all citizens who could individually use the proceeds to bid in a public sale managed by the state for all the property of the nation. When citizens died, their property would be sold at auction to finance dividends for a patrimony for the new generation. Skidmore's proposal represented a radical plan for truly "starting over" and initiating a regime of equal opportunity of which the Jacksonians spoke.

The urban radicals, however, were not the only group in America determined to start over. During the 1820s and 1830s there emerged hundreds of utopian communal experiments throughout America. Composed largely of farmers and religious dissidents, these utopias were attempts to reconstruct new societies on a small scale. One group, the Shakers, had existed as a religious sect since the Revolution. In the Jacksonian era, however, Shaker membership increased dramatically. The organization set up communes in New York, Ohio, and Kentucky. The central goal of a commune was simplicity. Shakers invented a whole series of practices and tools to celebrate this tenet. They designed new furniture, wrote hymns without music, and attempted to form a self-supporting community of equals. The Shakers felt that celibacy was the only alternative to the selective affection offered by kin and competition among families. They replenished their numbers by adopting orphans. The Perfectionists, another group that emerged in this period, celebrated sexuality, but insisted that dyadic relationships were a source of conflict; hence, they created a system of *complex marriages*. Secular utopian experiments also arose in this period. Robert Owen, a British industrialist, attempted to replicate his success with community organization in Scotland by starting a commune in Indiana. New England intellectuals attempted various communal experiments based in part on the writings of Charles Fourier, a French socialist; One of these communes, Brook Farm, had such august participants as Nathaniel Hawthorne and Margaret Fuller.

The first genuinely American literary movement also came into existence in the Jacksonian period. A collection of individuals in New England, sometimes called the *Concord circle*, included such men as Ralph Waldo Emerson, Henry David Thoreau, and Nathaniel Hawthorne as well as such women as Louisa May Alcott and Margaret Fuller. In New York Walt Whitman produced the first distinctly American poetry in terms of style and content. It would be incorrect to refer to these men and women as Jacksonian Democrats. Hawthorne was a Democrat, as was Whitman, but Emerson was studiously neutral in regard to partisan controversy. He once concluded that the Democrats had the best cause and the Whigs the best men. Thoreau consistently declared a plague on both parties. Despite their marginality in terms of party politics, the New Englanders and Whitman searched for what they regarded as a deeper and broader conception of individualism than the pursuit of economic success. As editor of the *Brooklyn Daily Eagle*, Whitman defended the Democrats. He also extended implicitly the democratic agenda by discovering sources of untapped energy in American life in *Democratic Vistas* and exploring his own liberation as a homosexual in *Leaves of Grass*. Emerson persistently insisted that individualism meant more than profit taking. He reportedly was enthralled by the activity of skipping a stone across a frozen pond; the pings were suggestive to him of eternity.

No figure of the Concord circle, however, has captured the American imagination across generations more than Thoreau. He was a self-professed failure in an era that celebrated success. The townspeople of Concord, claimed Thoreau, had no jobs for a "self-appointed inspector of snow storms" or a tender of huckleberry bushes and red pine. Thoreau celebrated a sense of place in an age of transportation and mobility. He rarely traveled beyond Concord and its environs. Thoreau even turned away from utopian experimentation, contending that all cooperative ventures cramped the human spirit.

Thoreau's *Walden*, an account of his individual experiment in living "free" for two years in the woods, was written in part as an attempt to show Americans that they could live simply and without reliance upon others. Thoreau begins his account by posing a question the French political philosopher Jean Jacques Rousseau had asked a century earlier: Why if individuals were born free do they live lives of such enslavement? Thoreau, in repeating this question, catalogs the ways Americans have become enslaved. The New England farmers have become "serfs of the soil." But they have also lost their freedom in other ways. They have become chained to their houses, to the pursuit of profit, to machines, to respectability. Most Americans, concluded Thoreau, lead lives of "quiet desperation." Rousseau, in his *Social Contract*, argued that only through a political system in which all citizens were equally dependent upon one another could true freedom become possible. Thoreau's solution proceeds from a very different direction. He argues that only when each individual rejects fame, fortune, and conformity and creates a life "shaved close" to necessity can he hope to be free. "Simplify! Simplify! Simplify!" is Thoreau's injunction to his generation. *Walden* includes stirring passages on the sense of peace and harmony that reward a life devoted to the contemplation of nature. But it is also very much a "how to" manual. Thoreau describes how to build a house cheaply and functionally, how to plant and tend a garden, how to eat, how to build furniture, and how to budget.

In many ways Thoreau's political thought represents one road traversed by New England moralistic republicanism after the Revolution and the founding. Thoreau was too independent and too poor to be a Federalist, too committed to a sense of place to be a nationalist Whig like Daniel Web-

ster, and too modernist for the clergy. Thus he fashioned a sense of individualism for his own generation of New Englanders. Nowhere do the political
implications of this form of individualism emerge more prominently than
in his famous essay, "Civil Disobedience." The discussion begins with the
standard Jeffersonian-Jacksonian motto, "That government is best which
governs least." Thoreau, however, adds a radical note by asserting that his
motto is "that government is best which governs not at all." Angered by the
Democrats' defense of slavery and the Whigs' willingness to compromise,
Thoreau declares war on the political process itself. Why should majorities
govern? Voting itself, declares Thoreau, is simply participation in a lottery.
"Cast your whole vote, not a strip of paper merely but your influence." Thoreau recommends extraconstitutional action—civil disobedience—to force
a majority to assess its own conscience. Yet on the verge of recommending
a concert of engaged, anarchistically inclined citizens, Thoreau retreats: "I
simply wish to refuse allegiance to the State, to withdraw and stand aloof
from it. . . ." Thoreau is an unusual radical in the sense that politics is
essentially an intrusion upon his central project—the understanding and
creation of his own self.

WHIGS

The Whigs struggled for a generation to overcome the elitist political
thought that had characterized the old Federalist party. As late as 1834 a
Whig editorialist wrote in the *Boston Courier:*

> A farmer never looks so well as when he has a hand upon the plough,
> with his huge paw upon the statutes what can he do? It is as proper
> for a blacksmith to attempt to repair watches, as a farmer, in general,
> to legislate.

But gradually and often fitfully the Whigs began to develop their own ideo-
logical alternative to the Democrats—one that did not rely upon the old
Federalist idea of a government by gentlemen for the benefit of the "lower
orders." The two figures largely responsible for performing this task are
Henry Clay and Daniel Webster. The presidency eluded both Clay and
Webster (although the former ran for it six times between 1824 and 1848).
But both men managed through political skill and ideological ingenuity to
share the national political stage with Jackson.

Whig political thought can be summarized in terms of three basic
ideas: nationalism, government planning, and moralism. First, the Whigs,
like the Federalists, were what Everett Ladd has called the party of the
national idea. Jackson may have spoken and acted forcefully during the
nullification crisis, in which South Carolina declared the 1828 tariff act
null and void, but the Democrats as a party were firmly committed to states'

rights, individualism, and limited government. The Whig concept of nationhood was a corporate, even a mystical, one. The American nation was neither a collection of states nor a collection of individuals. As Webster declared, "The Union is part of the religion of the people."

The most dramatic example of the Whig presentation of this national idea is the Webster-Hayne Senate debate in 1830. The conflict came unexpectedly. Senator Sam A. Foote of Connecticut asked for an inquiry into the suitability of delaying the sale of public lands. Senator Thomas Hart Benton of Missouri rose to charge that any delay was part of a New England plot to keep workers bottled up in the East and thus depress wages. Senator Robert Y. Hayne of South Carolina spoke in support of the commonality of the interests of the South and West. Webster then rose to demand a reply. The Senate was about to adjourn, and Webster was forced to wait until the next day to deliver his remarks. In his first reply to Hayne, Webster defended a careful approach to land policy, pointing out that Ohio, which was once a wilderness, was now a populous and thriving state. He also defended the altruism of the New England states. "The East! the obnoxious, the rebuked, the always reproached East! . . . Sir!, I rise to defend the East," began Webster. New Englanders had voted for roads to the West; a person from Massachusetts wrote the Northwest Ordinance of 1787, which had the virtue of banning slavery from the territories.

Webster then theoretically expanded the debate by asserting that the real issue was between state authority and national authority. There were those who regarded the Union in utilitarian terms and constantly calculated the value of its maintenance. "I deprecate and deplore this tone of thinking. . . . I am a unionist. . . . I would strengthen the ties that hold us together," replied Webster. He would mourn the day

> when our associated and fraternal stripes shall be severed asunder, and when that happy constellation under which we have risen to so much renown shall be broken up, and sink, star after star, into obscurity and night!

As to Hayne's charge that a federally managed land policy would lead to corruption, Webster replied:

> Can there be nothing in government except for the exercise of mere control? Can nothing be done without corruption, but the imposition of penalty and restraint? Whatever is positively beneficent, whatever is actively good, whatever opens channels of intercourse, augments population, enhances the value of property, and diffuses knowledge—must all this be rejected and reprobated as an obnoxious policy. . . ?

Senator Hayne took up Webster's theoretical challenge and left behind the issue of land policy itself (which may have been Webster's plan in the first place). For two days Hayne spoke before the Senate. He asked how Webster could characterize New Englanders as nationalists after the experience of the Hartford Convention (1814). Any criticism of slavery drove southern politicians to apoplexy, and Hayne was not an exception. Webster had "crossed the border, he has invaded the State of South Carolina, is making war upon her citizens, and endeavoring to overthrow her principles and institutions." In fact, charged Hayne, it was this philosophy of "meddling" which Webster epitomized that has "filled the land with thousands of wild and visionary projects, which can have no effect but to waste the energies and dissipate the resources of the country."

By the time Webster rose to give his second speech, the Senate chambers were overflowing. The senator from Massachusetts spoke for two afternoons. He quickly dismissed the Hartford Convention as an irrelevant historical episode. He denied criticism of slavery: "I go for the Constitution as it is, and for the Union as it is." Webster returned to his exposition of the national idea. Hayne had asked, "What interest has South Carolina in a canal in Ohio?" Webster replied: "We look upon the states, not as separated but united. . . .We do not impose geographical limits to our patriotic feelings. . . ." The ideal American legislator "is bound to regard with an equal eye the good of the whole, in whatever is within our power of legislation."

The second reply concluded with the kind of oratorical flourish that enthralled nineteenth-century audiences. Webster hoped that when he beheld "the sun in heaven for the last time" he would see:

> the republic, now known and honored throughout the earth, still full high advanced, its arms and trophies streaming in their original lustre, not a stripe erased or polluted, nor a single star obscured, bearing for its motto, no such miserable interrogatory as "What is all this worth?" nor the words of delusion and folly, "Liberty first Union afterwards"; but everywhere, spread all over in characters of living light, blazing on all its ample folds, as they float over the sea and over the land, and in every wind under the whole heavens, that other sentiment, dear to every true American heart,—"Liberty and Union, now and for ever, one and inseparable!"

As Merrill Peterson (in *The Great Triumvirate*) notes, Webster's conception of a single organic republic was something of a novelty in 1830. Haynes's view of the Union as a partnership, perhaps minus the doctrine of nullification, represented the received wisdom of the period. But Webster and the Whigs were not simply mystical nationalists. They had a plan. In fact, the Whigs consistently advocated national planning as the proper path to develop a more perfect Union. Webster, in his first reply to Hayne, defended the feasibility of beneficent planning. The precept that embodied this faith in planning was developed by Henry Clay, who called for the creation of an *American system*.

The Democrats consistently charged that the American system was nothing more than an ideological cover for high tariffs, a tax on the producing class. Clay, however, defended tariffs as a prudent policy for American economic growth and economic independence. "The truth is, and it is vain to discuss it, that we are . . . Independent colonies of Great Britain—politically free, commercially slaves," said Clay in 1820. The political theory of free trade and laissez-faire were ideological formulations designed to keep America a vassal state. Clay readily admitted that free trade was the ultimate goal, but only after America was in a position to compete with industrialized nations. Britain, after all, had employed the same policies in the past.

Clay denied that his American system would create the Jeffersonian nightmare of a country overflowing with Manchesterlike cities. Manufacturing centers would hardly be noticed in the vast American landscape. Besides, which policy alternative was more damaging to republicanism, high unemployment or a scattering of manufacturing centers? But the basic argument for the American system that Clay repeated year after year before the House was that a managed policy of national industrialization would increase the *national wealth*, which was in the interest of every region and every individual, rich or poor.

The second component of the American system was the federal government's subsidy or direct financing of what were called *internal improvements*. According to Whig doctrine, the tariff would assure America's economic independence, and internal improvements would be the economic foundation for an American sense of nation. John Calhoun became a Democrat and shortly later a regionalist because of his support of slavery (see chapter 5). But in 1816, writing as a National Republican in support of his proposed legislation for a permanent fund for internal improvements, he stated:

> [W]e are under the most imperious obligation to counteract every tendency to disunion. . . . [T]he more enlarged the sphere of commercial circulation, the more strongly we are bound together, the more inseparable our destinies. . . . Let us bind the Republic together with a perfect system of roads and canals. Let us conquer space.

Tariffs and internal improvement formed the structure of Whig political economy. But conquering economic space was only part of the Whig agenda. They also proposed a structuring of morality as well. The Jacksonian Democrats represented the libertarian alternative epitomized by the slogan of equality of opportunity. According to Daniel Walker Howe (*The*

Political Culture of the American Whigs, 1979), "Whig rhetoric emphasized 'morality'—or 'duties' rather than 'rights.'"

In order to appreciate the Whig conception of morality and duty, it is necessary to briefly review a cultural development during the period called the *Great Revival*. Early in the nineteenth century, a profound alteration in religious beliefs occurred in American society. The Puritan Congregational churches had given way in many towns to a more secular and rational faith called *Unitarianism*. In the West, however, a movement arose which criticized the Unitarians as too given to a secular vision of life. Adherents of this movement also rejected the traditional Calvinist doctrine of predestination. New religious sects among the Baptists and Methodists, and schisms within the Presbyterian churches, competed for the religious support of western settlers. A standard vehicle for this new environment of evangelism was the *camp meeting*.

It is difficult to convey the enthusiasm and sense of meaning that these new religious structures created among the people in attendance. The Great Revival began in Kentucky and Tennessee and then moved east. The number of participants at camp meetings, ostensibly nondenominational but in reality a battleground among various Protestant denominations, was quite large. Over 20,000 people attended the Cabin Creek and Cane Ridge meetings respectively. The camps were makeshift structures designed to permit ministers from different denominations to present their views of salvation to participants. James Finley, a skeptical observer at Cane Ridge who was converted and became a Methodist minister, provides an account:

> We arrived upon the ground and here a scene presented itself to my mind not only novel and unaccountable, but awful beyond description. A vast crowd, supposed by some to have amounted to 25,000, was collected together. The noise was like the roar of Niagara. The vast sea of human beings seemed to be agitated as if by a storm. I counted seven ministers, all preaching at one time, some on stumps, others on wagons. . . . Some of the people were singing, others praying, some crying for mercy in the most piteous accents, while others were shouting vociferously.

The point of the camp meetings, aside from adding to the members of competing sects, was to effect an instant conversion on the part of participants. Thus the Great Revival represented the same tension at a religious level that Jacksonian democracy represented at the political level. The camp meeting ministers railed against secularism and a modernist religion like Unitarianism. At the same time they also abandoned Calvinism. Through a sheer act of will a person could be saved. Charles Finney, an enormously popular minister, claimed that under the right conditions he could save a person in less than an hour. Puritans had waited a lifetime for some sign of grace.

Whigs carefully cultivated the support of the new evangelists. Cautious not to alienate the established clergy, which looked nervously upon the unbridled enthusiasm of the new converts, Whigs praised the revival and the conception of morality it espoused. As Daniel Walker Howe observes:

> [T]he evangelical movement supplied Whiggery with a conception of progress that was the collective form of redemption: like the individual, society as a whole was capable of improvement through conscious effort.

Jacksonians were Democrats, but it was the Whigs who supported public education and federal aid to mental hospitals and prisons.

Perhaps the high point of Whig moralism (since the question of slavery ultimately broke up the party) was its criticism of Jacksonian Indian policy. Despite the demonstrated peacefulness and commitment to accommodation with white settlers of the Cherokee Nation, Georgians were determined to evacuate the Indians to Oklahoma, regardless of numerous treaty commitments. Democrats had no sympathy for Indian rights. Jackson, a westerner, had no sympathy for Indian nations and was anxious to open up more land for settlement. He was quite willing to use states' rights to ignore a Supreme Court decision declaring Georgia's action unconstitutional. The Whig reply was based on a kind of paternalistic moralism that characterized their approach to all social questions. The Whigs considered the Indians a "redeemed" people who, in the words of Edward Everett, "are civilized, not in the same degree that we are, but in the same way that we are." The evacuation was a "gigantic crime"; Whigs, in fact, raised the specter of genocide.

SUMMARY AND COMMENT

Despite the Republican aversion to faction and the spirit of party, in the two generations after the second founding Americans managed to create four great political parties. These parties competed in attempts to outline and implement a political ideology for the new nation without disintegrating into armed conflict.

Federalists envisioned a national, executive-dominated government managed by a culturally and economically superior elite which would receive periodic approval from the deferential masses. The Republicans organized against what they saw as monarchical and aristocratic tendencies, and presented an image of a more locally centered polity managed by enlightened agrarian elites. In power, the Republicans returned to the Federalist dream of a factionless, partyless national polity. The Democrats transformed Republican party principles under the guise of reinstituting them. Democrats, like Republicans, were localists with little faith in the ability of the federal government to act in the interest of the population at large. But any successful reform movement must have the power to change economic and political practices, and the Jacksonians turned to the presidency as a reliable antigovernment political institution. Thus Jackson, the great dismantler of federal policy initiatives, relied in part upon Hamiltonian and Federalist conceptions of the presidency. The Whigs took on the task of the party of the national idea, asserting that virtuous representation was not only possible but indispensable for a stable and prosperous political system. In a broad sense, each of these two-party systems offered voters a choice—admittedly a circumscribed choice—between regimes promising to emphasize order (Federalists and Whigs) and freedom (Republicans and Democrats).

There were other consequences of party competition unanticipated by republican theory, even the chastened variety that appeared in the 1780s. Amidst this party conflict, which gradually came to be recognized as an inevitable, if not necessary, feature of national politics, there were certain basic consensual beliefs that all parties accepted (even if each of them charged the others with violating them). Federalists, Republicans, Democrats, and Whigs accepted the principles of constitutionalism, private property, political participation, and increasingly the idea of progress. Some Americans, such as Thoreau, found this framework confining, and this framework did impose restrictions on democratic politicians. Nevertheless, government leaders were able to make important, and often profound, statements of political thought. It is certainly true that faction and party competition do not assure the development of political theories, as many periods in our history demonstrate. Nor does ideological competition (what later came to be called the *marketplace of ideas*) assure that the best argument will win. But faction and the spirit of party are one way, as this period of our history shows, for citizens and leaders to talk, argue, and interact with one another—sometimes with profundity and purpose.

Note

1 The full name of the organization formed by Madison and Jefferson was the Democratic Republican Party, which produced a complex genealogical history. In 1824 all contestants for the presidency accepted the designation *Democratic-Republican*. In 1832 Andrew Jackson ran for the presidency as a candidate for the "Democratic Party," claiming himself heir to the (Democratic) Republicans. John Quincy Adams in 1828 and Henry Clay in 1832 used the label *National Republican*, which was replaced by Whig for the remainder of the 1830s until a new third party appropriated the Republican title and emerged with Abraham Lincoln as

its successful presidential candidate in 1860. Despite these convolutions, the generic names, *Republican, Whig,* and *Democrat,* formed into distinct ideological positions.

☆ *Bibliographic Essay*

Theoretical analyses of the management of faction include Seymour Lipset, *Political Man* (Garden City, NY: Doubleday, 1960), chaps. 2 and 3; E. E. Schattschneider, *The Semisovereign People* (New York: Holt, Rinehart & Winston, 1960); Samuel Huntington, *American Politics: The Promise of Disharmony* (Cambridge: Harvard University Press, 1981; Robert Dahl, *A Preface to Democratic Theory* (Chicago: University of Chicago Press, 1956); Mancur Olson, Jr., *The Logic of Collective Action* (New York: Schocken Books, 1968). Lipset, Olson, and Dahl emphasize the social and economic bases of factional conflict; Schattschneider, its dynamics; and Huntington, its basis in political culture.

Ralph Ketcham's *Presidents above Party* (Chapel Hill: University of North Carolina Press, 1984) ably reviews the republican opposition to party (chaps. 1–4) and argues that the model of nonpartisan leadership extended through the first six presidents. Glen A. Phelps challenges this view, contending that Washington was "the first partisan president" despite his own public protestations about faction: "George Washington and the Paradox of Party," *Presidential Studies Quarterly 19* (Fall 1989). Both William Nisbet Chambers, *Political Parties in a New Nation* (New York: Oxford University Press, 1963), and Richard Hofstadter, *The Idea of a Party System: The Rise of a Legitimate Opposition in the U.S., 1780–1810* (Berkeley: University of California Press, 1969), trace the development of parties in America and the revisions of republicanism necessary to accept the new practice. Important descriptions of early nascent factionalism are Jack N. Rakove, "The Structure of Politics at the Accession of George Washington," in Richard Breen, et al., eds., *Beyond Confederation* (Chapel Hill: University of North Carolina Press, 1987), and James P. Young, *The Washington Community* (New York: Columbia University Press, 1966). Young's study is a neglected minor classic in that it analyzes the creation of a "governmental community," its "inner life," and its relationship to public policy. Also see Thomas P. Slaughter's *The Whiskey Rebellion* (New York: Oxford University Press, 1987) for a sophisticated attempt to assess the significance of the violence of rising faction.

There are several histories of the Federalist party: John C. Miller, *The Federalist Era* (New York: Harper & Brothers, 1960); David Hackett Fisher, *The Revolution of American Conservatism* (New York: Harper & Brothers, 1965); Shaw Livermore, *The Twilight of Federalism* (Princeton: Princeton University Press, 1962). Each emphasizes the inability of many Federalist leaders to accommodate their beliefs to the realities of electoral politics. Russell Kirk, *The Conservative Mind* (South Bend, IN: Gateway, 1978), chap. 3, offers a more sympathetic reading. The two-volume collection of

Fisher Ames's writings is available in reprint as *The Works of Fisher Ames* (New York: Lennox Hill, 1971). Like Jefferson, Hamilton's status as a politician and thinker has risen and declined over the years. Morton Frisch offers an appreciative assessment in the introduction to his collection of Hamilton's writings, *Selected Writings and Speeches of Alexander Hamilton* (Washington, DC: American Enterprise Institute, 1985). Also see Gerald Stourzh, *Alexander Hamilton and the Idea of Republican Government* (Stanford: Stanford University Press, 1970). Vernon Parrington, however, describes Hamilton as "the most modern" of eighteenth-century leaders but one "from who our democratic liberalism owes nothing": *Main Currents in American Thought* (New York: Harcourt Brace Jovanovich, 1930), vol. I, pp. 279–307.

The rise of the Republican party is skillfully presented in Noble Cunningham's *The Jeffersonian Republicans* (Chapel Hill: University of North Carolina Press, 1957). Charles Beard placed John Taylor at the center, rather than at the periphery, of Republican party ideology in *Economic Origins of Jeffersonian Ideology* (New York: Macmillan, 1915). For a workmanlike and still valuable study of Taylor, see Eugene T. Mudge, *The Social Philosophy of John Taylor of Caroline* (New York: Columbia University Press, 1939). Also see Robert E. Shalope, *John Taylor of Caroline: Pastoral Republican* (Columbia: University of South Carolina Press, 1980). *An Inquiry* has been reprinted under the editorship of Roy Franklin Nichols (New Haven: Yale University Press, 1950). Liberty Press reissued *Arator* in 1977 (Indianapolis: Liberty Classics)with a thoughtful introduction by M. E. Bradford, who describes Taylor as "a Virginia Cato." The interpretations of Jefferson are nearly endless. The best place to begin is with John C. Merrill's *The Jeffersonian Image in the American Mind* (New York: Oxford University Press, 1960). Peterson discusses every major reinterpretation of Jefferson up to the New Deal. Richard K. Matthews, *The Radical Politics of Thomas Jefferson* (Lawrence: University of Kansas Press, 1984), emphasizes the radical, even eccentric, views of Jefferson. Pauline Maier questions Jefferson's contribution to the Declaration in *American Scripture* (New York: Knopf, 1997). Lance Banning, *The Jeffersonian Persuasion* (Ithaca, NY: Cornell University Press, 1978), sees Jefferson and the Republicans as given over to country ideology, while Joyce Appleby, *Capitalism and a New Social Order: The Republican Vision of the 1790s* (New York: New York University Press, 1984), describes Jefferson as a liberal who abandoned his early country and republican theory. Drew McCoy, *The Elusive Republic* (Chapel Hill: University of North Carolina Press, 1980), emphasizes the attempts by Jefferson to combine republicanism with liberalism.

See Richard McCormick, *The Second Party System* (Chapel Hill: University of North Carolina Press, 1966), and Everett Carl Ladd, *American Political Parties* (New York: W.W. Norton, 1970), (chap. 3 for analyses of the impact of party competition on officeholders and ideology. Arthur Schlesinger, Jr., *The Age of Jackson* (Boston: Little, Brown, 1945), portrays the Democrats as crusading modern liberals. Examples of the entrepreneurial school which presents Jacksonian democracy as a revolt of the *petite bourgeoisie* rather than the working class are Bray Hammond, "Jackson, Biddle and the Bank of the United States," *Journal of Economic History* 7 (May 1947), and Richard Hofstadter, *The American Political Tradition* (New York: Alfred A. Knopf, 1948), chap. 3. Marvin Meyers's creative interpretive synthesis, *The Jacksonian Persuasion* (Stanford: Stanford University Press, 1957), is a masterpiece of ideological analysis. Also see John William Ward, *Andrew Jackson: Symbol for an Age* (New York: Oxford University Press, 1962), for a fascinating attempt to ascertain what Jackson meant symbolically to American citizens. To Ward, Jackson represented "nature," "providence," and "will." Joseph L. Blau has collected major theoretical statements of the Jacksonians in *Social Theories of Jacksonian Democracy* (Indianapolis: Bobbs-Merrill, 1954). The anthology includes a selection from Skidmore's *The Rights of Man to Property!* For other aspects of Jacksonian reform, see Edward Pessen, *Most Uncommon Jacksonians* (Albany, NY: SUNY Press, 1967); Michael Paul Rogin, *Fathers and Children: Andrew Jackson and the Subjugation of the American Indian* (New York: Vintage, 1975); Mark Halloway, *Heavens on Earth: Utopian Communities in America* (New York: Dover, 1966). There are innumerable editions of Thoreau's writings. Owen Thomas's *Walden and Civil Disobedience* (New York: W.W. Norton, 1966) is a useful one since it also contains essays on Thoreau. For differing interpretations of Thoreau, see Philip Abbott, "Henry David Thoreau, the State of Nature, and the Redemption of Liberalism," *Journal of Politics* 47 (February 1985); Nancy Rosenblum, "Thoreau's Militant Conscience," *Political Theory* 9 (1981); Leo Staller, *After Walden* (Stanford: Stanford University Press, 1957). Jane Bennett's *Thoreau's Nature* (Thousand Oaks, CA: Sage, 1994) is noteworthy in its attempt to treat Thoreau as a major political theorist.

Whig political thought has been relatively neglected, at least in terms of the attention given the Democrats. Two fine works have helped remedy this deficiency: Daniel Walker Howe, *The Political Culture of the Whigs* (Chicago: University of Chicago Press, 1979), and Merrill D. Peterson, *The Great Triumvirate* (New York: Oxford University Press, 1987). Also see Howe's anthology, *The American Whigs* (New York: John Wiley & Sons, 1973), and Bertha M. Roethe, ed., *The Daniel Webster Reader* (New York: Oceana, 1956).

☆ Major Works

1805	"The Dangers of American Liberty," Fisher Ames
1796	"Farewell Address," George Washington
1790	"Report on the National Bank," Alexander Hamilton
1791	"Report on Manufactures," Alexander Hamilton
1813	*Arator,* John Taylor
1814	*An Inquiry into the Principles and Policy of the Government of the US,* John Taylor

1787	*Notes on the State of Virginia*, Thomas Jefferson
1801	"First Inaugural Address," Thomas Jefferson
1837	"First Inaugural Address," Andrew Jackson
1829	*The Rights of Man to Property!*, Thomas Skidmore
1854	*Walden*, Henry David Thoreau
1849	"Resistance to Civil Government," Henry David Thoreau
1830	"The Webster-Hayne Debate," Daniel Webster
1832	"The American System," Henry Clay
1827	"Colonization Address," Henry Clay

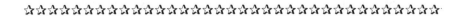

Civil War

INTRODUCTION

When Abraham Lincoln closed his first inaugural address in 1861, he pleaded with the secessionist states to avoid hasty action before they broke the "mystic chords of memory" that held the nation together. The events that followed were complex, but Lincoln almost certainly knew when he delivered his speech that the chords had already broken. Four years later over 600,000 Americans were dead from battle or disease. But even this figure, as calamitous as it is, cannot convey the special nature of the killing. *Fratricide* is a designation used to describe internal war. The depiction is apt because it attempts to symbolize the horror of familial violence. Fratricide as a metaphor evokes the murder not only of individual human beings but a violent assault on society itself. Behind the image of civil war always lies the Hobbesian terror that society will collapse completely and that men and women, living in a war of all against all, will be incapable of putting society back together again.

But as each civil war is the same, each is also different. England in the 1640s, America in the 1860s, Spain in the 1930s, Nigeria in the 1970s, and Lebanon in the 1980s are all societies in which killing seems to expand exponentially as political, social, and economic institutions crumble. But in each case the culture and history of a nation also create a particular character to the conflict. There were three important defining features of the fratricide that began in 1861. In America the force that drove what Seward called the *irrepressible conflict* was race. It was the recognition of the horror of the institution of slavery based upon color that drove middle-class northern men and women to reject gradual plans for emancipation. Once *imme-*

143

diatism was accepted as a public policy demand, these protesters were the first to suggest that secession was an appropriate alternative. And it was the defense of slavery that led Southerners to reexamine the culture of their region and its differences from the North and to question the viability of the Union. It was slavery that hampered the growth of the country, making Kansas in the 1850s a miniature of the Civil War itself. It was slavery that destroyed the American party system. The great party of the Jacksonians split in two in 1860; the party of Clay and Webster died; and the candidate of a third-party movement won the American presidency.

If race was the central and defining feature of the ideological conflict that drove the nation to civil war, both sides in the fratricide developed their own interpretations of republicanism to justify the killing. Nearly every student of the Civil War recognizes a Homeric character to this conflict. There was certainly a great deal of draft evasion and desertion on both sides, but the heroism displayed is still a subject of awe. The nature of the Civil War military strategy—two lines of advancing soldiers, often across open terrain—could not have been implemented without extraordinary courage. Casualties in the major battles of the war were 25 percent, including noncombat details. It was not uncommon for regimental losses to approach 80 percent. The First Minnesota Regiment at Gettysburg began the battle at a strength of 262 men; at the end of the day, only 47 were alive, and those 47 participated in the successful effort to repel Pickett's charge the next afternoon.

Honor was an operational rationale of the volunteers. It is honor that explains Ulysses S. Grant's treatment of Robert E. Lee and the Army of Northern Virginia at Appomattox as well as Lee's own decision to join the Confederacy in the first place. In fact, Lee himself was a combination of Hector and Achilles, fighting to defend his family and questioning southern honor as he himself epitomized it. Lee nearly alone among Southerners referred to the conflict as a civil war rather than a war between the states. Of Agamemnons there were plenty, from the South's Thomas J. (Stonewall) Jackson, John S. Mosby, and P. G. T. Beauregard to the North's William T. Sherman and George A. Custer. Civil War generals on both sides often led their troops; neither side gave medals. But with these similarities noted, it must be remembered that southern honor represented the more archaic, more Homeric form since it was derived from a conception of the southern demes—family and kin, friends and farm. The northern version was developed magnificently by Abraham Lincoln, who could be seen as the Odysseus of the war. It was more modern and more abstract. Northerners fought for human rights, religious retribution and redemption, and the idea of nation. Even Civil War songs seemed to reflect this difference. "The Battle Hymn of the Republic" with its refrain, "His truth is marching on" (based upon Isaiah 63), can be counterposed to "Maryland, My Maryland," with its announcement that "the despot's heel is on thy shore." As the war dragged on, it seemed that neither side could understand the other's motivation.

Finally the American Civil War is a war transformed from a premodern to a modern war as the killing progressed. In fact, Bruce Catton contends that the American Civil War was the first of the world's really modern wars. Some of the causes were technologically driven. When the war began, the infantry weapon was the smoothbore rifle. A muzzle-loading instrument, the smoothbore had an effective range of less than 150 yards. The Springfield, which came into wide use as early as 1861, was still a muzzle loader but had a range of up to a mile or more. The infantry line charges then soon became suicidal, even when the attackers vastly outnumbered the defenders (as was the case with Pickett's charge at Gettysburg). Generals on both sides moved slowly in recognizing this change, but it was clear that the role of the cavalry as an adjunct to the infantry assault was obsolete early in the war. Artillery had originally been thought to be the great equalizer in regard to assault columns, but the new rifle subjected the artillerymen to devastating losses by snipers and neutralized their role. Most important of all, however, was the inability of attackers and defenders to fail to "see" one another. When a veteran of the Army of the Potomac wrote his memoirs, he noted the novelty at Antietam of actually seeing and fighting the enemy at close quarters. Gallantry and honor certainly existed in the killing, but they were being erased by the anonymity of modern war.

The other change in the war was cultural. Early politicomilitary strategies had assumed a limited war. Bull Run, the first battle, was thought by both sides to be a decisive contest that would lead the Confederacy back to the Union or enable the South to go its own way. When the rout of Union forces produced neither scenario, the North adopted the "anaconda" strategy of forcing accommodation, and the South began to rely upon war weariness in the North. Neither approach worked. Politics in the North seemed to demand a decisive victory, while southern strategy increasingly was directed toward a battlefield victory that would destroy northern will.

The breakthrough to modern warfare came from the North. Union strategists came to realize that winning battles was less crucial than destroying the economic structure of the South. The new northern strategy involved tearing up rail lines, destroying iron foundries and textile mills, burning barns, and killing horses and pigs. General Sherman, in the midst of the Atlanta campaign, matter-of-factly reported:

> We have devoured the land and our animals eat up the wheat and corn fields close. All the people retire before us and desolation is behind. To realize what war is one should follow our tracks.

Bruce Catton has drawn the historical implications of this early form of total war:

> From sending a Sherman through Georgia, with the avowed objective of destroying that state's productive capacity . . . From doing that to dispatching a flight of bombing planes to reduce a manufacturing city to smoking rubble is only a small step.

It is certainly possible to reconstruct the events that led to the Civil War in America. The failure of a series of political compromises, including major legislation in 1820 and 1850, the institution of slavery and its inter-action with technological advances like the cotton gin, the beginnings of industrialization in the North, the election of Lincoln and the paranoia it created in the South, and the bombardment of Fort Sumter are all part of an important narrative that still needs to be reexamined and reinterpreted. But what can an analysis of American political thought and culture in this period tell us about why, in Richard Hofstadter's words, "the political order that was supposed to be the best in the world broke down completely"? There are three primary forms of political thought that can help understand the conflict that led to the Civil War: the abolitionists, the southern political theorists, and the political thought of Abraham Lincoln. Each can also help explain why in victory the North was unable to "reconstruct" the defeated South.

ABOLITIONISTS

Edmund Wilson began his classic study of Civil War thought, *Patriotic Gore*, with the line, "Let us begin with *Uncle Tom's Cabin*." Of course, the Civil War was not caused by Harriet Beecher Stowe, the author of the novel, despite Lincoln's remark about the "little lady" who started the "big war." But Wilson's decision to begin with this novel, which was first pub-lished in serial form in the abolitionist paper *National Era* in 1851 and 1852, was well conceived. Abolitionism had been in existence for over twenty years when Stowe's novel appeared. Novels exposing the evils of slavery had been published as well as nonfictional reports, such as Theodore Weld's *Slavery As It Is* (1839) and autobiographies of former slaves like Frederick Douglass's *Narrative* (1845). Stowe relied upon these accounts to create an indictment of slavery that was powerful because it spoke to all elements of abolitionism that had developed over a generation.

It is difficult to appreciate the novel's impact today, in part because of the important objections African Americans have raised to the white self-definition of race. Uncle Tom, the Christlike figure in the novel, is now a term of derision, and the young Topsy, who so charmed northern audi-ences, is often regarded as little more than a minstrel character. Some of

these characterizations, however, are more the result of innumerable melo-
dramatic presentations of the novel in the form of plays. George Aikens, for
example, added bloodhounds to challenge Eliza's escape across the Ohio
River, and directors often added additional Topsys to please audiences. But
Uncle Tom's Cabin is an unusual novel in that it combines the elements of
a roman à clef (Stowe later even added a companion volume as a "key" to
its historical authenticity) and archetypal structure. The speeches of the
genial Augustine St. Clare defending slavery as part of the southern way of
life are so effective that some critics have argued that Stowe had to kill the
character off to remove his voice from the pages of the novel. Miss Ophelia,
Augustine's sister, is a New Englander who never quite understands the
South. Tom is, of course, the passive sufferer, but Stowe also drew other
portraits of blacks, including the talented and militant George, husband of
Eliza, who is described as a genius comparable to Eli Whitney.

Overlaid with these Dickensian characterizations is the structure of
the narrative itself. The novel begins in the border state of Kentucky, but
Tom is soon sent "downriver" to a series of slaveowners, while Eliza flees
north on the underground railway. These two journeys—one to freedom
and one to degradation and death—have obvious parallels to the fate of the
Christian in general. Eliza is not free until she arrives in Canada, although
various Americans help her along her way, and this strong woman in revolt
is reunited with her husband and family. Tom, on the other hand, is given
the solitary fate of martyrdom on an isolated and grotesque Louisiana plantation.

Uncle Tom's Cabin, then, provides a guide to the nature of abolitionist
thought. Innumerable southern rejoinders to the novel were written,
including fictional accounts by southern women. George Frederick Holmes
wrote a caustic review in the southern *Literary Messenger*, complaining that
"fiction is the form and falsehood the end" of the novel. He argued that the
suppressed premise of the book was that "any organization of society . . .
which can possibly result in such instances of individual misery, or gener-
ate examples of individual cruelty as are exhibited in this fiction, must be
criminal in itself, a violation of all laws of Nature and of God, and ought to
be universally condemned, and consequently abolished." But like most
southern writers in this period, Holmes both saw and missed the point of
abolitionism.

Except for William Lloyd Garrison, the abolitionists were neither revolutionaries nor utopians in terms of general economic and political theory.
Many, perhaps most, harbored racist attitudes themselves. A young abolitionist debater in his 1836 report wrote to the Anti-Slavery Society: "I further stated that we did not claim for the slave the right of voting immediately, or eligibility for office." Most abolitionists were aware of the bad
conditions in the new textile factories in New England as well. But they

drew a line, which in their minds was a simple and minimal one, as to what constituted an unacceptable denial of human freedom. Slavery violated that minimal line and thus could not be tolerated. Failure to oppose the institution meant complicity in the crime of slavery itself. Stowe's portrayal of Eliza's ascent to freedom and Tom's descent downriver was meant to parallel the individual Christian's own inevitable journey. Stowe fought in all her works against what she regarded as the fatalism of Calvinist theology and emphasized the individual moral choice imposed upon all Christians. In fact, if there is any villain more sharply drawn than the monstrous Simon Legree in *Uncle Tom's Cabin*, it is the inactive northern ministry.

The central feature of abolitionist thought that Stowe's novel reiterated was the acceptance of an absolute minimum level of personal freedom as a natural right. The "right to enjoy liberty is inalienable," declared the signers of the "Declaration of Sentiments" in 1833. "To invade it is to usurp the prerogative of Jehovah." As defined by the Anti-Slavery Society, the minimum was the "right to control one's body and one's labor"; on these terms the society declared slavery a model of unfreedom. Historical precedent had no moral weight: "If [slaves] had lived from the time of Pharaoh down to the present period, and had been entailed through successive generations, their right to be free could never be alienated, but their claims would have constantly risen in solemnity. . . ."

Abolition became the perfect public policy solution to a crisis that the reformers saw as a minimum demand. The American Colonization Society was in existence as early as 1816, with its goals of manumission from slavery, compensation to slaveholders, and colonization in Africa. Henry Clay supported the goals of the society, as did many reform-minded Southerners. When William Lloyd Garrison, who was to become the leader of the most radical wing of abolitionism, responded to Clay's "Colonization Address" (1830), he complained that Clay "consults nothing but policy and forgets that justice should first be interrogated." The Colonization Society had freed 100 slaves in 13 years, Garrison noted, as he withdrew from the organization and formed the New England Anti-Slavery Society and set out to publish *The Liberator.* The public policy goal of the new society and *The Liberator* became abolition. Garrison, basing his argument upon the self-evident illegitimacy of slavery, declared that the opponents of slavery had no moral obligation to propose a plan for emancipation. "Duty is ours and events are God's," he told his readers. "To be without a plan is the genius and glory of the Anti-Slavery enterprise." Similarly, Frederick Douglass insisted that the biblical precedent and the Declaration of Independence were so compelling that there was no need to argue the utility of abolition. An instructional circular presented to abolitionist lobbyists in 1834 warned:

Do not allow yourself to be drawn away from the main object, to exhibit a detailed PLAN of abolition; for men's consciences will be greatly relieved from the feeling of present duty, by any objections or difficulties which they can find or fancy in your plan.

If for the abolitionists no plan was their perfect plan for ending slavery, they did devote a great deal of energy to eliciting personal commitment as a means of adding to their numbers. The American Anti-Slavery Society, formed in 1833 as an expansion of Garrison's organization, claimed over 250,000 members by 1838. Supported by such wealthy benefactors as Lewis Tappan, the society distributed almost a million copies of abolitionist publications. The American Anti-Slavery Society was a loose coalition of state and local auxiliaries that sought converts by sending agents to communities. An instructional pamphlet to members published in 1834 illustrates how the society functioned. Agents were cautioned to avoid proposing plans, as noted above, and to avoid exaggeration. "Ministers are the hinges of the community," the instructors noted, "and ought to be moved, if possible." The speaker was to seek permission to use a church to present his views but was warned not to take collections because this practice would decrease attendance. At a minimum, proselytizers were urged to try to get a commitment to prayer the last Monday evening of each month "as a season of special prayer in behalf of the people of color." The central goal of the visitor was to gain a commitment to create an auxiliary society, "both male and female." "Even if such societies are very small at the outset, they may do much good as centers of light, and means of future access to the people." Speakers were also encouraged to sell the *Anti-Slavery Reporter* at two dollars per 100 copies.

This evangelical approach to emancipation, which used all the techniques of the Great Revival, created what Ronald Walters has called a *community of believers*. "For those who became abolitionists," continues Walters,

> exposure to abolition often came at a crucial point in their lives and helped them find direction, meaning and companionship. To be an abolitionist was to declare allegiance to the principles of brotherhood and equality of opportunity, to suffer for those ideals, and band together with like-minded individuals. It was to find a moral community in a society that appeared increasingly immoral.

This moral communitarianism was an extremely effective vehicle for advancing the abolitionist cause. But it also placed severe limitations upon the strategic flexibility of the movement. Some abolitionists, notably Garrison and his followers, argued that since the country was in the grip of a "slaveholding power," the Constitution was itself morally tainted. He urged abstinence from voting and publicly burned the Constitution. The image of a nation held in the clutch of a conspiracy of southern plantation owners with allies among northern Democrats in Congress was a potent image for the abolitionist. Congress had passed a series of compromises, each of which was presented as a final concession to the South. Legislation had been proposed to prohibit abolitionist literature through the federal mail. Local authorities seemed to stand by when mobs attacked post offices and abolitionists. Garrison himself had been dragged through the streets by a Boston mob; Charles Sumner had been physically attacked by a southern senator on the legislature floor; and Elijah Lovejoy, an abolitionist publisher, had been killed in an antiabolitionist riot. These incidents and others convinced the abolitionists that the South was an alien, barbarous, and threatening culture that was spreading its venom throughout the country. The "Declaration of Sentiments" referred to the South as a *great brothel.* The charge was meant to be taken literally, but it also conveyed the belief that the absolute power granted the slaveholder was a corrosive institution that removed the moral restraints necessary for civilization. It is important to note that the cruel and lascivious Simon Legree of Stowe's novel was a New Englander, who presumably had been corrupted by the "opportunities" afforded by the southern slave culture.

Other abolitionists, even while accepting the conspiracy thesis, insisted that political action, including support for antislavery politicians and third-party movements, was essential to the promotion of the cause. Frederick Douglass was one of these *political abolitionists.* According to Douglass, Garrison's doctrine of "no union with slaveholders" was admirable as a "mere expression of abhorrence of slavery," but it "expresses no intelligible principle of action, and throws no light on the pathway of duty." In fact, carried to its logical conclusion, the Garrisonian position "dissolves the Union, and leaves the slaves and their masters to fight their own battles in their own way. . . . It ends by leaving the slave to free himself."

But Douglass's own political abolitionism was put to the test in 1856. In an editorial entitled "What Is My Duty as an Anti-Slavery Voter?" he urged voters to refuse to cast their ballot for the new Republican ticket of John C. Fremont and William Lewis Dayton. Unlike the Liberty party, the Republican party took an equivocal position on slavery. Although opposed to slavery in the Kansas-Nebraska territories, the party was silent on the Fugitive Slave Act and abolition. Douglass urged abolitionists to refuse to "allow themselves to be transferred from one demagogue to another, until all vitality shall have departed from them." But what if refusal to support the rising Republican party led to the establishment of Kansas as a slave state? Douglass responded:

> [G]reat as the misfortune to liberty should Kansas be given to slavery, tenfold greater would be the misfortune, should Kansas be saved by

any means which must certainly demoralize the Anti-Slavery sentiment of the North, and render it weak and inefficient for the greater
work of saving an entire country to Liberty.

But four months later Douglass changed his mind. In a new editorial he
urged abolitionists to vote the Republican ticket on the grounds that "right
Slavery action is that which deals the severest deadliest blow upon Slavery
that can be given at that particular time." The Republicans represented a
rising political force, and Douglass told his readers to "take them . . . not
merely for what they are, but for what we have good reason to believe they
will become. . . ."

Douglass's two editorials show the agonizing political decisions over
ways and means that a morally inspired reform group faces in a representative democracy. Other choices also plagued the abolitionist movement.
Garrison had opposed any political activity, even formation of a third party,
in part on the principle that the abolitionists were not yet morally prepared
for political action. But he did open up the pages of the *Liberator* to all sorts
of other issues involving the abolition of private property, capital punishment, and religious questions, such as the doctrine of original sin and
women's rights. Garrison's approach raised an important question for the
movement: Should abolitionists extend their critique of society, or focus
only on the most pressing moral problem, slavery? The former course
risked reducing the number of people in the movement. From Garrison's
viewpoint, the raised moral consciousness activated by recognition of the
horror of slavery demanded attention to other injustices. To fail to explore
them was hypocritical.

The most significant of these new issues involved women's rights.
Women had been extremely active in the abolitionist movement, and many
had come to question the restricted status of women in the movement and
in society in general. The *woman question*, as it was called, came to focus
over the society's position on the Grimké sisters of South Carolina. Angelina and Sarah Grimké were very effective abolitionist speakers, in part
because they were members of a prominent southern slaveholding family.
Originally the sisters spoke only before female audiences, but curious men
later began to attend their talks. The issue was raised as to whether it was
proper for women to speak before what were called *promiscuous assemblies*. A pastoral letter circulated to the New England Congregationalist
churches chastened the Grimkés for speaking before mixed audiences.
Indeed, it asserted that women should not speak in public at all. The
Grimkés themselves were feminists, but they were careful to avoid discussion of issues other than slavery. Other women in the movement accepted
traditional roles. Garrisonians pushed the woman question, and the American Anti-Slavery Society split in 1840 when a woman was elected to the

previously all-male board. Some members joined the new Liberty party. Others created a new abolitionist society. The organization, in general, never regained its position as the center of the slavery debate.

THE SOUTHERN "REACTIONARY ENLIGHTENMENT"

If the political task of the abolitionists was a difficult one, the burden facing the South was even more challenging. A stream of books, pamphlets, and editorials poured from southern presses in response to abolitionist demands. Louis Hartz has called this theoretical effort of the South to justify slavery the *reactionary Enlightenment.* The *Enlightenment* is a generic term used to describe the outpouring of philosophical, cultural, and scientific criticism of traditional society—an outpouring that advocated reason and skepticism as new measures of moral right. By using the term in conjunction with *reactionary,* Hartz was trying to convey the nature of the concerted effort on the part of Southern intellectuals to reexamine the entire nature of America as a liberal society based on the triumph of the Enlightenment. Hartz asks: "Had America suddenly produced, out of nowhere, a movement of reactionary feudalism?"

Southern writers began by seeking to find historical precedents that would justify slavery. Men like George Fitzhugh, Thomas R. Dew, and J. D. B. DeBow pointed to the existence of slavery in the Old Testament, in Greek and Roman democracy, and under feudalism. In their search for models the southern writers began to turn against modernity itself. They attacked the doctrine of individualism; they attacked Locke and Jefferson; they attacked capitalism; they attacked what they called free society itself. On the floor of the U.S. Senate in 1858, James Henry Hammond used what became known as the *mud-sill theory* to justify slavery:

> In all social systems there must be a class to do the menial duties, to perform the drudgery of life. That is, a class requiring but a low order of intellect and but little skill. Its requisites are vigor, docility, fidelity. Such a class you must have, or you will not have that other class which leads progress, civilization, and refinement. It constitutes the very mud-sill of society and of political government; and you might as well attempt to build a house in the air, as to build either the one or the other, except on this mud-sill. Fortunately for the South, she found a race adapted to that purpose to her hand. A race inferior to her own, but eminently qualified in temper, in vigor, in docility, in capacity to stand the climate, to answer all her purposes. We use them for our purpose, and call them slaves. We found them slaves by the common "consent of mankind," which, according to Cicero, "lex naturae est." The highest proof of what is Nature's law. We are old-fashioned at the South yet; slave is a word discarded now by "ears

polite"; I will not characterize that class at the North by that term; but you have it; it is there; it is everywhere; it is eternal.

The characterization of *mud sill* to the overwhelming majority of humanity must have been shocking to Northerners, even accustomed as they were to social status and deference. But Hammond's speech illustrates the extent to which Southerners had gone in pursuit of a reactionary Enlightenment.

Perhaps the most theoretically bold of the southern writers was George Fitzhugh, a Virginia journalist known affectionately in his region as the *Sage of Port Royal*. In *Sociology for the South* (1854) and *Cannibals All!* (1857), Fitzhugh attempted to demolish the very concept of a free society.

What is so striking about Fitzhugh's arguments is the extent to which he was driven to criticize the moral basis of a liberal view of society. Assessing the moral implications of the political economy of the North, Fitzhugh concluded that the conception of the "public good, the welfare of society, the prosperity of one's neighbors, is according to them, best promoted by each man's looking solely to the advancement of his pecuniary interests." "A beautiful system of ethics this," Fitzhugh continued, "that places all mankind in antagonistic positions, and puts all society at war." Here is a complete portrait of the kind of society that Fitzhugh thought the North was promoting (despite the abolitionist rhetoric of human rights):

> In free society none but the selfish virtues are in repute, because none other help a man in the race of competition. In such a society virtue loses all her loveliness, because of her selfish aims. Good men and bad men have the same end in view: self promotion, self elevation. The good man is prudent, cautious, and cunning of fence; he knows well, the arts (virtues, if you please) which enable him to advance his fortunes at the expense of those with whom he deals; he does not "cut too deep"; he does not cheat and swindle, he makes only good bargains and excellent profits. He gets more subjects by his course; everybody comes to him to be bled. The bad man is rash, hasty, unskillful and impolitic. He is equally selfish, but not half so prudent and cunning. Selfishness is almost the only motive of human conduct in a free society, where every man is taught that it is his first duty to change and better his pecuniary situation.

For Fitzhugh, there is a diminution of human character in capitalists themselves, even successful ones, since they devote their lives only to selfish pursuits while the majority of the population are "cheated by everybody" for whom they work.

The above quotation illustrates the extent to which the southern reactionary Enlightenment would reach for any source as part of its critique of modern society. The depiction of the "good" and "bad" man borrows from Aristotle's discussion in the *Nicomachean Ethics*. According to Aristotle, each regime provides its own conception of virtue, and thus the good citizen may not correspond to the good man. Fitzhugh was not likely to have read Marx, but he was familiar enough with the European utopian socialists to develop a labor theory of value. The workers "produce everything and enjoy nothing," Fitzhugh asserted. Wages are no more an embodiment of supply and demand and fair competition than the portion of the economic product afforded the southern slave:

> We say allowance, not wages; for neither slaves nor free laborers get wages, in the popular sense of the term; that is, the employer and the capitalist pays them from nothing of his own, but allows them a part, generally a very small part, of the proceeds of their own labor. Free laborers pay one another, for labor creates all values, and capital, after taking the lion's share by its taxing power, but pays the so-called wages of one laborer from the proceeds of the labor of another.

Fitzhugh closed his analysis with a warning to both capitalists and would-be socialists. To the latter he concluded:

> Our only quarrel with Socialism is, that it will not honestly admit that it owes its recent revival to the failure of universal liberty, and is seeking to bring about slavery again in some form.

Slavery was the "oldest, the best and most common form of Socialism." As soon as the European socialists realized that what they needed was "to procure good practical overseers from Virginia" to implement their plans, they would be assured of success. To northern capitalists he said that you "need not institute negro slavery" but need to realize that "the masses and the philosophers equally require more control."

Fitzhugh's political theory contained portions of a republican critique of capitalism and industrialization. By asking questions about a society in which "virtue loses all her loveliness," he had raised issues about the importance of community and rural life for the republic that had been voiced by Jefferson and Taylor. But Fitzhugh's policy goal of defending slavery drove him wildly all over the political map of Western thought. Rejecting Jefferson and Locke, he selectively embraced Aristotle and then sought out (admittedly presciently) the imminent authoritarian features of socialism.

Louis Hartz argues that the Southerners, instead of attacking Jefferson, should have clung to him and denounced themselves. This is, in essence, what Hinton Helper attempted to accomplish in *The Impending Crisis* (1857). Helper argued that the institution of slavery was eroding the economic status of the non-slaveholding yeoman class in the South. It is estimated that about 80 percent of white Southerners owned their own land in 1850, a diffusion of property that would have pleased Jefferson and indeed is far higher than farm ownership today. But slaveholders held the richest land, the largest number of acres, and controlled the political systems of each southern state. Helper argued that slavery was reducing the number of yeoman farmers and retarding southern economic development and culture. He advocated the creation of a southern nonslaveowners' party and a heavy tax on slave plantation labor to make it unprofitable. While Helper was an avowed racist, his book was banned throughout much of the South. Northerners (somewhat opportunistically) used *The Impending Crisis* as partisan propaganda for the Republican presidential campaign in 1860. If any lesson can be learned from Helper's effort, it seems that it is that race beats class as a trump in a debate over public policy.

One southern writer almost avoided the theoretical path of wild departure from American political tradition that beset Fitzhugh and the appropriation by the North that was Helper's fate. That writer was John C. Calhoun. Calhoun espoused many of the principles that became the theoretical core of the reactionary southern Enlightenment. In his 1837 Senate speech on the receipt of abolitionist petitions, he became the first southern politician of national prominence to declare slavery a "positive good" rather than a necessary evil. Calhoun's open defense of slavery as an institution was a turning point in the growth of southern nationalism. He angrily denied the abolitionist contention that slavery had led to the degeneration of southern culture. The South, he proudly proclaimed, was "equal in virtue, intelligence, patriotism, courage, disinterestedness" to the North. The only "virtue" in which the South was "inferior" was in "the arts of gain." He warned the northern senators that there was an impending crisis more serious than the one promoted by the abolitionists, the "conflict between labor and capital." The South had thus far been exempted from "the disorders and dangers resulting from this conflict," and the North would do well to examine the source of the South's "quiet" rather than "blindly" attacking it.

It was, however, in Calhoun's search for institutional mechanisms for preserving slavery that his genius as a theorist appears. Hofstadter thus describes Calhoun as "the last American statesman to do any primary political thinking." In numerous speeches and in two posthumously published theoretical treatises (*Disquisition on Government* and *Discourses on the Constitution and Government of the United States*), Calhoun imaginatively employed liberal arguments derived from Jefferson and Madison to protect the slave interest. The idée fixe of Calhoun's theory was the concurrent majority. Although he altered his definition of the concept in his various writings, Calhoun's central definition was as follows: a state must be permitted to nullify federal legislation within its borders that directly adversely affects its core political and economic interests. In effect, Calhoun thus reserved national legislation to only those areas in which there was unanimity. Calhoun insisted that the concept was not "anarchical or revolutionary," and that there was historical precedent in America for the practice. Both Madison and Jefferson had employed the practice in their opposition to legislation in the Adams administration by writing the Kentucky and Virginia resolutions declaring state nullification. The concurrent majority was "truly and emphatically American, without example or parallel."

In the *Disquisition on Government* Calhoun also offered precedent in ancient republican practice as well, pointing to the Roman system of tribunes, who could declare senatorial legislation nullified on behalf of the people. But his primary focus was directed toward the philosophical premises of the founding itself. Calhoun announced his admiration for Madison's political science. America had "happily" been freed of the existence of artificial classes such as those in Europe. But Madison recognized that factions are sown in human nature and can emerge over an infinite number of issues. The Constitution was thus designed as an instrument to curb majority factions. The separation of powers and the federal system were ingenious devices that recognized what was, for Calhoun, Madison's great insight: "[P]ower can only be restrained by power, and not by reason and justice."

But however magnificent the Constitution was in recognizing "universal experience," it still failed to fully protect the interests of a minority. Factions, institutionalized as political parties, could capture Congress, the presidency, and eventually the courts, and they could make minority interests their "subject." Early in his career Calhoun provided an example of how group interests can coalesce in a pluralist society to plunder a majority. In an 1828 report protesting federal tariffs which he authored for the South Carolina legislature, he described the history of recent legislation:

> The woollen manufacturers found they were too feeble to enforce their extractions alone, and of necessity, resorted to the expedient, which is ever adopted in such cases, of associating other interests until a majority is formed—and the result of which, in this case, was, that instead of increased duties on woollens alone—which would have been the fact if that interest alone governed, we have to bear equally increased duties on more than a dozen other of the leading articles of consumption.

The brilliance of Calhoun's arguments is difficult to deny. Whatever reservations one might express about the practicality of the concurrent majority (Calhoun insisted that the threat of recognition would make the recourse of nullification rare and actually promote regional comity), he had presented his case within the parameters of American political thought by employing and extending the positions of Madison. In fact, just as Madison had urged citizens to regard the Constitution as a "republican remedy for republican defects," Calhoun had presented his case for the concurrent majority. But there is a gaping hole in Calhoun's theory. How can one base a whole philosophy on the rights of a minority in order to suppress a minority (in this case, African Americans)? Calhoun died in 1850, but it seems as if his commitment to reactionary principles could not remain wedded to his constitutional theory, which was based on liberal and republican principles. Louis Hartz recognized this severe internal tension in Calhoun's system. How asks Hartz, can one denounce Locke (as Calhoun did when he dealt with racial questions) and then offer a Lockean solution to the conflict over slavery? Hartz's assessment is quite different from Hofstadter's. For Hartz, Calhoun is a "profoundly disintegrated political theorist," a man with a "brilliant mind gone haywire."

LINCOLN'S RESOLUTION

It is in the context of the abolitionist struggle between ways and means and the rise of southern nationalism that Abraham Lincoln emerged as a national political figure. Lincoln's definition of the threat of slavery to the republic and his interpretation of the theoretical significance of the Civil War have given him a central place in the American political tradition—a place perhaps second only to Jefferson's. But despite this exalted status, Lincoln remains a controversial and enigmatic figure, as indeed he was in his own day.

Lincoln became deified in popular American political culture upon his assassination. The historian David Donald refers to this as the *Black Easter* Lincoln tradition. The northern clergy portrayed Lincoln as the "savior" of America, as Washington had been its founder. Lincoln, through his vision of America as an indissoluble Union, suffered and died for a cause many did not understand as fully as he did. One New England minister, noting that the assassination had taken place on Good Friday, concluded that "it is no blasphemy against the Son of God that we declare the fitness of the slaying of the second Father of our Republic on the anniversary of the day on which He was slain. Jesus Christ died for the world, Abraham Lincoln died for his country." Lincoln, the Great Emancipator, freed an oppressed people and also thus freed a nation from dissolution.

In other generations, however, the Lincoln legacy has been treated more skeptically. Richard Hofstadter, for example, portrays him as a talented, even consummate, politician who was always just behind the changing northern consensus on slavery. During the civil rights protests of the 1960s, Lincoln's racist remarks were taken as proof of the historical origins of white hypocrisy. Many writers, while sympathetic to Lincoln, have objected to the Black Easter tradition. William Herndon, a law partner of the president and early biographer, wrote in 1899 that he hoped to take the memory of Lincoln away from the "nice, sweet smelling gentlemen." His account shows a democratic but ill-educated politician whose limited legal talents were becoming obsolete in a more sophisticated, industrial Illinois. Carl Sandburg, the poet, wrote popular biographies in the late 1920s and 1930s, portraying Lincoln as a prairie populist. It was from speaking on the stump at county fairs and country stores that, according to Sandburg, Lincoln imbibed an appreciation of the essence of American democracy.

But there has also always been an anti-Lincoln tradition in America. Southern writers could never decide whether Lincoln was a crafty tyrant or a buffoon. Lincoln's mild treatment of the Confederates before his death softened these assessments somewhat, but in 1904 Elizabeth Mary Meriwether still offered her readers an assessment of Lincoln as a frontier bully:

> Is it insanity or pure mendacity to liken a man of this nature to the gentle and loving Nazarene? Who can for an instant imagine Jesus swinging a bottle of whiskey around his head, swearing to the rowdy crowd that he was the "big buck of the lick"? Who can imagine Jesus sewing up hog's eyes? . . . What act of Lincoln's life betrays tenderheartedness? Was he tender-hearted when he made medicine contraband of war? When he punished Southern women caught with a bottle of quinine going South?

Lincoln's concentration of executive power during the war years made even his sympathizers skittish. Without consulting Congress, he declared that a state of war was in effect and enlarged the army, appropriated funds without congressional appropriation, and suspended the writ of habeas corpus. Historian David Donald, who argues that in general Lincoln's exercise of power was prudent, admitted: "It required but a line from the President to close down a censorious newspaper, to banish a Democratic politician, or to arrest suspected members of a state legislature." Albert Bledsoe, the editor of the *Southern Review,* offered a psychological interpretation of Lincoln's use of power. Lincoln's success, according to Bledsoe, was not based upon a love of freedom or hatred of oppression, but upon his "ruling passion" for personal distinction. Without a faith in God, "the one thought . . . which haunted and tormented his soul, was the reflection that he had done nothing, and might die without doing anything to link his name and memory forever with the events of his time." Bledsoe's approach has been duplicated by modern scholars. Indeed, Lincoln has been the most psychologized American president, except perhaps for Richard M. Nixon. For example, Charles B. Strozier argues in his *Lincoln's Quest for Union* that the president's powerful rhetoric and decisive action during the war were the result of his effort to resolve the failure to find union in his personal life: "His own ambivalent quest for union—with his dead mother, his bride, his alienated father—gave meaning to the nation's turbulence as it hurtled toward civil war."

A review of Lincoln's political thought reveals aspects of all the assessments noted above. Lincoln could be a cautious, guileful politician who would not challenge and indeed appealed to racist sentiment; he could be an astute admirer as well as a critic of the personal exercise of power; and he could be an eloquent interpreter of the essence of American political culture. A focus upon two issues—the institution of slavery and the nature of the Union—can help illustrate the many facets of Lincoln. Invariably, the slavery question for Lincoln was instrumental to his effort to preserve the United States as a single political entity. Lincoln's success as a political theorist lay, then, in his ability to present a set of arguments and symbols that resolved the abolitionists' ends-and-means problem and challenged the principles in the southern reactionary Enlightenment.

Although there is certainly a pattern of development in Lincoln's political thought, his first major speech—the Lyceum address delivered in 1838—contains all the elements of his later theory. The speech has fascinated scholars for generations, not only because of a belief that it represents a key to Lincoln's thought but because for some it offers tantalizing insights into Lincoln's psychology. In 1838 Lincoln was a two-term representative in the Illinois legislature and a rising young politician in the Whig party. The subject upon which he chose to speak was "The Perpetuation of Our Political Institutions." Lincoln reviewed a series of recent violent incidents that had occurred in the country. These included accounts of black lynchings and the murder of abolitionist editor Elijah Lovejoy. But Lincoln also discussed the hanging of a group of gamblers in Vicksburg, thus treating both politically motivated and ordinary crimes as part of a general problem of law and order. A "mobocratic spirit" was "now abroad in the land." Some men had "no restraint but the dread of punishment"; some, "having ever regarded government as their deadliest bane, make a jubilee of its suspension"; some "good men" who "love tranquility" and "who desire to abide by the laws and enjoy their benefits" see their property and families endangered and "seeing nothing in prospect that forebodes a change for the better . . . imagine they have nothing to lose."

Lincoln, at this point in his career, exclusively focused upon the effects of antislavery activity rather than upon its immediate causes. And what were the effects? For Lincoln, under such conditions "men of sufficient talent and ambition will not be wanting to seize the opportunity, strike the blow, and overturn that fair fabric which for the last half century has been the fondest hope of the lovers of freedom throughout the world."

According to Lincoln, the republic was at a crucial juncture. His speech began with a recitation of familiar July fourth rhetoric. America was "in the peaceful possession of the fairest portion of the earth" and "under a government of a system of political institutions more essentially to liberty than any of which the history of former times tells us." But Lincoln reminds his audience that the present and future generations are not responsible for this fortune: "We toiled not in the acquirement or establishment of them; they are a legacy bequeathed to us by a once hardy, brave and patriotic, but now lamented and departed race of ancestors."

Employing both republican symbols of virtue and corruption, Lincoln argued that the very success of the American experiment in free government was in danger in its third generation. In the first and second generations the success of the republic was itself at stake. "Theirs was the task," said Lincoln, "to create an edifice of liberty and equal rights." Ours is to "transmit these . . . undecayed by the lapse in time." The problem of maintaining a republic across time had long been a preoccupation of republican political theory. Lincoln reiterates this republican theme and suggests that the threat to the stability of the political system comes not only from the decline in virtue (the traditional republican argument) but also from a disjunction between the political ambition of leaders in the third generation and the requirements of the republic. The republic requires a shoring up of its foundations by its leaders and a reminder to the people of their duties. But what ambitious person would be satisfied with this chore of tending established institutions? In the first two generations, personal fame coincided with the needs of the republic:

> Their ambition aspired to display before an admiring world a practical demonstration of the truth of a proposition which had hitherto been considered at best no better than problematical—namely the capability of a people to govern themselves. If they succeeded they were to be immortalized; their names were to be transferred to counties, and cities, and rivers, and mountains; and to be revered and sung and toasted through all time. . . .

But now the "field of glory is harvested, and the crop is already appropriated." For Lincoln, however, human nature is unchanging. Each generation produces ambitious men, and leadership is now a threat to the republic:

> [N]ew reapers will arise, and they too will seek a field. It is to deny what the history of the world has told us is true, to suppose that men of ambition and talents will not continue to spring up amongst us. And when they do, they will as naturally seek the gratification of their ruling passion as others have done before them. The question is: Can that gratification be found in supporting and maintaining an edifice that has been erected by others? Most certainly it cannot. Many great and good men, sufficiently qualified for any task they should undertake, may ever be found to aspire to nothing beyond a gubernatorial or a presidential chair; but such belong not to the family of the lion, or the tribe of the eagle. What! think you these places would satisfy

an Alexander, a Caesar, or a Napoleon? Never! Towering genius disdains a beaten path. It seeks regions hitherto unexplored. It sees no distinction in adding story to story upon monuments of fame erected to the memory of others. It denies that it is glory enough to serve under any chief. It scorns to tread in the footsteps of any predecessor, however illustrious. It thirsts for distinction; and if possible, it will have it, whether at the expense of emancipating slaves or enslaving free men.

How were the American people to "fortify" (to use Lincoln's expression) against this danger? In the early days of the republic, memories of the sacrifices in the Revolution acted as a barrier against usurpation by ambitious men. "Nearly every adult male had been a participator in some of its scenes . . . in the form of a husband, a father, a son, or a brother, a living history was to be found in every family—a history bearing the indubitable testimonies of its own authenticity, in the limbs mangled, in the scars of wounds received. . . ." Now "the silent artillery of time" had accomplished what "invading foeman could never do." These memories functioned as "pillars of the temple of liberty," but they had crumbled. Unless this generation found "other pillars," the republic was imperiled.

The memory of the Revolution had functioned successfully for Lincoln as a natural support for republican institutions. Battlefield death and valor had made the revolutionary experience an immediate and concrete symbol of American political culture. Lincoln admitted that those memories would never be "entirely forgotten," but they would never again be "so universally known nor so vividly felt as they were by the generation just gone to rest." To the extent to which political culture could still function as an important foundation, it must now emanate from an exercise of rational will. "Passion has helped us," said Lincoln, but "in the future it will be our enemy." Only "reason—cold, calculating, unimpassioned reason" could help us now.

Lincoln, in essence, calls for a reaffirmation of the American social contract which emphasizes obedience to the law.

> Let every American, every lover of liberty, every well-wisher to his posterity swear by the blood of the Revolution never to violate in the least particular the laws of the country, and never to tolerate their violation by others. As the patriots of seventy-six did to the support of the Declaration of Independence, so to the support of the Constitution and laws let every man remember to violate the law is to trample on the blood of his father, and to tear the charter of his own and his children's liberty.

So important is this pledge to the future of the republic that Lincoln insists that it must become the "political religion of the nation" taught by every family, every school and college, every clergyman and legislator.

The Lyceum speech rises to the level of an innovative political philosophy. Lincoln places current political problems in the context of universals in human nature ("the jealousy, envy and avarice incident to our nature") and in the context of challenges that face a postrevolutionary regime. His premises are clearly Hobbesian, but he expresses faith in a rekindled republican virtue to combat the tendencies of humans to revert to a state of nature. In fact, just as Hobbes insisted that reason offers an alternative to anarchy, so does Lincoln, although the latter's social contract is republican in form.

One interpretation, then, emphasizes the extent to which Lincoln saw very early in the conflict the threat to the Union that the slavery issue posed. He was able to envision the significance of the struggle in broad terms through the application of principles of political philosophy to the particular problems facing a new nation that relied upon mass beliefs for its support. But other interpretations are also possible. Was Lincoln's focus on the rise of a towering genius and his threat to the republic a projection of his own ambitions? No towering genius emerged in the following years, except perhaps Lincoln himself. Or should the speech be seen as the clever effort of a young politician to avoid, and even silence, the issues raised by the abolitionists? By subsuming moral protests under the general question of law and order, Lincoln had been able to conclude indirectly that the abolitionists were contributing to the law-and-order peril facing the republic. A less critical, but still Machiavellian, view might be that Lincoln came to see, at least after the war began, that the armed conflict was an opportunity to create the political religion he had recommended in 1838.

Lincoln was elected to Congress in 1848 but served only a single term. His political career had reached a hiatus. The impending crisis, however, reawakened his political imagination. He later stated in his presidential campaign autobiography (written in the third person in 1860) that "the repeal of the Missouri compromise aroused him as he had never been before." In the 1850s Lincoln's speeches reveal two related but contradictory themes: a carefully constructed political critique of slavery and a jeremiadic vision of America as a society in crisis and in need of redemption. The elucidation of the first theme represented an effort to revise the Whig agenda, which was crumbling under the challenge of the slavery question; the other involved an adaptation of the abolitionist arguments.

In the Missouri Compromise of 1820, Congress permitted Missouri to enter the Union as a slave state, provided that in all territory north of the thirty-sixth parallel slavery should be banned. Senator Stephen A. Douglas of Illinois, however, introduced legislation permitting the Kansas-Nebraska territories to decide for themselves whether slavery should be permitted. Douglas argued that slavery was a local issue and used the principle of popular sovereignty to justify his legislation. Douglas's arguments were part of a plan to remove slavery as a national issue. His own policy he defined as "don't care" in regard to slavery.

In Peoria, Illinois, Lincoln delivered an address attacking Douglas's position. It was the first public speech in which Lincoln condemned slavery: "This declared indifference, but, as I must think, covert real zeal, for the spread of slavery, I cannot but hate." In following years and during a series of senatorial debates with Douglas, Lincoln carefully developed a set of arguments against Douglas's popular sovereignty position. Lincoln never challenged Douglas's own racism. Whenever the question of racial political or social or economic equality was raised, Lincoln responded by affirming white superiority or repeated Clay's support of colonization.[1] His central argument was that slavery could be tolerated as a regional institution that, one might hope, would gradually disappear; that Douglas's policies with southern support, however, were placing the institution "on a new basis, which looks to the perpetuity and nationalization of slavery."

Lincoln used a wide variety of arguments to support this judgment that slavery was in danger of becoming a national institution and, as such, was eroding the principles of the republic. In Peoria he presented an economic argument that slave and free labor could not coexist in the new territories: "Slave states are places for poor white people to remove from, not move to. New free states are the places for poor people to go to, and better their condition." The nation "needs these Territories," warned Lincoln, in order to maintain equality of opportunity.[2]

But Lincoln's primary supporting arguments rested on the assertion that nationalized slavery would require the repudiation of those central beliefs that made America a free nation. Southern writers had already challenged the validity of the Declaration of Independence, and Douglas himself had said that the document had been intended to apply only to white British subjects. To Lincoln this paring down of the shining abstract truth of the document represented a threat to everyone. He argued that the founding fathers who had framed the principles that defined us as Americans had been uncomfortable with slavery and always meant slavery to be a local institution. The Declaration had asserted the doctrine of self-government as an "absolute and eternal right." "If the Negro is a man, is it not to that extent a total destruction of self-government to say that he too shall not govern himself?" He closed his Ottawa, Illinois, address in the debate with Douglas by quoting Henry Clay. Clay once said that those who wished to repress liberty in America would have to "go back to the era of our independence, and muzzle the canon which thunders its annual joyous return; they must blow out the moral lights around us; they must penetrate the human soul, and eradicate there the love of liberty. . . ." Douglas, in his policy of not caring whether slavery was voted up or down, was of necessity attacking the "sacred right of self government" itself. He was "blowing out the moral lights around us."

In the debates with Douglas, Lincoln contended that there were compromises and appeals to self-interest that a political system could not accommodate without losing its self-identity. Lincoln's minimal line was drawn differently from that of the abolitionists (he objected only to the extension of slavery). In the late 1850s and throughout the war, however, Lincoln, borrowing directly from the abolitionists, created a broader, more powerful political theory that was a more complex conception of political religion than the one he had recommended in 1838. The first indication of this additional theme is Lincoln's 1858 speech before the Republican state convention in Springfield, Illinois. During the ensuing debates Lincoln cautiously interpreted his own address under questioning by Douglas. But the central metaphor of the speech represented the core of his subsequent political thought: "A house divided against itself cannot stand." The symbol of a house divided was not lost upon the biblically oriented nineteenth-century audience. The phrase Lincoln employed is derived from Matthew's account of the questioning by the Pharisees of Jesus' healing power. Jesus' response, "Every kingdom divided against itself is brought to desolation; and every city or house divided against itself shall not stand," is an extremely complex statement that explores the nature of belief, faith, and motivation. Simply summarized, the house-divided metaphor seeks to show the confusion, desperation, and fear that accompany actions undertaken in the absence of divine guidance. Lincoln, by employing the phrase, was contending that people will pay a price for ignoring "ancient truths" in their common heritage and tolerating evil. "Satan cannot cast out Satan" was part of Jesus' defense of his divine powers, and Lincoln was applying this New Testament lesson to those who would accommodate the spread of slavery.

Throughout the next two years Lincoln continued to present his own constitutional history of slavery. Intertwined with it, however, was the broader theme that slavery constituted a moral crisis for the American people that would require national expiation. In his Cooper Institute speech (1860), Lincoln reviewed the efforts of the founding fathers to restrict slavery, much as he had done in Peoria six years earlier. His address ended with the ominous words, "Let us have faith that right makes might."

In his message to a special session of Congress in April 1861, Lincoln spoke before a house that had divided. In the chamber the seats of southern representatives were vacant. He told the assembled body that the upcoming war was a "people's contest," and he urged Americans to "renew our trust in God, and go forward without fear and with manly hearts." As battlefield deaths mounted, Lincoln began to explicitly interpret the war as a providential test for America. At Gettysburg he stated his conception in terms so simple and eloquent that the address is regarded as a masterpiece of political discourse. He first touched upon *birth* ("Four score and seven years ago our fathers brought forth on this continent a new nation, conceived in liberty. . . "). Next he spoke of *trial* ("Now we are engaged in a great civil war, testing whether that nation, or any nation, so conceived and so dedicated, can long endure. . . ."). And finally he touched upon *rebirth* ("[W]e here highly resolve that these dead shall not have died in vain; that this nation, under God, shall have a new birth of freedom. . . ."). These were the meanings he attached to the war.

Lincoln's second inaugural, delivered near the end of the Civil War, is generally regarded as a conciliatory document. The address does close with the biblical injunction to behave with malice toward none and charity to all. But the body of the speech interprets the war as the result of divine retributive justice. Both sides had "read the same Bible" and prayed to the same God; both had invoked "his aid against the other." But Lincoln is clear about the righteousness of the northern cause:

> It may seem strange that any men should dare to ask a just God's assistance in wringing their bread from the sweat of other men's faces. . . .

He also warns:

> [I]f God wills that it continue until all the wealth piled up by bondsman's two hundred and fifty years of unrequited toil shall be sunk, and until every drop of blood drawn with the lash shall be paid by another drawn with the sword, as was said three thousand years ago, so still it must be said, "The judgments of the Lord are true and righteous altogether."

THE DILEMMA OF RECONSTRUCTION

Lincoln's interpretation of the war as providentially willed did not prevent him from declaring lenient peace terms with the defeated Confederacy. The divine scourge that had greeted the South had been the result of the region's defense and promotion of slavery. Out of political expediency Lincoln himself had moved slowly toward implementing emancipation. Preservation of the Union had always been his central political objective. With the war won and the South effectively without slaves, the president welcomed the rebels back into the Union. By 1865 three southern states had accepted Lincoln's requirement that 10 percent of its citizens take an oath of loyalty and recognize the end of slavery as a condition for readmission. Fate eliminated the opportunity for Lincoln to link his apocalyptic interpretation of the Civil War to the problems of peace. Thus it was left to other actors to attempt to interpret or revise Lincoln's vision. The surrender of Lee at Appomattox ended the fratricide but opened up staggering constitutional, economic, political, and moral problems.

What was the constitutional status of the states that had seceded? Were they still states, since the Confederate States of America (CSA) was never recognized by the North? Or had they forfeited their status as states and now assumed the role of conquered provinces? Who should decide this question and the terms of readmission, the president or Congress? Lincoln assumed that the initiatives would come from the office of the president, but Congress did not recognize his plan and offered its own, which Lincoln subjected to a pocket veto.

Whatever the legal status of the former CSA, the economic problems of the defeated South were enormous. When Carl Schurz, a northern Republican, surveyed the region for the president immediately after the surrender, he was shocked by the effects of this new kind of war. Some parts of the South had escaped devastation, but in others the countryside

> looked for many miles like a broad black streak of ruin and desolation—the fences were all gone; lonesome smoke stacks, surrounded by dark heaps of ashes and cinders, marking the spots where human habitations had stood; the fields a sickly patch of cotton or corn cultivated by Negro squatters.

Political problems involved in readmission were readily evident. The South had been soundly defeated, but the nationalism that emerged in the 1850s had not disintegrated. As historian W. J. Cash noted in *The Mind of the South*, the war had left the Southerners

> far more aware of their differences and of the line which divided what was southern from what was not. And upon that line all their intensified patriotism and love, all their high pride in the knowledge that they had fought the good fight and had yielded only to irresistible force, was concentrated, to issue in a determination . . . to hold fast to their own, to maintain their divergences, to remain what they had been.

Northern Republican politicians worried about the possibility of a resurgent Confederacy and the possible emergence of guerrilla warfare. They worried about the impact of southern representation in Congress. Would readmitted southern representatives again align with northern Democrats, stronger in numbers if the black population were included as part of the census? Would African American citizens, if enfranchised, vote at the bidding of their former masters?

Then there was the moral issue of slavery itself as well as the economic and legal status of African Americans. The abolitionist strategy that no plan was a plan had coincided with Lincoln's own goals. The Emancipation Proclamation ended slavery only in the states in rebellion. Lincoln worked very diligently with Congress in the enactment of the Thirteenth Amendment, which abolished slavery. The South acquiesced in ratification, although several southern states added codicils insisting that their accession did not foreclose in their minds the issue of compensation. Generally in the South emancipation created a panic. Calhoun had warned that abolition would make "the last first" in the South. Southerners were adamant in rejecting the most minimal social and economic implications of abolition. Emerson Etheridge, a prominent Tennessee politician, said in 1865 that "negroes are no more free than they were 40 years ago, and if one goes about the country telling them that they are free, shoot him." The South had no national representation, but the participants of the southern reactionary Enlightenment a decade before insisted either that the mass emigration of African Americans from their region was imperative or argued that some "home rule" plan of white "tutelage" was necessary. For many in the North the ratification of the Thirteenth Amendment meant that their moral mission was completed. Garrison recommended in 1865 that the national Anti-Slavery Society be dissolved.

The series of policies that attempted to deal with these problems is referred to as Reconstruction. Briefly, Reconstruction can be divided into two policy experiments. Presidential Reconstruction in which the executive branch assumed the initiative in policy formation was begun under Lincoln and revised by his successor, Andrew Johnson. Congressional Reconstruction can be said to have started in 1867 with the passage of the First Reconstruction Act, which divided the former CSA into five military districts and ended officially in 1877 when the last federal troops were removed from the South. Of course, Congress had significant influence in the presidential Reconstruction, as did the president in the congressional Reconstruction, but the two experiments do reflect different approaches. They give us a convenient way to review the discussion and debate over Reconstruction. Although the exchanges between the president and Congress were shaped in terms of specific policies and partisan politics, they reveal important theoretical questions.

The central figure in the first, or presidential, Reconstruction was Andrew Johnson. In many ways Johnson's career was a replica of Lincoln's. The vice president had been raised in a border state in very modest circumstances. He was economically a self-made man and had taught himself to read as an adult. But there was an essential difference between Johnson and Lincoln, aside from different political and intellectual talents and psychological proclivities. Lincoln had become a Whig and later a Republican. Johnson's party ideology was derived from a more conventional route, given his economic background. He was a Jacksonian Democrat.

Lincoln's choice placed him among the affluent elites of antebellum America. His ability to create ideological bridges between the men and women of his origins and the agenda of the Whigs was part of his genius as a politician. Johnson, on the other hand, nurtured his personal class resentments. Early in his career he had announced his goal: "Some day I will show up the stuck-up aristocrats who is running this country." But class anger was not the only source of difference between Lincoln and Johnson. As a Democrat, Johnson accepted fully the Jacksonian vision of America as an equalitarian society of yeoman farmers and small businesspeople betrayed by the efforts of the "money power," who used the government to take over the fruits of their labor.

The outbreak of the Civil War made Johnson an ideal vice presidential choice. Lincoln had complained in 1858 that "much of the plain old Democracy is with us, while nearly all the old exclusive silk-stocking Whiggery is against us." When Tennessee joined the CSA, Johnson refused to give up his Senate seat and remained in the Union. In 1862 Lincoln appointed him military governor of the state. Johnson had such a hatred of the southern aristocracy, which he saw as a force that had a political and economic stranglehold on the small farmer, that the Republicans eagerly looked forward to his leadership after Lincoln's assassination.

Johnson's plan for Reconstruction included an amnesty for those who had taken an oath of allegiance to the Union, as did Lincoln's proposal. But Johnson's plan also included an important revision. Confederates who owned more than $20,000 worth of property were ineligible for amnesty. Johnson explained to a Virginia delegation that the exceptioned class could appeal individually for special pardons to the president, but he reminded them, "You know full well it was the wealthy men of the South who dragooned the people into secession."

When various states began to hold constitutional conventions, however, voters elected as delegates members of the planter aristocracy that Johnson so detested. His dream of a restored yeoman South shattered, Johnson seemed to move toward another ideological position. If the small farmers were unable or unwilling to wrest political control of their states from the old landed aristocracy, he would be certain that his beloved farmer would not be forced to share power and status with African Americans. He swiftly granted numerous pardons to the planter class. When the new state governments enacted a series of Black Codes that restricted freedmen's movement without permission of their employers and provided imprisonment for African Americans who quit work before the expiration of their contracts, and when numerous terrorist groups emerged in the South, including the Klan, Johnson refused to act. His decisions precipitated congressional attempts at Reconstruction.

An acrimonious exchange between Frederick Douglass and Johnson in 1866 illustrates the president's position. Douglass appealed to Johnson to support measures to give African Americans the right to vote, in light of recent events in the former CSA. Johnson replied that slavery had been abolished with a "great national guarantee." He asked Douglass if it was not true that, as a black slave, he looked upon "a large family, struggling hard upon a poor piece of land" with less esteem than the large slave-owning planter. This in itself was a cruel question to ask a former slave, but Douglass politely but emphatically disagreed. Johnson, insisting that the affirmative was the case in his experience in Tennessee, continued:

> The colored man went into this rebellion a slave; by the operation of the rebellion he came out a freeman. . . . The non-slaveholder who was forced into the rebellion, who was as loyal as those that lived beyond the limits of the State, but was carried into it, lost his property, and in a number of instances the lives of such were sacrificed, and he who has survived has come out of it with nothing gained, but a great deal lost. Now, upon what principle of justice, should they be placed in a condition different from what they were before? On the one hand, one has gained a great deal; on the other hand, one has lost a great deal, and in a political point of view, scarcely stands where he did before.

Douglass attempted to argue that the small white farmer and the new African American freeman could use the ballot to overturn the plantation aristocrat, but Johnson found this scenario inconceivable and ended the exchange.

To northern Republican representatives in Congress and some former abolitionists, it seemed as if Hinton Helper had become president. Immediately after the war, the Republican party was composed of two groups: the conservative or moderate Republicans who were willing to accept Lincoln's and Johnson's proposals in principle, and the radical Republicans who hoped for a more comprehensive Reconstruction. Johnson's emerging position drove the former into the radicals' camp. Enraged by Black Codes and the patterns of terror in the South, radicals proposed constitutional remedies. The Fourteenth Amendment, which guaranteed every citizen due process and equal protection under law, was designed to enable the federal courts to protect African Americans from injustices by the states. This nationalization of civil rights made legislators in northern states skittish and would not have passed had it not been made a condition for readmission on the part of the southern states.

It seems that the limits of the northern consensus had been reached on the question of abolition. It became the task of radical Republicans to push this consensus further. After Congress refused to seat southern representatives elected under the presidential Reconstruction plan and drew up its own plan, two important issues emerged. One was the enfranchisement of African Americans; the other, the redistribution of private property.

Lincoln had never publicly supported black suffrage. Few northern states extended the vote to African Americans, although several state Republican conventions had been on record for extending the franchise. Both Douglass and Wendell Phillips spoke eloquently for the franchise as a logical extension of the abolitionist program. Phillips described the general liberating effects of voting:

> The Ballot is opportunity, education, fair play, right to office, and elbow-room. Compare the New England of 1820 with the England of that year—one, after two hundred years of timid and heartless caste, and you see the fruit of the ballot. . . .What the Alphabet is in Literature the Vote is in the State.

Douglass faced a new and poignant ends-and-means problem. He had always been an ardent supporter of extending the ballot to women as well as to African Americans, but the Fifteenth Amendment submitted to the states for ratification by Congress did not mention gender discrimination. He reaffirmed the ballot as an essential means of protection of the right "to own one's body," and reaffirmed the restriction of the franchise as a violation of the principle of consent of the governed: "Woman is not a consenting party to this Government," he wrote in the *New National Era* in 1870:

> She has never been consulted. Ours is a Government of men, by men. . . . So far as respects its relation to woman, our Government is in essence, a simple usurpation, a Government of force, and not of reason. We legislate for woman, and protect her, precisely as we legislate for and protect animals, asking the consent of neither.

But nevertheless Douglass stressed the unique character of racial oppression:

> When women because they are women, are dragged from their homes and hung upon lamp-posts; when their children are torn from their arms and their brains dashed upon the pavement; when they are the objects of insult and outrage at every turn; when they are in danger of having their homes burnt down over their heads; when their children are not allowed to enter schools; then they will have an urgency to obtain the ballot.

When a member of the Equal Rights Association to which Douglass was speaking shouted, "Is that not true of the black woman?" Douglass replied, "Yes, yes, yes, it is true of the black woman, but not because she is a woman but because she is black." For Douglass a historical opportunity was available now for African-American men, and thus racial injustice must be addressed before gender injustice.

The Fifteenth Amendment was ratified, but many radical Republicans and abolitionists thought that property redistribution was essential to

Reconstruction. Thaddeus Stevens, the radical Republican leader in the Senate and the nightmare of the South, declared in 1865 that "the whole fabric of southern society must be changed. . . ."

> How can republican institutions, free schools, free churches, free social intercourse exist in a mingled community of nabobs and serfs; of the owners of 20,000 acre manors with lordly palaces, and the occupants of narrow huts inhabited by "low white trash"? If the South is ever to be made a safe republic let her lands be cultivated by the toil of the owners or the free labor of intelligent citizens.

Stevens was aware of the consequences of his position. Perhaps the southern nobility must be driven "into exile." "All great improvements in the political and moral world" require "a heavy impetus to drive forward a sluggish people." Phillips, near the Civil War's end, proposed that large southern plantations be broken into small pieces and sold to "the sons of Vermont and New York," who would employ free "Negro Labor."

There are some indications in the congressional Reconstruction Acts (1867) of an intent to make, in Phillips's words, the South into a "garden" of free labor. Early legislation promised every freedman forty acres of confiscated plantation property. When Congress attempted to extend the life of the Freedmen's Bureau in 1866, it provided for the allocation of public land to African Americans. But the northern public again became skittish about interference with private property, however it might have originally been attained. The *New York Herald-Tribune,* for example, complained that the granting of land would "destroy that very feeling of manhood, by making them [freedmen] dependent upon the government." The *Nation,* generally sympathetic to the black cause, declared that the freedman must proceed on his own "on the dusty and ragged highway of competition." After reviewing the experiment in congressional Reconstruction in South Carolina, its editors concluded, "This is . . . socialism."

The promise of forty acres was not met. The isolated instances of confiscation and freedman ownership undertaken by northern generals were overturned by President Andrew Johnson. The Supreme Court so narrowly construed the Fourteenth Amendment that it became inapplicable as a juridical solution to problems in race relations for a century. The Fifteenth Amendment, which guaranteed voting rights to all male citizens, was nullified by state legislation and terror. When Hilary Herbert, a congressman, edited and contributed to a collection of essays entitled *Why the Solid South?* in 1890, he declared that the South had solved the "Negro problem" despite Reconstruction, and that the "new South" eagerly awaited capital investment from the North. The image of Reconstruction as either a policy of revenge or a failed utopian experiment in race relations quickly took hold in the North.

SUMMARY AND COMMENT

All wars are difficult to justify. The aims of the victors never seem fully capable of implementation. The defeated never are fully able to accept the terms of surrender. The sacrifice of human life never seems fully defensible. Lincoln recognized the nature of the unpayable debt to the dead when he said at Gettysburg that "in a larger sense, we cannot dedicate, we cannot consecrate, we cannot hallow this ground." Civil war, despite its special ferocity, leaves even a greater sense of regret and recrimination. To the extent to which the nation-state has come to be seen as a family, fratricide seems a crime barely capable of exculpation.

It is still possible, of course, to see elements of a vindicatory defense of the conflict. It is possible that America may have divided even further had the CSA been successful in creating on the continent a contentious set of small states, none of which could be secure from the other. It is possible that the South as an independent state could have managed to retain slavery indefinitely as a garrison state with institutions of control similar to those more recently employed in South Africa.

Each of the major political theorists discussed above appreciated the gravity of a civil war. But for abolitionists, for writers in the southern reactionary Enlightenment, and for Lincoln there was an unacceptable radical incongruity in the idea of a nation dedicated to freedom and the institution of slavery. For men and women like Garrison and Angelina and Sarah Grimké, the institution challenged their identity both as human beings and as citizens. For writers like Fitzhugh, the defense of slavery led to a general abandonment of a free society. For Lincoln, slavery represented a threat to the nation itself since a house divided cannot stand.

For all the insights offered by these three groups, there were also serious failings. There was an unmistakable strain of solipsism in abolitionism. With the exception of Frederick Douglass, who himself had been a slave, many abolitionists seemed more concerned about protecting the purity of their motives than finding institutional outlets for their goals. It is true, as we have emphasized, that for abolitionists legal emancipation was a minimal line and hence not subject to compromise. But the very individualism that gave abolitionists the courage to devote themselves to the cause and create their community of believers also led to policy pronouncements calling for secession in the 1840s ("No Union with Slaveholders"). There were calls to refuse to vote or participate in politics at all; a pamphlet circulated by the American Anti-Slavery Society in 1845 entitled "Can Abolitionists Vote or Take Office under the Constitution of the US?" answered the question negatively. In addition, for Garrisonians there was a belief in the illegitimacy of any government. Richard Hofstadter thus concludes that proposals like those listed above would not have helped end slavery but would have permitted the abolitionists to "wash away their personal sin of participating in a slaveholding commonwealth."

The estrangement of Southerners from the North did manage to create an intellectual opening that permitted them to critically survey the kind of inequality that a fully industrialized society could produce. Fitzhugh's description of a society in which virtue has lost its loveliness was a powerful indictment of the cultural impact of unrestrained economic competition. But driven by an obsession to justify slavery, Fitzhugh used his insight to explore the possibilities for enslavement rather than for liberation. Calhoun, too, who began his career as an ardent nationalist, discovered the oppressive impact of majority decisions reached by a pluralist compromise. He refused to see, however, that regional minorities cannot use their autonomy to oppress others in their midst.

Lincoln came to see and appreciate the consequences of the arguments of both the abolitionists and the southern writers. He used the full force of national sentiment to move the abolitionist critique to more general goals. If there is any enduring legacy to Lincoln's political thought, it is that there are some actions that even a decentralized and tolerant society cannot accept without losing its identity as a nation. But the political religion he employed to implement his insight has its own liabilities. Should the presidency be the focus for the interpretation and enforcement of basic American values? Can a political religion, however benevolently defined, itself become oppressive and unduly restrict regional diversity and innovative ideas? Should even important policy disputes be translated into a complex cosmology of national trial and rebirth?

The experience of Reconstruction illustrates how both abolitionist protest and Lincolnian political religion could not assert themselves effectively when confronted by the more complex problems of implementing justice and equality in a multiracial society. Radical Republicans, after much struggle, were able to advance the minimal line from emancipation to citizenship. They were not able, however, to extend the consensus to a property distribution nor continue for long the draconian measures of military occupation. The trump that beat the efforts at Reconstruction involved the reassertion of the general precepts that govern American political culture—that is, belief in the inviolability of private property, federalism, and individualism. But the failure of Reconstruction was also the result of the North's own ambivalence concerning race, which was epitomized by Andrew Johnson's reading of the Civil War's meaning.

Notes

[1] At the first joint debate with Douglas in Ottawa, Illinois, Lincoln assured his audience that he had no intention to "introduce political and social equality between

the white and black races." A "physical difference" prevented, "probably forever," living together in "perfect equality." Lincoln affirmed his agreement with Douglas that he was "in favor of the race to which I belong having a superior position." Four months before announcing the Emancipation Proclamation, Lincoln revealed to a group of African Americans a plan for colonization to Central America.

2 At the fifth debate in Galesburg, Illinois, voters appeared to appreciate this implied rejection of Fitzhugh. One sign read: "Small-fisted farmers, mud-sills of society, greasy mechanics for A. Lincoln."

☆ *Bibliographic Essay*

Estimates of the number of books on the American Civil War range in excess of 50,000. Bruce Catton's essay *America Goes to War* (Middletown, CT: Wesleyan University Press, 1958) is an attempt to assess the evolving nature of what he called the world's first modern war. Catton's trilogy (*Mr. Lincoln's Army, Glory Road, A Stillness at Appomattox*), based on regimental memoirs of the conflict, is highly readable. Shelby Foote's three-volume *The Civil War: A Narrative* (New York: Random House, 1958–74) leans more heavily on southern sources. James M. McPherson's *Battle Cry of Freedom* (New York: Oxford University Press, 1988) is an able one-volume historical synthesis. For explorations of honor, see Gerald F. Lindeman's *Embattled Courage* (New York: Free Press, 1987), as well as chap. 2 of Bertram Wyatt-Brown's *Southern Honor: Ethics and Behavior in the Old South* (New York: Oxford University Press, 1982). Also see Thomas Keneally's novel *Confederates* (New York: Harper & Row, 1979), which examines the war from the southern viewpoint in 1862. Burke Davis in *Sherman's March* (New York: Vintage, 1980) is a historical narrative of the Georgia and Carolinas campaigns in which Sherman redefined the nature of war.

Edmund Wilson's *Patriotic Gore* (New York: Galaxy, 1966) is regarded by many historians as eccentric in its emphases, but it is a powerful account by a person both fascinated and repelled by Civil War political thought and culture. George Fredrickson, *The Inner Civil War*, is particularly helpful in its analysis of the impact of Lincoln's interpretation of the war on northern intellectuals.

Harriet Beecher Stowe's relationship to the abolitionist movement is examined in John R. Adams, *Harriet Beecher Stowe* (New York: Twayne Publishers, 1963). Leslie A. Fiedler offers a brief but provocative reading of Stowe's famous novel in *Love and Death in the American Novel* (New York: Dell Publishing, 1960), pp. 259–65. Also see Kenneth Lynn's essay on *Uncle Tom's Cabin*, in *Visions of America* (Westport, CT: Greenwood Press, 1973). Assessments of the abolitionists have changed radically as new generations compare their efforts to current problems and often reach different conclusions. Compare, for example, Stanley Elkins, *Slavery* (Chicago: University of Chicago Press, 1959), with Aileen S. Kraditor,

Ends and Means in Abolitionism (New York: Vintage, 1969), and Merton
L. Dillon, *The Abolitionists: The Growth of a Dissenting Minority* (New
York: W.W. Norton, 1974). Also see Howard Zinn, "Abolitionists, Freedom
Riders and the Tactics of Agitation," in Martin Duberman, ed., *The
Anti-Slavery Vanguard* (Princeton: Princeton University Press, 1965), and
Bertram Wyatt-Brown, "The New Left and the Abolitionists: Romantic
Radicalism in America," *Soundings* 54 (Summer 1971): 147–63. Ronald
Walters's discussion of the abolitionists as a community of believers is
contained in chap. 4 of *American Reformers, 1815–1860* (New York: Hill
& Wang, 1978). John L. Thomas's collection of abolitionist writings, *Sla-
very Attacked* (Englewood Cliffs, NJ: Prentice-Hall, 1965), is a valuable
initial primary source.

Louis Hartz's characterization of the southern defense of slavery as a
reactionary Enlightenment is in chap. 6 of his *The Liberal Tradition in
America* (New York: Harcourt Brace Jovanovich, 1955). Also see William
Sumner Jenkins, *Pro-Slavery Thought in the Old South* (Chapel Hill: Uni-
versity of North Carolina Press, 1935), and Eugene Genovese's interpreta-
tion of Fitzhugh in *The World the Slaveowners Made* (New York: Pantheon
Books, 1969). Richard Hofstadter's discussion of Calhoun is in his *The
American Political Tradition* (New York: Alfred A. Knopf, 1948). Also see
Ralph Lerner, "John C. Calhoun," in Morton Frisch and Richard Stevens,
eds., *American Political Thought* (Itasca, IL: F. E. Peacock, 1983). Emory M.
Thomas examines the paradox of a new society devoted to conservatism
but driven by the demands of war to develop radical policies in *The Con-
federacy as a Revolutionary Experience* (Englewood Cliffs, NJ: Pren-
tice-Hall, 1971). Excerpts from both Fitzhugh's major works and Helper's
Impending Crisis are available in *Ante-Bellum*, ed. Harvey Wish (New
York: Capricorn, 1960). Also see Eric L. McKitrick's anthology, *Slavery
Defended* (Englewood Cliffs, NJ: Prentice-Hall, 1963), which contains
selections from Hammond, Dew, Holmes, DeBow, and others.

Where does one begin to study Lincoln? The standard collection of
his writings is Roy P. Basler's nine-volume edition, *The Collected Works of
Abraham Lincoln* (New Brunswick, NJ: Rutgers University Press, 1953–
55), but Philip Van Doren's one-volume anthology, *The Life and Writings
of Abraham Lincoln* (New York: Modern Library, 1940), which includes a
biography, contains Lincoln's major speeches. William Herndon, who was
Lincoln's crusty law partner, published a biography in 1889. The work
often tells more about Herndon's complex relationship with the president
and his wife than it illuminates Lincoln's life. But it does contain many
insights which later writers have embellished. See David Freeman
Hawke's abridgement, *Herndon's Lincoln* (Indianapolis: Bobbs-Merrill,
1970).

Michael Davis, in *The Image of Lincoln in the South* (Knoxville: University of Tennessee Press, 1971), reviews the various assessments of Lincoln in the region in the ante- and postbellum period. Roy P. Baster, *Lincoln Legend* (Boston: Houghton Mifflin, 1935), is an early attempt to trace
the various "Lincolns" in American political culture. Also see David

Donald, *Lincoln Reconsidered* (New York: Vintage, 1967), and Stephen B. Oates, *Abraham Lincoln: The Man behind the Myths* (New York: Harper & Row, 1984), for discussions of the "Black Easter" and other aspects of Lincoln. Examples of psychologically informed interpretations of Lincoln are Charles B. Strozier, *Lincoln's Quest for Union* (New York: Basic Books, 1982), and George B. Forgie, *Patricide and the House Divided* (New York: W.W. Norton, 1979). Forgie argues that Lincoln's career and political thought were the result of a politically induced Oedipal complex. His psychologically ambivalent relationship with the founding fathers led to the pursuit and "symbolic murder" of Douglas. Harry Jaffa, in *The Crisis of the House Divided* (Garden City, NY: Doubleday, 1959), accepts some of the psychological implications of Lincoln's own quest for immortality in relation to the founders, but he forcefully argues that Lincoln's belief that the Kansas-Nebraska Act represented a real possibility of the nationalization of slavery was well founded and not psychologically motivated nor the result of political opportunism. Don E. Fehrenbacher, *Prelude to Greatness: Lincoln in the 1850's* (Stanford: Stanford University Press, 1962) and David Zarefsky, *Lincoln, Douglas and Slavery* (Chicago: University of Chicago Press, 1990) provide a useful close reading of the issues discussed in the Lincoln-Douglas debates. Douglas has not had many defenders since George Fort Milton's 1934 biography, but Robert W. Johannsen's *The Frontier, the Union, and Stephen A. Douglas* (Urbana: University of Illinois Press, 1989) contends that it was Douglas who epitomized the new West more than Lincoln. Glen E. Throw's *Abraham Lincoln and American Political Religion* (Albany, NY: SUNY Press, 1976) contains thoughtful analyses of the Lyceum speech, the Gettysburg address, and the second inaugural. Many of these interpretations are defended and debated in Gabor S. Boritt and Norman O. Forness, eds., *The Historian's Lincoln* (Urbana: University of Illinois Press, 1988). Frank J. Williams and William D. Peterson have collected essays which examine Lincoln's influence today, particularly among U.S. presidents in their *Abraham Lincoln: Contemporary* (Campbell, CA: Savas Woodbury, 1995).The case for Lincoln as an opportunistic politician is made in Hofstadter's *The American Political Tradition*, and accepted in part in Gore Vidal's novel, *Lincoln* (New York: Random House, 1984).

Early histories of Reconstruction advanced the view that the policies of the radicals were grossly ill conceived. The most influential of these accounts was William A. Dunning, *Reconstruction: Political and Economic, 1865–1877* (New York: Harper & Brothers, 1907). Gradually historians began to question the racial theories of Dunning and his followers. One of the first responses was W. E. B. Du Bois's *Black Reconstruction* (New York: Harcourt Brace Jovanovich, 1935). Du Bois's account of attempts at empowerment by African Americans was persuasively presented, but his Marxist interpretation of Reconstruction as a failed dictatorship of the proletariat was theoretically forced and reduced the study's general impact. Recent accounts have emphasized the spottiness of military occupation and African-American rule; Virginia, the home of the

CSA, had only about a thousand federal troops deployed in the state in 1869, and the only state with a black legislative majority was South Carolina. More recent accounts also have emphasized the responsible and diligent efforts of African-American representatives and citizens to set up public schools and expand government services. See John Hope Franklin, *Reconstruction: After the Civil War* (Chicago: University of Chicago Press, 1961), and Kenneth M. Stamp, *The Era of Reconstruction, 1865–1877* (New York: Vintage, 1965). LaWanda Cox and John H. Cox have collected major documents of the Reconstruction, including reports of the Freedmen's Bureau and speeches of Johnson, Stevens, and others, in *Reconstruction, the Negro and the New South* (Columbia: University of South Carolina Press, 1973).

☆ *Major Works*

1852	*Uncle Tom's Cabin*, Harriet Beecher Stowe
1845	*Narrative of the Life of Frederick Douglass*, Frederick Douglass
1852	"Fourth of July Oration," Frederick Douglass
1856	"What Is My Duty as an Anti-Slavery Voter?", Frederick Douglass
1833	*"Declaration of Sentiments of the Anti-Slavery Society," William Lloyd Garrison
1854	*Sociology for the South*, George Fitzhugh
1857	*Cannibals All!*, George Fitzhugh
1857	*The Impending Crisis*, Hinton Helper
1837	"Speech on the Reception of Abolitionist Petitions," John C. Calhoun
1853	*A Disquisition on Government*, John C. Calhoun
1827	"Colonization Address," Henry Clay
1838	"Lyceum Speech," Abraham Lincoln
1854	"Peoria, Illinois, Speech," Abraham Lincoln
1861	"First Inaugural Address," Abraham Lincoln
1863	"Gettysburg Address," Abraham Lincoln

*A collaborative effort

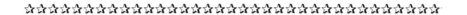

Industrialization

INTRODUCTION

When Charles Francis Adams returned to the United States from Britain in 1871, he observed a silent revolution occurring in America after the Civil War. He was surprised to see "a greatly enlarged grasp of enterprise and increased facility of combination" in the country:

> The great operations of war, the handling of large masses of men, the influence of discipline, the lavish expenditure of unprecedented sums of money, the immense financial operations, the possibilities of cooperation were lessons not likely lost on men quick to receive and to apply all new ideas.

The "new" America that Adams described and whose origins he traced to the unanticipated consequences of the war between the states had created conditions that challenged American beliefs about acceptable social and political arrangements. These arrangements were as disturbing as those of slavery a generation earlier.

The changes in American society were sudden and drastic. The number of manufacturing workers rose by four times between 1859 and 1899; the number of factories doubled between 1879 and 1899. The number of people living in cities increased five times from 1860 to 1900. U.S. steel companies produced 200,000 tons in 1867. By 1895 the steel output of 6 million tons passed that of the British, and 10 million tons a year were produced in America before the turn of the century. The roads, rails, and canals that had been part of the Whig political agenda of "internal improvements" now carried steel and coal to new manufacturing cities, such as Fall River, Bridgeport, Paterson, Scranton, Troy, Youngstown, and Akron.

This transformation placed enormous strains on American political culture. The practice of republican virtue that had been seen as the fabric binding Americans together had been torn on many occasions. We saw how mightily Lincoln strove to identify and preserve a sense of moral purpose even at the cost of civil war. Now it seemed, however, that new men had emerged in American society—men whom Lincoln, even with his fear of "towering genius" that "thirsts and burns for distinction," had never imagined. The new men of business seemed to accept no rules that might halt or slow the creation of their own economic empires. Jay Gould and Jim Fisk, with the complicity of high government officials, attempted to corner the gold market. Oakes Ames and Thomas C. Durant, stockholders in the Union Pacific Railroad, set up a construction company called Credit Mobilier of America and made contracts with themselves for profits ranging from $7 million to $23 million. When a congressional investigation seemed possible, Ames sold stock to congressmen at par. The transactions were made public during the 1872 presidential campaign. A congressional investigation followed, but there were no prosecutions. State politics seemed even more scandal-ridden. Fisk and Gould watered stock in the Erie Railroad; the St. Louis "Whisky Ring" defrauded the government of millions in tax dollars; Collis P. Huntington bribed California state congressmen to support his railroad ventures.

Nor was the task of politics limited to the question of how to assess what some writers would call the new *robber barons* in terms of republican virtue. Nearly 17 million immigrants arrived on American shores between 1850 and 1900. Large numbers coming from European countries were strange and threatening to the "old pioneers." Jacob Riis, himself an immigrant whose photographs did much to awaken a sense of sympathy for the plight of the newcomers, described New York City as a map which, if "colored to designate nationalities, would show more stripes than the skin of a zebra, and more colors than any rainbow." Many Americans failed to see these new settlers as another generation of pioneers, but rather regarded them as bearers of an alien culture who were contributing to the decline of republican values.

This new America also directly challenged other tenets of republicanism. Jeffersonian republicanism had assigned the farmer a central role in the maintenance of republican values. But agricultural workers had declined from 50 percent to 37 percent of the population in the thirty years after 1870, and agricultural daily wages had fallen by 1880 to the level of 1862 wages. Farm prices continued to decline in the postwar period, and shipping costs, manipulated in part by the new rail barons, eroded profits. Sometimes farmers refused to send their produce to market under these conditions. Vernon Parrington, whose own histories were to represent a protest against the decline of agricultural America, wrote in his autobiography that in his boyhood days in Kansas many a time he had warmed himself by the kitchen stove "in which ears were burning briskly, popping and crackling in the jolliest fashion. And if while we sat around such a fire watching the year's crop go up the chimney, the talk became bitter . . . who will wonder?"

Equality of opportunity too seemed to have been shattered in the new America. The *Chicago Evening Post* in 1887 reported a disillusioned immigrant saying, "Land of Opportunity, you say. You know damn well my children will be where I am—that is, if I can keep them out of the gutter." Meanwhile, Marshall Field, the Chicago department store magnate, earned a reported $575 an hour. His employees were paid $12 for a 59-hour work week.

Such disparities of income and opportunity are generally accepted today, when reports of the enormous salaries of corporate CEOs and sports and rock celebrities are routine. But in the nineteenth century such differences in wealth, as opposed to social deference, were regarded as shocking. Theodore Roosevelt, himself a man from a family of considerable wealth, complained about "a riot of individualistic materialism, under which complete freedom of the individual turned out in practice to mean perfect freedom for the strong to wrong the weak. . . ."

But most disturbing of all the discrepancies between traditional American values and the new America created by industrialization was the sheer size of the new economic structures. The name *trust*, which had once connoted belief, faith, and reliability, now became the description of a new kind of industrial organization which challenged the very principle of democratic governance. Trusts were collections of businesses bound legally to one another that in their perfect form captured the entire market for a product through *vertical controls* on the procurement, manufacturing, and retailing of a product. John D. Rockefeller's Standard Oil Company became for many Americans the archetypal model of the trust. When Rockefeller entered the oil business in the late 1860s, he found a highly volatile industry subject to booms and busts. The oil that sold for $20 a barrel in 1860 brought only 10 cents on the 1861 market. Starting with five small refineries, Rockefeller worked out arrangements with railroad companies to lower rates for long hauls. Companies with local markets now struggled with higher costs. To apply even more pressure, Rockefeller developed agreements, called *drawbacks*, with rail officials. Under these agreements, the railroad companies that moved oil for other businesses paid a portion of those rates to Standard Oil! Moving across the country like a conquering general, Rockefeller gobbled up his competitors state by state. Henry Demerest Lloyd wrote in the *Atlantic Monthly* in 1881, after Rockefeller had broken the resistance of independent drillers, that Standard Oil had "done everything with the Pennsylvania legislature but refine it."

Rockefeller's oil empire was not the only instance of successful trust building. Trusts were created in tobacco, sugar, steel, chemicals, and other products. *Holding companies,* a new economic structure that emerged in the late 1880s to avoid antitrust restrictions, continued these consolidations. Between 1895 and 1904 an average of 300 firms disappeared every year. As a result, a single business accounted for 60 percent of the production of a product in fifty different industries. Moreover, the trusts, holding companies, and mergers helped create a new set of huge national economic institutions. Bankers who profited from the sale or merger of business came to supervise this new surplus capital.

How could these features of industrialization be explained? Could this new America accommodate the beliefs in republican virtue, equality of opportunity, and self-governance? Numerous new political theories emerged to answer these questions. And Americans, according to Robert Wiebe, "like so many floating particles" cast about by these changes, "attached themselves to a cause."

THE PROMISE OF SOCIAL DARWINISM

One theory, or more properly one set of theories, that attempted to argue that the changes wrought by industrialization represented a fulfillment rather than a repudiation of American beliefs was social Darwinism. Charles Darwin's publication of *The Origin of Species* in 1859 promised a whole new theory of biological development. Changes in the number and variety of species could be explained in terms of adaptation to changes in the environment. The process by which these changes occurred was characterized by Darwin as *natural selection.* During his famous trip aboard the *Beagle,* Darwin had dinner with the governor of one of the Galapagos Islands, who told him that he could identify what island a tortoise came from by looking at the markings and shape of its shell. Darwin pondered this remark and began categorizing finches by island. He soon discovered that he could correlate beak shapes according to the availability and location of food on an island. Darwin concluded that different species of finch had adapted to different environmental niches.

Darwin's theories remained controversial throughout the century, particularly when he supported the evolutionary theory of human origins in *The Descent of Man* in 1871. By imaginatively borrowing from the theoretical insights of Thomas Robert Malthus, Sir Charles Lyell, and others, and by casting his hypotheses in terms of painstaking empirical research, Darwin created a whole new cosmology of the universe. The mysteries of life itself, including its origins and future, were at least partially revealed in his system.

It is not surprising, then, that others would seek to apply the theory of evolution to the patterns and problems of industrialization. Students of American political thought have marveled at the ideological success of these collective efforts. Eric Goldman has described social Darwinism as a "steel chain of ideas" that prevented reform of the new industrial system for decades. Thomas Cochran and William Miller, in their *Age of Enterprise*, contend that social Darwinism gave "cosmic significance" "to the process of industrialization." "In the age of science, it 'scientifically' justified ceaseless exploitation." Richard Hofstadter has remarked that American business leaders were attracted to the theory "almost by instinct." Yet without denying the hegemony of Darwinist ideas in postbellum America, it should be noted that the social Darwinists were remarkably variable in their applications of evolutionary theory. Perhaps the "steel chain of ideas" was more like a series of nets patched together over the public's mind, sometimes raggedly but still effectively.

Foremost among the social Darwinists was Herbert Spencer. Henry Holt, a New York editor, wrote in his memoirs in 1923 that "probably no other philosopher ever had such a vogue as Spencer had from about 1870 to 1890." Spencer's *Social Statics* sold almost 400,000 copies between 1864 and 1903. When he visited the United States in 1882, he was treated by both business leaders and intellectuals as a hero.

Spencer was born in 1820 in Derby, England, which has often been described as the English *Middletown*. His background was decidedly British lower-middle-class. The son of a dissenting schoolmaster, Spencer was a self-educated man who worked briefly on the railways before finding a position with the *Economist* in 1848. He was a prolific writer *(A System of Synthetic Philosophy* has ten volumes) and less than a warm person. When an admirer told him that his works filled up several yards of space on his shelves, Spencer replied that several yards meant at least three, and that at the moment his books occupied only twenty-one inches, less than three-fifths of a yard.

Social Statics, certainly his most readable work, was, in fact, published eight years before Darwin's *Origin of Species*. In this work Spencer had used the phrase *survival of the fittest* to describe the evolution of societies. He later regarded Darwin's principle of natural selection as a confirmation of his own theory. There is a sense, then, in which Darwin could be regarded as a biological Spencerian. Spencer offered two natural laws to describe this evolutionary process. One he called the *law of equal freedom;* the other, the *law of conduct and consequence*. Spencer asserted that both were expressions of the will of God, thus avoiding the direct theological assault on his theory that so plagued Darwin's formulation.

The law of equal freedom stated that "every man has freedom to do all that he will, provided he infringes not on the equal liberty of any other man." This principle was not, at least in broad outline, any different from the harm principle that John Stuart Mill was to advocate in his famous essay *On Liberty* in 1859. Mill, of course, drew none of the Darwinist implications from his principle, largely reserving the rule to protect freedom of speech and association. Spencer, however, attached to his law of conduct and consequence the principle of the survival of the fittest, which he then applied to liberalism. Spencer argued that only if individuals received the benefits or suffered from the consequences of their actions, could actions most advantageous to the environment be ascertained so that the most fit individuals would survive. To the extent that individuals were not held responsible for their actions, the "good-for-nothings" in society would increase, delaying "that natural process of elimination by which society continually purifies itself."

From these two laws, which were modified slightly in later works, Spencer drew extremely wide-ranging conclusions. He opposed virtually all governmental regulations of the economy, including not only antitrust legislation but also sanitary laws and building codes. Even public schools were a violation of the law of conduct and consequence. Private charity might be permissible to alleviate "superfluous sufferings," but it must take a form in which the sick, "degenerate," or "incapable" would not be encouraged to multiply. It was, he insisted in *Social Statics*, an "impious imprudence" for "political schemers" to attempt to "supersede the great laws of existence." Who could dare to "announce that he and certain of his colleagues have . . . found out a way to improve upon the Divine arrangements!"

Often overlooked, however, in Spencer's system were his later attempts to ascertain the role of industrialization in terms of some larger evolutionary paradigm. In his *Principles of Sociology* he constructed two broad types of human society. Militant societies were based upon the ethical principles of enmity; they survived and grew in terms of their ability to wage war. The use of deadly force was thus socially sanctioned, and the hierarchy required for its success was reinforced through moral codes external to the individual (divine sanction, law, and custom). Submission to authority was demanded. Industrial societies, on the other hand, were based upon the ethical principle of amity and derived their morality from an internal source, which Spencer called *conscience*. Its citizens were industrious, peaceful, and (in Spencer's Victorian mind) also chaste and temperate; they were able to largely ignore the state. Spencer, in fact, suggested that the state itself was likely to disappear among the industrial societies of the future.

How could the proponent of the principle of survival of the fittest speak of societies without conflict and competition? Spencer apparently believed that the industrializing societies of his day were hybrids of his two models; hence, they suffered from the strains of an evolutionary transition. He feared that resort to state regulation in this period of temporary economic strain would cause the new industrial forms of society to revert to the principles of militant societies. Increase the powers of the state under modern conditions of technology, warned Spencer, and there will appear tyrannies more appalling than those of the ancient empire of the Assyrians.

THE AMERICANIZATION OF SPENCERISM

Despite the enormous popularity of Spencer's general theory, Americans were reluctant to accept portions of it. Many of his admirers objected to his attack on public schooling. Others found his anarchist tendencies disturbing. Andrew Carnegie, who considered himself a disciple of Spencer, disagreed with his position on charity and insisted that a good portion of America's economic success could be traced to democratic institutions.

The chief academic interpreter of Spencer in America was William Graham Sumner. Sumner began his career as a clergyman, accepted a position at Yale University in 1872, and spent the next thirty years attacking those who insisted on pursuing "the absurd effort to make the world over." He demanded that socialists, anarchists, reformers, and all those spouting the "gospel of gush" leave the stage of world history. "It is evident," he declared, "that God alone could give distributive justice; and we find, in the world in which we are, that God has not seen fit to provide for it at all." But if social Darwinism was capitalism's version of the Enlightenment, for Sumner it was very short on optimism. Spencer certainly had his moments of gloom, but Sumner often appeared as an old Calvinist divine in Darwinist garb. He refused to justify industrialization as a stage in the progress of freedom. Industrial society requires extreme organization:

> It controls us all. . . . It creates the conditions of our existence, sets the limits of our social relations, determines our conceptions of good and evil, suggests our life philosophy, molds our inherited political institutions, and reforms the oldest and toughest customs, like marriage and property.

The gain in economic organization was won "by narrowing individual range." Modern capitalism was then pulling some institutions into its grasp and at the same time tearing others asunder. Americans must stoically accept the new conditions and not "cry out that liberty is a delusion and a puzzle," but understand that liberty is an "intelligent acceptance of the conditions of earthly life, conformity to them and manful effort to make life a success under them."

Sumner even refused to glorify the new capitalists. Most were "idle or silly or vulgar." He challenged the assumption of the dignity of labor: "It is a good safe phrase, because it sounds well. . . . In truth, dignity is just what labor does not possess; for it always forces a man into strained posture, ungraceful motions, dirt, perspiration, disorder of dress and manner. It is leisure which has dignity."

But like Spencer, Sumner saw no exit from the conditions of the new industrial society. The eight-hour day was a utopian delusion. And while he showed a great deal of sympathy for what he called the "forgotten man" in America, that is, the "industrious self-supporting men and women who have not inherited much to make life luxurious for them," he warned that if Americans were to place more demands on its citizenry, "it will fail to get what it expects." Democracy extended to the economy would create in Sumner's model a *plutocracy*. Many Americans might have concluded that a rule by the rich had already arrived. But Sumner contended that regulation would only produce a "lamentable contest":

> . . . the contest between numbers and wealth is nothing but a contest between two sets of lawyers, one drawing acts in behalf of the state, and the other devising means of defeating those acts in behalf of their clients.

The latter set of lawyers, concluded Sumner, is "far better paid in security and in money." In the end, reformers would only create a new kind of capitalist, a "plutocrat" who, "having possession of capital, and having the power of it at his disposal, uses it not industrially, but politically; instead of employing laborers, he enlists lobbyists" in order to form new organizations "half political and half industrial." There was, then, a sense of the tragic beneath Sumner's polemical essays that may have been lost upon his audiences. Individuals want "perfect happiness" and individual creativity, but nature only cares for the "maintenance of the race."

Other American social Darwinists saw the world in less stark terms. Andrew Carnegie provided one theoretical alternative. Carnegie epitomized both the rags-to-riches model of the new industrial capitalist (he had worked as a bobbin boy in a cotton mill) as well as that model's ruthlessness (he violently suppressed the Homestead steel strike of 1892). In his most well-received essay, entitled "Wealth" (1889), Carnegie took the conditions of industrial society as a given. Industrialization indeed was a mixed blessing. It had created goods that were cheaper and better constructed. "The laborer has now more comforts than the farmer had a few generations ago." But employers now know little about the lives of workers in their factories; there is "great inequality" of wealth and the "concentration of business, industrial and commercial," is "in the hands of the few." These develop-ments have been "hard on the individual" but "best for the race, because it insures the survival of the fittest in every department." "It is a waste of time," concluded Carnegie, "to criticize the inevitable." To socialists who argued for the nationalization of wealth, Carnegie replied that the falsity of that alternative had been established at the dawn of history when individ-uals learned the following golden rule: "If thou dost not sow, thou shalt not reap."

The policy question of the day then could be stated only in these terms: "What is the proper mode of administering wealth after the laws upon which civilization is founded have thrown it into the hands of the few?" Carnegie offered three alternatives: wealth could be left to the fami-lies or descendants of successful industrialists; wealth could be bequeathed for public purposes; or wealth could be given to charities and foundations by those who amassed fortunes. Carnegie adamantly rejected the first alter-native. While he did not believe that the sons and daughters of the wealthy should be cast "adrift in poverty," he felt that inheritance was simply the result of the "vanity" of the parents and often led, as in Europe, to the dis-solution of fortunes through the "follies" of the sons. It was far better, Car-negie argued, for the state to heavily tax the estates of the wealthy to encour-age millionaires to make bequests, or better yet, to encourage the wealthy to give away their "surplus" wealth to noble causes: "By taxing estates heavily at death the state marks its condemnation of the self millionaire's unworthy life."

By advocating the reduction, if not the elimination, of inherited wealth, Carnegie offered a way in which Americans could receive the ben-efits of industrial society and still receive intergenerationally the benefits of equality of opportunity. Moreover, Carnegie's description of the exemplary behavior of the new capitalist (he should "set an example of modest, unos-tentatious living") attempted to incorporate the principles of republicanism into his version of social Darwinism.

APPLIED SOCIAL DARWINISM

How did Americans respond to this interpretation of a new America? Many would reject the entire social Darwinist framework or struggle to revise it. But a lot of other Americans "consented" to this interpretation by attempting to discover ways in which they could survive in the new environment.

One person who provided guidance was a Civil War veteran, former lawyer, real estate agent, and Baptist pastor named Russell Conwell. Con-well gave a speech entitled "Acres of Diamonds" to perhaps as many as 10 million people between 1861 and 1915. The theme of Conwell's address, which was delivered over 6,000 times, was: "You ought to get rich, and it is your duty to get rich." "Money printed your Bible, money builds your churches, money sends your missionaries, and money pays your pastors," Conwell reminded his audience. Only the love of money for itself was an evil, and Conwell urged his audiences against a misplaced sense of overpiousness regarding the accumulation of capital.

Conwell's lecture is often regarded as evidence of the collapse of Christian doctrine in the face of social Darwinism. But this interpretation misses the rapture that enveloped the audiences listening to the evangelist. For while Conwell accepted portions of social Darwinism (for example, he contended that people were poor because of their own "shortcomings"), he drew chiefly a portrait of the beneficent aims to which capital could be directed. Conwell himself donated virtually all his lecture fees to college students (an estimated $8 million) and founded Temple University for students who could not afford to attend traditional colleges.

The utopian appeal of the Acres of Diamonds speech also rested upon Conwell's assertion that opportunities were still available for the American middle class. While he never promised fortunes, he told his audiences that "there is wealth right within the sound of your voice." Assuring his listeners that money could be obtained honestly (or it would be a "withering curse"), Conwell offered a middle-class version of Carnegie's unostentatious millionaire.

Perhaps the most significant popular application of social Darwinism in America was given in the writings of Horatio Alger, Jr. (1832–99). Alger, a Unitarian minister, published over 125 novels, and other writers continued his stories after his death. Even today, while the memories of Raggedy Dick, Tattered Tom, and Matchboy Mark (the heroes of some of the Alger books) have faded, Horatio Alger or *Algerism* is synonymous with the belief that a dedicated and energetic person, however modest his or her origins, can rise to fame and fortune in America.

In actuality, Alger's young heroes rarely rise to the level of a Carnegie or a Rockefeller. Instead, they find middle-class, white-collar positions in the new industrial order. Nevertheless, competition and the struggle for survival are readily apparent in all the Alger novels. His young men are most often cast into the city from an early childhood on the farm and faced with unscrupulous employers, amoral street boys, and not infrequently drunken fathers. In many of his introductions to the novels, Alger points out that his hero is worse off economically than many of his readers. Throughout these works, Alger's characters are reminded that the world does not owe them a living; the difference between the "rich merchant" and the "ragged fellow" lies "not in natural ability, but in the fact that the one has used his ability as a stepping-stone to success, and the other has suffered his to become stagnant, through indolence, or dissipation."

Even with this advice, however, Alger's young heroes need a great deal of help—help from ministers, help from fellow workers, help from the family, and most important of all help from capitalists who see something of themselves in the young men. These potential benefactors are frequently reminded of their obligations to youth in many Alger novels. In *Forging Ahead* he describes the fate of a banker who took no interest in the ambitions of the next generation:

> Joshua Starr was found dead one day in his barn. The property which he had accumulated by miserly ways and unscrupulous dealings, went to a cousin whom he hated. Was his life worth living?

Careful not to overpraise the new captains of industry and finance, but mindful of the treachery and competition in this new America, Alger offers, in the words of Carol Nackenoff, "not a recipe for spectacular success . . . but a map for survival."

THREE CHALLENGES

Although American interpretations of social Darwinism differed considerably as writers attempted to adapt their outlook to the demands of American political culture, its appropriation of the symbols of American political discourse was nearly complete. John L. Commons, who later became a famous labor economist, remembers that in his childhood in Indiana he had been "brought up on Hoosierism, Republicanism, Presbyterianism, and Spencerism." Indeed, Lawrence Goodwyn's observation about populism could be applied to all those in the generation who participated in the various reform movements after the Civil War: "Though the economic realities of their own daily lives made them question the universal beneficence of the new era, so thoroughly had the cult of forward motion infused itself into the very structure of the American idiom" that protesters "encountered great difficulty finding language that could convey their individual disenchantment."

Men and women who attempted to deconstruct social Darwinism and create their own alternative vision of a new industrial America clustered around three major political movements: populism, progressivism, and socialism. Roughly, their efforts form a narrative of the reaction of portions of the farming, middle, and working classes to this new America.

Populism

Perhaps the group that suffered most from the dislocations created by industrialization were America's farmers. The construction of the railroads had opened new markets, and technological advances had increased output. Yet these developments were also paralleled by the struggle to control rail rates and agricultural output. In a sense farming had become commercialized, and farmers themselves had become business leaders. They were no longer producing for their own subsistence and a local market but for the new cities of America. Agricultural output increased dramatically in the years after the Civil War. For example, the wheat harvest rose from 152 million bushels in 1866 to 675 million in 1898. But as Paul Glad reports, the farmer "did not have the market power of the industrialist, the implements manufacturer, and the others who sold to him." Nor did he have the market power of the grain dealers, and at many locations he could not bargain effectively with the railroads. Whether the farmer's plight resulted from overproduction, excessive debt, the power of the rail companies, or some combination of these factors, this group became less and less sympathetic to the images of a new America. A Kansas farmer complained: "There never was, nor can there be, a more brutal, utterly selfish, and despicable doctrine than the Darwinian's 'struggle for existence' when applied to the social relations of man." Farmers began to struggle to create new organizations of political and economic empowerment. Farmer *alliances* were formed in the Northwest and Southwest in an attempt to sell produce to intermediaries and rail officials in blocks. They accepted protest leader Mary Lease's challenge to "raise less corn and more hell" by organizing a third-party movement called the People's party in the 1890s. The high-water mark of this protest was reached in 1896 when the new party was merged with the Democratic party under the leadership of William Jennings Bryan.

What kind of political thought emerged from these struggles? Scholars are divided in their assessment of populism. One view emphasizes the populists' rejection not only of Darwin and social Darwinists but of many features of modern life in general. For example, Edward Shils, in *The Torment of Secrecy*, argues that the populists' proclamation that "the will of the people as such is supreme over every other standard, over the standards of traditional institutions, over the autonomy of institutions and over the will of other strata" is a frighteningly dangerous doctrine. Shils argues that Nazism and fascism in Europe were also forms of populism. In this view populism in its attempt to turn back the clock and return to a simpler age through the collective actions of an uncorrupted "plain people" is an understandable but disastrous response to the problems of industrialization.

A quite different assessment is offered by Norman Pollock in *The Populist Response to Industrial America*. Pollock, largely drawing from his examination of editorials from populist magazines and newspapers, rejects the view that the movement had anything in common with fascist developments in Europe. He contends that Populism's critique of social Darwinism enlarged into a general critique of capitalism. He concludes:

> Is Populism then a socialist movement? Here labels become unimportant; it was far more radical than is generally assumed. Had Populism succeeded, it would have fundamentally altered American society in a socialist direction.

Lawrence Goodwyn, too, in *The Democratic Promise* emphasizes what he regards as the positive contribution of American populism. Arguing that the key to the movement can be discovered in the farmer alliances of the 1880s of which the People's party represented only the "shadow" of the main struggle, he concludes that neither the "capitalist [nor] . . . socialist languages of political description in the twentieth century" adequately characterizes the core of populist theory. For Goodwyn, the populists had grasped a view of how democratic life could be organized under modern conditions that people in neither today's capitalist nor today's socialist societies can grasp.

Still another interpretation has been offered by Richard Hofstadter in *The Age of Reform*. Hofstadter presents a model of two aspects of populist protest, a "soft" and a "hard" side. The former was represented by the *agrarian myth*. Populist rhetoric "looked back to the lost agrarian Eden, to the republican America of the early years of the nineteenth century in which there were few millionaires, and as they saw it, no beggars, when the laborer had excellent prospects and the farmer abundance. . . ." But farmer protest, particularly in its organizational efforts and use of business tactics and political pressure, had also a "hard" side. While the soft portion of populist theory indeed failed (the America of a nation of small farmers would never return), the non-Edenic aspects of populism were relatively successful. Farmers gained control of many state legislatures and congressional committees in Congress. During the Progressive and New Deal eras they obtained protection for their agribusinesses through credits and subsidies. Another version of populism might take the populist rhetoric of the agrarian myth more seriously than Hofstadter had and attempt to see the populists as people trying to use the principles of republicanism as a critique of social Darwinism. But let us take a brief look at populist theory and attempt to see how well these interpretations explain this form of postbellum protest.

Two novels that appeared in America at the close of the 1880s express in dramatic fashion the hopes and fears of the populist movement. One,

Edward Bellamy's *Looking Backward, 2000–1887,* presents an image of a postindustrial utopian America. Another, Ignatius Donnelly's *Caesar's Column,* is an antiutopian prediction of the future of the country.

Bellamy, the son of a Baptist minister, had established himself as a successful novelist when he began work on *Looking Backward,* which he originally conceived as a romance, a "mere literary fantasy, a fairy tale of social felicity." As the work progressed, however, he became convinced that he had discovered the "cornerstone of the new social order." The opening chapter of the book illustrates the juxtaposition of these two aims. Julian West, a well-to-do Bostonian, falls asleep in 1887, and awakes in 2000 to a vastly different social order. This Rip Van Winkle motif permits Bellamy to allow Ward, through his guide, Dr. Leete, to introduce the time traveler to all manner of technological innovations. Bellamy's anticipation of airplanes, radios, credit cards, and shopping centers replete with Musak-like transmissions wafting music through the malls must have fascinated the nineteenth-century reader. But these marvels are not the fulfillment of social Darwinist prophecy. Leete tells Ward that the great trusts of the last century had bred great unions until the people finally discerned the nature of the evolutionary pattern and through a bloodless revolution inaugurated the era of the "Great Trust."

Bellamy outlines the nature of this historical process through the metaphor of a stagecoach:

> The driver was hungry and permitted no lagging, though the pace was necessarily very slow. Despite the difficulty of drawing the coach at all along so hard a road, the top was covered by passengers who never got down, even at the steepest ascents. These seats on top were breezy and comfortable. Well up out of the dust, their occupants could enjoy the scenery at leisure, or critically discuss the merits of the straining team. Naturally such places were in great demand and the competition for them was keen, everyone seeking as the first end in life to secure a seat on the coach for himself and to leave it to his child after him. . . .

When the ascent became especially treacherous, riders in the lower seats of the coach often fell off and were forced to grab at a tow rope. Many "were trampled in the mire." "At such times the passengers would call down encouragingly to the toilers of the rope, exhorting them to patience, and holding out hopes of possible compensations in another world for the hardness of their lot. . . ."

Dr. Leete then proceeds to explain the irrationality of nineteenth-century capitalism. Entrepreneurs could only guess at the marketability of their products. The competitive system bred a "mutual hostility" that prevented the formation of common efforts to discern the most valuable methods and focus for new production. As a consequence, gluts and crises were endemic, creating unnecessary unemployment and idle capital. Capitalists actually discovered that this competition, based upon the "instinct of self-ishness," was "another word for the dissipation of energy." They organized trusts as their "secret of efficient production." "Capital," Bellamy's Dr. Leete explained, "had proved efficient in proportion to its consolidation." When "strangely late in the world's history," the people realized the "obvious fact" that to entrust these new cooperative structures into the hands of "private persons to be managed for private profit" was a "folly similar in kind to that of surrendering the functions of political government to nobles and kings to be conducted for their personal glorification," the state was given authority to become the Great Trust.

Bellamy's explanation borrowed extensively from the social Darwin-ists' theory of industrialization. History was an evolutionary process, as Spencer and Sumner argued; the trusts were a rational development, as Carnegie asserted. But according to Bellamy, the social Darwinists had seri-ously misapplied the logic of their own system. If, as Sumner said, the methods of preindustrial capitalism were so "loose and slack" that they needed to be replaced by the economy of scale offered by large enterprises, there was an irrationality in the present system that evolutionary processes were also destined to overcome. The stagecoach image of society would have to be superseded by new forms of economic organization. Spencer himself had foreseen a utopia emerging just beyond the strains of industri-alization. Bellamy was, in fact, arguing that his own version was based upon a more scientific perception. For Bellamy, part of the reason for the delay in the natural progression of evolution rested upon two common mis-taken beliefs in the nineteenth century, both of which were actually social Darwinist axioms. One was the assertion that "there was no other way in which Society could get along, except the many who pulled at the rope and the few who rode, and not only this, but that no very radical improvement even was possible, either in the harness, the coach, the roadway, or the dis-tribution of the soil." The other was the "singular hallucination which those on the top of the coach generally shared, that they were not exactly like their brothers and sisters who pulled at the rope, but of finer clay in some way belonging to a higher order of beings who might justly expect to be drawn."

But Spencer's industrial society was one in which the state was largely irrelevant. For Bellamy, the state now assumed the functions of all the trusts combined. When Bellamy began writing *Looking Backward* as a fantasy, he had come upon the idea of an "industrial army" as a structure for organizing society. "Instead of a mere fairy tale of social perfection" the book became "the vehicle of a definite scheme of industrial organization." Bellamy combined the practice of universal public education, primarily an American invention, with universal conscription, a Napoleonic innovation, to redefine citizenship under new economic conditions. All men were obligated to serve the state for twenty-four years from the ages of twenty-one to forty-five.[1] Each male citizen would receive as his right a publicly financed education, including food, clothing, and shelter. Upon graduation from school he would be obliged to work for three years in unskilled work as a service to society.

When his service requirement was fulfilled, the member of the industrial army could complete his education in a trade or industrial school. After a period of apprenticeship, he would be free to pursue a career in accord with his talents. Jobs in high demand would be regulated by increasing the number of hours of labor rather than by the market mechanism of selective compensation. Each citizen would receive equal remuneration for his work. There would be no money in Bellamy's utopia. Each citizen was to be given a credit card that could be drawn upon. The figure would be set by dividing the estimated wealth from the next year's production by the number of citizens. In order to prevent the accumulation of wealth, credit accounts could not be carried over from year to year.

The political structure of this new society would be vastly different from both the premises and conclusions of the founding fathers. Political corruption would be minimized, not through federalism and a separation of powers but by reserving decisions to those who have retired from the industrial army. States would be abolished. Having implicitly rejected Madison's maxim that the seeds of conflict are sown in the nature of man, Bellamy assumes that the defeat of economic want has removed the prime source of political discord. Retirees elect a president and Congress whose major functions appear to be limited to accepting or rejecting the reports of ten department heads responsible for the management of the economy.

How should we evaluate Bellamy's Great Trust? From the vantage point of the late twentieth century, *Looking Backward* contains all the features of a totalitarian state. In organizing an entire society as an army, Bellamy ignored an important aspect of military structure. Armies require a hierarchy of command, concentration of power, and obedience to authority. But Bellamy clearly conceived the industrial army as a structural vehicle for promoting a sense of service and communal solidarity. In fact, the Jacksonian slogan, "Equal Rights for All, Special Privileges for None," appears to be the animating motif of the new society. Defending himself from the charge of militarism, Bellamy admitted:

> I confess an admiration of the soldier's business as the only one in which from the start, men throw away the purse and reject every sordid standard of merit and achievement. . . . Is it any wonder that war has a glamour? That glamour we would give to the peaceful pursuits of industry by making them, like the duty of a soldier, public service.

The focus of the book is nearly always upon the equal service that each citizen would perform. In his mind Bellamy had created an army without generals. He was so unconcerned about the bureaucratic and political problems of a planned economy that he devoted only a single chapter to the political structure. The state, at least as Bellamy conceived it, is as limited as the state conceived by Madison. Congress only meets once every five years, and then only to approve or reject administrative reports. Bellamy himself appears to have reevaluated his assumptions regarding a benevolent state. In his companion work, *Equality*, written in 1897, he introduced a number of constitutional safeguards into his system, including the right of recall of public officials.

Nineteenth-century Americans, however, seemed relatively unconcerned about the militarist aspects of *Looking Backward*. There were concerns about the position of women in the utopia, and overpopulation, as well as questions about exactly how the evolutionary process would produce such a society in such a period of time. There was disagreement over Bellamy's abolition of the states. The conservative Atlanta *Constitution* worried that just as *Uncle Tom's Cabin* had led to the "downfall of our property in slaves," Bellamy's book would result in "a new crusade against property and property rights in general." But Bellamy had carefully framed his utopia to appeal to middle-class sentiments. He avoided any mention of socialism because it was a "foreign word" that "smells to the average American of petroleum, suggests the red flag with all manner of sexual novelties, and an abusive tone about God and religion. . . ." His character, Julian Ward, is a comfortable bourgeois, who quickly sees the reasonableness of the premises of the new society as explained by Dr. Leete. The English socialist William Morris had, in fact, complained about the book on precisely these grounds. The "only ideal of life" portrayed by Bellamy was "that of the industrious professional middle class men of today purified from the crime of complicity with the monopolists class, and become independent instead of being, as they now are, parasitical. . . ."

Almost immediately after the publication of *Looking Backward*, over 150 Nationalist Clubs were formed to study the feasibility of Bellamy's proposals. Hundreds of reform newspapers and magazines were created to provide forums of discussion. A. E. Morgan, one of Bellamy's early biographers, writes that "the word 'Nationalism,' as descriptive of Bellamy's movement, was commonly used in current literature, on a par with 'socialism' and 'capitalism.'" *Looking Backward* provided a new language for the ministers, lawyers, and farmers who joined these groups to examine the impact of industrialization. Nationalists created their own party tickets in communities with candidates who campaigned for municipal control of utilities. But the most dramatic impact of Bellamy's book can be found in its influence upon the new People's party. When Daniel De Leon spoke in

Kansas in 1891, he was surprised that the "name of Bellamy brought forth prolonged cheers." When the new party met in Omaha in 1892, Bellamy's ideas were very much in evidence. Nationalists, fresh from creditable initial showings in local elections in Massachusetts, Rhode Island, Michigan, Ohio, and California, formed a significant number of delegates on the platform committee. Farmers were already acquainted with Bellamy since his book had been recommended by leaders of the Farmers' Alliance. Bellamy himself was somewhat ambivalent about the success of his ideas within the new party since he hoped that the Nationalist Clubs would be nonpartisan. Still he proclaimed the Omaha platform, which called for government ownership of the railroads and telegraph companies and the creation of government postal savings banks, Nationalist "in spirit."

Another major and even more direct figure in the populist movement was Ignatius Donnelly. His novel *Caesar's Column*, published in 1891, reveals another aspect of late nineteenth-century protest. Set in the year 1988, Donnelly's work presents a picture quite different from Bellamy's of what social Darwinism had wrought. *Caesar's Column*, like *Looking Backward*, features such technological marvels as airplanes, elevators, electric trains, air conditioning, and glass-roofed restaurants where sumptuous food is served by "star-eyed maidens." But these extravagances are surrounded by a poverty-stricken, brutalized, international labor force whose members are kept under control by an air fleet of "Demons," operated by mercenaries, who fire poison gas at the masses below upon the first sign of resistance. Society is managed by a secret group of plutocrats.

Perhaps the most disturbing aspect of America in Donnelly's presentation is the character of the American citizenry. Donnelly's masses are anything but a downtrodden yet unbowed people. "Brutality above," Donnelly explains, "had produced brutality below." The farmers are not the "honest yeomanry" of the days of Washington and Jackson but their "brutalized descendants . . . cruel and bloodthirsty serfs." The climax of the story occurs when a small secret revolutionary organization buys off the Demon mercenaries and sparks a revolution. The looting and killing reach enormous proportions. New leaders force the plutocrats to pile the bodies of the dead onto an enormous funeral pyre, which is then covered with cement to form a pyramidal monument commemorating the revolution. The city itself is so destroyed by the general conflagration that only a few survivors remain. They capture a plane and fly to Africa, where they create a Christian socialist state.

In many respects *Caesar's Column* is an ugly book. Richard Hofstadter described the novel as "sadistic and nihilistic." *Caesar's Column* demonstrates the basis of concerns about populism. But without excusing the nature of Donnelly's fantasy, the book illustrates what for many populists was the likely consequence of the destruction of republican values.

Nowhere is this more vividly presented than in the preamble to the People's party platform written by Donnelly himself:

> The conditions which surround us best justify our cooperation; we meet in the midst of a nation brought to the verge of moral, political, and material ruin. Corruption dominates the ballot-box, the Legislatures, the Congresses, and touches even the ermine of the bench. The people are demoralized. . . . The newspapers are largely subsidized or muzzled, public opinion silenced, business prostrated, homes covered with mortgages, labor impoverished, and the land concentrating in the hands of the capitalists. . . . The fruits of the toil of millions are boldly stolen to build up newspaper fortunes for a few, unprecedented in the history of mankind; and the possessors of these, in turn, despise the Republic and endanger liberty. From the prolific womb of governmental injustice we breed the two great classes—tramps and millionaires.

Despite the apocalyptic symbolism of both *Caesar's Column* and the preamble to the party platform, the resolutions adopted at Omaha in 1892 were hardly revolutionary or even socialist. Delegates selectively adapted portions of the Nationalist program, such as government ownership of the railroads, but did not recommend either Bellamy's political structure or the abolition of property. One plank recommended that the revenue obtained from a graduated income tax be used to reduce the burden of taxation on domestic industries.

The person who worked to bring together these two features of populist protest—apocalyptic fear for the future of the republic and political reform—was William Jennings Bryan. Bryan's reputation as a leader, let alone as a political theorist, has not fared well. He has been alternately portrayed as a country bumpkin (by Hofstadter) or as an opportunistic politician who dissipated the democratic potential of the populist movement (by Goodwyn).

In his three unsuccessful campaigns for the presidency, Bryan accumulated more affectionate monikers than any other American political leader. The "Great Commoner," the "Nebraska Cyclone," the "Knight of the West," the "Boy Orator of the Platte," the "Silver-Tongued Orator" were some of the descriptions that normally suspicious populist farmers gave to Bryan. Willa Cather, the novelist, reported seeing "rugged, ragged men of the soil weep like children" at Bryan's speeches. Both Hofstadter and Goodwyn attribute this adoration to the simple demagogic nature of Bryan's mind. Thus Hofstadter writes: "He spoke for them so perfectly that he never spoke to them. In his lifelong stream of impassioned rhetoric, he communicated only what they already believed."

It is true that Bryan's political thought stemmed from two fundamental ideas he had received as a child in Illinois. According to John Thomas,

Bryan held to the two pillars of his philosophy of life—natural law and the Christian faith, as exemplified respectively by the Declaration of Independence and the New Testament. There was for Bryan, as well as for his followers, simply nothing else worth believing in. Within this context we need to consider Bryan's remark during his 1892 campaign for Congress that he knew nothing about free silver, but that if the people of Nebraska were for it, he would support it and "look up the arguments later."

Anger over what many Americans regarded as the rejection of these values had reached ugly proportions by the late 1880s, as our review of Donnelly's work suggests. Bryan's innumerable speeches in three national campaigns reiterated these two pillars of his philosophy in two important ways. He reduced the cultural intimidation that many farmers had experienced, and he attempted to define ways in which republican and fundamentalist religious commitments were still relevant to American life. Throughout this effort Bryan's rhetoric might have been hyperbolic, but his interpretation of Christianity was nearly always a gentle one and his republicanism generous. A different sort of populist leader might have carried the movement in the directions outlined by Shils. For example, Tom Watson, the Georgian populist, culminated his career as a virulent racist, and Mary Lease turned to anti-Semitism.

Bryan's "Cross of Gold" address in 1896, which helped him win the Democratic party nomination and its fusion with the People's party, illustrates the nature of his contribution. Bryan began the speech with the assertion that there were those in the country who would give the definition of a businessman too limited an application:

> The man who is employed for wages is as much a businessman as his employer; the attorney in a country town is as much a businessman as the corporation counsel in a great metropolis; the merchant at the crossroads store is as much a businessman as the merchant of New York; the farmer who goes forth in the morning and toils all day—who begins in the spring and toils all summer—and who by the application of brain and muscle to the natural resources of this country creates wealth, is as much a businessman as the man who goes upon the board of trade and bets upon the price of grain. . . . We come to speak for this broader class of businessmen.

Bryan's formulation did not reject but attempted to transform Algerism. If the banker, farmer, and worker were all businessmen, then their activities must be measured by the respective contribution that each of them makes to the nation's wealth. Indeed, for Bryan, the small-town attorney, farmer, and local merchant had as much a claim to national respect as corporate businessmen. "Burn down your cities," he told the crowd that had behaved as a "trained choir" during the address, "and your cities will spring up again as if by magic; but destroy the farms and the grass will grow in the streets of every major city in the country."

There was a measure of assurance in Bryan's conception. He did not advocate socialism but simply demanded a capitalist order in which all individuals could participate economically and politically in a fair way. Andrew Jackson, not Robespierre as critics charged, was the exemplar of the movement. For it was Jackson who had stood for the working capitalist against the "encroachments of organized wealth." Beneath the assertion that in America we all are capitalists and will fight to keep opportunities open was another implied image of the place of economic activity in a republic. Bryan would never deny that economic mobility—even the accumulation of wealth—was not a prime motivation of his expanded definition of businessmen. But his speeches emphasize the efforts of families to engage in other activities. Americans rear children, "erect schoolhouses for the education of their young, churches where they praise their Creator, and cemeteries, where rest the ashes of their dead. . . ." Bryan attempted to paint a portrait of what might be called "neighborhood capitalists," men and women who "employed their skills to better themselves, their offspring, and the communities they lived in."

The cross of gold metaphor that closed his 1896 speech can be understood as a political symbol more complex than the demand for free silver. Bryan is often criticized for emphasizing the silver issue at the expense of other portions of the populist program. But in an important sense the demand for free silver in addition to gold as a monetary standard represented something more than just a misplaced panacea for easy credit and inflated prices on the part of farmers and greed on the part of western mining interests. What Bryan attempted to articulate was a model for America of a nation of capitalists without a capitalist class. To the populists, the gold standard represented the growth of finance capital as an economic structure beyond the influence or control of the average American. "Property is and will remain the stimulus for endeavor and the compensation for toil," insisted Bryan, but the Declaration of Independence had also declared that all men are created equal:

> Our ancestors, when but three millions in number, had the courage to declare the political independence of every other nation; shall we, their descendants, when we have grown to seventy millions, declare that we are less independent than our forefathers?

For Bryan both republicanism and religious values were a legacy that should never be surrendered. They were analogous to the legacy each farmer or merchant left to his children and community in the form of property and religious conviction. When he cocked his head and held out his arms before a hushed convention and declared, "You shall not press down upon the brow of labor this crown of thorns, you shall not crucify mankind upon a cross of gold," he was attempting to assert the cultural power of these twin pillars of faith.

Bryan was not always successful in applying these values to American life nor in living up to his own standards. His opposition to anti-lynching legislation and an anti-Ku Klux Klan plank in the 1924 Democratic party platform are glaring examples of this failure. More complex was his testimony supporting the restriction of teaching evolutionary theory at the Scopes trial in 1925. Leroy Ashby, a biographer of Bryan, traces some of these positions to what he calls "inverted boosterism" on the part of the Great Commoner. Many small towns had adopted a "booster ethos" of "local collective goals, self-sacrificing citizens and a strong public spirit." This expression of community pride, according to Ashby, contained "remnants of the revolutionary era's celebration of classical republicanism in which virtuous citizens were to subsume purely personal gain to community needs." When these efforts failed, as they often did, communities would frequently revert to an inverted boosterism in which any change was regarded as a threat to community values. Bryan did, however, recommend clemency for Leo Frank, a Jewish businessman convicted of the murder of an Atlanta factory girl. Bryan also courageously opposed President William McKinley's imperialist policies in the Philippines, arguing that "a republic can have no subjects."

Despite Bryan's efforts, he lost presidential elections in 1896 and 1900 against McKinley and in 1908 against William Howard Taft. The 1896 election is frequently regarded as a watershed campaign, not only because it featured many of the modern campaign strategies but also because it established a period of Republican presidential dominance that, with the exception of Woodrow Wilson's administration, lasted until 1932. It is important to note that, despite Bryan's crusades, another synthesis of American values had become dominant.

McKinley, guided by his brilliant campaign manager, Mark Hanna, attracted enormous amounts of corporate contributions for his effort, but the candidate's message openly rejected class conflict (or conflict of any kind). America, argued McKinley, could create a "progressive society" (not to be confused with the *progressive movement* that was soon to emerge) in which both corporations and workers could live in harmony. Unlike many business leaders, McKinley and Hanna supported unionization as a legitimate avenue for stabilizing relations between capital and labor. McKinley largely ignored the image of society as the survival of the fittest and instead offered voters a vision of America as a society with a *harmony of interests*. He did retain, however, Alger's basic premise that economic mobility was still possible in a corporate society through the careful supervision of the economy. "I believe," he told Pennsylvania miners, that "the business of this free government is to preserve the American market to the American producer, whether in the factory or the farm, and to preserve the American mines and the factories of the American workingmen." Describing himself as the worker's "best friend," McKinley attacked the Democrats' adoption of a silver standard by arguing that only "sound money" was in the interest of the worker: "When the miners of West Newton have dug their coal by their honest toil, they want to be paid in dollars that are equal to the best dollars of the world. . . ." The Republicans employed two symbols to counteract Bryan's cross of gold. One was the dinner pail to designate prosperity; thousands of replicas were passed out at campaign rallies. The other symbol was the American flag. McKinley remained at his home in Canton, Ohio, during the campaign, but Hanna had brigades of Civil War veterans travel throughout the country proclaiming that "1896 is as important as 1861." Distraught Democrats came to see the flag itself as a party banner and often ripped them from the trains.

Progressivism

The populist movement collapsed in 1896, although Bryan carried his version of some of its themes in subsequent campaigns. Goodwyn concludes that the populists "became deferential, either consciously or unconsciously" after the election, while the McKinley forces "advanced from confidence to arrogance." But this particular Republican synthesis was short-lived. Another stratum in American society emerged with amazing rapidity to challenge the premises of the new industrial order.

The American middle class had been openly hostile to the populist movement. The People's party and Bryan's fusion ticket were not portrayed as besieged Jeffersonian yeomen but as dangerous "anarchists, howlers, tramps, highwaymen, burglars, crazy men, wild-eyed men . . . men with long beards matted together with filth from their noses" whose body odor "would have knocked down a brazen bull." But often the very same people who proclaimed the need for order in the 1890s led the ranks of reformers a few years later. Theodore Roosevelt, who had once volunteered to head a regiment to repress the populists, led the reform movement as a third-party presidential candidate in 1912. William Allen White, the Kansas newspaper editor, complained bitterly about the Farmers' Alliance with its "demagogic rabble rousing" in 1890, only to confess ten years later that "as a child of the governing classes" he had been "blinded" by his own birthright.

There had been a brief reform impulse in the 1870s as many middle-class Republicans came to be so repelled by political corruption that they bolted the party in 1884. But the *mugwumps*, as the nickname implied, were men of high economic stature who were quite conservative. What created the massive shift in opinion and theory away from social Darwinism and Algerism that moved across the middle class at the turn of the century?

Richard Hofstadter argues that the origins of progressivism were primarily psychological. As a "status revolution," progressivism resulted from the realization that the old middle class was being replaced in power and prestige by new corporate elites. Small-town business leaders were being pushed aside by franchises and chains. Ministers found that their positions on college boards of trustees were being taken by the new philanthropic robber barons. Lawyers found themselves driven to accept positions in large corporations rather than settling into private practice. For Hofstadter, progressive thought was so driven by this status deprivation that its goals tended to be moralistic, culturally intolerant, and given to the acceptance of "ceremonial" resolutions of political and economic problems. Another view, offered by Robert H. Wiebe, traces progressivism to the emergence of a new middle class created by industrialization. Wiebe argues that progressivism emerged from people with outlooks created by the new industrial structure. Physicians, business leaders, academics, scientists, engineers, and social workers—the representatives of new or transformed professions—attempted to provide solutions to problems caused by industrialization through the application of scientific methods. For Wiebe, the new middle class hoped to "fulfill its destiny through bureaucratic means."

Gabriel Kolko offers a decidedly critical assessment of progressivism in *The Triumph of Conservatism: A Reinterpretation of American History, 1900–1916*. Kolko argues that since many nineteenth-century robber barons supported the progressive movement, the entire reform period can be explained as a result of their efforts to rationalize the chaos of the production process and the structures of capital accumulation. According to Kolko, the new corporations were the main beneficiaries of government regulation. Kolko may have mixed cause and effect in his analysis; but his study, as well as Hofstadter's and Wiebe's, does raise the question, "What did the progressives want?" An answer to this question is difficult because of the tremendous size and scope of the movement. As historians Arthur S. Link and Richard L. McCormick conclude:

> Progressivism was the only reform movement ever experienced by the whole nation. Its national appeal and mass base vastly exceeded that of Jacksonian reform. . . . Wars and depressions had previously engaged the whole nation, but never reform.

We can gain some appreciation for the validity of these interpretations through a brief analysis of three progressive thinkers: Jane Addams, Thorstein Veblen, and Herbert Croly.

Jane Addams's social background fits well with Hofstadter's description of a progressive. She was the daughter of a Cedarville, Illinois, mill owner. Her house, she remembers in her autobiography, was the largest in the town. As Christopher Lasch notes in his study of reformers, the young Addams, whose heroes were her father and Abraham Lincoln, realized that America was turning away from men of "entrepreneurial appetites and republican zeal" for leadership and toward robber barons and big-city bosses. Graduating from Rockford Seminary and briefly attending medical college after her father's death, Jane Addams then traveled through Europe as many young well-to-do women did in her generation in search of "culture." But Addams became disgusted with her aimless pursuit of the arts and returned to the United States in 1889. She was determined to set up a settlement house in Chicago, which she later called *Hull House*. Her efforts served as a model for thousands of reformers across the country. Young men and women, many from similar family backgrounds to Addams's, worked at the settlements for a few years before taking up professional careers. Others, like Addams herself, made reform into a profession. *Twenty Years at Hull House* is Addams's own account of the activities of the settlement house on Chicago's West Side. In reviewing the activities of Hull House, Addams shows how truly innovative the settlement workers were. The movement provided impetus for the establishment of neighborhood playgrounds; it created shelters for battered women; it worked for housing reform; it ran voter registration and education campaigns; and it provided child-care services and meeting places for union members.

In England, settlement workers referred to their movement as *practical socialism*, but Addams preferred to see her efforts as part of an attempt to rebuild urban neighborhoods suffering from industrial dislocation, overcrowding, and ethnic antagonisms. Progressives in general, while taking an interest in immigrants, were unable or unwilling to see the new Americans at least partially on their own terms. As Richard Hofstadter writes:

> The reformer was a mystery. Often he stood for things that to the immigrant were altogether bizarre, like women's rights and Sunday blue laws, or downright insulting like temperance.

Addams, too, could be insulated by middle-class sensibilities. She confesses in her memoirs that once she brought to Hull House a temperance speaker who was listened to politely by a group of Italian women. After the speech was over, the women brought out some bread and wine and offered both to the horrified guest! But Addams's message was that people must come to understand the hopes and fears of others in order to fully transform society.

Addams's essays explore this theme. Her accounts of the social problems that progressives focused upon—urban corruption, poor housing, and factory conditions—attempt to understand the underlying conditions for the disintegrative tendencies of modern urban life. They seek to offer new forms of community to overcome those problems. In "Why the Ward Boss Rules" (1898), she insists that the identification of the immigrant with corrupt party machines is not the result of "corrupt and illiterate voters." Aldermen give presents at weddings, buy "tickets galore" for benefits for widows, distribute turkeys on holidays. "Indeed," Addams asks, "what headway can the notion of civic purity, of honesty, of administration, make against this stalking survival of village kindness?" Not until reformers develop a "like sense of identification can we hope to modify ethical standards." In "Immigrants and Their Children" (1910), she addresses the problem of cultural disintegration at the personal level. Noting how the Italian women who visited Hull House felt despair over the "loss" of their "Americanized children," she asks why "should the chasm between fathers and sons, yawning at the feet of each generation, be made so unnecessarily cruel and impassable among these bewildered immigrants?"

As a small effort to remedy this situation, Addams created a Labor Museum at Hull House, which was designed to demonstrate the vernacular domestic culture. Women would give presentations to their own children and to other children about their handicrafts and culinary skills. To Addams the museum provided an opportunity for parents to become teachers— "a pleasant change from the tutelage in which all Americans, including their own children, are apt to hold them."

Like nearly all middle-class reformers, Addams had a special repugnance for the use of alcohol, but she struggled to restrain her own feelings in *The Spirit of Youth and the City Streets* (1909). The "gin palaces" of Chicago were indeed "lurid places" that preyed upon youth. But these young people had daily been herded into factories that demanded labor "continually more monotonous and subdivided"; in the tenements there were no village greens or peasant festivals where the youth could congregate. Society did not care at all how the youth might fulfill "their immemorial ability to affirm the charm of their existence." For Addams, the gin palaces would fade away only when some alternative kind of social life could be provided.

Perhaps the most effective of all Addams's essays is her interpretation of the Pullman strike of 1894. In fact, "A Modern Lear" (1894) is a neglected masterpiece of American political thought. Unlike many of the new corporate leaders, George Pullman took a special interest in the workers employed at the Pullman Palace Car Company. He had created a model company town outside Chicago that was, in the words of one admirer, a place from which "all that is ugly, discordant, and demoralizing is eliminated." When he insisted upon successive wage reductions, however, workers in his company demanded arbitration. Pullman refused. Workers struck and were soon supported by the American Railway Union, led by Eugene V. Debs. The strike was broken when President Grover Cleveland sent federal troops to Chicago to enforce a court injunction. Many Americans were terrified at the realization that a whole nation could be paralyzed by a strike, especially a strike against an internationally recognized "model" employer. As a result, they welcomed Cleveland's action. Addams herself was somewhat ambivalent. She supported the workers' cause but was skeptical of the value of strikes. In her essay, which was originally read before the Chicago Women's Club, Addams drew upon Shakespeare's play to interpret the event. In the first act King Lear demands elaborate expressions of gratitude from his three daughters. When one of them, Cordelia, who loves her father more than the others, refuses to acquiesce in this spectacle, Lear responds violently. The result is a tragedy for Lear, Cordelia, and the whole kingdom. Pullman was a modern Lear, and the strikers were modern Cordelias. The lesson of Lear modified and softened Addams's judgment of the workers. Pullman was in many respects a great man but, like Lear, he had "ignored the common ancestry of Cordelia and himself." And, like Cordelia, gratitude royally demanded had produced a rejection and a transformation of the workers. For Addams, the Pullman workers, however generously they may have been treated compared to employees in other industries, had not been treated with the dignity required by independent human beings. "The president of the Pullman company," concluded Addams, "thought out within his own mind a beautiful town. He had power with which to build this town, but did not appeal to nor obtain the consent of the men who were living in it." Herein lay Pullman's failure (and though Addams does not say so directly, his culpability):

> The most unambitious reform, recognizing the necessity for this consent, makes for slow but sane progress, while the most ambitious of social plans and experiments, ignoring this, is prone to the failure of the model town of Pullman.

"A Modern Lear" was such a powerful address that Addams's friends urged her not to publish it. Not only had Addams applied the political principles of consent to economic structures and demystified Pullman's public persona by comparing him to the foolish and arrogant Lear, but she had also supplied a warning that was probably not lost upon the women's club audience; reformers must look into their own hearts for evidence of paternalism lest it lead to tragedy.

In later years Addams lost a good deal of political influence by opposing America's entry into World War I (although she received the Nobel Peace Prize in 1931). But her public life and writings provided a powerful moral exemplar for reformers in the progressive movement.

Thorstein Veblen was in many ways the antithesis of Addams in personality and sentiment. While Addams was a public and engaged person, Veblen was retiring and committed to what he regarded as a scientific solution to the problems of the newly industrial America. So eccentric, in fact, was Veblen that he had difficulty finding a niche in the relatively tolerant confines of the academy. Sometimes Veblen would give all his students As; at other times he would give them all Cs, regardless of their personal effort. But Veblen had a caustic, incessantly inquiring mind—a trait illustrative of the progressive reformers.

Veblen, probably the most trenchant critic of capitalism among the progressives, was ironically also a social Darwinist. He had studied at Yale under William Graham Sumner and written extensively about the superiority of Marxism over Darwinism. Veblen always assumed in his works that the needs of a viable social order inevitably take precedence over the individuals that compose it. But Veblen's Darwinism was of a unique kind. Eric Goldman has called it *reform Darwinism*, and David Reisman has called it *Socialist Darwinism*. Perhaps *technocratic Darwinism* might be an appropriate characterization, but even this doesn't quite capture the nature of Veblen's system.

Like the Darwinists, Veblen asserted the existence of certain instincts. But unlike the Darwinists, he added workmanship and curiosity to the instinct for survival. Moreover, instincts could be repressed and redirected (*contaminated* was Veblen's term) for centuries. Like the Darwinists, Veblen asserted that human societies progressed through stages. But unlike Spencer, who posited the emergence of an industrial society over a militant society, Veblen hypothesized the existence of a savage society that had been overtaken by a predatory one.

Veblen's anthropology is important for an understanding of his economic thought. Savage societies, of which the Neolithic form is his most common example, are small, equalitarian, and peaceful communities. Veblen describes a *fall* from savagery and its replacement by a barbaric society that extended through the Middle Ages. In this barbaric society male gods replaced female ones; because an economic surplus could be produced, a new form of human behavior emerged, which Veblen calls *predatory emulation*. Individuals, tribes, armies, classes, and states preyed upon people who were militarily or economically weaker. The display of the triumphs of the predators became a standard for imitation by other groups.

The Theory of the Leisure Class (1899) applies this anthropological speculation to the American economy of the Gilded Age. The new industrial elite, for Veblen, is a product of predatory emulation in a society in which pecuniary displays, rather than military ones, are the dominant forms of activity. The portrait he paints of this new elite is detailed and merciless. Every activity of the new industrialists—from their schooling to their pets, homes, silverware, and clothes—is portrayed as a form of display. To describe these activities, Veblen invented a series of terms that are still part of contemporary social science: *conspicuous consumption* (the display of material possessions); *conspicuous waste* (the display of destroying material possessions); and *conspicuous production* (the creation of factories as means of display). What Veblen attempted to do was to show that Spencer's Darwinism was a faulty theory. The new captains of industry were closer to Spencer's warring Aztecs of a militant society—with their reckless displays of power and "quasi-peaceful" methods of competition—than to the productive geniuses of an industrial society. According to Veblen, their activities were largely irrelevant to the Darwinist injunction of survival of the fittest.

Many contemporary critics of Veblen have argued that, for all its satirical insight, *The Theory of the Leisure Class* was more a description of the cultural tastes of a single *nouveau riche* elite in a particular period of time and country. The corsets, elaborate picnics, and numerous servants described by Veblen are, after all, not activities of today's rich. But Veblen would have been the first to accept this criticism, for he thought he saw the beginnings of a new economic and social order in this emerging industrial society. Imbedded in its structure were the really productive individuals of a new order. The secret of industrial society was machinery; the engineers who designed machines and the workers who ran and fixed them were the economically functional class.

Veblen thought the days of the robber barons were numbered. In support of this assertion, he relied upon his own interpretation of Darwinism. For if the captains of industry engaged in no significant economic activity, society would eventually recognize the members of the truly useful class. At his most optimistic, he envisaged a return to the principles of a savage society with a technological base. The instincts of workmanship and curiosity would again be recognized; a "democratic commonwealth" would emerge in which people would again live under the "ancient and altogether human rule of Live and Let Live." But at other moments Veblen seemed to posit a technological version of Darwinism. He developed a theory of technological lag, according to which technological change is modified by cultural constraints. When imported by a different society, however, Veblen argued that technology is "stripped of most or all of its anthropomorphic or spiritual values and limitations." Thus he suggested that a future world economy would be propelled by severe competition and instability.

If Veblen attempted to *deconstruct* the new men of industry for the cause of reform, Herbert Croly, cofounder of the *New Republic*, aimed at American politicians. *The Promise of American Life* (1909) was an extremely influential book in the progressive movement. Judge Learned Hand sent a copy to Theodore Roosevelt, who was on safari in Africa. TR, an inveterate if casual reader, was enthralled by the book and, upon his return to America, immediately invited Croly to lunch at his home on Oyster Bay. It would be fascinating to know the nature of the conversation that took place between the man Louis Hartz called "our only Nietzschean president" and the retiring Croly. For the author of what Roosevelt called "the most profound and illuminating study of our national conditions which has appeared for many years" was intellectually an unusual man. The son of British immigrants and eccentric political reformers, Croly had a political vision that was greatly influenced by European thought, especially the writings of French philosopher Auguste Comte. This background contributed to a distinctive emotional distance from the progressive movement. Writing from the perspective of an outsider-insider, Croly managed to combine both moral fervor (which one critic characterized as "Crolier than thou") and analytic detachment in his critique of American life. Eric Goldman has described Croly's attitude toward the American progressives as "the way foreign ambassadors often talk about American baseball games." "He was there, he wanted to be part of it all, but he remained an outsider who could not help wondering at some of the antics he saw."

The basic argument of *The Promise of American Life* involves a direct attack on one of the central political figures of American culture, Thomas Jefferson. The Sage of Monticello had been (and still is) regarded by most American reformers as the quintessential democrat. Croly, however, takes another look at the battles between the Republicans and the Federalists, especially between Jefferson and Hamilton, and concludes that Jefferson's "conception of democracy was meager, narrow and self contradictory" while Hamilton's vision was "one of energetic and intelligent assertion of the national good." Jefferson's distrust of the state, his emphasis on localism, and his commitment to the principle of "equal rights for all, special privileges to none" had corrupted every democratic reform movement that followed him. The Jacksonians had replicated Republican errors, as had the populists and the progressives.

Hamilton, on the other hand, held a national vision that Jefferson lacked. He understood the positive role that the federal government can perform in promoting economic prosperity. He convinced the powerful propertied interests to support the Constitution, and he had a conception of America as a great world power. Croly too had kind words for the Whigs as the party of "national ideas." While he was quick to remind his readers that the ideas of Hamilton and the Whigs were flawed by their adherence to aristocratic concepts, Croly insisted that the "nationalism of Hamilton . . . was more democratic . . . than the indiscriminate individualism of Jefferson."

What was the "promise of American life" ? According to Croly, Americans have historically defined the promise in terms of individual economic prosperity, but the promise also implies certain responsibilities:

> [T]he American national Promise . . . demands . . . that individuals shall love and wish to serve their fellow countrymen, and it will demand specifically that in the service of their fellow countrymen, they

shall reorganize their country's economic, political, and social institutions and ideas.

Hamilton had discerned a national purpose beyond "the parade of individualism," and Croly desperately hoped to convey this insight to the
progressives. Somehow reformers must capture the conservative insight of
America as a national community and attach it to programs of democratic
reform.

The political agenda outlined by Croly involved the regulation of corporations as well as unions by the federal government (trust busting was
another anachronistic Jeffersonian mistake), a national inheritance tax, and
what we would now call an industrial policy of encouraging business initiatives. But most of all Croly called for the emergence of a new political leadership. Unlike many progressives, he distrusted reforms that extended
democracy since he thought that by themselves they would only be corrupted by Jeffersonian politicians. Croly's open admiration for men like
Hamilton, Clay, Webster, and Lincoln led to his plea for "exceptional" individuals to educate in the public sentiments of brotherhood and national
purpose in "a popularly interesting manner." And, of course, as Machiavelli
had his Cesare Borgia, Croly had his Theodore Roosevelt. "More than any
political leader, except Lincoln, his [TR's] devotion both to the national and
to the democratic ideas is thorough-going and absolute."

Both Veblen and Croly represented in important ways Wiebe's interpretation of progressivism. Veblen exalted a new figure in the industrial
order, the technocrat, and attempted to give to him the status the public had
reserved for the robber barons. Croly, too, insisted that the economy could
not be turned back and that industrialization offered new opportunities for
the creation of national leaders and bureaucracy. Progressive politics
would, however, prove to be more complex than either writer anticipated.

Woodrow Wilson defeated TR in 1912, at least in part on the principle
that Jeffersonianism could be applied to national problems and that the
"new nationalism" was a form of paternalism. "Free men need no guardians" was Wilson's campaign theme, and while both TR and Croly looked
to war as a mixed blessing that invigorated nationalism, it was precisely
American participation in the European conflict in 1917 that led to the
rapid dissipation of the progressive movement. After the war, conspicuous
consumption seemed to pervade the whole population, not just the captains of industry.

Socialism

In 1912, when the entire nation seemed enveloped in progressive reform,
Eugene V. Debs polled nearly a million votes as the Socialist party's candidate for president of the United States. More than a thousand Socialists

held elected office, including a congressperson from Wisconsin and mayors of Flint, Michigan; Butte, Montana; and New Castle, Pennsylvania. There were five English-speaking daily Socialist newspapers and eight in other languages, nearly 300 weeklies, and ten monthly magazines. The total circulation of the Socialist press may have reached 2 million. America, which had proved a fertile ground for utopian communal experiments in the antebellum period, now seemed to be in the process of creating a Socialist movement as powerful as those that had emerged earlier in many European nations. In 1912 many Socialists predicted that progressives would soon join their movement. But while the period from 1900 to the First World War is often referred to as the *golden age* of American socialism, in a few short years the movement would be dead and the Socialist party nearly moribund.

Why did the movement fail? Many writers contend that the party's opposition to the war effort not only split the movement but also placed the party in a position that made it vulnerable to government repression. Others blame the rapid decline upon factionalism within the movement over such questions as the use of violence, the role of trade unions, support for the Russian Revolution, and the inability of Socialist leaders to respond constructively to middle-class progressive concerns. Explanations of this sort can be grouped as *internal factors*. That is, so these arguments go, had Socialists avoided a confrontation with the government in 1917, or had they spent more effort appealing to the American public at large and to progressives than arguing among themselves, the history of American socialism would have been different. Another set of explanations emphasizes *external factors*. Socialists looked to Europe for models of movement building and the creation of a Socialist agenda, although conditions in America demanded an indigenous response. The most critical version of this argument suggests that no ideology advocating a significant expansion of state power, the replacement of individualism with collectivism, and the abandonment of equality of opportunity can succeed in America, even in a period of crisis. Socialists were destined to remain in the wilderness in terms of participation in American political culture, however united and strategically gifted they might have been.

One way to resolve the debate over internal and external factors is to look at the responses of Socialist leaders to industrialization. We can then attempt to assess the potential of their theories. Even before World War I and the Bolshevik revolution placed enormous strains upon American Socialist theory, there were, in fact, several competing visions within the movement. Within the Socialist party there was a right wing led by Victor Berger, leader of the Wisconsin Socialists. Closely allied to Berger on many issues were the New York Socialists, led by Morris Hillquit from his base in the garment workers' union. In many ways the theoretical focus of the right-center wing of the party came from Europe. Both Berger and Hillquit envisioned an American social democracy led by a worker-based electoral coalition. Berger had actually anticipated many criticisms of Marxist economic and political theory before Eduard Bernstein published his famous *Evolutionary Socialism* in 1899. Both Berger and Bernstein argued for the abandonment of revolution as a goal of the movement; they deemphasized class conflict and committed themselves to free speech and elections. In 1905 Berger declared that he was "proud of being called the 'American Bernstein'" and refused to sign the 1904 party platform until all references to *The Communist Manifesto* were deleted (which they were).

The Wisconsin Socialists were quite effective in winning reform campaigns in American cities. Running on a platform of better services and schools, municipal ownership of utilities, and civil service reform, these Socialists were often able to defeat both Republican and Democratic candidates. Building theoretically on local successes, they saw a Socialist future gradually emerging from a growing collection of small- to medium-sized Socialist cities. More radical members of the party referred to this approach as *sewer socialism*, but Hillquit defended the program by insisting that the capitalist parties' reforms were ad hoc while municipal socialists' reforms were like a table d'hôte dinner in which each course logically followed the next.

Miles away, both theoretically and literally, were the southwestern Socialists. Nearly 17 percent of Oklahoma's citizens voted for Debs in 1912, and Oklahoma, Texas, Arkansas, and Louisiana together accounted for a tenth of the Socialist party's national vote in 1912. The rank and file of the right-center wing was composed largely of skilled craftsmen and organized labor; the southwesterners were small farmers or sharecroppers who had turned to socialism after the collapse of the populist movement. As James Green notes, these Socialists looked back to the radical traditions of the nineteenth century—not just to populist agrarianism, but further back to the natural rights philosophy articulated by Tom Paine and Thomas Jefferson. As a revivalist crusade it created a kind of religious enthusiasm. Green argues that the southwestern Socialists enriched socialism by "relating their radicalism to these native traditions." But this wing of the party also placed major strains upon the national movement. Socialism was primarily an urban movement, and Marxism had little to say about the farm *problem* save for collectivization, which was anathema to the struggling farmers. These tensions are illustrated in an article written for *American Magazine* in 1908 by a journalist surveying the growth of socialism in the region:

> "You city people don't realize how deep the old passion for democracy still is in the country region," said the Socialist organizer. "He sees that democracy is going; he sees the power converging into that Wall Street group. And he has about made up his mind that the only way

to get that power back is by government ownership of the trusts and railroads. He showed it by his vote for the populist party. That party sold him out. And now he is coming our way."

"But," I argued, "as far as I can find, you people want not only the trusts but every man's private business, give it all to the politicians. How about the farmer's vote then?"

"That's way off in the future," he said. "We're busy these days with a string of concrete issues. Times have changed. We're getting votes. And the farmer agrees to enough."

"First," said one old codger, "I don't want every blamed thing put under the government, but I do like the idea of Uncle Sam bein' the big dog again an' Wall Street bein' the pup. Second, I don't believe in this here class struggle if you mean only them union strikes. But if you mean the democracy agin the men who are stealing its independence, then I'm with you hard."

"You took him in on that basis?" I asked. He nodded. "Isn't that stretching Marx a bit?"

"Let him stretch," said the Socialist stoutly. "Stretching means growth, doesn't it? On the road I'm always picking up rattling good points from new kinds of recruits."

Another wing of the party was the International Workers of the World (IWW), who were also known derisively as the *Wobblies, I Won't Work, I Want Whiskey, Irresponsible Wholesale Wreckers*, and during World War I as *Imperial Wilhelm's Wreckers*. The IWW was formed in 1905 when the Western Federation of Mine Workers left the American Federation of Labor (AFL). Frustrated by their experiences with the conservative AFL led by Samuel Gompers, which was committed almost exclusively to organizing only skilled workers, the IWW proclaimed itself a *revolutionary union*. It adopted a political theory called *syndicalism*, derived in part from French radicalism. The conventional definition of a union strike called for withholding services in order to gain union recognition as a collective bargaining agent for workers and to increase wages and improve working conditions. For the Wobblies, the strike was not a strategy for winning concessions from business, but for destroying and eliminating employer ownership. The IWW held to the belief that if workers could form a single union, one massive strike could destroy capitalism. America, and eventually the world, would then be governed by a federation of worker-owned industries. To that end its leaders often advocated the use of violence to further the success of strikes. In reality, IWW strikes (when they were won) did lead to settlements, but IWW unions refused arbitration, fact-finding, and even contracts. They simply insisted that when their demands were met they would return to work.

The Wobblies did make a significant theoretical point in their analysis of the transformation of work at the beginning of the century. Unionization was largely confined at the time to craft unions of skilled workers (the CIO was not formed until the 1930s); increasingly workers at the turn of the century were becoming "de-skilled" by the use of technology in the factory. As the authors of the 1905 preamble of the IWW observed, the "laborer's home" as a skilled craftsman was rapidly disappearing: "Laborers are no longer classified by differences in trade skill, but the employer assigns them according to the machines to which they are attached." The IWW attempted to organize the unorganized, western miners and lumberjacks, immigrant textile workers, and itinerant laborers whom no other union could or would attempt to reach. But the IWW's anarchism, its open talk of violence and revolution, and its own general bravado angered and terrified the American middle class. Community after community in the West adopted antisyndicalist statutes to keep the IWW from organizing in their towns and cities. For Socialists like Berger and Hillquit, the IWW was a threat to their attempts to make American socialism legitimate. At the 1912 Socialist party convention a plank was passed calling for expulsion of any member who "opposes political action or advocates crime, sabotage, or other methods of violence as a weapon of the working class to aid in its emancipation." A year later Bill Haywood, the leader of the IWW, was expelled from the executive committee of the party and soon left the Socialist party altogether.

Most of the eastern Socialists were supportive of the Berger-Hillquit wing of the party, but a group of influential intellectuals centered in Greenwich Village frequently supported the IWW within the Socialist party. Led by Max Eastman, Floyd Dell, and John Reed, who edited the iconoclastic *Masses* magazine, this group advocated a modernist, aesthetic concept of socialism that, in reality, was far removed from both the trade-union radicalism of Berger and Hillquit and the cowboy anarchism of Haywood. Dell had once referred to 1912 as the *lyrical year* in which love, sexual freedom, and artistic expression seemed to wash over the literary community of which he was a part. For these *lyrical Socialists*, as they are now sometimes called, Haywood was a romantic figure and the IWW a romantic movement. In the words of the poet Harry Kemp, who traveled from New York to support the IWW-led Paterson strike in New Jersey in 1913, there was "an unsmoothed vigor or rough balladry" in the songs they sang and a "direct contact with life, as invigorating as strong drink that took us captive."

Presiding over and attempting to unify these competing strands of socialism was Eugene V. Debs. The skilled, intellectual, relatively comfortable German-born workers in Milwaukee, the Jewish garment workers on the lower East Side of New York, the men of western silver mines and lumber camps, the dispossessed Oklahoma farmers, the urban New York radi-

cals on a moral holiday from the small towns from which they had emigrated—all these groups represented cultural enclaves in the American
political culture that organizationally coalesced around the general symbols of socialism. There was, in fact, very little specifically to unite them
since the sources of their alienation from American society were objectively
disparate. The internal factors were the products of American culture itself.
Debs's burden was to create a framework that was meaningful to these
alienated segments. At the same time he was to attempt to expand the ideology of socialism beyond the enclaves from which it had emerged.

Debs had come to socialism as a result of the strains of industrialization. Born in Terre Haute, Indiana, as the son of a grocery store owner in
1855, Debs's early career could fit well into an Alger novel. He left high
school at fourteen to take a job as a paint scraper in a railroad yard, rising
later to the positions of a locomotive fireman and a billing clerk. He
returned to the railroad industry as an official of the conservative Brotherhood of Local Firemen, worked for the local Democratic party, and was
elected to the Indiana state legislature in 1885. As a leader of the new American Railway Union, he achieved national prominence for his management
of a successful strike against James J. Hill's Great Northern Railroad. His
remarks to a crowd at Terre Haute after the strike revealed a conservative
labor leader. He assessed the strike not as part of the antagonism between
labor and capital but as part of an effort to create "an era of close cooperation" between management and workers in which "strikes will be a thing of
the past." The Pullman strike dramatically altered Debs's political theory.
His union was drawn into the strike; troops were called out by President
Grover Cleveland; the strikers lost badly; and Debs was sentenced to prison
in 1885 for refusing to obey a court injunction for the workers to return to
work. Debs supported Bryan in 1896 before entering Socialist politics, but
Debs was careful to point out that he favored Bryan as a populist, not as a
Democrat.

As the five-time Socialist party candidate for president of the United
States between 1900 and 1920, Eugene V. Debs attempted to offer a version
of socialism congenial to American political culture by intermingling three
strands of political thought. One, of course, was Marxism. But while Debs
almost always tended to side with the left wing of the party (he was a founding member of the IWW and occasionally openly attacked Berger and Hillquit), his Marxism was eclectic to the point of incoherence. He reported
that his reading of Marx's *Capital* while in jail set the "wires humming in
my system." He also read, however, Bellamy and Donnelly with equal com-
pliments. Returning from his imprisonment at the Woodstock, Illinois, jail
in 1897, he went on a western tour with a plan for utopian, not Marxist,
socialism. Debs's plan was to "colonize" a western state, to form a "cooperative commonwealth," and to invite the "laborless thousands" in America

to join the colony in "life, liberty and the pursuit of happiness." He formed a Colonization Commission to raise money for the project and appealed to industrialists to make contributions, writing John D. Rockefeller "to join hands with us in our emancipating and ennobling mission."

Far more pronounced in Debs's written and spoken words was his attempt to conceive of socialism as the fulfillment of the Protestant Christian tradition. He would ask himself in speeches, "What is Socialism?" and reply, "Merely Christianity in action. It recognizes the equality in men." Certainly Debs's imprisonment in 1897 had a profound effect upon his own ideology. It is the embellishment of his period in jail as a conversion experience, however, that made many members of his party wince while it drove crowds to tears. The jail in Woodstock became, in Debs's rendering, his road to Damascus. Sitting in the twilight in his cell on his fortieth birthday, Debs would tell audiences, "I was to be baptized in Socialism in the roar of the conflict . . . in the gleam of the bayonet and the flash of every rifle the class struggle was revealed." A 1904 speech suggests that Marxist dialectics has been transformed into Christian millenarianism by Debs. Religious symbol follows religious symbol: "Intellectual darkness is essential to industrial slavery." "The Socialist Party is the herald of Freedom and Light." "Death to Wage Slavery!"

The third strand in Debs's thought was republicanism. To a conventional Marxist, the thought of Jefferson and even Paine could be regarded, at best, as examples of bourgeois reform now outmoded by new economic conditions. Debs, however, attempted to employ the same argument against "wage slavery" that Lincoln had used to criticize chattel slavery. In fact, Debs once compared the Socialist party's electoral status in 1908 to that of the Republicans in 1856. Wendell Phillips, William Lloyd Garrison, and Elijah Lovejoy made their way into his speeches more than any Marxist figures. He urged workers to assume their rightful role as citizens, to refuse to wait for "a Moses to lead you out of this capitalist wilderness," and "to begin by respecting yourselves." To Nick Salvatore, a recent biographer of Debs, his belief in the "redemptive power of the ballot" was staggering. Debs, Salvatore concludes, "took the republican tradition seriously and stressed the individual dignity and power inherent in the concept of citizenship."

This combination of Marxist symbolism, Christian moral witness, and republicanism was an unstable mix that did not always hold the movement together or convince Americans in general in great numbers. Jailed for his opposition to American participation in World War I, Debs was later pardoned by President Warren G. Harding. A third of the population of his home town of Terre Haute petitioned for his release, and he was greeted with enthusiasm at the railroad station, where he had worked as a young man. Old and infirm, Debs spoke of how often he had yearned for his "beloved community of Terre Haute, where all were friends and neighbors."

SUMMARY AND COMMENT

Wherever and whenever industrialization occurs, it creates havoc in people's lives and beliefs. New cities and new kinds of cities seem to grow overnight as others die. Work is transformed. Conceptions of time are even altered, as both workers and employers respond to the rhythm of the machine rather than of nature. The most intimate of human relations change. Most historians believe that the modern family and the sexual revolution were a consequence of industrialization. New classes are created, and some old ones die. In Europe whole new ideologies emerged as a result of industrialization as well. A distinctive working-class culture rapidly arose in Britain, the first country to industrialize. In Europe revolutionary ideologies, Marxism, anarchism, and later fascism, sought to explain and to direct the course of industrialization. After 1917 the Soviet Union offered a new model of industrialization. Today countries in the Third World struggle to industrialize without sacrificing political stability.

In the United States industrialization seemed to place a special strain on political stability. American political thinkers had nearly always conceived of their country as a nation of villagers, homogeneous in cultural outlook, relatively equal in economic and political status. The trust, the robber baron, the metropolis, and the immigrant dramatically and irrevocably altered or smashed this vision. The new America would be an urban, pluralist society with large national, political, and economic institutions and disparities in wealth. If we place the transition in terms of an analogy to classical history, America came to resemble Rome, with its cosmopolitan culture and complex economic structure, more than the relatively isolated, homogeneous, and small polities of Greece.

Nearly every major political theorist we have discussed in this chapter seems to have recognized this fact without fully accepting all its consequences. The social Darwinists, who held the trump position throughout most of this period, accepted aggressively the changes industrialization was creating. Equality and economic decentralization were outmoded values that must give way to a more modern society and scientific theory. But each of the American Darwinists we have discussed sought to partially legitimize his theories through the insertion of some republican values. William Graham Sumner continued to celebrate the *forgotten man* while insisting that the new captain of industry was the objective agent of scientific progress. Andrew Carnegie assured his readers that through inheritance taxes disparities in wealth would be temporary. Russell Conwell and Horatio Alger showed Americans how equality of opportunity could still be operative under new conditions.

The progressives saw more clearly than any ideological group the consequences of industrialization. Articulate, reflective, and possessed of organizational skills to implement their vision, these men and women turned from supporters of the new order to its critics. While over a decade of reform had managed to undermine portions of the social Darwinist position and to bring about ameliorative legislation, the trusts had not been smashed at the close of the Wilson administration, and economic inequality remained largely the same as it was in 1900. Part of the reason for the failure of progressivism lay in the reformers' unwillingness to confront the fact that effective political control of the economy would require the formation of a state more powerful than the trusts. Progressives (except perhaps for Herbert Croly) were too Jeffersonian to accept this challenge. Trustbusting rather than economic control seemed a more palatable alternative. But given the degree of economic consolidation reached by 1900, such a strategy would have required a revolutionary commitment. This was a commitment the progressives never even pretended to have. Perhaps as important an explanation for the limited success of the progressives, however, can be traced to their privileged position in the new order. While they may have suffered status anxieties from industrialization, as Hofstadter argues, the progressives had the talent and skills to find and create important and comfortable positions in the new order. Veblen's work, for all its caustic attacks on capitalism, draws the picture of a future in which the robber barons will be replaced by engineers, that is, the sons and daughters of the middle class. Jane Addams late in her career complained that the men and women now coming to volunteer for service at Hull House seemed to be more interested in studying the poor than in helping them.

Populist and Socialist protest can perhaps be understood as the ideologies of marooned populations. Most significant in both ideologies was the appearance of republicanism as an ideology of protest and nostalgia directed toward groups left behind economically and politically by industrialization. Debs may have spoken for the workers of the world, but his primary frame of reference was the American small town, as it was for Bryan. In 1924 Debs complained to a friend that in the "enchanting little village" in which he was born, the maple trees and grass had been replaced by concrete and "hideous" modern buildings. But "we can at last thank God that the profit pirates can't reach into our consciousness and despoil us of our sweet and priceless memories." Nevertheless, the populist "democratic moment" and the "golden age" of socialism passed as more and more individuals were able to leave their maroonage and fit into the new America.

Throughout this long debate about the nature of an industrialized America, it is important to note that however much Americans might have resented the new captains of industry and the trusts, the diminution of the small town, and the threat to equality of opportunity, one eye of America seemed always focused on the possibilities afforded by this new society. McKinley's evocation of the symbol of the full dinner pail in 1896 captured this eagerness, as did the speeches of Conwell and the novels of Alger. Industrialization did create desperate men and women, but it more often created the kind of stressfulness that seeks a way out. There was among all ideological groupings in America from the 1870s to World War I a genuine concern for republican values, but there was also a certain acquisitive appetite for the blessings of industrialization. Nearly every spokesperson in the debate seemed to want both Americas, the Greek model as well as the Roman. Herbert Hoover, whom we shall discuss in the next chapter, stated this dual purpose in 1928 when he reminded Americans that, despite the convulsions of the past four decades, the American system had "added electric lights, plumbing, telephones, gramophones, automobiles" to our daily life. These new "comforts" began as luxuries for the upper classes and were now widely diffused. "Seventy or eighty per cent of our people participate in them."

Note

[1] Women were formed into a separate corps. In his companion work, *Equality*, Bellamy integrated his industrial army.

☆ *Bibliographic Essay*

General conditions during America's Industrial Revolution are surveyed in Edward Kirkland, *Industry Comes of Age* (New York: Holt, Rinehart & Winston, 1961). For the student who wishes to explore the impact of industrialization on economic and political institutions in international context, see Charles Moraze's *The Triumph of the Middle Classes* (Garden City, NY: Doubleday, 1961) and David S. Landes, *The Unbound Prometheus* (Cambridge: Cambridge University Press, 1969), are helpful. Nell Irvin Painter's *Standing at Armageddon: The United States, 1877–1919* (New York: W.W. Norton, 1987), is a very readable synthesis of the efforts of social historians to assess the period. She is also adept at discussing political and social theory. Mathew Josephson, *The Robber Barons* (New York: Harcourt Brace Jovanovich, 1934), is a very readable account of the ascendancy of Morgan, Rockefeller, Carnegie, and others. John Chamberlain's *The Enterprising Americans* (New York: Harper & Row, 1963) challenges assessments such as Josephson's by arguing that the "shameful aspects" of the new captains of industry have been exaggerated. Charles Wittke's *We Who Built America* (Cleveland, OH: Press of Case Western Reserve University, 1967) contains a useful review of the immigrants' dilemma. Also see Irving Howe's richly written *The World of Our Fathers* for an account of the Jewish immigration, and Oscar Handlin's sweeping account in *The Uprooted* (Boston: Little, Brown, 1951, rev. ed., 1973). Richard Lingeman, *Small Town America* (Boston: Houghton

Mifflin, 1980), chap. 7, contains a provocative analysis of the impact of industrialization on the American small town. Michael Lesy's *Wisconsin Death Trip* (New York: Pantheon Books, 1973) is a controversial documentary history of Black River Falls. But no account, prose or fiction, portrays the changes in towns like Debs's Terre Haute, Bryan's Jacksonville, and Addams's Cedarville more vividly than Booth Tarkington's novel, *The Magnificent Ambersons* (1918).

The standard histories of American social Darwinism are Richard Hofstadter's *Social Darwinism in American Thought* (Boston: Beacon Press, 1955) and Robert Green McCloskey, *American Conservatism in the Age of Enterprise, 1865–1910* (New York: Harper & Row, 1951). Loren Eisely's *Darwin's Century* (Garden City, NY: Doubleday, 1961) is a highly readable account of the general impact of Darwinism. Irvin G. Wylie's "Social Darwinism and the Businessman," in Carl Degler, ed., *Pivotal Interpretations in American History, vol.* 2 (New York: Harper & Row, 1966), contends, however, that apart from Carnegie and a few other new captains of industry, Darwinism had little influence on the American businessman. Alan Munslow credits Andrew Carnegie with providing a new language of political discourse in "Andrew Carnegie and the Discourse of Cultural Hegemony," *Journal of American Studies 22* (August 1988). Agnes Rush's early biography of Conwell, *Russell H. Conwell and His Work* (Philadelphia: John C. Winston, 1926), is hagiographic, but it does contain a reprint of his famous speech. The impact of Alger's novels has been a subject of some dispute. Louis Hartz in *The Liberal Tradition in America* (New York: Harcourt Brace Jovanovich, 1955) elevates the novels to an entire substratum of American ideology. John Cawelti in *Apostles of the Self-Made Man* (Chicago: University of Chicago Press, 1965) and Gary Scharnhorst and Jack Bales in *Horatio Alger, Jr.* (Metuchen, NJ: Scarecrow Press, 1981), contend that the novels are neither an apology for the robber barons nor a defense of industrialization. Carol Nackenoff's survival thesis is offered in *The Fictional Republic: Horatio Alger and American Political Discourse* (New York: Oxford University Press, 1994).

The competing assessments of populism discussed in this chapter include Richard Hofstadter, *The Age of Reform* (New York: Vintage, 1955); Lawrence Goodwyn, *Democratic Promise* (New York: Oxford University Press, 1976); Norman Pollock, *The Populist Response to Industrial America* (New York: W.W. Norton, 1962); Edward Shils, *The Torment of Secrecy* (Glencoe, IL: Free Press). Also see Michael Kazin's *The Populist Persuasion: An American History* (New York: Basic Books, 1995), which attempts to trace populist sensibilities to the present, and Margaret Canovan's *Populism* (New York: Harcourt Brace Jovanovich, 1981) which effectively places populist thought and practice in comparative context. Bellamy's *Looking Backward* is available in a number of paperback editions, as is Donnelly's *Caesar's Column* in reprint. There is no biography of Donnelly, but Bellamy has two able and sympathetic treatments: A. E. Morgan, *Edward Bellamy* (New York: Columbia University Press, 1944), and Sylvia Bowman, *The Year 2000* (New York: Bookman Associates, 1958).

Also see John Thomas's *Alternative America: Henry George, Edward Bellamy, Henry Demarest Lloyd and the Adversary Tradition* (Cambridge: Harvard University Press, 1983). Leroy Ashby's *William Jennings Bryan* (Boston: Twayne Publishers, 1987) is masterful and empathetic to the Great Commoner. Hofstadter's Reconstruction of Bryan is in *The American Political Tradition* (New York: Vintage, 1948), chap. 7. A convenient collection of Bryan's speeches is in Ray Ginger, ed., *William Jennings Bryan: Selections* (Indianapolis: Bobbs-Merrill, 1967). Paul Glad's *McKinley, Bryan and the People* (Philadelphia: J. B. Lippincott, 1964) is a fascinating analysis of the 1896 election that can be read along with Bryan's own account, *The First Battle* (Chicago: W. B. Conkey, 1896).

Interpretations of progressivism include Hofstadter's status revolution thesis in *The Age of Reform,* Wiebe's new middle-class thesis in *The Search for Order* (New York: Hill & Wang, 1967), and Gabriel Kolko's corporate capture thesis in *The Triumph of Conservatism* (New York: Free Press of Glencoe, 1963). These and other assessments are discussed in Arthur Link and Richard McCormick, *Progressivism* (Arlington Heights, IL: Harlan Davidson, 1983). Intriguing accounts that emphasize psychological strain in progressive thought are Jackson Lears, *No Place of Grace* (New York: Pantheon Books, 1981), and Robert M. Cruden, *Ministers of Reform* (New York: Basic Books, 1983). Cruden's analysis of what he calls a "Presbyterian foreign policy" is particularly interesting. David Noble's *The Paradox of Progressive Thought* (Minneapolis: University of Minnesota Press, 1958) contains a fascinating interpretation of Croly. Kevin C. O'Leary detects republican elements in Croly's thought in his "Herbert Croly and Progressive Democracy,"*Polity* (Fall, 1996). James T. Kloppenberg places American progressivism in comparative perspective with some insightful results in his *Uncertain Victory* (New York: Oxford University Press, 1986). David Reisman's assessment of Veblen is critical but balanced in *Thorstein Veblen* (New York: Scribner's, 1953). Also see John P. Diggins, *The Bard of Savagery* (New York: Seabury Press, 1978). Jane Addams's writings are conveniently excerpted in Christopher Lasch's *The Social Thought of Jane Addams* (Indianapolis: Bobbs-Merrill, 1965). Lasch's *The New Radicalism in America, 1889–1963* (New York: Alfred A. Knopf, 1965), chap. 1, advances an assessment of Addams similar to Hofstadter's general critique of progressivism. For more sympathetic accounts, see Jean Bethke Elshtain, *Meditations on Modern Political Thought* (New York: Praeger Publishers, 1986), chap. 7, and Philip Abbott, *States of Perfect Freedom* (Amherst: University of Massachusetts Press, 1987), chap. 6.

A number of recent writers now see progressive ideas as the basis for a new reform movement in the near future. See: Michael Lind's *The Next American Nation* (Glencoe, IL: Free Press, 1995) for a passionate argument along these lines. Jeffery Issacs has raised doubts about the contemporary utility of progressivism in "The Poverty of Progressivism," *Dissent* (Fall, 1996). His criticism brought both agreement and opposition in later issues by E. J. Dionne, Mark Levinson, Jane Mansbridge and others.

Sundry interpretations of the rise and decline of American Socialism are collected in Seymour Lipset and John Laslett, eds., *The Failure of a Dream?* (Garden City, NY: Doubleday, 1974). Irving Howe reviews many of these theories in his *Socialism and America* (New York: Harcourt Brace Jovanovich, 1985). Ira Kipnis's *The American Socialist Movement, 1897–1912* (New York: Monthly Review Press, 1952), is particularly well done on internal disputes within the party. Nick Salvatore's biography of Debs, *Eugene V. Debs: Citizen and Socialist* (Champaign: University of Illinois Press, 1982), is highly recommended for its effort to analyze the five-term presidential candidate in terms of American political culture. Patrick Wenshaw's *The Wobblies* (Garden City, NY: Doubleday, 1967) is a sympathetic history of the IWW, as is Salvatore Salarno's *Red November, Black November* (New York: SUNY Press, 1989). Loren Baritz's *The American Left* (New York: Basic Books, 1971) contains reprints of two illustrations of IWW, political thought, proceedings of the 1905 convention and the congressional testimony of Vincent St. John, an IWW official. James R. Green describes the adaptation of socialism to an American subculture in *Grass-Roots Socialism: Radical Movements in the Southwest, 1895–1943* (Baton Rouge: Louisiana State University Press, 1978). Richard W. Judd describes American Socialists in power at the local level in *Socialist Cities* (New York: SUNY Press, 1989). The best accounts of the lyrical Left can be found in Floyd Dell's memoirs, such as *Homecoming* (New York: Farrar and Rinehart, 1933), and *Love in Greenwich Village* (New York: Doran, 1926). Also see Robert E. Humphrey, *Children of Fantasy* (New York: John Wiley & Sons, 1978).

☆ *Major Works*

1883	*What Social Classes Owe Each Other*, William Graham Sumner
1889	"The Conflict of Democracy and Plutocracy," William Graham Sumner
1915	"Acres of Diamonds Speech," Russell Conwell
1867	*Raggedy Dick*, Horatio Alger
1889	"Wealth," Andrew Carnegie
1891	*Caesar's Column*, Ignatius Donnelly
1892	*"Populist Party Platform," Ignatius Donnelly
1888	*Looking Backward*, Edward Bellamy
1896	"Cross of Gold Speech," William Jennings Bryan
1894	"A Modern Lear," Jane Addams
1935	*Twenty Years at Hull House*, Jane Addams
1899	*The Theory of the Leisure Class*, Thorstein Veblen
1909	*The Promise of American Life*, Herbert Croly
1905	"Grand Central Palace Speech," Eugene V. Debs
1912	"Acceptance Speech," Eugene V. Debs
1918	"Canton, Ohio, Speech," Eugene V. Debs

* A collaborative effort

Depression

INTRODUCTION

There are few events in a nation's history so traumatic that they produce sudden massive changes in its belief system. One is revolution. We have seen how special circumstances served to attenuate the cataclysmic nature of that event in America. Another is civil war. We have seen how internal war hardens and magnifies cleavages in the body politic to such an extent that the nation itself ceases to exist as a source of common belief. It was in this context that Lincoln so brilliantly spoke. Another is military defeat or occupation. America has been fortunate in avoiding the demoralization, anger, and self-doubt that arise from such a defeat, although the South as a region has suffered under the banner of the "Lost Cause." As we shall see, the Vietnam experience has produced some of these characteristics. Another is economic collapse.

Beginning with the stock market crash in 1929, the nation's economy underwent a series of startling crises. Banks closed (10,000 of them between 1929 and 1934); drought conditions were reported in 300 counties in 30 states; 12 million people were unemployed by May 1932; and farmers lost their land to banks and/or tax collectors. In a single day in April 1932, one-fourth of the entire area of the state of Mississippi went under the hammer of auctioneers. Perhaps as many as a million men and boys left their homes, wandering the country looking for work. By January 1931 New York City operated 82 bread lines feeding 85,000 people a day. Farm income plummeted as corn prices fell to pre-Civil War levels. Many schools closed for lack of public funds.

It is difficult to portray the impact of these events on the American people. Observers were struck by the sudden appearance of conditions that had never existed on such a broad level in America. For instance, literary critic Edmund Wilson was horrified by what he saw in Chicago:

> [T]here is not a garbage dump . . . which is not diligently haunted by the hungry. Last summer in the hot weather, when the smell was sickening and the flies were thick, there were a hundred people a day coming to one of the dumps, falling on the heap of refuse as soon as the truck had pulled out and digging in it with sticks and hands.

As Americans lost their houses, shantytowns of makeshift homes began appearing throughout the country. They soon became known as *Hoovervilles*. Here is one description by Laurence Hewes, who later became an assistant to Rexford Tugwell, a member of FDR's *brain trust*:

> Each had built for his family a rickety shelter of salvage lumber, boxes, cardboard and tin cans. Each small holding was pitifully cultivated in a hopeless diversity of crops. Some were strawberry beds, others spindly orchards; here and there tobacco and cotton stalks evidenced either imagination or a cotton bed origin.
>
> The entire settlement was a dreary, sodden mess; stagnant rain water stood three to six inches deep; outdoor privies had overflowed shallow wells, sickness was rampant. I stared at the dismal scene in a steady autumnal downpour. Lank men in patched denim pants puttered lethargically; a few in groups whittled and spat. Half-clad urchins peered through windows or skittered through slop.

On novelist John Dos Passos' visit to Detroit he learned that the unused Fisher Body plant had been turned into an emergency shelter, but then closed for fear that it was turning into a "nest of Reds." Dos Passos saw homeless and unemployed everywhere, in shacks and in the back rooms of abandoned houses. "In one back lot," he reported, "they have burrowed out rooms in a huge abandoned sandpile. Their smokestacks stick out at the top."

Apple peddlers became the symbol of the early years of the Depression. Poems were written about them. Gene Fowler, a New York reporter, offered a comment that seemed to hit upon the mood of Depression-weary Americans. He spoke of "apple sellers crouched at the street corners like half-remembered sins sitting upon the conscience of the town." In actuality, apple peddling began as a commercial and public-relations enterprise on the part of growers in Oregon and Washington. Their apple production had actually increased in 1930, but there was no market for the surplus. An official developed the idea of selling apples on credit to the unemployed, who would then retail them at five cents apiece. The slogan, "Buy an Apple a Day and Eat the Depression Away!" was part of a campaign to market the produce and at the same time to show evidence of public-spiritedness. In a month there were 6,000 apple sellers in New York City. But prospects almost immediately dissipated for these new retailers. Competition required price reductions (two for five cents was common); spoiled and unsold apples as well as subway fares and the cost of paper bags ate into the profits of what was a twelve-hour day. Citizens began complaining, and police began to harass the vendors. What began as a typically American approach to renew equality of opportunity seemed to have ended in a parody of American ideals, as epitomized by President Herbert Hoover's famous comment: "Many persons left their jobs for the more profitable one of selling apples."

Every symbol, then, of American political culture seemed to be smashed by the Depression: belief in material abundance; belief in the individual's capacity to own property and make an independent living; belief in a beneficent future through individual saving and diligence. Not only the symbol of Horatio Alger seemed to be dead, but even those of Thomas Jefferson and John Locke.

How did Americans act through the early days of this crisis? For the most part the nation slipped into a mood of eerie despair. Paul Lazarsfeld, drawing upon cross-national data, described the unemployed as *die müde Gemeinschaft* (the weary community). Louis Adamic, writing for *Harper's* magazine in 1931, described the people of New England towns as having "something dead in them, as from exhaustion or perhaps too much idleness, without any personal winsomeness or any power of demand." A year later Elmer Davis, writing in the same magazine, said: "There is a strong feeling of suspense in the air, an overcast sultriness. Anything may happen."

But sporadic incidents of protest and violence had also begun to appear. Farmers blocked sheriffs' sales of homes by placing logs across highways and smashing the car windshields and tires of potential buyers. In Nebraska farmers carried signs that read "Be Pickets or Peasants," and commandeered a carload of cattle from a train. In cities there were hunger strikes, often organized by Communists; miners demanded at gunpoint food from the company stores; angry crowds began appearing on streets in attempts to prevent the eviction of tenants from apartments. Perhaps the most dramatic example of protest, and one that received the most national attention, was the encampment of the "Bonus Army" in Washington, D.C. When the petitions of veterans of World War I for a bonus were denied by Congress in 1932, the ax-soldiers built makeshift shelters outside the capital and even slept in unused government buildings on Pennsylvania Avenue. On July 28 Hoover ordered their dismissal. General Douglas MacArthur used cavalry to chase the protesters away and burned the shacks. Hoover justified his action by emphasizing that no one was killed, and that the veterans had been duped by "communists and persons with criminal records."

HOOVER, SERVICE INDIVIDUALISM, AND THE AMERICAN SYSTEM

The president of the United States during this collapse became, in the minds of many Americans for generations, the figure who, if not responsible for the Depression, was unable to cope with it. This man was Herbert Clark Hoover. In the words of historian Carl Degler:

> [H]is administration is usually depicted as cold hearted, when not pictured as totally devoid of heart, inept, or actionless in the face of the Great Depression.

Degler himself demurs from this assessment, but others confirm the generalization. Elliot Rosen writes:

> [Hoover's] American system [was] intended to preserve individualism and nineteenth century anti-statist, laissez-faire attitudes. His policies as Secretary of Commerce, then as President contributed substantially and directly to the Great Depression.

It is indeed an ironic turn of history that Hoover should be discussed in such terms. For whatever Hoover's failures were in dealing with the Depression (and he spent the remainder of his life justifying his actions in 1929–33), his political persona before the Crash was quite different. In 1928 he was known as the "Great Engineer," and *The New York Times* said his "office looked more like a machine shop than a room, in whose mind commanded all experience and whose wave of hand organized fleets of rescue vessels and millions of contributions." Because of his successful activities as an administrator of relief in Europe after World War I, his name had come "to mean food for the starving and medicine for the sick." The campaigner, who in 1932 was said to have a face that would wither a flower, was four years earlier "an idealist representing enlightened individualism, humanitarianism, harmony, liberty. . . ." It was Hoover who was so committed to an "open presidency" that he created a New Year's Day open house, and in 1930 shook the hands of 6,000 of his fellow Americans at the event. Historians who have studied both the pre- and post-Depression Hoover have attempted to reevaluate his ideological reputation. For instance, Martin Fausold, a Hoover biographer, has concluded that Secretary of Commerce Hoover was "the more liberal and progressive candidate in 1928." He received the support of Jane Addams, the Chicago reformer who had voted for Debs in 1920 and Robert H. La Follette in 1924. She endorsed Hoover's farm policy and his positions on collective bargaining. (Hoover had gone on record as favoring the curtailment of "excessive use" of injunctions in labor disputes.) Addams also admired his concern for the poor. Similarly, Joan Hoff Wilson concluded in her biography that "the great engineer and humanitarian still lived beneath the new mantle of the Great Depression president," and that Hoover was a "forgotten progressive and a remembered conservative."

Some historians believe they have detected in Hoover a political philosophy that was neither liberal nor conservative. William Appleman Williams describes Hoover as "the keystone in the arch that leads from Mark Hanna and Herbert Croly to such later figures as Nelson Rockefeller and Adolph Berle." For Williams, Hoover was one of the first American leaders to see that the competitive capitalism characterizing much of American history was operationally obsolete and needed to be replaced by a cooperative system of both labor and capital led by a "class conscious industrial gentry." Ellis Hawley, a historian of both the twenties and the New Deal, has taken Williams's observation one step further. Hawley calls Hoover's philosophy *corporativism*. Hawley is careful to point out that Hoover was not influenced by the "fascist perversion of the corporate ideal" but that, like his counterparts in Europe, he was concerned about the "destructive competition" and "social anarchy" in capitalism and envisioned a new order through "scientific coordination and moral regeneration."

Hawley concludes that the dividing line between Hoover and FDR is not one of a laissez-faire and a managed economy, as proposed by those who see Hoover as a conservative, but rather "one attempt at management, through informal private and public cooperation to other more formal and coercive yet also limited attempts." Murray N. Rothbard, the libertarian economist, concurs with this assessment. In *America's Great Depression* he argues that in such parts of Hoover's program as the Reconstruction Finance Corporation, which provided loans to banks and businesses, "laissez-faire was boldly thrown overboard and every governmental weapon thrown into the breach."

Was Hoover, who refused to use the full weight of the government to deal with social and economic problems, a believer in laissez-faire? Was he really a progressive caught in the storm of the Depression? Was he a *corporativist* seeking new kinds of partnership between government and business? An examination of Hoover's major theoretical work, *American Individualism*, suggests that in varying degrees all these contradictory assessments are correct.

American Individualism, published in 1922 when Hoover was secretary of commerce in the Harding administration, is a remarkable book. In fact, it is a neglected classic of American political thought. Hoover begins his essay by outlining his understanding of American exceptionalism. In his seven years of service overseas, he had seen nations "burned in revolution." These ideologies may be "clothed by the demagogue" in "the terms of political idealism," but they have unleashed the "bestial instincts of hate, murder and destruction." America, too, had an ideology, one which "partisans of some of these other schemes" insist is exhausted. Hoover defines this ideology as *individualism* but insists that "our individualism differs from all others" and is "not the individualism of other countries." The remainder of the book involves an attempt on Hoover's part to define the historical development of this ideology in America and to explain how much it contributes to America's political stability and economic well-being.

Hoover, who describes himself as an "unashamed individualist," divides his discussion of individualism into four aspects: philosophical, spiritual, economic, and political. The philosophical grounding of individualism is based upon the recognition of two basic instincts, selfishness and altruism. For Hoover, the dominant human instincts are selfish, and "the problem of the world is to restrain the destructive instincts while strengthening and enlarging those of altruistic character and constructive impulse." The "will-o'-the-wisp of all breeds of socialism" is that it asserts "motivation of human animals by altruism alone." In order to achieve a surface resemblance to other-regarding behavior, socialists find that they must create a "bureaucracy of the entire population." Similarly, autocracies, in which Hoover includes all forms of class rule, even unrestrained capitalism, suppose that "the good Lord endowed a special few with all the divine attributes." Autocrats treat others only as means. The proof of the futility of this idea lay with the "grim failure of Germany" and those in America "who have sought economic domination."

To date Americans had rejected both of these faulty conceptions of human nature. They have rejected the "clap-trap of the French Revolution," and they have rejected the ideas of the "frozen strata of classes." As proof of the latter, Hoover cites the twelve men comprising the presidency, vice presidency, and cabinet, nine of whom "earned their own way in life without economic inheritance, and eight of them started with manual labor."

The second aspect of individualism, the spiritual, assumes that there is a "divine spark" that can "be awakened in every heart." Hoover notes the impact of the religious origins of America in maintaining this idea. In this section he outlines his conception of what can be best called *service individualism* as the key element in the American individualism that "differs from all others." Proof of this spiritual spark is the "vast multiplication of voluntary organizations for altruistic purposes" in America. He continues:

> These associations for the advancement of public welfare improvements, morals, charity, public opinion, health, the clubs and societies for recreation and intellectual advancement, represent something moving at a far greater depth than "joining." They represent the wide-

spread aspiration for mutual advancement, self expression, and neighborly helpfulness.

The essence of American individualism, then, was service. Hoover stated that "when we rehearse our own individual memories of success, we find that none gives us such comfort as the memory of service given. Do we not refer to our veterans as service men? Do not merchants and business men pride themselves in something of service given beyond the price of their goods?"

In his section on the economic aspects of individualism, Hoover completed his designation of the businessperson as one engaged in the provision of a service. The principle of "every man for himself and the devil take the hindmost" may have been a code of conduct in the American past, but "our development of individualism shows an increasing tendency to regard right of property not as an object in itself but in light of a useful and necessary instrument in stimulation of initiative to the individual. . . ." The goal of economic activity was not "the acquisition and preservation of private property—the selfish snatching and hoarding of the common product." As a form of "self expression" it was an activity designed to produce "a high and growing standard of living for all the people, not for a single class. . . ." Hoover listed the "comforts" (electric lights, plumbing, telephones, gramophones, and automobiles) that had begun as luxuries and now had become so commonplace that 70 or 80 percent of the population could afford them.

Hoover admitted that when private property became concentrated in the hands of the few, "the individual begins to feel capital as an oppressor." But American individualism had devised a variety of mechanisms to prevent this occurrence. One was the "American demand for equality of opportunity" as "a constant militant check upon capital." Hoover cited the income tax as a means by which the "surplus" from profits could be shared. He also supported regulation to prevent economic domination and unfair practices. In his chapter on the political aspects of American individualism, Hoover discussed the faults in the American system. He was careful to point out that the achievements far outweigh the shortcomings, but nevertheless his list was not a short one:

> [T]he spirit of lawlessness; the uncertainty of unemployment in some callings; the deadening effect of certain repetitive processes of manufacture; the twelve hour day in a few industries; unequal voice in bargaining for wage in some employment; arrogant domination by some employers and some labor leaders; child labor in some states; inadequate instruction in some areas; unfair competition in some industries; some fortunes excessive far beyond the needs of stimulation to initiative; survivals of religious intolerance; political debauchery of some cities; weakness in our governmental structure.

One can see even from this brief summary of a brief book how commentators can draw different conclusions from Hoover's political philosophy. An emphasis on his interpretation of American exceptionalism serves to underline the limits to governmental intervention in the economy. Hoover was so impressed by the failure of European governments and so impressed with the success of the American system that any measure that borrowed from socialism was to be rejected. There is a "deadline between our system and socialism," he wrote in *American Individualism*. "Regulation to prevent domination and unfair practices, yet preserving rightful initiative are in keeping with our social foundations. Nationalization of industry or business is their negation." It is often noted that Hoover in 1932 insisted that grass would grow in the streets of New York if FDR's programs were enacted. But in 1928, against the counsel of his advisers, Hoover accused Al Smith, the Democratic presidential candidate, of promoting socialism by his support of state purchase and sale of liquor. "Shall we depart from the principle of our American system," Hoover asked a crowd at Madison Square Garden, "upon which we have advanced beyond all the rest of the world, in order to adopt methods based on principles destructive of its very foundation?"

Yet despite Hoover's profession of having discovered the essence of the American system in the concept of individualism, there clearly is a collectivist strain in his thought. He warmly embraced the corporation as a new form of economic organization that was more efficient, more rational, more innovative, and even more public-spirited than the small farm or firm. In 1928, for instance, he told residents of his hometown of West Branch, Iowa, that, despite the bravery and kindness of the early settlers, we "must avoid becoming homesick for the ways of those self-contained farm houses of 40 years ago." These yeomen had "lower standards of living, greater toil, less opportunity for leisure and recreation, less of the comforts of home, less of the joy of living." Besides, there was no way to go back to simpler times. It was no more possible to "revive those old conditions than it was to summon back the relatives in the cemetery yonder." Farming was now a business with 80 percent of production for market use. Once self-sufficiency was transcended through improved feed and livestock and a "long list of mechanical inventions for saving labor," the economy of scale changed and the farmer joined an "economic system vastly more intricate and delicately adjusted than before."

Hoover's model, then, envisioned groups of farmers, labor unions, corporations, chambers of commerce, bankers, all nationally organized and motivated, as he had said in *American Individualism*, by a mixture of self-interest and altruism. The government would foster the conditions for their cooperation. In this aspect we can see the elements of progressivism in Hoover's political thought. He never advocated a "greed is good" ideology. In fact his central defense of capitalism was always based upon its ability as a system to promote a sense of service to the community. He mirrored the progressive's commitment to discovering ways to promote the public good through a rational approach to solving social problems. No fault in the American system was not potentially remediable for Hoover. Even poverty could be abolished through a general increase in the standard of living and volunteer efforts of communities. The list of social problems he drew up in 1922 was "becoming steadily more local." "That they are recognized and condemned is a long way on the road to progress."

Seen from different angles, then, Hoover's American system was laissez-faire liberal, progressive, *and* corporativist. In fact, it could be argued that the glue that provided the synthesis was Hoover's reinterpretation of the nature of republicanism, which we have discussed in chapter 2. The republican political theorist, too, insisted upon the private ownership of property and the uniqueness of American institutions but justified both in terms of republican virtue; for Hoover, this concept became service individualism. But Hoover was convinced that the Jeffersonian farmer had been superseded by other institutions more capable of guaranteeing the foundations of the American system under modern conditions.

Of course, Hoover's synthesis was short-lived. He barely had a moment to implement his ideas when the Crash and the Great Depression smashed the American system as he understood it. The very aspects of his thought that had looked so irresistible in 1928 seemed limited and inflexible by 1930. Despite Hoover's famous dictum after the Crash that the economy was fundamentally sound, he expressed belief that the downturn would be a long, hard one. He refused to accept his treasury secretary's view that the Crash provided social Darwinist opportunities for the elimination of inefficient business and the liquidation of unnecessary labor. Wages must remain stable and the unemployed provided for, according to Hoover. Business must accept some of the responsibility for the Depression because of "over-optimism as to profits."

Hoover believed that the cause of the Depression rested with the unstable economies of Europe; hence, to copy measures undertaken in Germany and France or Britain would only compound America's problems. His approach to relief for the unemployed paralleled his approach as a relief administrator after World War I. In both cases he saw the government's role as one in which private relief funds were coordinated. When a Democratic Congress demanded direct relief monies for the unemployed, he admitted that the impulse came from a "natural anxiety for the people of their states," but he insisted that direct appropriations would "break down" the "sense of responsibility and mutual help." The issue was not one of financial integrity. But Hoover feared that the "cost of a few score millions" would create "an abyss of reliance in the future upon charity in some form or another."

Only the mobilization and organization of "the infinite number of agencies of self help in the community" could be the basis of "successful relief in national distress." In 1932, however, Hoover had acted more boldly in dealing with what he called the "temporary mobilization of timid capital." The Reconstruction Finance Corporation, initially capitalized at $500 million by the federal government, was created to lend funds to railroads, banks, insurance companies, building firms, and loan associations. But the administrators of the program tended to be overly cautious in their lending policies, at least in terms of the emergency at hand, and the public at large began to perceive the program as money spent on "plutocrats." By the late spring Hoover seemed to have almost given up on the plan.

The problem with Hoover's American system was that after 1929 its major premises no longer seemed operational. Local communities and volunteer organizations had nothing more to give. The prosperity that Hoover had guaranteed would be the inevitable result of the growth of the corporation vanished to a memory. The divine spark seemed to have flickered and gone out. Still Hoover believed that the country would have pulled out of the crisis had not European banks defaulted in 1931. Then he blamed the persistence of the Depression on Roosevelt's policies. In fact, in spite of his unpopularity, the former president continued throughout the 1930s to advance his belief in the verities of the American system.

THE CHALLENGE OF THE DEPRESSION

What was the state of political theory in the early 1930s? We noted how by 1932 the Depression had reached to nearly every stratum of American society and how the American people seemed to have sunk into a kind of despondency with occasional sparks of violence and anger. As the Depression deepened and Hoover's efforts seemed to have no effect, America's intelligentsia began to search feverishly for solutions. A pattern quickly emerged in the scores of books and articles that diagnosed the causes and proposed cures for the Depression. First, writers began to see the Depression in terms other than a severe but temporary economic slump or even as a consequence of economic dislocations in Europe. Something was seriously wrong with the American system as a whole. In late 1929 the *New Republic* asked "whether capitalism can survive as we know it." In 1931 Edmund Wilson, writing in the same journal, questioned whether liberals should continue "betting on capitalism" as the basic structure within which reform should take place. George Soule, the author of several influential books in the 1930s, argued that the sources of the Depression could be found in the prosperity of the 1920s. Technological advances, expansion in the auto industry, installment buying, and loans all stimulated production past the point at which products could be consumed. Wages had not risen as profits had, nor had retail prices been lowered. Now in the context of glutted markets, Soule could foresee no immediate possibilities for an increase in wages and farm prices. He predicted a revolution in America by 1934 as the most likely consequence.

In 1932 Adolph Berle and Gardiner Means, a law professor and an economist, respectively, both of whom were later to assume important posts in the Roosevelt administration, published a book entitled *The Modern Corporation and Private Property.* The work placed a large part of the blame on the new structures of capitalism that Hoover had so admired. Berle and Means argued that the modern corporation had transformed capitalism in ways that few Americans understood. While it was true that the financing of corporate enterprise required large numbers of stockholders, investors had little or no influence on corporate decisions. The control of the corporation rested with a "dozen or so men." This separation of ownership from control had eroded the mechanism of the market and made the corporation "not only on an equal plane with the state, but possibly even superseding it as the dominant form of social organization." Berle and Means were vague about what to do with the corporation. They clearly rejected the progressive panacea of trust-busting, but they also avoided the question of public ownership. Not so Rexford Tugwell, an economist and also a member of FDR's brain trust. After reaching many of the same conclusions as Berle and Means, Tugwell announced in 1933 that it was a "logical impossibility to have a planned economy and to have business operating its industry."

What this sampling suggests is that many writers in the early 1930s had come to the conclusion that capitalism in its present form simply did not work and that the Depression was overwhelming evidence of this fact. But how was one to shape the future in light of the historic American commitment to individualism? Tugwell had written in March 1932 that "the contemporary situation has explosive possibilities. The future is becoming visible in Russia. . . ." In the same year Stuart Chase published a book which concluded with the question: "Why should Russians have all the fun of remaking a world?" Writers of the early Depression struggled to reevaluate the premises of individualism with a sense of urgency.

By the early 1930s Hoover may have already become a discredited figure among the American intelligentsia, but the warning he expressed in 1928 was not easily ignored. The president had said that free speech "does not live many hours after free industry and free commerce die." Bureaucracy will not tolerate the "spirit of independence"; it will "spread the spirit of submission into our daily life." Of course, Americans had already experienced a different kind of submission in breadlines and shelters, but the issue raised by Hoover—what kind of economic system other than capitalism preserves individualism—was not taken lightly even in the depths of the Depression. Out of this crisis over the value of individualism, there emerged three classic works of American political thought: Lewis Mumford's *Technics and Civilization* (1934); John Dewey's *Individualism: Old and New* (1930); and Reinhold Niebuhr's *Moral Man and Immoral Society* (1932).

Lewis Mumford's work is an unusual one in the history of American political thought in that its scope and reading of history are quite wide. Mumford redrew Marx's categorization of historical periods (feudal, capitalist, and socialist) on the basis of historical change and its impact upon culture. One period, which he called the *eotechnic*, had lasted from the fall of feudalism to the Industrial Revolution. This phase rested upon wind and water power, and its major inventions were the clock, printing press, and blast furnace. Features of the next phase were already present in the eotechnic period, including the factory system and the decline of a craft economy. Mumford praised the connection between technology and culture: "In every department of activity there was an equilibrium between the static and the dynamic, between the rural and the urban, between the vital and the mechanical."

If the eotechnic period combined the best of medieval culture with the new technology, the next phase, the *paleotechnic*, was nightmarish in its competitiveness and the triumph of the machine over the needs of an "organic" social experience. Worst of all its features, however, was the rise of individualism. Men and women were alienated from each other, from their work, and from nature; they were forced to compensate by "egocentric getting and spending for the absence of collective institutions and a collective aim." But a new age was dawning. The outlines of the *neotechnic age* could be seen in the invention of the telegraph, telephone, phonograph, radio, and motion picture, for the "organic was becoming visible again . . . within the mechanical complex." The new age put a premium on the senses; electric power allowed for new forms of communication; new forms of play could enrich lives. With the new techniques a *collective economy* and a *planned society* would permit the growth of new forms of fellowship and community.

Mumford's *Technics and Civilization* is part of a long line of American forecasts that see technology as a liberating force for American society. Some of his predictions bear striking resemblance to contemporary works that see the computer as the agent for a new age. In the context of the early 1930s, Mumford's analysis served a number of important functions. It argued that the form of economic individualism at that moment was only a passing phase (much as Hoover himself had argued). The new technology would usher in a new form of individualism that bore more similarities to traditional American values than the recent appetitive version. Thus, while there is talk of collectivism and socialism in *Technics and Civilization,* one could read in Mumford's analysis the message that the transformation was already under way without the necessity of revolution in a political sense and without an abandonment of individualism in the traditional sense of the term.

John Dewey's *Individualism: Old and New,* originally published as a series of articles in the *New Republic* in 1929 and 1930, is a less ambitious work but no less searching in its analysis of American values. Dewey used Lincoln's biblical metaphor of a *house divided* to explain the current state of American society. Uncharacteristic of Dewey's other efforts, the work drips with a sense of cynicism about America:

> Anthropologically speaking, we are living in a money culture. Its cult and rites dominate. . . . This, of course, is as it should be; people have to make a living, do they not? And for what should they work if not for money, and how should they get goods and enjoyments if not by buying them with money—thus enabling someone else to make money, and in the end to start shops and factories to give employment to still others, so they can make more money to enable other people to make more money by selling goods—and so on indefinitely.

This description is in a broad sense a parody of Hoover's American individualism, and Dewey goes on to give the satirical Panglossian conclusion: "So far, all is for the best in the best of all possible cultures: our rugged . . . or is it ragged? individualism." The author dismisses as so much "cant" the "Rotarian applause" of service. Ours is a "pecuniary culture," and the "whole idea of individualism" is made to conform to it. He describes America as the "United States, Incorporated." The "business mind" determines "the tone of society at large as well as the government of industrial society." Americans are "exposed to the greatest flood of mass suggestion that any people has ever experienced. . . . The publicity agent is perhaps the most significant symbol of our present social life."

Given the dominance of corporate ends, in what sense, according to Dewey, is the house divided? Dewey responds on two points. Although he is writing at the beginning of the Depression, he sees a gap between the promise of United States, Incorporated, and its practice. Satirically, he discusses Robert and Helen Lynd's study of Muncie, Indiana, in *Middletown:*

> If a few workers know what they are making or the meaning of what they do, and still fewer know what becomes of the work of their own hands . . . in the largest industry of Middletown perhaps one-tenth of one percent of the product is consumed locally . . . this is doubtless because we have so perfected our system of distribution that the whole country is one. And if the mass of workers live in constant fear of loss of their jobs, this is doubtless because our spirit of progress, manifest in change of fashions, invention of new machines and power

of over-production, keeps everything on the move. Our reward of industry and thrift is so accurately adjusted to individual ability that it is natural and proper that the workers should look forward with dread to the age of fifty or fifty-five, when they will be laid on the shelf.

But even if this gap were closed (and for Dewey this is not possible), there is something wrong with the American system. The spirit of corporate culture has "obscured and crowded out" true individualism in the American tradition. As to the latter, Dewey speaks of the values of equal opportunity, free association, and free speech. Since there are few institutional supports for nurturing the old version, genuine individuality is lost almost as soon as it is asserted. Work is no longer meaningful; the churches tend to support the pecuniary culture; thrift is discouraged in favor of consumption; and role models are all taken from the captains of industry.

Dewey is reluctant to call for a return to the older individualist tradition, however. In this respect *Individualism: Old and New* perfectly fits with the genre of early Depression political theory. Both the old individualism (the Jeffersonian ideal of equality for all and privileges for none) and the new one ("ruthless and self-centered energy") must be transcended. Dewey was not enthusiastic about the Soviet experiment, although he credited the Russians with imagination and resourcefulness. Instead, he called for a planned society on different principles. He mentioned the Interstate Commerce Commission and the Federal Reserve Board as "a socialistic undertaking on a large scale sponsored by the party of individualism." "The probabilities seem to favor," he continued, "the creation of more such boards in the future, in spite of all concomitant denunciation of bureaucracy. . . ."

In Dewey's defense, it must be said that he was successful in terms of a major part of the project he set out to complete. For he had insisted that what passed for individualism in America was not worthy of its name and that it was possible, contrary to the communists' claim, to envision a form of individualism in a planned society. There was, he insisted, an "inexpungible" essence to individuality that could be discovered under new conditions. In describing the "lost individual" in United States, Incorporated, he asserted that individuals "who are not bound together in associations, whether domestic, economic, religious, political, artistic or educational, are monstrosities." Corporate America had gone a long way toward destroying these associations, but Dewey could not envision with any precision what would be their replacement in a "socially planned" order.

Niebuhr's *Moral Man and Immoral Society* had many of the same premises and sensibilities of Mumford's and Dewey's efforts. Privileged groups in America really had no interest in society save the protection of their status; Marxian socialism's "dreams . . . have an immediate significance, which the religio-ethical dreams of the Christians lack." We can no longer afford to "build our individual ladders to heaven and leave the total human

enterprise unredeemed of its excesses and corruption." But these common-
alities aside, Niebuhr, through his activities as a pastor for thirteen years in
Detroit and his own theological anchors, developed a political theory different from those of Mumford and Dewey. Using St. Augustine's famous distinction between the City of God and the City of Man as the basis for his
analysis, Niebuhr rejected both theories of determinism, whether technological or economic, as well as any theory that placed too high a reliance
upon ethics or reason as a motivating source for social change.

Augustine had argued that, while in the City of God individuals gave
up their own interests for God, even the church was infected with the premises of the City of Man, which placed individual interests before all others. From this Augustinian theology, formulated in terms of the metaphor of
two cities and positing a dualist conception of human nature (in which
both good and bad are permanently intermixed), Niebuhr developed his
political theory. It is possible, Niebuhr argued, for individuals in their personal relationships to behave with some measure of justice and empathy
toward other individuals. As members of groups (for example, a class, race,
nation, or gender), we have a diminished ability to comprehend the needs
of others; instead, we develop stereotypes that function in ways that
oppress others. One of Niebuhr's many examples includes his citation of
Mahatma Gandhi on the English. "An Englishman in office," Gandhi said,
"is different from an Englishman outside. Similarly an Englishman in India
is different from an Englishman in England. Here in India you belong to a
system that is vile beyond description. It is possible, therefore, for me to
condemn the system in the strongest terms, without considering you bad
and without imputing bad motives to every Englishman." Niebuhr reminds
his readers, however, that even relationships among individuals are not
always marked by goodwill; we cannot completely "disassociate an evil
social system from the moral responsibilities of the individuals who maintain it."

The morality of individuals (properly qualified) and the immorality of
groups means for Niebuhr that what he calls the two major approaches to
social change, the moralist approach and the realist approach, are faulty.
The moralist approach expects that the egoism of groups can be changed as
reason or goodwill is developed in society. Niebuhr cites Dewey's comment
that change can occur if only we "cease mouthing platitudes" as a prime
example of this approach. Dewey had advocated the development of experimental procedures in social life, and Niebuhr concludes that "no class of
industrial workers will ever win freedom from the dominant classes if they
give themselves completely to the 'experimental techniques' of modern
educators." The author finds the same attitudes in the Social Gospel movement of the early twentieth century, which tried to implement reform by
appealing to the principles of Christian love and to the progressive move-

ment, which based its goal upon reason and science. The privileged classes of that time were so certain of their superiority or so worried about their loss of status that they would never accept these appeals to reason and love. Similarly, political realists (Niebuhr places many Marxists and Socialists in this group) who eschew moral motives also ignore human nature. Force and violence may be necessary, but an exclusive reliance on them creates new forms of tyranny. Niebuhr notes that "if the Russian oligarchy strips itself of its own power, it will be the first oligarchy of history to do so." Moreover, Niebuhr argues that many Marxists, despite their professions of realism, hold to the same naive belief in reason in parts of their theories as liberals and religious reformers do. We cannot expect the class of workers to espouse a perfect morality, for in his or her oppression the "proletarian is not enough of a whole person." Just as the privileged classes use morality as a cloak for hypocrisy, the workers' morality is a cloak for vengeance.

In light of the promises of moral man and an immoral society, what does the activist do? Niebuhr insists that the drive for justice must never cease; it must sometimes be pursued through violence, but we must never forget that complete justice is never possible. *Moral Man and Immoral Society* is a unique book, especially in light of the historical moment in which it was written. Niebuhr argued that individualism, in the sense of individual capacity for goodwill, was always threatened either by our own individual capacity for self-deception or through the group will, which always treads over the needs of others. The book contains an impassioned plea for social justice as well as a warning to both those seeking to maintain their power and those seeking to overturn it. If there is a fault to Niebuhr's approach, however, it lies in the fact that nowhere does he outline what kinds of institutions can preserve some measure of morality in politics. This absence is especially glaring when we consider the fact that the very struggle for equality urged by Niebuhr requires an increase in the scope and number of institutions that, on his own terms, will inevitably restrict moral behavior.

America, of course, has its own revolutionary tradition—even though it is a special kind of revolutionary theory—and, as we have seen, the history of America is very much the history of political reform. But the political writers of the early 1930s found little help within the American tradition—at least in this respect. The crisis seemed so large and the possibility of the complete collapse of American society so real that conventional models of reform appeared irrelevant. We have noted how vague the critics tended to be in their promotion of planning and socialism. Equally frustrating for 1930s writers was the task of getting from the present to the future.

In a very popular book published in 1932 and entitled *Farewell to Reform*, John Chamberlain hammered away at the American reform tradition. From Jefferson to Jackson and the progressives, American reform always has had a "return connotation," according to Chamberlain. Some-how Americans must restore the "methods and possibilities of a more prim-itive capitalism." But the Depression showed that nothing had really delayed or halted the growth and concentration of capital. Chamberlain was particularly critical of the progressive tradition. He argued that writers like Thorstein Veblen, Herbert Croly, and Charles Beard had ignored funda-mental problems by relying upon technicians and enlightened business leaders without preparing any real plan as to how "to oust the high priests of profit." In fact, Chamberlain angrily found the same approach in the cur-rent works of George Soule and John Dewey. Similarly, Edmund Wilson complained that writers from the progressives to those of the 1930s seemed to constantly talk about the desirability of a planned society without mak-ing the task ahead plain. According to Wilson, only when theorists stated that their goal was "ownership of the means of production by the govern-ment" would Americans begin to listen.

Many writers focused upon the apparent indifference to radical ideas on the part of the American people. The American system was in collapse, and while there was anger and sporadic protest, where were the militant organizations? V. F. Calverton, an imaginative independent radical and edi-tor of the *Modern Quarterly,* blamed this state of affairs on what he called the *agrarian mind* in America. While it was true that some of the most vio-lent forms of protest were undertaken by farmers, Calverton argued that the American agrarian was too imbued with the individual pioneer spirit, the taste for cheap land, and the lack of experience in dealing with a feudal landlord class to undertake any truly collective action. The farmer's outlook was actually closer to the ideals of the lower-middle class than to the ideals of the worker. Calverton concluded that the rise of fascism was a greater possibility in America than a worker-based socialist revolution. Shopkeep-ers and farmers could be manipulated by bankers and industrialists into accepting restrictions on dissent and unionization.

If Calverton raised the specter of fascism American-style as a possible result of an embattled agrarian and middle-class America, Lewis Corey, a former member and founder of the American Communist party in the 1920s, tried to refashion Marxism in the American context in other ways. Anticipating by generations the idea of the *new class* offered by C. Wright Mills, Daniel Bell, and others, Corey identified a large stratum of American society (salaried employees, clerks, government bureaucrats, and profes-sionals) whose members had no real property to protect. Corey detailed what he called the *proletarianization of the middle class.* For instance, years ago a clerk was an "honored employee" in a small firm:

> His position was a confidential one, the employer discussed affairs with him and relied on his judgment; he might, and often did, become

a partner and marry the employer's daughter. The clerk was measurably a professional and undeniably a member of the middle class. But all this was changed by the collectivism of large-scale industry. Specialization and division of labor, mass education, increasingly deprived clerks of their old skills and scarcity value, particularly after office appliances began to mechanize not only skill but intelligence itself. The mechanization of clerical labor becomes constantly greater; a typical large office is now nothing but a white-collar factory. Real clerical earnings were practically stationary in 1914–26, but real wages rose. In 1929 the average clerical salary was $1400 yearly, not much more than the wage worker's $1200, while many organized skilled workers earned more than the great majority of clerical employees.

For Corey, members of this stratum of the middle class were already "objectively" part of the proletariat. They had no property to protect, had lost their individual craft functions at work, and were always threatened with unemployment. It was now possible to create an American middle class/worker coalition that would support the principles of freedom and democracy for everyone and not just for property owners, as the old middle class had done. But despite this relatively optimistic analysis, Corey expressed concern that the "objective" interests of this new middle class might not prove to be determinative and that these individuals would choose the "nightmare" of fascism.

In summary, then, the political thought of the early 1930s was a period of ferocious theorizing in which the major tenets of the American system were under sustained attack. While writers in this period were often frustrated in their efforts to outline the features of a new social order, they seemed to agree that the Depression had created a crisis like no other in American history. For them, capitalism had failed, and the American values of individualism had failed along with it.

FDR, THE NEW SOCIAL CONTRACT, AND THE NEW DEAL

Franklin Delano Roosevelt began his campaign for nomination and election in 1932, and then confronted the problem of governance by borrowing many ideas of the Depression-era political theorists and by rejecting others. Most significantly, however, he developed his own theory of the nature of the Depression and the kind of new society that could grow out of it.

If Hoover's reputation in regard to the Depression emphasizes ideological rigidity, Roosevelt's reputation largely rests upon his opportunism and general lack of attention to political thought. Although he had served two terms as an innovative governor of New York, he was regarded by many in 1932 as a candidate who was little more than a Democratic Harding.

Walter Lippman described FDR as "a pleasant man who, without any important qualifications for the office, would very much like to be President." Hoover, who later would see Roosevelt in demonic terms, emphasized his vacillations and inconsistencies. According to Hoover, Roosevelt was a "chameleon in plaid." The Communist party, which later made an uneasy peace with the New Deal, saw him as the last American president, an American Kerensky. Roosevelt himself did little to dispel assessments about his ideological sophistication. When a reporter once asked him to what ideology he was committed, he hesitated a moment and said, "I am a Christian and a Democrat." After his election in 1932 and throughout the New Deal, FDR came to be credited as a strategic genius, but rarely as a political theorist. Even the famous sympathetic assessment by Arthur Schlesinger, Jr., that the New Deal was an exercise in experimentation and a middle course between fascism and communism is based on the premise that the president had no "rigid ideology." Schlesinger did admit that Roosevelt might hire "bold and imaginative subordinates," but he did so in order to "balance the right and the left." All of these assessments, however, miss the major theoretical achievements of Franklin Roosevelt. For he was not simply a "country squire" from a distinguished family in Hyde Park, New York, or simply a brilliant political strategist. Roosevelt redefined the very nature of American liberalism, always staying within the bounds of the American political tradition, at a time when all existing variations were being declared dead.

The basic outlines of Roosevelt's approach can be found in his first speech in the race for the nomination. The address is quite brief and was delivered nationally on radio. Raymond Moley, an early trusted adviser in the candidate's brain trust, who broke with FDR in 1936, composed the draft for the speech. Ironically, he used William Graham Sumner's concept of the forgotten man in American society as the organizing theme. Sumner, as we have discussed, was a social Darwinist. Nevertheless, he had reminded his readers in one of his essays of the importance of "the simple, honest laborer" and the "clean, quiet citizen" in maintaining the capitalist system. Moley and Roosevelt took this idea and pushed it in very different directions. The candidate argued that Americans had had experience with crisis and experience with planning that could be used to fight the current Depression. In World War I America had faced a challenge and had responded to it by a national commitment to planning for war production. But Hoover had "either forgotten or does not want to remember" the success of this effort. In that war the United States had had a "great plan" because it was built "from the bottom to top and not from the top to bottom." Hoover had begun to plan for the "big banks, the railroads and the corporations." But FDR asked, "How much do the shallow thinkers realize that approximately one-half of our population, 50 or 60 million people, earn a living by farming or in small towns . . .?" Roosevelt did not say exactly what kind of planning he had in mind, but he assured his radio audience that it would include the participation of, and focus upon, "Main Street," "farm owners," "little local banks," and "local loan companies."

The themes intimated in the Forgotten Man speech—the American precedent for planning, the need for democratic action, the focus on problems facing the middle class, the charge that the Depression was being prolonged (if not precipitated by elites)—all these themes were drawn upon through the 1932 campaign and, indeed, throughout the entire New Deal. In a Jefferson Day address in St. Paul, Minnesota, FDR spoke of the role of the federal government in the promotion of economic policy. He described the men he called two great planners, Jefferson and Hamilton, and their respective approaches. Hamilton, though a "financial genius," believed that only certain sections of the country and certain individuals were fit to conduct government. Jefferson, on the other hand, rode across the young country on horseback, "slowly and laboriously accumulating an understanding of the people in this country." He learned of the "yearnings and lack of opportunity, the hopes and fears of millions" of Americans and built a political party in support of the common principles of the people. Roosevelt then briefly described the conflicts between Hamiltonian and Jeffersonian approaches throughout American history. He called for a "new concert of interests" based on "imaginative and purposeful planning" in accord with the model provided by Jefferson. The speech contained few examples of just what was to be planned, although FDR mentioned his policies as governor on the use of public power on the St. Lawrence River. He went on to assure his audience that he did not speak of an "economic life completely planned and regimented."

The Concert of Interest address was a brilliant speech, even if FDR's reading of history may have been suspect. Aside from articulating the themes mentioned above, Roosevelt outlined a general approach to the Depression that was different from Hoover's in terms of American political thought. A new administration would resemble more the revolution of 1800 than the Russian model that was of increasing interest to the early Depression writers. FDR had appropriated the Jeffersonian symbol, one of the most powerful in American political culture, as a model for national reform. The conservative opposition within the Democratic party had come to regard themselves as "Jefferson Democrats," and Hoover himself had cited Jefferson as proof of the need for local governments to solve problems. But Roosevelt asserted that Jefferson was "no local American." Jefferson had galvanized a whole people under threat of domination by aristocrats; he had been "willing to stake his fortunes on the stroke of a pen" when he purchased Louisiana, which "trebled the size of the nation over night." Not so subtly Roosevelt intimated that Hoover was the modern-day Hamilton.

In his speeches Roosevelt suggested that the Depression could be ended by symbols and methods within the American political tradition. He also "Americanized" the sources of the Depression. It would have been surprising, indeed, in an election campaign if FDR had not blamed the Depression on Hoover. FDR used Hoover's analogy of the Depression as a storm sweeping across American shores from Europe to attack the Hoover administration's competence: "[T]here are glimpses through the clouds, of troubled officers pacing the deck wondering what to do. . . ." But the candidate's critique quickly broadened not only to include Hoover and the Republicans but also the entire corporate business elite. His Oglethorpe University address, which is famous for its injunction that the country required "bold, persistent experimentation," also contained a picture of the "rose-colored days" of the 1920s when every American was told he "could sit back and read in comfort the hieroglyphics called stock quotations which proclaimed that their wealth was mounting miraculously without any work on their part." But this prosperity was a "mirage" fostered by financial leaders and men in high public office. Corporate leaders had engaged in "gigantic waste," "superfluous duplication," "questionable methods of raising capital," "continual scrapping of useful equipment," and the depression of wages despite huge profits. They were "selfish" and "opportunist." In his nomination acceptance speech, FDR described the 1920s as a "period of loose thinking, descending morals, and an era of selfishness." "Let us be frank to admit," he told the delegates, "many of us too have made obeisance to Mammon."

Roosevelt's inaugural address, delivered in the depths of the Depression, announced the abdication of the entire business class:

> The money changers have fled from the high seats in the temple of our civilization. We may now restore the temple to the ancient truths. The measure of the restoration lies in the extent to which we apply social values more noble than mere monetary profit.

Roosevelt had accepted the assessment of Dewey and other writers that America was a money culture, but only in part. For FDR insisted that the "unscrupulous money changers" now "indicted in the court of public opinion" represented only an aberrant period in American history.

Late in the 1932 campaign Roosevelt gave a speech to a group of business leaders in San Francisco and pulled all these elements into a general philosophical approach to government. The Commonwealth Club address has been treated skeptically by historians. Arthur Schlesinger, Jr., for instance, admits that it was a powerful speech but believes that it represented Berle's thinking more than Roosevelt's. Yet there is evidence that FDR encouraged his speech writers to draft an address that would directly refute Hoover's philosophical understanding of individualism. The original title of the address was "Individualism: Romantic and Realistic."

The speech is structured around sets of pairs. Roosevelt compares the growth of central governments to that of centralized industry. He compares the rise of European monarchies to the new "princes of property." He compares Jefferson to Hamilton. He compares the needs of a country with a frontier to those of one whose "plant is built." The theme of the essay deals with one of the central preoccupations of political philosophy: How are rights preserved and exploitation avoided across time?

Often overlooked in analyses of the address is Roosevelt's presentation of great leaders. They are portrayed here in ambivalent terms, not unlike in Lincoln's Lyceum address. Lincoln had spoken of the need for men of great ambition at the time of the founding and of the threat they posed in an established republic. Roosevelt recounts the contributions of the "creators of national government" in Europe. "The people preferred the master far away to the exploitation and cruelty of the smaller master near at hand." The people, by and large, wanted "a strong stable state to keep the peace, to put the unruly nobleman in his place, and to permit the bulk of individuals to live safely." There were, however, "ruthless" men, and when there came a growing feeling that "ambition and ruthlessness" had "served their term," the people sought a "balancing—a limiting force." Roosevelt describes the new institutional forms created for this purpose—town councils, trade guilds, national parliaments, constitutions, and elections—as well as the formulation of the tenet that rulers bore a responsibility to their subjects.

America had come into existence as part of this struggle. Our own institutions reflected this concern with the oppressive consequences of centralized political power. But new kinds of creators came to fulfill a similar role in this country. Roosevelt traces their emergence to the Industrial Revolution and the "new dream" it created:

> The dream was the dream of an economic machine, able to raise the standard of living for everyone; to bring luxury within the reach of the humblest; to annihilate distance by steam power and later by electricity, and to release everyone from the drudgery of the heaviest manual toil.

But there was a "shadow over the dream." "To be made real, it required use of the talents of men of tremendous will and tremendous ambition. . . ." The American people accepted these men "fearlessly" and "cheerfully." "It was thought that no price was too high to pay for the advantages which we could draw from a finished industrial system." The methods of these men were "not scrutinized with too much care." The "financial Titans" were "always ruthless, often wasteful, and frequently corrupt." FDR estimates that investors paid for railroads three times over. But the railroads were built, and "we still have them today." With this task now completed, however, these American creators threaten the people like the old feudal barons: "great uncontrolled and irresponsible units of power within the State" are a danger to everyone's ability to earn a living.

As with all of Roosevelt's speeches, Jefferson is turned to for a solution. He had beaten back the Hamiltonian challenge that only a "great and strong group of central institutions" led by "a small group of able and public-spirited citizens" could best govern. In its place Jefferson had devised two sets of rights. Those of "personal competency," such as freedom of speech, required limitations on governmental power. Property rights, so argues Roosevelt, are historically variable in their implementation.

"But even Jefferson realized that the exercise of the property rights might so interfere with the rights of the individual that the Government, without whose assistance the property rights could not exist, must intervene, not to destroy individualism, but to protect it." Now a "re-appraisal of values" was necessary. FDR's solution is presented in Jeffersonian terms. A new "social contract" is required. "Every man has a right to life; and this means that he has also a right to make a comfortable living." "Every man has a right to his own property; which means a right to be assured, to the fullest extent available, in the safety of his savings." If the economic elite cannot meet these requirements, the "Government must be swift to enter and protect the public interest." The "apparent Utopia which Jefferson imagined for us in 1776" was still obtainable.

Perhaps Roosevelt had held true to the essence of Jeffersonianism; perhaps all he was doing was applying Jeffersonian principles to "new conditions." Or had he used Jefferson to reach a Hamiltonian solution in which "a great and strong group of central institutions" led by a "small group of able and public spirited citizens" would be the guardians of happiness? Throughout the 1930s critics would ask similar questions.

Despite the philosophical smoothness of Roosevelt's transition from the rights of competency to the new social contract, the New Deal in practice struggled mightily in implementing the new order. The attempt to form a "concert of interests" in the form of the National Recovery Administration (NRA) proved to be a failure. The NRA permitted the suspension of antitrust restrictions for business in return for their promise to improve working conditions and pay a living wage. Roosevelt seems to have abandoned this approach even before it was declared unconstitutional by the Supreme Court in 1935.

The idea had been to reach an accord with corporations in which wage-and-price agreements would be set by the government in exchange for exemption from antimonopoly restrictions. Aid to farmers in the form of the Agricultural Adjustment Act (AAA) was more successful, but critics were often astounded by the policy of reducing food production in such a time of need. The president spent millions of dollars on various relief projects. Its participants almost uniformly agree that such projects saved the lives of their families, and the range of public work was quite impressive. Unemployed individuals hired by the government built medical centers, water supply systems, amphitheaters, bridges, and air fields; they also performed plays and wrote books. FDR always regarded these programs as temporary, twice reducing funding for them before they were all eventually dismantled by more conservative Congresses in the late 1930s.

The new rights to make a living and to have safe savings accounts were not pursued until 1935. Much of this legislation, including social security, unemployment insurance, and the federal guarantee to labor of the right to organize unions, came after prodding by the president's advisers and Congress. Moreover, no efforts seemed to cure the country of Depression. When the president, in frustration over the Supreme Court's lack of sympathy with his programs, proposed to "pack" the court, the momentum of reform rapidly dissipated. By 1937 the New Deal was, for all practical purposes, dead.

NEW DEAL CRITICS

Even with these limitations the New Deal had no absence of critics. It was FDR who largely set the agenda for the politics of the 1930s. Theorizing about the nature and implications of the Depression continued—accompanied henceforth by assessments of the New Deal itself. Very broadly speaking, some critiques centered around a concern that the New Deal might have strayed too far from the American political tradition. Other critics argued that FDR had not departed far enough.

Hoover continued his debate over Roosevelt's premises. After 1932 the former president talked less about FDR's vacillation than about his plan to Europeanize America. A typical formulation of Hoover's argument can be seen in a speech he delivered to the Colorado Young Republican League in 1936. According to Hoover, in Europe after World War I and at this very moment, "Liberty has been dethroned and dictatorship erected by men greedy for power." These leaders (whom Hoover leaves unnamed) blamed the "tragic miseries of the times" on "some party or class":

> They made great promises. They demanded violent action against human ills that are only slowly curable. They claimed that sporadic wickedness in high places had permeated the whole system of liberty. They shouted new destructive slogans and phrases day by day to inflame the people. They implanted hates in the souls of men. They first grasped at power through elections which Liberty provided. Then be-

gan most of the emergency instruments of power to "save the nation." The first demands were powers of dictation over industry and agriculture and finance and labor. Legislatures were reduced to rubber stamps. Honest debate was shut off in the halls of deliberation . . . these men insisted the civilization had begun all over again when they came to power.

Finally, Hoover argued, "Liberty died," and men were "goose-stepped in a march back to the Middle Ages." The New Deal "has imitated the intellectual and vocal technique of typical European revolution." The NRA and AAA were the first steps in this process. A second step, and this one angered Hoover most of all, was the New Deal's claim that it was now the party of liberalism. He urged youth to reject this "false liberalism":

> The spirit of liberalism is to create free men. It is not the regimentation of men. It is not the extension of bureaucracy. You cannot extend mastery of government over the daily life of people without somewhere making it master of people's souls and thoughts.

Less well known but important in terms of American political thought (since it was an attack on what were perceived as the excesses of the New Deal from a different direction than Hoover's) was the position taken by the Southern Agrarians. In some ways the arguments of these writers were a minor recurrence of the reactionary Enlightenment we described in chapter 5. In 1930 twelve southern writers, many of them associated with Vanderbilt University and some with the literary journal *The Fugitive*, published a statement of principles and individual essays. Collectively these writings are entitled *I'll Take My Stand*. The Southern Agrarians, of course, were not devoted to a defense of slavery as Fitzhugh and others had been. Yet there was more than a dollop of racism in the Southern Agrarians' essays. For instance, Frank Lawrence Owsley complained bitterly about the Reconstruction and the northern belief after the Civil War that "the South had no history, or its history was tainted with slavery and rebellion." Robert Penn Warren's "The Briar Patch" argued that blacks were better off in a rural economy than an industrial one. (Warren later retracted this position.) The Southern Agrarians took for granted a southern culture for whites only. But the bulk of their argument was that the South was still an identifiable culture quite different from that of the North and far superior to it. Central to their position was the belief that agricultural labor was vastly preferable to its industrial counterpart. The latter was alienating; it was "mercenary and servile" while the former was connected to nature and designed for use. The Southern Agrarians accepted the poverty of their region (in fact, they romanticized it). Like their nineteenth-century counterparts, they compared this poverty favorably to the "overproduction, unemployment, and growing inequality" in the North. They declared their opposition to benevolent capitalists as well as to labor and socialist agitators who might come to reform their region. The Southern Agrarians hoped to provide a philosophical rationale for the "little agrarian community" attempting to "resist the Chamber of Commerce of its county seat, which is always trying to import some foreign industry that cannot be assimilated to the life pattern of the community."

The authors of the manifesto also saw religion threatened by industrialization. For them, "religion is our submission to the general intention of nature." But perhaps most of all, the Southern Agrarians drew a picture of a "Southern way of life." It consisted of "such practices as manners, conversation, hospitality, sympathy, family life, romantic love." In these kinds of "social exchanges which reveal and develop sensibility in human affairs," the South developed an alternative to the "strictly-business or industrial civilization" of the North.

Franklin Roosevelt had carefully attempted to avoid a clash with the Southern Agrarian viewpoint by moving cautiously on race questions as they affected the region and by catering to the needs of powerful congressional chairs for projects in their districts. But for some Southern Agrarians, the New Deal was at base simply another form of Yankee imperialism over the region. The most effective critic in this regard was Donald Davidson. *The Tennessee*, his two-volume history of the region, is very much an American masterpiece of regional history. In the second volume of the work, Davidson evaluated the Tennessee Valley Authority (TVA), a multistate federal project that provided electricity, water irrigation, and support for farmers in the region. The TVA was one of the most popular New Deal programs nationally. Even Norman Thomas, the head of the Socialist party, described it as a flower in a bed of weeds. Its third director, David Lilienthal, an indefatigable promoter of the project, wrote a book entitled *TVA: Democracy on the March*. Lilienthal argued that the program was a model not only for America but for the world since it showed that public planning could be efficient and democratic. For his ideological slogan he borrowed from Tocqueville, claiming that the TVA proved the virtues of a "decentralized administration of centralized authority."

For Davidson, however, the TVA had showed little interest in democracy. The administrators were like "kings"; the TVA was like the Yankee gunboats of the past; "happily armored," they "had chugged stolidly on." Administrators believed that the region had no real economy or culture. (A. E. Morgan, a former TVA administrator, had said that "a man seldom sees conditions as bad as in the city slums.") But Davidson insisted that an indigenous culture had managed to survive in the region despite Indian wars, slavery, and the Civil War. He horrifyingly described the evacuation procedures used to make room for the dams. Fourteen thousand people had been removed (more than four times the number of people evacuated in the

Cherokee removal of the 1830s). Nearly 500,000 acres had been flooded, 300,000 of which were farmland (more than the enclosures in England at the time of Henry VIII). Remaining farming was limited to dairying and raising cattle, sheep, and poultry. Here is Davidson's description of the remaking of the region:

> Green fields would be many, and tillage would be small. The Tennessee farmer would become a cattle raiser, a dairyman enslaved to the aching, compulsive teats of a herd of cows and to the trucks and price scale of Borden, Pet, Carnation. And then he might also become a forester, a mountain guide, an operator of tourist homes and hot-dog stands, a tipped purveyor and professional friend to tippling fishermen, hunters of ducks unlimited, abstracting artists, tired neurotics, and vacation seekers of all sorts. Under the TVA agricultural plan it might even turn out, eventually, that the various rural dialects of the valley would acquire a marketable value and could be entered among the farm assets, along with the blooded bulls, hogs, alfalfa, and refrigerators.

For Davidson the concerns and fears of the authors of *I'll Take My Stand* had become a reality under the New Deal.

Many individuals and groups who complained that the New Deal was too cautious had plans of their own. The new radio technology FDR used so effectively in his fireside chats to explain his program was, of course, available to others. Father Charles Coughlin, the radio priest from Royal Oak, Michigan, was an initial supporter of Roosevelt. "Roosevelt or ruin" was the choice as Coughlin saw it. His National Union for Social Justice was funded by listeners' contributions. Coughlin's early broadcasts were an unusual combination of reformist Catholicism and populism. Arthur Schlesinger, Jr., describes the radio orator thus: "For a season, Father Coughlin seemed a point of fusion between Populism and the Encyclicals, between William Jennings Bryan and Cardinal Gibbon." Bankers were Coughlin's nemesis, and his major critique of the New Deal was that it had not attempted to nationalize finance capital. As Coughlin's break with FDR became wider, his attacks became more eccentric and chillingly anti-Semitic.

Perhaps the most significant political threat to Roosevelt as the Depression wore on was Huey Long, a former governor and later U.S. senator from Louisiana. If any figure fit Hoover's description of men "greedy for power," it was Long, not Roosevelt. In fact, the president himself regarded Long as one of the two most dangerous men in America. Running for governor in 1928, Long, who was known as the *Kingfish*, adopted a slogan of Bryan's, "Every Man a King, but No One Wears a Crown." The slogan carried him to victory and later became the basis for his critique of the New Deal. As governor, Long initiated significant public works and welfare programs that were financed through taxes on the oil industry. He ruthlessly suppressed dissent, and his years as governor were rife with corruption. Long built up what Schlesinger contended was "the nearest thing to a totalitarian state the American republic had ever seen." Still many intellectuals were fascinated by this man's ambition and verve. (Robert Penn Warren's novel about Long, *All the King's Men*, is a classic American study of power as both a means and an end.) The poor farmers of Louisiana seemed to adore Long.

The Kingfish turned against Roosevelt early in the New Deal and developed a national organization of locals around a plan called "Share the Wealth." Although Long insisted that he had "never read a line of Marx or Henry George or any of them economists," the plan showed an amazing ideological ingenuity. Like all political panaceas, its attraction lay in its apparent practicality and simplicity. Long proposed a tax on all income over $1 million that would be used to finance what we would call today a *negative income tax* (Long called it a *homestead allowance*) of $5,000 and an annual income of $2,000. Long spoke in great detail about this capital endowment and the benefits it could provide. A radio, washing machine, and automobile could be in every home. The plan had certain ideological affinities to the Jeffersonian idea of property for every American and plans in the Jacksonian era for redistributing private wealth. There was no hint of public ownership in the plan. Hence Share the Wealth steered away from conventional socialism, and there was the beauty of the absence of bureaucratic structure. At least as Long saw it, checks were to be sent to the government by the wealthy and mailed out to millions of Americans.

Since Long died at the hands of an assassin in 1935, FDR was spared the prospect of Long as a third-party presidential candidate. But FDR still borrowed heavily from aspects of Long's program through his focus on the maldistribution of wealth in America. In his 1935 annual address to Congress, the president spoke of "weeding out" the "overprivileged" and shortly later proposed his *soak-the-rich* tax plan. FDR also redefined the goals of the New Deal in response to a reporter's question as a way of providing people "more of the good things of life, to give them a greater distribution not only of wealth in the narrow terms" but "places to go in the summertime recreation; to give them assurance that they are not going to starve in their old age. . . ."

In regard to the last objective cited by Roosevelt, a challenge to the New Deal emerged. Dr. Francis E. Townsend led a movement for a national pension plan that attracted widespread support not only among the elderly but also among those that saw it as a wedge to end the Depression. Townsend, unlike Long and Coughlin, was a man of quiet presence. (E. B. White uncharitably described him as a "skinny bespectacled little savior, with a big jaw, like the Tin Woodman.") Townsend proposed a monthly pension of $200 to all Americans over the age of sixty to be financed by a 2 percent business tax. The only catch was that each retiree must spend the money within the month. "And mind you," the doctor told his audiences, "we don't care a rap what you spend it for!" The idea, of course, was to provide care for the elderly while at the same time creating consumer spending and a demand for business activity. This was a principle that many New Deal economists from Gardiner Means to Rexford Tugwell championed in general terms. But the attraction of the Townsend plan rested on the same basic ideological terms as the proposals of Coughlin and Long: the redistribution of wealth without nationalization and bureaucratic planning.

As with so many New Deal critics, FDR outflanked the Townsend movement with his own plan. It was to be financed by a tax on workers' incomes, not from taxes on business; it exempted from coverage large groups of workers, including farm laborers and domestics. In fact, William E. Leuchtenberg, a sympathetic Roosevelt biographer, described it as an "astonishingly inept and conservative piece of legislation." But it was more than enough to derail the Townsendites, who tried to create a third-party movement in 1936, failed, and then disintegrated as a result of bickering and scandal among their leaders.

One of the most surprising stories of the Depression Era concerns the Socialists, a group that should have provided a sustained challenge to the New Deal. Ironically, the Communist party, while originally violently opposed to the New Deal in 1932, soon decided to cooperate with Roosevelt. Its membership rose dramatically throughout the 1930s. The Socialists, on the other hand, the more moderate left party, opposed the New Deal and saw their membership disintegrate. Norman Thomas, leader of the Socialist party and heir to Eugene V. Debs, received only 0.4 percent of the presidential vote in 1936, the lowest Socialist vote since 1900.

The causes of the collapse of a movement that had long predicted the collapse of capitalism at a time when enterprise nearly did collapse are multiple and complex. The failure of socialism in the 1930s did not entirely rest with Thomas's lack of theoretical originality, although he was certainly not an innovative thinker. In fact, in fundamental ways he was not even a Marxist. Bernard K. Johnpoll, a biographer of Thomas, concludes that he was "more Christian than Marxist, more pacifist than revolutionary." Nor did the failure of socialism result exclusively from Thomas's strategic errors, even though Thomas made plenty of mistakes. He failed to act as an honest broker between factions at the 1934 Socialist party convention in Detroit; as a result, the party suffered from massive defections. He also refused to support Upton Sinclair's 1934 campaign for governor of California as a Democrat despite the fact that Thomas admitted that, in all its fundamentals, Sinclair's platform was Socialist. Sinclair lost the election; the Socialist candidate did miserably; and the Socialist party membership in

California declined to 105 people by 1935. Nor did the failure result from Thomas's inability to provide a critique of the New Deal. He pointed out the fascist possibilities of the NRA and described the New Deal in general as "state capitalism," a system of government in which the state "makes concessions to workers in order to keep them quiet a while longer and so stabilize the power of private owners." He could be judicious in praising aspects of the New Deal. Thomas supported the TVA and said all workers should be grateful for the Wagner Act, which provided workers the right to organize into unions. He fought tirelessly for tenant farmers, who had been left out of the subsidy programs of the AAA.

But despite his own uniquely American moral vision, Thomas failed just as all the New Deal critics had. In fact, he admitted that his failure and the failure of his party could be explained in one word—*Roosevelt*. But it was not simply FDR's craftiness that defeated the Socialists in the 1930s. (Thomas in his unpublished autobiography complains that when he argued with the president in person, FDR had once answered, "Norman, I'm a damn sight better politician than you are.") However much Thomas might insist that Roosevelt was carrying out the Socialist platform "on a stretcher," the president had in fact carried out enough major reforms to satisfy the beleaguered American farmers and workers. As Johnpoll points out, "Thomas ran on the issue of socialism versus capitalism because he had no other issues left—Roosevelt had swept the ground from under him." To the unemployed, the question of the relative superiority of socialism over capitalism was much less important than a weekly paycheck. They were not interested in the fact that socialism had been proposing unemployment insurance for over thirty years. Irving Howe gave an assessment of Thomas in *Socialism in America*. According to Howe, the arguments of Thomas had a certain abstract remoteness about them; "they were too chilly in relation to the hopes the New Deal set off among workers" because in a certain way they were not theoretical enough. Howe contends that while the Socialists had a clear view of the nature of capitalism, they had "come to think of it as a fixed entity rather than as a developing system." What FDR had created was a theory of the welfare state which Howe defines as a "capitalist society partly transformed and humanized through the pressure of internal, democratic insurgencies and also through the improvisatory changes by a segment of the society's elite." In Thomas's defense, Howe admits that Thomas had seen the implications of this transition and named it *state capitalism*. But Howe thinks that the concept did not fully take into consideration the particulars of Thomas's own reactions to the New Deal. In any case, Thomas lost the argument—badly—perhaps in part because Americans saw the New Deal not as state capitalism or even as the welfare state but simply as a *concert of interests.*

SUMMARY AND COMMENT

From the vantage point of two generations after the Depression, much of the political thought of the period appears as dated as Hoover's optimistic pronouncements on the perfectibility of the American system. Belief in the imminent collapse of the old order, vague and often incomplete thinking about planning as a panacea, undue faith in particular plans (including those of the New Dealers), hyperbolic assessments of the motivations of competing groups, classes, and leaders—all of these are features of Depression political thought. The enthusiasm the New Deal brought seems a bit puzzling now (in fact, it wore thin by 1937) because Roosevelt's observations and programs seem either commonplace or mistaken.

But it is important to note that the Depression created an important debate over the current consensus on the American political system. Like all debates, the arguments are uneven. What is distinctive about Depression political thought is that the debate was more intense, and the examination of the premises of the American system more thorough, than any in American history. For even in the days before the Revolution and the period of the founding, the American system itself was not in danger of immediate disintegration. The American Civil War, of course, produced a sense of that same immediacy. But in a certain sense the argument could be closed, as indeed it was, by battlefield resolve. Depression writers, too, liked to think of their task and that of the American people in terms of the metaphor of war. Walter Lippman recognized the complexity of this aspect of the problem when he wrote in 1931 that "in war the objectives are concrete and simple. You have to mobilize men and munitions at a point where you can force the enemy to sue for peace. The whole nation is agreed on the objective, and minorities are silenced." Of course, war is only the outcome of an ideological debate, a point Lincoln knew well. But still, who was the enemy in the 1930s? And how was the nation to fight the war? Lippman saw the essence of the problem. There was a false analogy in thinking that "human society could be planned the way an ocean liner, for example, could be planned."

But if the war analogy confused rather than aided the debate to end the Depression, there were still clear-cut winners and losers. Hoover lost, but so did Norman Thomas. Depression intellectuals like Dewey, Niebuhr, and Mumford saw their visions modified and transformed in major ways. The Southern Agrarians lost, perhaps in the worst of all ways. Like the northern reaction to the southern Enlightenment, men like Davidson were largely ignored. Coughlin, Long, and Townsend, the leaders of incipient mass movements, lost after brief periods of ideological ascendancy. Only FDR and the New Dealers won. Why?

One reason is that Roosevelt was able to take major portions of the critiques of the American political system from people as diverse as Long and Dewey and fashion them into, if not a fully coherent political theory, at least a comprehensible vision. In constructing that vision, FDR found an elasticity in the American political tradition that few Depression writers had discovered or were even willing to admit. The concert of interests and the new social contract may not have been accurate readings of Jefferson, but they made the nature of the Depression and its end culturally understandable. The Depression, according to Roosevelt, was the outcome of a historic battle in America between Jeffersonians and Hamiltonians; it could be fought through a rededication to Jefferson "under modern conditions." In 1937 the president explained that the spirit of the barn railings and quilting bees of the frontier was now embodied in "carefully constructed statutes" that provided economic security. Of course, the winners of the 1930s were not to be permanently victorious. The New Deal consensus would have vigorous and able challengers who faced the victors under new circumstances and conditions. It is to that series of debates that we now turn.

✫ *Bibliographic Essay*

Conditions during the Great Depression are portrayed kaleidoscopically in Edward Robert Ellis, *A Nation in Torment: The Great American Depression, 1929–1939* (New York: McCann, 1970). Also see Broadus Mitchell, *Depression Decade* (New York: Harper & Row, 1947). Examples of eye-witness accounts discussed in the text are Laurence Hewes, *Boxcar in the Sand* (New York: Harper & Brothers, 1957); Edmund Wilson, *The American Earthquake* (New York: Doubleday, 1958); Louis Adamic, "Tragic Towns of New England," *Harper's* 162 (1931); Elmer Davis, "The Collapse of Politics," *Harper's* 165 (1932). Robert Lowitt and Maurine Beasley have collected the observations of the peripatetic Lorena Hickock, a New Deal assistant to Harry Hopkins, in *One Third of a Nation: Lorena Hickock Reports of the Great Depression* (Champaign: University of Illinois Press, 1981). Also see Studs Terkel's engaging and heartbreaking oral history, *Hard Times* (New York: Random House, 1970).

Herbert Hoover's major speeches are available in a reprint of a 1934 edition: *State Papers and Other Public Writings of Herbert Hoover*, 2 vols. (White Plains, NY: Kraus International, 1970). Also see Hoover's *The New Day* (Stanford: Stanford University Press, 1928) for speeches in his presidential campaign; *The Challenge to Liberty* (New York: Scribner's, 1934); *Addresses upon the American Road, 1933–1938* (New York: Scribner's, 1938); *Memoirs of Herbert Hoover*, 3 vols. (New York: Macmillan, 1951–52). For Hoover as a laissez-faire conservative, see Arthur Schlesinger, Jr., *The Crisis of the Old Order* (Boston: Houghton Mifflin, 1955); John Kenneth Galbraith, *The Great Crash* (Boston: Houghton Mifflin, 1955); Elliot

Rosen, *Hoover, Roosevelt and the Brain Trust* (New York: Columbia University Press, 1977). Reevaluations include Carl Degler, "The Ordeal of Herbert Hoover," *Yale Review* 52 (Summer 1963); Ellis W. Hawley, "Herbert Hoover and American Corporativism, 1929–1933," in Martin L. Fausold and George T. Mazuzan, eds., *The Hoover Presidency: A Reappraisal* (Albany: State University of New York Press, 1974); William Appleman Williams, *The Contours of American History* (Cleveland, OH: World, 1961); Joan Hoff Wilson, *Herbert Hoover: Forgotten Progressive* (Prospect Heights, IL: Waveland Press, 1992); Martin L. Fausold, *The Presidency of Herbert Hoover* (Lawrence: University of Kansas Press, 1985).

Depression political thought is brilliantly reviewed in Richard H. Pells, *Radical Visions and American Dreams* (Middletown, CT: Wesleyan University Press, 1973). Also see T. V. Smith, "The New Deal as a Cultural Phenomenon," in E. S. C. Northrup, ed., *Ideological Differences and World Order* (New Haven: Yale University Press, 1949); and Warren I. Sussman, "The Culture of the Thirties," in *Culture and History* (New York: Pantheon Books, 1984), for provocative interpretations of the period. The highly polemical atmosphere of the 1930s has produced some exceptional memoirs of the ideological battles of the period. See, for example, Alfred Kazan, *Starting Out in the Thirties* (New York: Vintage, 1980); Richard Wright, *American Hunger* (New York: Harper & Row, 1977); Sidney Hook, *Out of Step* (New York: Harper & Row, 1987).

A convenient collection of FDR's speeches is *Rendezvous with Destiny*, J. B. S. Hudson, ed. (Garden City, NY: Doubleday, 1974). There are some extraordinary biographies of Roosevelt and the New Deal: Arthur Schlesinger, Jr., *The Age of Roosevelt*, 3 vols. (Boston: Houghton Mifflin, 1957–1960); Frank Friedel's *Franklin Roosevelt*, 3 vols. (Boston: Little, Brown, 1973); James McGregor Burns's *Roosevelt: The Lion and the Fox*, and *Roosevelt: The Soldier of Freedom* (New York: Harcourt Brace Jovanovich, 1956, 1970). The best one-volume accounts are William E. Leuchtenburg's *Franklin Roosevelt and the New Deal* (New York: Harper & Brothers, 1963), and Robert J. McElvaine, *The Great Depression* (New York: Times Books, 1984), although Rexford Tugwell's *The Democratic Roosevelt* (Garden City, NY: Doubleday, 1957) is full of insights. Bruce Miroff, in his *Icons of Democracy* (New York: Basic Books, 1993), also has an interpretation of FDR as a leader who typifies "the possibilities and paradoxes in modern democratic leadership" which is well worth reading.

For assessments of the New Deal and FDR from theoretical perspectives, see Arthur Ekirk, Jr., *Ideologies and Utopias: The Impact of the New Deal in American Thought* (Chicago: University of Chicago Press, 1969); Paul Conkin, *The New Deal* (New York: Crowell, 1967); Harvard Sitkoff, ed., *Fifty Years Later: The New Deal Evaluated* (Philadelphia: Temple University Press, 1985); Morton Frisch, Jr., *Franklin D. Roosevelt* (Boston: Twayne Publishers, 1975). One can also discern ideological tensions within the New Deal by reading accounts of its participants. Most revealing are Hugh Johnson, *The Blue Eagle from Egg to Earth* (Westport, CT: Greenwood Press, 1968); Rexford Tugwell, *The Brain Trust* (New York:

Viking, 1968); Frances Perkins, *The Roosevelt I Knew* (New York: Viking, 1946); Raymond Moley, *The First New Deal* (New York: Harcourt Brace Jovanovich, 1966).

The Southern Agrarians' *I'll Take My Stand* has been reprinted with biographical essays by Louis D. Rubin (New York: Harper & Row, 1962). The agrarians and related ideological movements are perceptively discussed by Edward Shapiro, "Decentralist Intellectuals and the New Deal," *Journal of American History* 58 (1972). There have been some intriguing reexaminations of the Agrarians in recent years. See: Eugene Genovese, *The Southern Tradition* (Cambridge: Harvard University Press, 1994); Thomas Daniel Young, *Waking Their Neighbors Up* (Athens: University of Georgia Press, 1982) and William C. Havard and Walter Sullivan, eds., *A Band of Prophets* (Baton Rouge: Louisiana State University Press, 1982). The latter includes an imaginative essay by John Shelton Reed comparing the Southern Agrarians to later nationalist theorists and activists in comparative perspective. Long and Coughlin receive balanced treatment in Alan Brinkley's *Voices of Protest* (New York: Random House, 1982). Also see Charles Bull, *Father Coughlin and the New Deal* (Syracuse, NY: Syracuse University Press, 1965). Norman Thomas receives sympathetic treatment from Murray Seidler, *Norman Thomas: Respectable Rebel* (Syracuse: Syracuse University Press, 1961), while Bernard Johnpoll is quite critical in his biography, *Norman Thomas: Pacifist's Progress* (Chicago: Quadrangle, 1970). Thomas's revealing autobiography has never been published, but an example of his own views is contained in his *A Socialist's Faith* (New York: W.W. Norton, 1951). The role of the Communists in the 1930s is exhaustively treated in Harvey Kehr's *The Hey Day of American Communism* (New York: Basic Books, 1984).

✰ *Major Works*

1922	*American Individualism*, Herbert Hoover
1934	*The Challenge to Liberty*, Herbert Hoover
1932	*The American Jitters*, Edmund Wilson
1930	*Individualism: Old and New*, John Dewey
1935	*Liberalism and Social Action*, John Dewey
1934	*Technics and Civilization*, Lewis Mumford
1932	*Moral Man and Immoral Society*, Reinhold Niebuhr
1934	"Every Man a King Address," Huey Long
1932	"Concert of Interests Speech," Franklin D. Roosevelt
1932	"Commonwealth Club Address," Franklin D. Roosevelt
1933	"First Inaugural Address," Franklin D. Roosevelt
1930	*"I'll Take My Stand," Donald Davidson
1946-48	*The Tennessee*, Donald Davidson
1936	"Why I Am a Socialist," Norman Thomas

*A collaborative effort

Cold War

INTRODUCTION

In the late 1930s, Roosevelt carefully attempted to draw America away from an ideological commitment to isolationism. After his election to a third term, Roosevelt delivered an address that borrowed from Lincoln's assertion that American society could not endure "half slave and half free." FDR denied that "wars in Europe and in Asia are of no concern to us." Nazi conquest was "a modern form of slavery" and there could be "no ultimate peace between their philosophy of government and our philosophy of government." America, announced Roosevelt, could not endure in a world half slave and half free. A year later America was fighting a war on two fronts.

As allied forces neared victory, FDR began planning a new international order for the postwar world. To the American president, the peace in 1917 had failed because the great world powers failed to act in concerted fashion. Roosevelt led the planning for a more effective world organization than the old League of Nations. The United Nations, created in a series of meetings beginning with the 1944 Dumbarton Oaks Conference, was predicated upon the cooperation of the great powers. A Security Council was formed that included five permanent members (Britain, the United States, the Union of Soviet Socialist Republics [U.S.S.R.], France, and China), each with a veto power. Smaller nations were assigned a subordinate role in the organization through participation in a General Assembly.

By the time of Roosevelt's death in April 1945, this design for a new international system based upon great-powers cooperation was seriously disintegrating, and a new international system was emerging far different from the one FDR envisioned. Serious conflicts appeared at the Yalta Conference of the allied powers in February. Churchill was distrustful of Stalin's motives in Eastern Europe, especially in Poland. Roosevelt acted in the role of mediator. A generally worded communiqué promised interim governments "broadly representative of all democratic elements," followed by "free elections" throughout Eastern Europe (although the Soviets had refused to recognize the non-Communist Polish government in exile).

At the Potsdam Conference in July, President Harry S. Truman complained publicly about the failure of the Soviets to respect the Yalta accords with regard to Eastern Europe. Stalin's reply to these kinds of objections was that "whoever occupies a territory also imposes his own social system . . . as far as his army can reach. It cannot be otherwise." In March 1946 Winston Churchill delivered a speech at Westminster College in Fulton, Missouri. He declared: "From Stettin in the Baltic to Trieste in the Adriatic, an iron curtain has descended across Europe."

The first crisis that resulted from the antagonism between the United States/Britain and the U.S.S.R. occurred in Iran. Soviet troops refused to withdraw from northern Iran as scheduled in March. Truman sent an ultimatum to the Soviets, urged Iran to take its case to the United Nations, and informed the press of his actions before he received a response. A week later a troop withdrawal agreement with Iran was announced by the Soviets. American-Soviet disagreements, conflicts, and competition seemed to appear everywhere and on every issue. No agreement on German reparations could be reached. Truman said that the Russians could take what they wanted only from their zone of occupation. Action on a Soviet request for loans from the United States was delayed. Truman refused to permit the Soviets to share in the allied occupation of Japan. The Red Army's grip on Eastern Europe tightened; there were daily conflicts between the Western allied forces and Soviet occupation troops in Berlin.

Open war between the Americans and the Soviets seemed imminent. That war did not occur, and there is a new international system developing. But for over thirty years, with brief periods of limited cooperation, the United States and the Soviet Union fought a *cold war*. The international system that emerged from the devastation of World War II created a new world for Americans. The United States, of course, had engaged in international conflicts throughout its history. But participation was sporadic and usually limited to the Western Hemisphere. America had clearly attained great power status as a result of World War I, but it largely refused to accept that role. In the words of John G. Stoessinger (*Crusaders and Pragmatists*), "[O]nce the sinner was punished and evil was purged, the United States could once more withdraw into itself, certain in the knowledge that force had been used in the cause of righteousness. The 'city on the hill' was once again secure." World War II produced an international system that sheared away the competitive multipolar dominance of European powers. Germany was in ruins. Britain and France could no longer maintain their colonial empires. The international system had become bipolar. "Not since Rome and Carthage," concluded Dean Acheson, secretary of state in the Truman administration, "had there been such a polarization of power on this earth."

Multipolar international relations can certainly lead to war (as they did in 1914) and mete out harsh treatment to lesser states. But the number of great powers can also lead to shifting alliances and some political maneuverability through attempts to maintain a *balance of power* among participants. A bipolar system, however, is much more intense and limiting, since it leads to the perception on the part of both parties that conflict is a *zero-sum game* in which one side must win and the other suffer defeat. In 1947 President Truman, in what became known as the Truman Doctrine, outlined the nature of the new struggle in his request to Congress to aid Greece in its fight against communist guerrillas. He announced that "at the present moment in world history nearly every nation must choose between alternative ways of life." One way of life "is based upon the will of the majority, and is distinguished by free institutions . . . the second way of life is based upon the will of the minority . . . terror and oppression."

Bipolarity was not the only feature of this new international system. Air warfare had already revolutionized international politics by making any nation vulnerable to some kind of attack. According to John H. Herz, with the perfected level of airborne destruction reached in World War II, "the roof blew off the territorial state." The development of the atomic bomb radically altered international politics. The United States held a monopoly briefly on the weapon. When the Soviets produced their own bomb in 1949, Harold Lasswell, a political scientist, concluded that a U.S.-U.S.S.R. war at that time "might not end with one Rome but with two Carthages." Strategists disagree about the extent to which nuclear weapons prevented a war between the new superpowers in the late 1940s and early 1950s. But this much was certain: for nuclear weapons to function as deterrents against war, neither side could enjoy dramatic advantages in its arsenal or delivery systems. Such a lead might encourage one power to engage in nuclear blackmail (that is, the other side must accede to certain demands or face destruction). Alternatively, one of the powers might risk a "first strike." Only two basic alternatives are available in this dilemma: a mutual arms reduction, or a race on each side to match the perceived future advantages on the other side. The first alternative was largely impossible to achieve throughout most periods of the Cold War. The second led to the creation of what was called a *mutually assured destruction* (MAD) strategy, that is, the building of huge arsenals and extensive delivery systems to create a

balance of terror that would guarantee a protection against the temptation
to initiate a first strike on both sides.

Another aspect of this new bipolar international system was its pronounced tendency to produce crises. In a two-party conflict, particularly
one in the nuclear age, miscalculation of the will or strength of the other
party creates almost immediately a destabilization of the system. The Cold
War was strewn with serious international crises. Stalin miscalculated the
West's resolve when he ordered a blockade of Berlin in 1948 and when he
accepted North Korea's plan to militarily unite Korea in 1950. The United
States miscalculated the chances of China's entry into the war in Korea. Frequently, conflicts in the Third World would not bend to bipolar resolution,
as the United States learned in Vietnam and with the U.S.S.R. in Afghani-
stan. In one instance, the Cuban missile crisis of 1962, the two superpowers
came to the brink of nuclear war.

How did Americans respond to the responsibilities and frustrations of
such a central participation in this new international system and to carrying on the Cold War for over thirty years? One group of theorists, by no
means unanimous in their assessments, attempted to justify American participation in this struggle. Another group—again far from uniform in their
approaches—attempted to gauge the price Americans were paying for their
assumption of these new international commitments.

COLD WARRIORS

The term *cold warrior* became a negative description among Cold War critics, particularly during the Vietnam War. But for much of the period of
intense bipolar conflict, it was accepted with pride and honor. Martial met-
aphors such as *cold warrior* and *soldier of freedom*, imaginatively borrowed
from republican theory, were meant to characterize those who were
devoted to clarifying and implementing American policy in what President John F. Kennedy later called "a long twilight struggle."

One of the analysts who provided the theoretical bases for the Cold
War was George F. Kennan. A Soviet specialist and head of a newly formed
Planning Staff in the State Department, Kennan was asked by the secretary
of defense to respond to a paper on Soviet international objectives written
by a government official. Portions of Kennan's critique of this internal document were presented to the Council on Foreign Relations, an influential
organization of experts in international politics, in January 1947. The
enthusiastic reception by the council resulted in the publication of a version of the memorandum to the secretary in its journal, *Foreign Affairs*, as
"The Sources of Soviet Conduct." Since Kennan was a State Department

official and his position was not a settled government policy, the authorship was designated as "Mr. X."

The essay consisted of three parts: an assessment of the origins of Soviet conduct in the world, the nature of Soviet decision making in terms of Russian society, and recommendations for U.S. foreign policy. Kennan began by accepting the fact that Soviet actions were driven by its leaders' belief in the tenets of Marxism. He described these tenets as a belief in economic determinism ("[T]he central factor in the life of man . . . is the system by which material goods are produced and exchanged"); as a belief in capitalism as an exploitive system; as a belief that capitalism is a naturally self-destructive system; and as a belief that the last stages of capitalism require imperialistic policies that will eventually lead to war and revolution. Reinforcing these beliefs was a "Russian-Asiatic" worldview "unmodified by any of the Anglo-Saxon traditions of compromise." When the Russian leaders adopted Marxism, they "carried with them a skepticism as to the possibilities of permanent and peaceful coexistence of rival forces." Antagonism to capitalism was fortified by the traditional Russian hostility to the West.

These two sources of Soviet conduct had already created a police state in the U.S.S.R. Between 1917 and 1945 every possible remnant of capitalism and freedom had been erased from Russian society. Only with the adoption of the New Economic Policy (NEP) in the early 1920s had the Soviets retreated from this path. Faced with economic collapse, Lenin had temporarily permitted the reemergence of a small capitalist sector. Kennan suggested that had Lenin lived, "he might have been a great enough man" to reconcile the two economic systems in the country for the "ultimate benefit of Russian society." But Stalin reverted to the Marxist and Russian traits that Kennan believed were likely to characterize Soviet leadership for many years to come. Now the justification for continued repression was a fantasy, since a system of concentration camps and an enormous secret police apparatus had virtually exterminated any kind of opposition. But the Soviet leadership continued to insist upon the maintenance of organs of repression because of the alleged "menace of capitalism abroad."

Thus Kennan concluded that "we are going to continue for a long time to find the Russians difficult to deal with." The situation was made even more difficult because traditional diplomacy was practically impossible. The concentration of power in the Soviet Union was so complete that its diplomats had no leeway to negotiate. Borrowing from an RCA commercial, Kennan compared the Soviet diplomat to the white dog before the phonograph: both hear only their master's voice. Moreover, the Soviet Union was "under no ideological compulsion to accomplish its purposes in a hurry." Absolutely convinced of the validity of their beliefs about capitalism, its leaders could "afford to be patient." Kennan added that "again, these precepts are fortified by the lessons of Russian history." Russians had fought "centuries of obscure battles between nomadic forces over the stretches of a vast fortified plain."

What options, then, were available for an American foreign policy in regard to the U.S.S.R.? Kennan concluded that all was not lost. It was possible both to avoid war with the Soviets and to avoid the gradual but steady loss of ground in the face of their persistent pursuit of a Communist world empire. Two assessments were fundamental to Kennan's analysis on this crucial point. First, Soviet conduct contained an element of rationality. Since its leaders "looked forward to a duel of infinite duration," it was felt they could afford to compromise whenever necessity required caution. "Thus the Kremlin has no compunction about retreating in the face of superior force. And being under the compulsion of no timetable, it does not get panicky under the necessity of such retreat." Second, the Soviet economic and political system was, for Kennan, a vulnerable one. The military buildup and the terror created "a population which is physically and spiritually tired." Soviet economic achievements were formidable in certain areas, but overall economic development was "spotty and uneven." Work habits were sloppy; maintenance was inefficient; and construction was "hasty and poor in quality." Kennan felt that none of these features of the Soviet economy was likely to improve with "a tired and dispirited population working largely under the shadow of fear and compulsion." Since the Soviet system had no constitutional apparatus for leadership succession, the death of a leader always raised the possibility of "shak[ing] Soviet power to its foundations." Kennan concluded that Soviet power was not as secure as "Russian capacity for self-delusion would make it appear to the men in the Kremlin"; in the long term it was likely to become more precarious. An American policy of "long-term, patient but firm and vigilant containment of Russian expansive tendencies" would eventually lead to an American victory.

Kennan warned of two tendencies in American society that must be avoided in order to assure the success of his containment strategy. One was the proclivity to believe that a tactical retreat by the Soviets "when they want something from us" means that "the Russians have changed." In his speech before the Council on Foreign Relations, Kennan warned against the belief that policy could be formed on "a personal basis, by glad hand and a winning smile." Another concern was the tendency toward a histrionic foreign policy. Containment "has nothing to do with . . . threats and blustering or superfluous gestures of outward 'toughness.'" Like any government, argued Kennan, the U.S.S.R. "can be placed by tactless and threatening gestures in a position where it cannot afford to yield even though this might be dictated by its sense of realism."

In one way the reception of "The Sources of Soviet Conduct" was a theoretically informed policymaker's dream. Reporters quickly discovered that Kennan was the author of the essay. He almost immediately became known as the intellectual architect of the American policy of containment that was practiced through the decades of the Cold War. But for Kennan, the implementation of his strategy was so badly flawed that the essay sometimes became a personal nightmare. His complaints over the years corresponded roughly to the two tendencies he warned against as Mr. X. He approved of the goal of aiding nations threatened by communism but objected to the language of the Truman Doctrine. The justification for aid was hyperbolic and Manichaean—features of American policy that might produce a Soviet response opposite from American objectives. He offered a more moderate draft of Truman's speech before Congress. It was rejected. Kennan was both terrified and demoralized by the anti-Communist speeches of Senator Joseph McCarthy. In 1953 Kennan told the members of the Century Club:

> I do not see how you can have a satisfactory situation as long as an at-
> mosphere exists in which shibboleths are allowed to be established and
> to prevail, to the detriment of normal discussion—an atmosphere in
> which simple alternatives of foreign policy cannot even be discussed
> without leading to charges of subversion and treason—an atmosphere
> in which name calling and insinuation take the place of calm and free
> debate.

Kennan also warned policymakers in the 1970s not to raise their expectations about detente. Although he recognized that important changes had occurred in the U.S.S.R. and advocated more negotiation, he said: "The United States would do well not to indulge in unreal hopes for intimacy with either the Soviet regime or the Soviet population. There are deeply rooted traits in Soviet psychology—some of old Russian origin, some of more recent Soviet provenance—that would rule this out." Kennan included among these traits "the congenital disregard for the truth," "hysterical preoccupation with espionage," and "continued fear of foreigners."

David Mayers, an astute biographer of Kennan, has attempted to place his political thinking within the American political tradition. Mayers finds many strands in Kennan's thought: they range from a Puritan devotion to guardianship and asceticism to the moralistic republicanism of John Quincy Adams and to the theology of Reinhold Niebuhr. Kennan himself acknowledged Niebuhr as his greatest influence. But in Mayers's estimation, Kennan is fundamentally a twentieth-century Hamiltonian: "Like Hamilton, Kennan is by instinct and intellect a Federalist." Mr. X has a deep distrust of democracy (he once described America as a "raucous equalitarian republic"). Like Hamilton, Kennan has a vision of an executive-dominated government that would oversee America's interests, largely independent of the tides of public opinion. When the policy of containment is not followed with the coolness and patience Kennan demands, he blames departures from it on demagogues and restless citizens.

As influential as Kennan's containment policy was, the full theoretical justification of the Cold War came from individuals without Kennan's Puritan and Federalist outlook. It is a matter of some irony that the major intellectual achievements of Cold War political thought in America were realized by people who were members or *fellow travelers* (those individuals who had close ties to the Communist party and were sympathetic to many of its positions but who were not members) of the Communist party in the 1930s. This development is not as unexpected as one might first imagine. Many intellectuals broke with the party at some point in the 1930s. They spent the remainder of the decade battling the Communists from new ideological positions secured in the New Deal Democratic party or, more likely, in various groups among the American Left. These groups, which included the Socialist party and the Workers party or followers of Leon Trotsky, attacked the Communists and were attacked by them. Moreover, political philosophy and strategy in the 1930s were intensely and ferociously debated. Thus survivors of factional wars among the Left-wing parties of the decade were highly trained theorists and fierce debaters.

One such cold warrior was James Burnham, the son of a well-to-do railroad executive and a graduate of Princeton and Oxford universities. As a professor at New York University, Burnham focused on the intersection between philosophy and literature. He coedited a journal devoted to this theme called *The Symposium*. In the early thirties he sparred with the Communist party in the pages of the journal, complaining that the Communists were thoughtlessly subservient to the Russians and ignorant of American society and politics. After reading Trotsky's *History of the Russian Revolution* and Sidney Hook's reinterpretation of Marx (*Toward an Understanding of Karl Marx*), Burnham joined the newly formed American Workers party (AWP) led by Hook and A. J. Muste. When the AWP merged with the followers of Leon Trotsky to form the Workers party in 1934, Burnham, along with Max Schactman, edited a monthly journal called the *New International*. As a regular contributor and editor, Burnham became one of the most feared polemicists of the 1930s, criticizing New Dealers and members of both the Socialist and Communist parties. In 1939 Burnham broke with Trotsky over the latter's support for the Russian occupation of Poland and the war with Finland. To Burnham, it no longer made sense to call the U.S.S.R. a "degenerated workers' state" worthy of conditional support because of "capitalist encirclement."

Some of Burnham's most original work was written after his break with the Workers party. *The Managerial Revolution* (1941) was what John

Diggins called Burnham's "answer to Trotskyism and a farewell to Marxism as a philosophy of history and as a program of hope—but not as a mode of analysis." Since 1914 a new political-economic system had been emerging, according to Burnham, that owed little to the predictions of those committed either to a capitalist or a communist future. Control of the economy and hence of the political system (Burnham was still committed to the economic determinism of Marx) can be traced to four interrelated groups: those responsible for "the actual technical process of producing" (operating executives, production managers, and plant superintendents); those responsible for "guiding the company for profit," whom Burnham called finance-executives and whom we would call today chief executive officers (CEOs); finance capitalists; and stockholders. Burnham admitted that in the United States, the third group (finance-capitalists) was "still the ruling class." But events in both Nazi Germany and Soviet Russia had shown that the functions of this group could be effectively undertaken by state managers. As to stockholders, Burnham never gave them much thought. They were largely passive elements in the new society. Groups one and two formed the new ruling class of the future.

Burnham's *managerial society* had already been outlined in its various parts by Veblen, Corey, and others in the United States. In Europe, Simone Weil, Jan Machajski, and Bruno Rizzi (who accused Burnham of plagiarism) had already discussed the power of those who managed the means of production, whether they operated in a communist or a capitalist society. Burnham was not even a very good futurologist in the short term, although long-term international developments might still confirm his assessment. He predicted that after the war Germany and Japan would be the major international powers since they were the most advanced managerially. The United States, which was still only a "primitive" managerial society, would be a power in the Western Hemisphere and the U.S.S.R. would split in half. The novelty of Burnham's thesis, however, rested on his assertion that the necessity of modern production created a new class that was not only impervious to the capitalist and Marxist slogans of liberty and equality but also would severely limit democratic practice wherever it emerged. Burnham was still enough of a Marxist, despite his break with Trotsky, to regard these developments as inevitable.

In America, the book sold 100,000 hardcover copies and was featured by *Time* and *Fortune* magazines. Lewis Corey criticized *The Managerial Revolution* as the work of "a doctrinaire radical gone sour," and C. Wright Mills called the book "a Marx for managers." But for many Americans the book offered a peek into the future that represented an alternative to fascism, communism, and prewar capitalism; hence it was a theoretical breakthrough from the ideological battles of the 1930s.

Two years later Burnham carried his analysis to an even higher level in *The Machiavellians*. Here he identified a tradition of elitist political thought that divorced ethics from political considerations, rejected metaphysics, and concentrated upon developing a "science of power." The thinkers Burnham highlights, with the possible exception of Niccolo Machiavelli, were not well known to Americans and as far from the American political consensus as Marx and Trotsky: Gaetano Mosca, Michels, Vilfredo Pareto, and Georges Sorel. Yet Burnham was careful to show that these men, who showed the inevitability of elite rule, were in fact the true "defenders of freedom," for only through a clear-headed analysis of power relationships can certain elites protect the people from the new managerial class. He also learned from the Machiavellians that, in order to preserve liberty, the elites must foster myths they themselves cannot permit themselves to believe in. "In short," concludes Burnham, "the leaders, if they themselves are scientific, must lie."

Here then was Burnham's general political theory at the eve of the Cold War. The world was moving toward a form of collectivism unforeseen by both capitalists and Marxists. The only force able to maintain some measure of freedom consisted of trained Machiavellian leaders. For decades Burnham used these two truths, discovered from his journey through the Left, to outline the nature of the Cold War. Writing on contemporary events in the *National Review* under the ominously titled column, "The Third World War" (later retitled "Protracted Conflict"), he criticized administration policy from Truman to Nixon.

Burnham's books attempted to place the Cold War in theoretical perspective. *The Struggle for the West* (1947) was published the week in which the Truman Doctrine was announced. If Kennan regarded the administration's rhetorical support of the Greek government as too provocative, he must have been at a loss for words at Burnham's description. The opening line of the book read: "The Third World War began in April, 1944." Total open war between the United States and the U.S.S.R. could begin at any moment. It would be fought until one side had complete control of the world. As a first step the United States must create a "world federation" or "world democratic order," which would become a "universal empire" after victory. Burnham had great doubts whether the American people were up to the task of undergoing this "long, difficult and perhaps terrible process," but he urged intellectuals and political leaders to seize the moment and galvanize the population. According to Burnham, the opportunity for world empire comes only at certain moments in history. "After only one failure, or refusal, the offer is withdrawn. Babylon, Athens, Thebes, Alexandria, Madrid, Vienna sink back, and do not rise again."

The Struggle for the West was widely read in Washington and interpreted largely as theoretical support for containment. *Containment or Lib-*

eration?, published in 1952, criticized the containment strategy as based on false hopes of eventual Soviet moderation. Burnham recommended more aggressive tactics, such as covert action in the Third World, the formation and recognition of non-Communist governments in exile, and support for resistance movements in Eastern Europe. Again, Burnham's analysis came at a propitious moment. The book appeared during the 1952 presidential campaign and provided the Republicans with intellectual support for their campaign promise of ending the Korean stalemate and "liberating captive nations."

After American impotence during the Soviet suppression of the Hungarian revolution in 1956, Burnham engaged in a reappraisal of his position. He briefly entertained the idea of a demilitarized Europe. His hopes were raised for a Cold War victory when Kennedy was elected president in 1960. Much to the consternation of his conservative colleagues at the *National Review*, Burnham praised the new president's "brave and lofty words" and characterized him as "a young David facing the Soviet Goliath." He soon lost faith, however, when JFK refused to support a U.S.-backed invasion of Cuba by exiles with air cover at the Bay of Pigs. Later Burnham recommended using chemical warfare in Vietnam and carrying the battle into China.

In 1964 Burnham published his last theoretical book, *Suicide of the West*, which was derived from a series of lectures delivered at Princeton University. Burnham's latest theoretical enterprise again became intertwined with presidential electoral politics, although this time he was on the losing side. Charles Frankel, for example, said that "*Suicide of the West* is the pure Platonic form of which Barry Goldwater is only the pale stammering shadow." Briefly, Burnham's major argument was that the United States had missed an opportunity to create a Pax Americana in the immediate postwar period; it was now undergoing a steady process of contracting influence, which would be followed by eventual disintegration. Rome had "kept her strategic eye on the destruction of Carthage" for two centuries. But "even granted mass incomprehension" of the meaning of the bipolar struggle, no American leader would undertake "the necessary measures" for victory. Burnham contended that this drift was not because America did not have a superior economic or military system. The West under American leadership simply had lost "the will to survive." The cause of this loss of will was "liberalism." Young Goldwater supporters almost certainly interpreted the ideological villain in the analysis in terms of liberal Democratic party politicians. Burnham actually had a much broader definition in mind: liberals were those who believed in the malleability of human nature, held a "faith in intelligence," believed in progress, and had little faith in custom.

James Burnham was an innovative thinker who devoted his considerable talents to assessing the nature of the Cold War. His travels through various ideological homes enabled him to borrow imaginatively from many traditions of political thought. Although for different reasons Burnham was much like Kennan in his rejection of modern democratic society, the description of liberalism he offered in *Suicide of the West* is a somewhat exaggerated depiction of large portions of the thought of Locke, Jefferson, John Stuart Mill, and the Enlightenment in general. One is forced to ask, then what was the West fighting for in the Cold War if not for democracy, progress, and freedom?

Another cold warrior who became even more alienated from American society was Whittaker Chambers. Chambers was one of many figures in America who made sudden, dramatic public appearances during the Cold War. In 1948 a quiet, disheveled, overweight man, who was at the time a senior editor of *Time* magazine, appeared before the House Un-American Activities Committee (HUAC). Chambers announced that he had been a secret Communist party agent. Until 1938 he had engaged in espionage work for the Soviet Union as part of a network which included at least seventy-five U.S. government officials. The most important official named by Chambers as a fellow underground Communist was Alger Hiss, a career civil servant who was then president of the Carnegie Endowment for International Peace. Hiss had served in the Agricultural Adjustment Administration. Once a counsel to a congressional committee, Hiss, as an officer in the State Department, had traveled to Yalta with FDR and had helped in the formation of the United Nations. At first, Hiss refused to say he ever knew Chambers. Chambers later accused Hiss of engaging in espionage and produced microfilm copies (hidden in pumpkins in his backyard) of government documents allegedly copied by Hiss in the 1930s. The charge of espionage could not be brought against Hiss since the alleged activity had occurred so long ago, but he was indicted for perjury. One trial resulted in a hung jury; a second trial convicted Hiss, who was sentenced to five years in jail.

The testimonies of Hiss and Chambers divided a generation of Americans. Who was telling the truth? In 1952 Chambers published his autobiography, *Witness*. There were numerous instances of confessional literature by former Communists during the Cold War. Benjamin Gitlow's 1948 autobiography, *The Whole of Our Lives*, provided sketches of his fellow Communists. Elizabeth Bentley's *Out of Bondage* (1951) vividly described Communist sexual and espionage activities. But in *Witness* Chambers's project was more ambitious. He attempted to link the course of his own life as a Communist and ex-Communist to the Cold War, the future of Western civilization, and even the meaning of life itself.

Autobiography as a form of expression can itself form a political theory, as it did in St. Augustine's and Rousseau's *Confessions*. Chambers's work certainly does not rank with these classics, but his effort to do so has fascinated both his detractors and admirers. He once described *Witness* as a poem and was convinced that it was the poetic force of the autobiography that explained its success, although he complained that people "read into it the meanings they chose." The narrative of Communist activity, spying, and accusing Hiss is given a theoretical structure through Chambers's exploration of three meanings of witness.

The first involves an account of the witnessing on which most readers probably focused on. Chambers recounts in great detail his appearances before HUAC, before the grand jury, and at the Hiss trial, which he describes as his "witness to acts." In this concept of witness he is greatly disturbed by the moral implications of breaking faith with a friend, for which he feels he must somehow pay a price. He has now become an informer: "Men shrink from that word and what it stands for as something lurking and poisonous."

The second meaning of witness describes Chambers's participation in the activities of the two competing forces of the twentieth century: "It was my fate to be in turn a witness to each of the two great faiths of our time." For Chambers his two roles as an underground Communist and cold warrior gave him a unique vantage point for analysis. *Witness* then is designed to provide an educative function for American readers. The opening chapter of the autobiography attempts to convey this point in the form of a letter to his children. He states that some day his children will ask: "Who is my father?" Chambers gives an answer: "I was a witness." The meaning of his life was not in remembering the "short, squat, solitary figure, trudging through the impersonal walls of public buildings," but in recalling his attempt to "witness for something."

Chambers believed he had discovered the secret of communism's success to date because he himself had been an activist and believer. He argued that the appeal of communism rests not with its program of hope to the downtrodden, nor with its party discipline, nor with the grandeur of its philosophical system. Communism is successful because it is

> man's second oldest faith. Its promise was whispered in the first days
> of the Creation under the Tree of the Knowledge of Good and Evil: "Ye
> shall be as gods." It is the great alternative faith of mankind.

Communism was, for Chambers, a faith which envisioned "man's mind displacing God as the creative intelligence in the world." Thus the Communist party was "quite justified in calling itself the most revolutionary party in history." Many students of Marxism have noted the parallels in communism to religion, and the secular utopianism that underlies much of communism's economic and political analysis. Chambers, however, insisted that this element represented the essence of communism.

The third meaning of witness in Chambers's autobiography involves his own conversion to Christianity. After he left the party and before he appeared before HUAC, Chambers converted to Quakerism, the faith of his grandmother. He was fascinated and soothed by the mystical elements in what he described as his new religion and dedicated the rest of his life to Christian witness. It is the combination of these three meanings of witness—legal, political, and religious—that formed Chambers's conception of the meaning of the Cold War. Communism had so effectively challenged the West because its alternative faith was stronger than the declining religious faith of the West:

> The crisis of the Western world exists in the degree in which it is indifferent to God. It exists to the degree in which the Western world actually shares Communism's materialistic vision. . . .

He constantly insists in *Witness* and in his essays that the choice facing Americans is "Faith in God or Faith in Man."

Many religious communities in America endorsed the policies of the Cold War because of their opposition to *godless communism*. Chambers argued that in a fundamental sense America itself had already become godless. Perhaps the United States and the U.S.S.R. were on the same side as nations "indifferent of God." He supported capitalism because he saw this economic system as the only viable alternative to communism. But he regarded capitalism as a "profoundly anticonservative" force in history and opposed new techniques in factory mass production and machinery in agriculture. The optimism of American culture drove him to despair. Would Americans ever be capable of learning that evil is not something that can be "waved aside or smiled away" but is "coiled . . . within ourselves"? He once wrote conservative journalist William Buckley that he felt like a fly clinging to a "violently turning wheel, in the hope of slowing it" by a "fly's weight."

Kennan, Burnham, and Chambers each attempted to define the nature of the crisis facing America in the Cold War. Hannah Arendt also sought to define the nature of the regime confronting America. Unlike Burnham and Chambers, Arendt did not have organizationally close ties to the Left when she emigrated from Europe to the United States in 1941. She had studied under Martin Heidegger, a German philosopher who later collaborated with the Nazis. She did, however, have extensive experience with the German Communist party (her husband was, in fact, a member). While her works written in the United States are generally regarded as conservative, one of her lifelong heroes was the German revolutionary, Rosa Luxemburg (1870–1919). Arendt's political thought, then, represents an intriguing synthesis of insights and experiences derived from European culture and combined with a critical appreciation of the American political tradition.

We will concentrate here on what has become Arendt's most famous work, *The Origins of Totalitarianism*, published in 1951. *The Origins* is an extremely difficult book to summarize, not only because of the scope of its analysis (well over 300 years of world history) but also because her argument is presented in terms of concepts that interact with one another. The thesis offered by Arendt that became influential in Cold War thought is that a new kind of regime had emerged in history—a regime qualitatively different from traditional dictatorships. Both Nazi Germany and Soviet Russia were examples of this new "totalitarian" regime. The essential feature of totalitarianism is the incessant and total commitment of terror to alter and subdue the population. The concentration camps in Germany and the purges and labor camps in the U.S.S.R. were common attempts to destroy the "infinite plurality and differentiation of human beings."

Arendt argues that there are three sources of totalitarianism: anti-Semitism, imperialism, and racism. The discussion of anti-Semitism constitutes the most extensive part of her analysis. Why, Arendt asks, did both Hitler and Stalin devote so much attention to Jews in their totalitarian experiments? In an intricate inquiry Arendt contends that European Jews occupied an unusual position throughout the seventeenth and eighteenth centuries. Because of their isolation from Christendom, Jews were both the beneficiaries and victims of special state legislation. Some were offered freedom of travel in return for financial support. Nearly all the rights and duties of this group were directly bestowed by the state. Thus Jews assumed no clear status independent of the nation-state as this basic political unit of the world developed. They were neither aristocrats nor bourgeois nor farmers nor proletarians. Increasingly, the Jews were identified with the state itself. When each class came into conflict with the state, "the only group that seemed to represent the state were the Jews."

Arendt then adds to this analysis of the precarious and unusual status of European Jews a discussion of the rise of imperialistic policies on the part of European governments. Her narrative here closely follows a Marxian analysis. Capitalist impetus toward expansion for investment (the flag following the need for trade) radically altered the European nation-state. Imperialist policies of Great Britain, the Netherlands, France, and other nation-states foreshadowed totalitarianism. The bourgeois slogan of "Nothing Succeeds like Success" had its place in the economic development of the nation-state. But expanded to a justification of colonialism, such a slogan became the "first stage in the political rule of the bourgeoisie." "In the imperialistic epoch a philosophy of power became the philosophy of the elite, who quickly discovered and were quite ready to admit that the thirst for power could be quenched through destruction," concludes Arendt.

The incessant pursuit of power in pursuit of profit had the effect of destroying the territorial basis of the nation-state; it became an organization that subjugated peoples with cultures quite different from those of the mother country. Relationships between home country and colonies were thus defined in terms of bureaucratic subordination and racism. Racism might "indeed carry out the doom of the Western world." For Arendt, "when Russians have become Slavs, when Frenchmen have assumed the role of commanders of a *force noire*, when Englishmen have turned into 'white men,' as already for a disastrous spell all Germans became Aryans, then this change will itself signify the end of Western man."

After the era of imperialism, international politics was filled with what Arendt called "superfluous" people. Jews were no longer needed for the financial support of the nation-state, which had expanded its economic base by colonial conquest. Thus, for Arendt, Jews became the epitome of a new superfluous population, defined by an organization (the nation-state) that was radically transformed by imperialist acquisitions. But Jews were only the most prominent example of "stateless" persons. The drive toward colonization rendered obsolete the political unit of the nation-state with its protection of peoples under its authority. In its place there arose mass movements of Germans, who contended that their nationality transcended that of a nation, and of pan-Slavs who made the same case. Since these movements were transnational, the Jews, who became identified with particular state bureaucracies, were singled out as enemies. Thus for Arendt, totalitarianism was a consequence of the disintegration of people as members of a nation or as members of classes and their transformation into "masses."

Arendt classified the totalitarian movements that gave rise to these new regimes as *mass movements of people*. Their personnel was quite varied. Intellectuals were attracted despite both Hitler's and Stalin's aversion to the avant-garde. Totalitarian movements included people that the major parties had neglected as "too stupid" or too apathetic to deserve their attention. Thus totalitarian demagogues found recruits among all the major classes of European countries. Once in power, totalitarian leaders translated the characteristics of mass politics into public policy:

> In an ever changing, incomprehensible world the masses had reached the point where they would, at the same time, believe everything and nothing, think that everything was possible and that nothing was true.

This extreme disorientation gave rise to the essential features of the totalitarian regime: a boundless drive toward organized violence. In fact, this incessant impetus of the regime to maintain a constant motion in finding ever-new scapegoats, whether Jews or kulaks, was the central characteristic separating traditional despotism from modern totalitarianism. The most disturbing political implications of Arendt's analysis were her intimations that there was a separate and distinct totalitarian rationality. How else, asked Arendt, could one explain the diversion of military personnel to the concentration camps and the destruction by Stalin of an entire generation of professionals? Searching for reasons for terror within the totalitarian mind, Arendt discovered an internal rationality. Totalitarian regimes are built upon the premise that the world is divided between executioners and victims; the regime owes its total control to its ability to determine and redetermine which groups fall into each category.

The Origins of Totalitarianism is a masterpiece of political analysis. But it is, nevertheless, not immune to severe criticism. Unlike other cold warriors, Arendt placed little emphasis on Marxist ideology as the basis for Soviet conduct. For her, the origins of totalitarianism rested upon the moral and political failure of the European middle classes to uphold the values of Western civilization; they had little to do with Marx's predictions about the rise of class consciousness. In fact, communist revolutions were decidedly classless phenomena. In one respect Arendt shared Marx's perspective: the bourgeoisie, despite its high-minded invocations of human rights, was really only concerned about profit. But then why did not the great bourgeois imperialist states, Great Britain and France, become totalitarian regimes? Arendt's discussion of the Boers and British in South Africa is a chilling one, but this kind of racial model did not produce a totalitarian state in Great Britain. After all, the two examples Arendt focuses upon, Germany and Russia, had few colonies. Although Arendt attempts to argue that both Germany and Russia had analogues of racist and imperialist thought in the Pan-German and Pan-Slav movements, this construct is not convincing in terms of her own analysis. Moreover (and many critics have commented on this point), the bulk of Arendt's description of totalitarian movements and regimes rests upon the German experience. For example, Margaret Canovan, a friendly critic, concludes that Arendt's analysis is more an essay about Nazism with an analogy to Stalinism.

Despite these criticisms, Arendt's analysis provided a major theoretical contribution to the Cold War. Interpreters largely ignored her indictment of the ideology and behavior of the middle classes in Europe as a contributing factor in the rise of totalitarianism as well as her assertion in later editions that the U.S.S.R. had ceased to be a totalitarian state after the death of Stalin. What policymakers focused upon in Arendt's analysis was her depiction of the totalitarian state as an irrational regime with its own totalitarian logic based upon terror. Thus Jeane J. Kirkpatrick argued in an influential article in 1979 ("Dictatorships and Double Standards") that the West should not feel uncomfortable in supporting authoritarian governments, since these regimes were capable of democratization while totalitarian governments were not.

Hannah Arendt had attempted to identify and describe the nature of the Soviet political system. During the most intense period of the Cold War (1948–1962), Americans debated the concessions that must be made to freedoms at home. The presidential election of 1948 created an important demarcation in the character of the discussion itself. In 1948 the Democratic party split into three. A right wing separated itself from the party over opposition to the national organization's platform statement on civil rights. A left wing abandoned the party in opposition to President Harry S. Truman's foreign policy of containment. This latter group called itself the Progressive party and nominated Henry Wallace, former vice president under FDR and secretary of commerce in the Truman administration, as its candidate. Wallace insisted that there are no differences between the United States and the U.S.S.R. which "cannot be settled by peaceful, hopeful negotiation." The Progressive party opposed the Marshall Plan (a $13.5 billion U.S. aid program to rebuild Western Europe), the Truman Doctrine, and the draft. It denounced what it called *anti-Soviet hysteria*, which was "a mask for monopoly, militarism, and reaction."

Election debate did not turn entirely upon American foreign policy. The Republicans largely supported the Truman Doctrine. Truman himself focused his campaign on the assertion that his administration represented the legacy of the New Deal. Communists effectively assumed control of the Progressive party, which only managed to obtain a million votes. Without ignoring the important impact of Soviet actions in the international arena, electoral debate over the utility and necessity of the Cold War was closed for a generation.

What was debated, however, was the extent to which American civil liberties needed to be curtailed in light of what was a continuing international crisis. Was America effectively at war with the Soviet Union? Since this seemed to be the case, despite the fact that direct violent confrontation was continuously avoided, what were permissible restrictions on freedom of speech and association? Any nation at war restricts access to governmental information and criticism of the government. Moreover, any nation at war is especially sensitive to critics who might be in the employ or service of the enemy. The tensions in American society that these questions posed exploded when Joseph McCarthy (a Republican senator from Wisconsin) charged in a speech delivered in February 1950 that there were 205 "card-carrying Communists" in the State Department. In subsequent speeches McCarthy broadened his attack, contending that there was a "conspiracy so immense, an infamy so black, as to dwarf any in the history of man. . . ." The object of the conspirators was that the United States be "contained, frustrated and finally fall victim to Soviet intrigue from within and Russian military might from without."

For the next five years the nation was in the grip of a massive campaign to remove Communists and communist sympathizers from positions of authority in national, state, and local governments; trade unions; universities and schools; and the media. As McCarthy himself exclaimed to the delegates of the 1952 Republican convention:

My good friends, I say one Communist in a defense plant is one Communist too many. One Communist on the faculty of one university is one too many.

The effort was complicated by the fact that many Americans had been members of communist front organizations in the 1930s when the Communist party had adopted a "popular front" policy of cooperation with liberal causes. McCarthy himself was given to reckless charges, and the entire question became intertwined with partisan political competition between Democrats and Republicans.

Were individuals who were or had been members of the Communist party or its front groups a threat to national security? Few intellectuals supported Joseph McCarthy, but many did believe that some restrictions on free speech and association were necessary during the Cold War. Sidney Hook attempted to justify these restrictions, arguing that they were consistent with democratic theory. Hook himself had been very close to the leadership of the Communist party in the early 1930s. After breaking with the Communists, he formed the short-lived radical American Workers party before eventually joining the Socialist party. Hook, however, was a much stronger supporter of the war effort than most other Socialists.

Hook refused to appear before any congressional committee to identify Communists he had known or even to discuss American communism in general. Nevertheless, he was convinced that the Soviet threat placed intellectuals under a moral obligation to defend their country. Those who refused to take sides in the struggle, he remarked in 1949, became "unwitting accomplices of Stalinism." In 1952 he complained that he could not understand "why American intellectuals should be apologetic about the fact that they are limited in their effective historical choice between endorsing a system of total terror and critically supporting our own imperfect democratic culture with all its promise and dangers." Hook's support of restrictions on academic freedom is an important example of his attempt to theoretically redraw the limits to freedom of speech and association during the Cold War.

In the early 1950s a number of states required loyalty oaths for teachers and/or required educational institutions to fire teachers who were members of the Communist party. Many colleges and universities independently adopted their own statutes along the same lines. Fifty-eight teachers were fired in New York City. As many as 200 professors lost their jobs. The American Association of University Professors (AAUP) opposed these actions, and one historian (Edward C. Kirkland) in 1951 described the restrictions as a "reign of terror" that was "unexampled in the history of American higher education."

In a series of articles, Hook "with some reservations" supported these actions. His major theoretical point was that a democratic society must tolerate and even encourage dissent from the majority, as a matter of both moral principle and practicality. Hook, a student and interpreter of John Dewey, believed that only through experimentation and discussion could truth be discovered. But it is clear that for Hook, Communist party members represented the antithesis of this principle. He constantly criticized those who in his mind mistakenly compared American Communists to "honest and independent spirits like Thoreau and Garrison." He summarized his position as "heresy, yes—conspiracy, no."

In educational institutions teachers must be given the widest latitude to discuss controversial subjects in the classroom since, especially in the social sciences, arts, and philosophy, "one man's truth is often another man's propaganda." Thus any doctrinal restrictions, "no matter what their source," must be protected:

> If in the honest exercise of his academic freedom an individual reaches views which bring down about his head charges of "Communist" or "Fascist" or what not, the academic community is duty bound to protect him irrespective of the truth of the charges.

But, according to Hook, the situation in education involved challenges that John Dewey, who helped organize the AAUP, could not have anticipated. Members of the Communist party were not free agents but closely monitored agents of a hierarchical organization. Hook quoted the induction pledge of the party as printed in a 1935 issue of the *Daily Worker* as evidence:

> I pledge myself to remain at all times a vigilant and firm defender of the Leninist line of the party, the only line that insures the triumph of Soviet power in the United States.

Communists could not accept the theories of John Dewey or many other philosophers or criticize dialectical materialism and still remain members of the party. Moreover, the Leninist line could radically change (as it had done numerous times in the 1930s), and members were duty bound to accept the new version.

As to the charge that the firing of Communists entailed punishing people for their beliefs, Hook argued that membership in the party constituted an "act" and was hence beyond the protection of the First Amendment. Communists were ordered to promote their ideas in the classroom. Hook quoted a 1937 party directive: "Marxist-Leninist analysis must be injected into every class." However, he refused to support legislation that barred Communists from educational positions, arguing instead that faculties themselves were in the best position to take action based upon assessment of evidence of party membership. Hook endorsed the position adopted by Harvard University, which declared that faculty membership in the Communist party with its "usual concomitant of secret domination" is beyond "the realm of political beliefs and associations" and "cuts to the core ability" to perform academic "duties with independence of judgment." The document concluded that such membership by a professor constituted "grave conduct, justifying removal."

Hook, however, extended his restrictions further. He believed that an individual under investigation had no right to use the Fifth Amendment to avoid responding to queries about his activities. Thus he also supported Harvard's denunciation of the use of the Fifth Amendment by faculty members, which it defined as "misconduct, though not necessarily grave misconduct." Hook argued that while a teacher might have a constitutional right to plead the Fifth Amendment, "what is legally permissible may be morally impermissible." There are a number of activities (such as plagiarism) that are not illegal but nevertheless constitute professional misconduct. For Hook, using the Fifth Amendment was one of them.

Another related issue involved the question of fellow travelers of the Communist party. Some cold warriors insisted that membership in organizations devoted to specific political causes dominated by Communists (called *front groups*) constituted enough evidence of Communist sympathies to bar individuals from teaching positions or jobs in the government or media. Irving Kristol, for example, argued in 1952 that proven membership in three front groups constituted complicity in the crimes of Stalinism. Hook, however, took a somewhat more restrained position. "So long as they [fellow travelers] are not under the discipline of the Communist party, they still may be sensitive to the results of free inquiry." Hook recommended that faculties look at each case individually and apply "various sanctions short of dismissal."

In his memoirs, *Out of Step* (1987), Hook defended his positions taken in the late 1940s and 1950s. It was impossible, he wrote, "to ignore the presence and activity of members of the Communist Party when the nation hovered on the brink of all-out war with the Soviet Union." He argued that he had offered a reasonable and responsible position by outlining ways in which faculties themselves could correct "abuses of the academic ethic." Hook's critics, however, still contend that he misunderstood the larger consequences of his accommodation of freedom of speech. Irving Howe, for example, contends in his autobiography (*A Margin of Hope*, 1982) that party discipline "might seem uniform on paper but not so in fact" and contends that there are many other organizations which "exacted obedience to an authoritarian worldview—which, if true, would have required, by Hook's criterion, constant academic purges."

A more complex legacy of McCarthyism involved a discernible loss of faith in democracy on the part of a significant portion of American intellectuals. Many writers began to construct a pattern that traced the origins of support for McCarthy from a populist strain in American culture that they interpreted quite negatively. Thus Leslie Fiedler observed that "McCarthyism is . . . an extension of the ambiguous American impulse toward 'direct democracy' with its distrust of authority, institutions, and expert knowledge." McCarthy "inherits the bitterest and most provincial aspects of a populism to which smooth talking has always meant the Big City, and the Big City has meant the Enemy." Seymour Lipset, Daniel Bell, and Richard Hofstadter pursued Fiedler's line of argument by contending that despite the anxiety created by international events during the early years of the Cold War, McCarthy's popularity could be explained in terms largely independent of the question of communism. Various groups in American society (particularly upwardly mobile ethnic groups anxious to establish their *Americanism* and small-town elites apprehensive over the growing cultural and economic influence of cities) suffered severe status anxieties in the 1950s. According to these theorists, fears of possible loss of prestige and prosperity were displaced upon the threat of Communist subversion. The point of these interpretations of McCarthyism was that protection of free speech and civil liberties rested in the hands of responsible elites, not in the population as a whole. Ironically, it was precisely many of these same elites that had placed anticommunism on the political agenda in the first place.

COLD WAR CRITICS

During the height of the Cold War it seemed possible for writers to criticize American policy in its particulars, but rarely were there theoretical attempts to present alternatives. Walter Lippmann argued that Kennan's containment policy demanded too much American resolve. No nation, even one as militarily powerful as the United States, could maintain a global "unalterable counterforce" of infinite duration. Alan Barth, Henry Steele Commager, Zechariah Chaffee, Alexander Meiklejohn, and others offered narrower restrictions on free speech and association than those of Hook. But the impact of this new bipolar international struggle was so overwhelming that both conservatives and liberals settled rapidly into a Cold War consensus: Communism must be contained through large amounts of American military and economic resources; the Soviet Union represented a new and dangerous form of despotism in sharp contrast to the freedom of Western societies; and some restrictions on free speech and association must be accepted in order to deal with the threat of subversion at home.

To those who objected to this consensus, the theoretical alternatives seemed utopian or even inconceivable. For example, Dwight MacDonald, in examining the Truman Doctrine in 1947, complained about the disparity between the president's rhetoric and the fact that Turkey was "just another military-police state like Spain or Yugoslavia," and that Greece was a "monarchist oligarchy." It was "grotesque" to refer to aid in terms of "helping free peoples maintain their free institutions." But MacDonald had no illusions about the Soviets or extant American critics: "I think that if Henry Wallace had won out over Truman in Chicago in 1944, he would by now have evolved a 'Wallace Doctrine' along much the same lines." He concluded:

> Is it any longer possible for the individual to relate himself to world politics? Can these vast and catastrophic events be any longer conceived of in terms of radical choice and action? And if they cannot, must we not regard them as part of nature rather than human history, affecting us for good or ill like the weather—and also, like it, something everybody talks about but nobody does anything about?

Among some writers a sense of dispiritedness and alienation characterized their political writing. Paul Goodman, who later wrote several important books on social theory in the 1960s, claimed that in the 1950s he simply jotted down his thoughts in notebooks because he felt he "had no one else to write or talk to." A small counterculture emerged in the late 1950s, but the new "Beat" bohemians were resolutely antipolitical; they celebrated alienation and devised heroes who were either mute or inarticulate.

A rare theoretical challenge to this Cold War consensus is found in the works of two writers, C. Wright Mills and Herbert Marcuse. The two men could not have been more different. Mills was born a Texan; Marcuse was a German émigré. Mills drove to his classes at Columbia University on a motorcycle; Marcuse was a connoisseur of fine wines. Mills was an eminently accessible writer whose major concepts were derived from plain speech (*power elite* and the *new middle class*); Marcuse's prose is dense and complex, and his concepts (such as *repressive desublimation*) can only be fully understood in terms of G. W. F. Hegel, Karl Marx, and Sigmund Freud. Mills derived his theories from Max Weber, who regarded the growth of bureaucracy as the major determinant of modern life; Marcuse was a Marxist. But both men were committed radicals and both men analyzed American society at mid-century as *outsiders.*

The central dichotomy that formed Mills's theory in all his books was his contrast between nineteenth- and twentieth-century American society. In *White Collar* (1951) Mills describes the central role of the middle class in a historically unique society:

Europe's five-hundred year struggle out of feudalism has not absorbed the energies of the United States producer; a contractual society began here almost *de novo* as a capitalist order.

The "single most important fact" of this new kind of society of small entrepreneurs was that a substantial proportion of the people owned the property with which they worked. Thus there was a "linkage of income, status, work, and property" that produced a character type of an "'absolute individual,' linked into a system with no authoritarian center, but held together by countless, free, shrewd transactions."

Mills gives less emphasis than Veblen or even Marxist writers to industrialization as a process that had radically altered the world of the old middle class. The captain of industry was still "the active owner of what he created and then managed." The new middle class, for Mills, emerged in the twentieth century with the consolidation of capital into a single massive bureaucratic structure. The old middle class has been absorbed into this bureaucratic leviathan:

> In the established professions, the doctor, lawyer, engineer, once was free and named on his own shingle; in the new white collar world, the salaried specialists of the clinic, the junior partner in the law factory, the captive engineers of the corporation have begun to challenge free professional leadership.

Borrowing from Marx's concept of the *Lumpenproletariat* as a description of superfluous workers who have never been subjected to the new life in the factory, Mills argues that small entrepreneurs have now become a *Lumpenbourgeoisie* that relies upon family labor in attempting to find a marginal place in the corporate economy.

The heart of the new middle class, according to Mills, is in the salesrooms, whose atmosphere "seem(s) to coincide with the new society as a whole." Mills anticipates the rise of a service economy in which the bulk of employment would shift from wholesaling to retailing and from manufacturing to service. There are, of course, gradations of income and status among Mills' new middle class. He describes the "prima donnas" at the top of corporations, "the mobile salesmen of insurance," advertising men ("absentee salesmen helping others sell from a distance"), and "the stationary salesgirls in the department store." In the "lower reaches of the white collar world," there are the office operatives who "grind along, loading and emptying the file system; there are private secretaries and typists, entry clerks, billing clerks, corresponding clerks—a thousand kinds of clerks. . . ." Mills depicts the emergence of various personality types in each of the complex levels of this new middle class. He describes the organization and reorganization of the new white-collar offices and the salesrooms of department stores. But most of all, he emphasizes the severe alienation of the white-collar worker who sells things he or she does not make and provides services to an organization in which he or she has little or no form of expression. Mills concludes:

> The material hardship of the nineteenth century industrial workers finds its parallel on the psychological level among twentieth century white-collar workers. The new Little Man seems to have no firm roots, no sure loyalties to sustain his life and give it a center. He is not aware of having any history, his past being as brief as it is unheroic; he has lived through no golden age he can recall in time of trouble. Perhaps because he does not know where he is going, he is in a frantic hurry; perhaps because he does not know what frightens him, he is paralyzed with fear.

Part of the Cold War consensus in America involved a celebration of postwar American life. Theorists compared the terror and uniformity of totalitarian regimes to the economic vitality and pluralism of free societies. Daniel Bell argued that the relative indifference to political ideas in America was a result of the realization that the ideologies of the 1930s were "exhausted" because they had lost their "power to persuade." In a period of "the end of ideology," social problems could now be approached rationally and through a spirit of "pragmatic compromise." Daniel Boorstin contended that it was the "genius" of the American political tradition that made theory superfluous. Seymour Lipset explained that the low rate of political participation was evidence of satisfaction with the political system. Mills offered a different picture. A new middle class had emerged that was politically impotent. It could not "go politically 'proletarian'" because there was no proletariat in the Marxian sense in America. It could not form its own political bloc because the nationalization and transformation of work had robbed white-collar workers of an independent culture from which they could mount their own political vision.

White Collar described an American nightmare from the perspective of both republican and liberal theory. The independent property owner—hence the independent citizen—was gone. The pluralistic society had been replaced by a bureaucratic culture. In *The Power Elite* (1959) Mills carried his comparison between the nineteenth and twentieth centuries to even broader proportions. Elites had always existed in America. During the height of Federalist dominance, political life was controlled by an identifiable set of influential families. But the state at the national level was decidedly weak and limited and, as such, was an important but partial prize. For most of American history, the economy was "a scatter of small productive units in autonomous balance"; the political order "a decentralized set of several dozen states with a weak spinal cord"; and the military a "slim establishment in a context of distrust fed by a state militia." For the most part the military "was subordinate to the political, which in turn was sub-ordinate to the economic. The military was off to the side of the main driving forces of United States history."

According to Mills, both the consolidation and nationalization of the economy and the Cold War had dramatically transformed America. The Cold War placed the national political structure on a permanent war footing, creating an executive-dominated government and a military service that was a "sprawling bureaucratic domain." In place of limited and loose coalitions of elites now stood a "power elite." The CEOs of a few hundred corporations, the president and his intimate advisers, and the Joint Chiefs of Staff made all decisions of national consequence. The power elite decided how fast the economy would grow, where investment would be directed, and, most important, questions of war and peace. What was most striking of all for Mills was that this triad of elites (political, economic, and military) was interlocking (for example, the relationship between the president and the National Security Council). Its personnel was interchangeable (military figures became corporate executives, while corporate executives moved into the executive branch and back again to the corporations); its social backgrounds were similar (a common recruitment and training program that extended from prep schools to military academies to Ivy League colleges and law schools).

Mills found no centers of power in America capable of challenging this elite. At the "middle levels of power," the Madisonian system of checks and balances still worked. Congress provided the focal point for working out compromises on issues of local import after national priorities had been set. The president had already effectively made decisions about international commitments and the use of military force. Political parties might be effective in organizing Congress and elections, but there were in reality forty-eight state parties and none of them had much influence at the summit of national power, except as directed by the president himself. There was in America no tradition of a semi-independent national civil service, as in Great Britain, to serve as a check on the power elite. The new middle class described in *White Collar* was politically immobilized.

Mills was most troubled by the absence of public opinion as a check on the power elite. In fact, he argued that publics in America had nearly disappeared and had been replaced by "mass opinion." In order to make a distinction between public and mass opinion, he constructed a matrix. The existence of public opinion depended upon some ratio between giver and receiver. At one extreme was the two-person conversation; at the other, a single person talking to millions. In between were the assemblages of democratic theory, legislative chambers, political rallies, and discussion groups. Mills could find few instances of the latter not controlled or safely ignored by the power elite. Another dimension was the existence of avenues of "talking back" to governmental authorities. At one extreme was "a wide and symmetrical flow of opinion" between rulers and ruled; at the other was an "absolute monopoly of communication to pacified media groups." A free press was an important medium in facilitating this interaction, but Mills complained that its emphasis on images created a "psychological illiteracy" among Americans. Mills makes clear in his analysis that the negative end of the continuum toward mass opinion is a feature of totalitarian regimes and that America is "not yet at the end." But he warned that "many features of the public life of our times are more features of a mass society than a community of publics."

In *The Causes of World War Three* (1958) Mills attempted to apply his analysis of American society to the Cold War. This book, more a *cri de coeur* than sociology, was not well received. Even Mills's critics were driven to acknowledge the force of his sociological analysis in *White Collar* and *The Power Elite*. But *The Causes* simply relies on his previous work and pleads for some break in the Cold War impasse. The central, indeed the only, premise of the essay is that the elites of both the United States and U.S.S.R. were so independent and isolated from their populations that World War III was inevitable:

> In the two superstates the history-making means of power are now organized. Their facilities of violence are absolute; their economic systems are increasingly autarchic; politically, each of them is increasingly a closed world; and in all these spheres their bureaucracies are world-wide.

Human history was now in the hands of less than a thousand individuals. Mills believed that World War III would be "accidental." A mistaken blip on a radar screen, however, would be only the immediate cause of the war. The

> prime conditions of the "accident" are not themselves accidental; they are planned and deliberate. . . . The first cause of World War III is, obviously, the existence of these bureaucratic and lethal machines.

Mills, like most political theorists in the 1950s, had few recommendations for ending the Cold War. He suggested a Marshall Plan for developing nations as a replacement for the "military metaphysic" of the American power elite. But the bulk of Mills's counsel was framed for what he regarded as remnants of communities of publics in America that were not yet part of mass opinion. To Christian communities he said, "Do not these times demand a little Puritan resolve?" "Who among you," asked Mills, "is considering what it means for Christians to kill men and women in ever more efficient and impersonal ways?" To scientists he recommended the formation of "private forums and outlets." To secular intellectuals he suggested that their prime objective should be directed toward breaking the monopoly of ideas of the cold warriors.

For all his radical efforts, C. W. Mills was less concerned with naming and categorizing the transformation of America under the Cold War conditions than in returning the United States to its rightful place as a uniquely democratic society. In many ways Mills was an American Cicero. For him America was on the brink of a transformation from a republic to an empire. In *The Power Elite* he asked, "What was Caesar's power at its peak compared with the power of the changing inner circle of Soviet Russia or of America's temporary administrations?" Writing as a patriot, Mills, while realizing that America could never return to an antebellum society, sought, often inchoately, some functional equivalents. Mills consistently fought a personal battle to avoid romanticizing nineteenth-century America. Nevertheless, he was intellectually and emotionally absorbed by the idea of a "community of publics" as a check on the power elite.

Herbert Marcuse had none of these objectives. His intellectual position, doubly removed from American politics—first as a German émigré, and second as a radical—permitted him insights not available to Mills as well as screens that separated him from an appreciation of the redeeming features of American culture. Marcuse's writings must be understood in terms of the efforts of an influential group of independent German Marxists who founded the Frankfurt Institute of Social Research in 1923. The *Frankfurt school* attempted to theoretically respond to the failure of Marxism to account for the attraction of the working class to fascism. To the scholars at Frankfurt, Marxism failed to account for the cultural impact of modern society in general as a frame of reference for all classes. Perhaps new patterns of domination, located in technological sources, were stronger predictors of behavior and consciousness than economic class. In the absence of any independent bases of protest against this new technological order, the task of intellectuals was to expound a *critical theory* that exposed the forms of domination hidden beneath the idealized image of liberal democracy.

Critical theory was a pessimistic political doctrine dedicated to preserving what the Frankfurt theorists regarded as free thought during a period in which the very concepts of rationality had become, as Max Horkheimer asserted in his *Eclipse of Reason* (1947), tools of the ruling class and "individuality loses its economic basis." Many of the works of the Frankfurt school were pressed into the service of the Cold War. Theodor Adorno's study of working-class authoritarianism (*The Authoritarian Personality*, 1950), which attempted to unearth the sources of antidemocratic beliefs in the everyday lives of members of the German working class, was interpreted by American scholars as evidence of the failure of labor to absorb democratic ideals. Erich Fromm's *Escape from Freedom* (1941), which attempted to document the anxiety ordinary people exhibited in the face of a problematic future and hence their vulnerability to Nazi propaganda, was assessed by American scholars as evidence of the failure of European politics.

As a member of the Frankfurt school and as a critical theorist, Herbert Marcuse was unique in that in his works he forced American audiences to confront the question raised by the Frankfurt school: Was America itself somehow a totalitarian society? In his early works Marcuse attempted to provide theoretical foundations for a critique of all modern societies, capitalist and Communist. *Eros and Civilization* (1955) recognized Sigmund Freud's insight that all organized society was predicated upon the abdication of the *pleasure principle*, the instinctual drive to experience individual satisfaction, in favor of the *reality principle*, the realization that instinctual drives must be suppressed in order to attain such other important individual goals as security. Redefining Freud's concepts in economic terms, Marcuse argued that the reality principle was historically implemented by elites who demanded more self-restraint than was necessary for organized society. Elites reaped the advantages of *surplus repression*, that is, additional labor in defiance of instincts. Marcuse called the excess of renunciation of individual desires a necessary step to maintain the *performance principle* for society.

How much extra work was performed that was not necessary for the essentials of a good life? Marcuse never answered this question with any precision. But in *One Dimensional Man* (1964) he attempted to analyze American society as one in which this question was incapable of being addressed. Marcuse described America as a culture in which "a comfortable, smooth, reasonable, democratic unfreedom prevails. . . ." There were no agencies of social and political change; nonconformity was "socially useless." So convinced was Marcuse of the stability of the American regime that he asserted that "not even a catastrophe will bring about a change." He argued that the technological basis of American society had produced "new, more effective, and more pleasant forms of social control and social cohesion" and went so far as to call America totalitarian:

> For "totalitarian" is not only a terroristic political coordination of society, but also a non-terroristic economic-technical coordination which operates through the manipulation of needs by vested interests.

The most arresting portion of Marcuse's critique is his delineation of political discourse in America. Words in use have been limited to their function. Nouns such as *freedom, equality, democracy,* and *peace* implied a closed set of predicates that were "ritualized" and "immune from contradiction." Indeed, Marcuse argued, the most disturbing aspect of Cold War speech was the expression of opposites or contradictions in such a way as to avoid genuine political discourse. Expressions such as a *clean bomb, harmless fallout,* and *luxury fall-out shelter* represented not only the application of Madison Avenue techniques of advertising to political problems but the subjugation of the contradictions characteristic of any society to a rational silence of opposition. George Orwell, a British socialist who became an anti-Stalinist, fictionally chronicled a political language that violated and transformed reality in his antiutopia, *1984,* which was published in 1949. Marcuse argued that Orwellian language had now permeated American political discourse without the benefit of a secret police.

Had America become a totalitarian society different in technique than the regimes constructed by the Russians and the Germans, but nevertheless similar in its "closing of the universe of discourse," according to Marcuse? Was what Marcuse called *happy consciousness*—the acceptance of political impotence and the advantages of American technology—the same as citizen acquiescence to terror in totalitarian societies? This question had been raised by Dwight MacDonald and implied by C. Wright Mills. Critics of Marcuse regarded this assertion as nothing less than obscene. But the American military involvement in Vietnam and the apparent inability of dissidents to change American policy led some Americans to accept large portions of Marcuse's critique.

U.S. interest in the outcome of the anticolonial struggles in Southeast Asia formed an important part of Cold War history. FDR had largely negative reactions to the reassertion of European colonial political control in the Asian colonies after the defeat of Japan. With the emergence of the Cold War, however, the region quickly became a contested region. President Dwight D. Eisenhower refused to send American ground troops or provide air cover to aid France's attempt to regain its former colony of Indo-China when French forces became surrounded by the Vietnamese at Dien Bien Phu in 1953. He was willing, however, to provide economic aid to the French. After the French surrendered in 1954, the country was divided into two military zones. President John F. Kennedy provided 10,000 military advisers to South Vietnam in 1962, and President Johnson, after his election in 1964, rapidly escalated American troop commitments. In 1969 U.S. military personnel peaked at 543,000.

The debate over American involvement in Vietnam led to the first full-scale discussion of the theoretical premises of the Cold War consensus since 1948. Was containment as applied to Vietnam a rational and measured response to Soviet aggression by proxy? So argued Sidney Hook, with some reservations. Was the war in Vietnam an ill-advised commitment in terms of a policy that was essentially correct? So argued international theorists such as Hans Morganthau. Or was American military intervention in Vietnam evidence of some broader error? Was, perhaps, American intervention part of a policy of an international Pax Americana that needed to be reevaluated both morally and politically?

An early intimation of this larger critique can be found in the "Port Huron Statement," a position paper offered by the Students for a Democratic Society (SDS) in 1962. The organization had hundreds of chapters on university campuses before its collapse in the early 1970s. Drafted primarily by Tom Hayden, a University of Michigan student who wrote his master's essay on C. Wright Mills, the Port Huron Statement presented an image of an America that was psychologically and economically dependent upon the Cold War, independent of any objective Soviet threat: "Worker and family depend upon the Cold War for life." The SDS argued that America's "democratic institutions and habits have shriveled in almost direct proportion to the growth of her armaments." Her "pugnacious anticommunism and protection of interests" has led to an international alliance that is incorrectly called "the Free World." Only four democracies comprised the Western alliance (Canada, Great Britain, India, and the United States). The rest of the international coalition included dictatorships.

The SDS leaders described themselves as part of a new generation "bred in at least modest comfort, housed in universities, looking comfortably to the world we inherit." They admitted that they were a "minority" (most of their generation accepted the present organization of society as composed of "eternally-functional parts"), but they argued that a "tough-minded" acceptance of reality had already produced a sense of "emptiness of life" amidst prosperity. They hoped that a utopian vision of human beings as "infinitely precious and possessed of unfulfilled capacities for reason, freedom, and love" could overcome the "loneliness, estrangement, isolation" which described the relationships of individuals today.

The authors of the Port Huron Statement insisted that they had no "sure formulas, no closed theories," but one phrase in the document caught the imagination of a generation: *participatory democracy. As* James Miller (*Democracy Is in the Streets*) writes, the phrase came to "capture the spirit of the convention, the soul of the document, the essence of the New Left. It became, literally, a catchword—used, over and over again, to recruit, to convert, to convince." What did the quest for "the establishment of a democracy of individual participation" mean? To Miller the concept had a disturbing elasticity and volatility. No doubt to some activists participatory democracy came to mean the extension of the structure and élan of the civil rights movement to American politics in general. Thus Paul Booth, an SDS leader, wrote: "If everything could be restructured starting from the SNCC [Student Nonviolent Coordinating Committee] project in McComb, Mississippi, then we would have participatory democracy." To others participatory democracy meant socialism. Bob Ross, a University of Michigan student, contended that "the idea of democracy had embryonic in it the socialist idea. . . . Our problem was to find a way to talk about socialism with an American accent." To many others the concept meant nothing more than an expression of a yearning for a political and economic system within their individual control. The Port Huron Statement, which was handed out to college students with the simple invitation that SDS membership was "open to all who share our commitment to participatory democracy," spoke of a "kind of independence" that was not derived from an "egoistic individualism" but one involved in "common participation."

The student activists who signed the Port Huron Statement attempted to position themselves to the left of the Kennedy administration. Indeed, the concepts of service and idealism that were the emotional underpinnings of participatory democracy paralleled the rhetoric of the young president. But as the war in Vietnam escalated and dragged on, the New Left became more and more disillusioned with American society. Activists who demanded that audiences "Name the system!" moved from assessments of the United States as in the grip of Cold War liberalism or corporate liberalism to an acceptance of Marcuse's description of the nation as a kind of totalitarian society. By the late 1960s many student radicals came to promote the designation *Amerika* as a description of a society they felt was not only totalitarian but a brutal international military presence in the world. It was indistinguishable from the Nazis or Soviets in its behavior. Some demanded: "Bring the war home!"

There have been numerous explanations for the meteoric rise and fall of student radicalism. Some observers have contended that the New Left failed because the Cold War cut them off from the expertise and advice of the Old Left; others blame the Old Left for its unwillingness to respond sympathetically to the concerns of another generation. Some argue that the radicals were effectively eliminated by government repression and police violence. Herbert Marcuse once told a Berkeley crowd that "the movement did not die, it was murdered!" Others argue that the upper-middle-class background of the students limited their strategic and theoretical capacities. As children of a privileged class, the radicals could never fully comprehend the needs of either the Third World peoples or the minority groups in the United States whom they sought to represent. A harsher version of this explanation argues that their radicalism was motivated by self-interest (particularly in terms of the opposition to conscription) and overindulgence. Still others point to the failure of New Leftists to offer a political theory for a post-Cold War America. Often student radicals spoke in slogans, misapplied American symbols (such as the tendency to see the North Vietnamese as Jeffersonian farmers), or adopted heroes far removed from American culture partially for existential reasons, such as Ernesto "Che" Guevara or Mao Zedong.

Perhaps a central reason for the fall can be traced to the students' inability to create or reinvigorate the publics of which C. Wright Mills spoke. Todd Gitlin in *The Sixties* (1987) reminds his readers that throughout the period of protests New Leftists resolutely attempted to form "alternative" institutions in America. But "the thousands of communes, underground papers, free schools, food 'conspiracies,' auto repair and carpentry collectives, women's centers and health groups and alternative publishers" soon collapsed as most youths eventually entered traditional professions. Gitlin reports that many of his former Harvard classmates, in a 1973 anniversary report, wrote of their commitment to "cultivating our garden." He then asks: "Was the hip farm, with its freer-form style of family and conventional male-female division of labor, so different" from "the traditional middle class way of renouncing the world?" Gitlin denies that the whole generation of radicals moved en masse from "'J'accuse' to Jacuzzi," but he does admit the new publics the protesters attempted to create for the most part disintegrated into solipsism and materialism.

The collapse of the New Left did not, however, end the debate it had begun about the impact of the Cold War on American institutions. The last U.S. troops left Vietnam in 1973. While the Cold War was far from over, subsequent American discourse about the aims and limitations of American policy was considerably broadened. Moreover, this discourse reemerged in different forms after the end of the Cold War.

THE REAGAN REVOLUTION AND THE END OF THE COLD WAR

For many of the cold warriors with radical pasts in the 1930s, anti-communism was simply to be added to the domestic political agenda of extending the New Deal in the post-war world. This political position, which eventually became known by critics as Cold War liberalism, remained the dominant ideology in America until the protests of the sixties. When William F. Buckley founded the *National Review* in 1955, he and his contributors began a concerted attack on "liberalism" from the right that actually anticipated some of the themes of the New Left. Buckley, for example, wrote in *God and Man at Yale* (1951) that the university curriculum was stultifyingly conformist and dominated by a "Liberal orthodoxy." In the first issue of the *National Review*, he promised to expose the enemy—liberals—"who run this country."

But the implementation of this critique faced problems. While many ex-radicals like Whittaker Chambers and James Burnham were now willing to call themselves conservatives and there were talented writers like Buckley from the new post-war generation who questioned the liberal anti-communist consensus, they defined conservatism in quite different ways. Although there are many complex variations, the major split in American conservatism was between *traditionalists*, who emphasized the need for order and even hierarchy in society and placed their hopes on the stabilizing influences of religion and elites; and *libertarians*, who supported the market and were willing to grant wide latitude to individual choice in cultural areas as well. Libertarians accused traditionalists of making too many accommodations with Cold War liberals in the areas of welfare and trade union policy and were deeply suspicious of the traditionalist's fascination with community. Traditionalists accused libertarians of not being conservative at all (libertarians did often refer to themselves as the "true" liberals) and of being indifferent to the corrosive impact capitalism can have on traditional institutions like the family and churches.

Two examples of this division are Milton Friedman's *Capitalism and Freedom* and Irving Kristol's essay, "When Virtue Loses All Her Loveliness." Friedman, an economist at the University of Chicago who worked in the U.S. Department of Treasury during World War II, participated in a series of seminars at American universities featuring internationally known libertarian scholars such as Friederich Hayek (Austria) and Bruno Leoni (Italy) in the 1950s. *Capitalism and Freedom* summarized some of the thinking of this group. In many respects, Friedman's approach was quite similar to Herbert Hoover's. Friedman denied, for example, that the Depression was caused by any inherent flaw in capitalism. He charged that the Federal Reserve Board made disastrous decisions in monetary policy that converted what "would have been a moderate contraction into a major catastrophe." Like Hoover, he too raised questions about the relationship between economic and political freedom.

Unlike Hoover and his own mentor Frederick Hayek, who in his *Road to Serfdom* (1944) contended that the post-war economic planning of the Labor government in Britain would lead to totalitarianism, Friedman placed much less emphasis on the negative consequences of government activity than on the positive consequences of an expanded free market. It was this reformist, even utopian, attitude toward market solutions to political and social problems that so captured the hearts of libertarian conservatives. Friedman contended that political resolution of problems requires conformity and thus tends to destroy consensus. He gave as an example government attempts to control religious choice as a "bloody testament" to the results of this approach. Letting the market resolve individual differences, on the other hand, "reduces the strain on the social fabric." Appealing to American exceptionalism, Friedman said that "in the United States, 'free' has been understood to mean that anyone is free to set up an enterprise, which means that existing enterprises are not free to keep out competitors except by selling a better product at the same price or the same product at a lower price"; while in Europe the meaning has generally been that enterprises are "free to do what they want, including the fixing of prices, division of markets, and the adoption of other techniques to keep out potential competitors."

Leaning upon an American conception of capitalism, Friedman proposed the elimination of tariffs, price-support programs for agriculture and government-authorized monopolies like railroads. But he did not stop there. Although he contended that the "consistent liberal is not an anarchist," Friedman proposed the elimination of rent control, public housing (including veterans' mortgage programs), the minimum wage, social security, national parks, and conscription. In 1962 these proposals were shocking. But citizens and politicians kept returning to Friedman's list. Anti-war activists found the proposal for a volunteer military force persuasive. Friedman's substitute plan for welfare, a "negative income tax," was eventually supported by Richard Nixon. And, of course, in the Reagan years, Friedman's proposals on economic regulation received a thorough review.

As we have noted, Irving Kristol, who briefly dallied with Trotskyism as a college student in the 1930s, participated in the debates over McCarthyism and free speech in the 1950s. Among New York intellectuals he is still known for this concluding sentence in a 1952 article in *Commentary* magazine: "There is one thing that the American people know about Senator McCarthy; he, like them, is unequivocally anti-communist. About spokesman for American liberalism, they feel they know no such thing." Kristol became one of the leaders of a movement called *neo-conservatism*. Like their immediate forebears in the 1950s who referred to themselves as the "new conservatives" (to distinguish themselves from the libertarians), the neo-conservatives emphasized the need to consider the basis of social order in society. Unlike their predecessors, many neo-conservatives were disillusioned liberals who reacted with alarm to the protests of the sixties. Daniel Bell, for example, argued in *The Cultural Contradictions of Capitalism* (1976) that the sixties were a reflection of a moral degeneration. Liberalism was inherently unable to critique this "cultural contradiction" between capitalism's economic success and the hedonism that it also spawned.

In "When Virtue Loses All Her Loveliness," Kristol began his argument with an acknowledgement that the sixties radicals' antagonism to "liberal, individualist, capitalist culture" was actually understandable. While he was clearly disturbed by the radical critique as well as the inability of post-war liberalism to acknowledge that government programs like welfare were creating economic dependency, Kristol reserved a large portion of his criticism for the libertarians. The choice of the title of the essay seemed to be an odd one, since the phrase was borrowed from George Fitzhugh's defense of a slave economy that was discussed in chapter five. But for Kristol this spokesman for the "reactionary enlightenment" had hit upon the central problem of American capitalism, for Fitzhugh's charge was becoming more and more valid: "From having been a capitalist, republican community, with shared values and a quite unambiguous claim to the title of a just order, the United States became a free democratic society where the will to success and privilege was severed from its moral moorings." Libertarians were, for Kristol, part of the problem. He focused upon Hayek's argument that there was no relationship between economic success and moral desert, since any such correspondence was a step toward reorganizing society according to some plan and Milton Friedman's contention that the free person "recognizes no national purpose." These "extreme libertarian positions" only served to promote the "inner spiritual crisis of our time." Only through a return to the study of the classics—Plato, Aristotle, Aquinas, Hooker, Calvin—could one begin to see that individual gain was not the only value necessary for a just society. Leading a virtuous life was essential to individual happiness as well as social stability.

These two strands of conservatism both spoke to the problems America faced in the 1970s. "Stagflation" (inflation plus high unemployment), America's relative loss of a hegemonic global economic position (particularly in terms of Japan), doubts about the value of detente with the Soviets, and unsolved problems of race and gender all produced what Jimmy Carter called a "national malaise" in 1979. Libertarians promised a solution through expansion of the free market and traditionalists through a moral revival. It was the political genius of Ronald Reagan to eclectically combine both outlooks in what became known as the *Reagan revolution*.

While it is too early to gauge the full impact of the initiatives of this "revolution," commentators have often been reluctant to give former President Reagan much credit. This polite remark in 1986 by François Mitterand (socialist president of France) is typical: "[Reagan] is a man of common sense, gracious and pleasant. He communicates through jokes, by telling ultra-California stories, by speaking mainly about California and the Bible. He has two religions: free enterprise and God—the Christian God. . . . He is not a man who dwells on concepts, yet he has ideas and clings to them." Assessments like these are not unlike those continuously made about FDR in the 1930s. FDR was a "pleasant man," an affable "country squire" from upstate New York and self-described simply as a "Christian and a Democrat." Since both men were clearly underestimated politically and since Reagan systematically attempted to erase FDR's achievements, it will be useful to briefly compare Reagan's "revolution" to the New Deal.

The monumental status of FDR had stood as an obstacle to all post-war presidents and presidential aspirants as well as the conservative critics of whom we have just spoken. Even Democratic successors found this status a burden. Political necessity required obeisance to FDR's New Deal but, as John Kennedy once complained, 1933 is not 1963 and "what was fine for Roosevelt simply would not work today. . . ." For Republicans, however, FDR's achievements (from the creation of the American welfare state to U.S. participation in the United Nations) were centrally contested. Dwight Eisenhower, for example, wrote in his memoirs that he hoped that his administration would be remembered as "the first break with the political philosophy of the decades beginning in 1933." Nevertheless, Republican presidents were forced to reach accommodations with "New Deal socialism" and to reinterpret FDR's internationalism.

The notable exception to this pattern of begrudging accommodation is Ronald Reagan. More than any other post-Roosevelt president, Reagan successfully challenged the authority of FDR and initiated his own revolution in American politics. Yet the achievements of the "Reagan revolution" were constructed from unusual elements. Reagan always referred to Roosevelt as his "idol." His "Time for Choosing" speech in 1964, however, indirectly associated New Deal politics with Marxism; later he contended that New Dealers used fascism as their policy model. This paralleling of strident critiques of the New Deal and imitative gestures toward FDR characterized Reagan's entire presidency. Reagan repeatedly and readily admitted that he was a Roosevelt supporter and yet portrayed the New Deal in the satanic mode of the new American right. This propensity puzzled even his supporters. Peggy Noonan, a Reagan speechwriter, insisted that Reagan's Roosevelt was derived from a scene in the 1942 film *Yankee Doodle Dandy*, in which an actor playing FDR gives a presidential medal to George M. Cohan (played by Jimmy Cagney). Cohan/Cagney is rendered speechless by Roosevelt's comments about love of country as the president awards the medal for Cohan's authorship of "Over There" and "Grand Old Flag."

Reagan constantly acknowledged the influence of FDR in his own youth. He recalled Roosevelt's election victories, his father's jobs in New Deal relief programs, FDR's speeches, and his personal appearances. Reagan's remembrances of the Depression and FDR's heroic actions are quite vivid. The Depression hit his boyhood town of Dixon "like a cyclone" and "one of its first casualties was my father's dream." The Depression "had such an oppressive effect that it cast a dreary pall over everything." In these "cheerless, desperate days," Reagan remembered the "strong, gentle, confident voice" of FDR, who "brought comfort and resilience to a nation caught up in a storm and reassured us that we could lick any problem. I shall never forget him for that."

This seemingly frank and fond oral history, however, also contained a critique. In his autobiography, Reagan tells the story of his father's job as New Deal relief administrator and then as local head of the WPA. Although Reagan described the WPA as "one of the most productive elements of FDR's alphabet soup agencies," he notes his father had difficulty signing up participants. Jack Reagan later had found that relief administrators discouraged able-bodied men from applying. Reagan the son concludes: "I wasn't sophisticated enough to realize what I learned later: The first rule of bureaucracy is to protect bureaucracy. If the people running the welfare program had let their clientele find other ways of making a living, that would have reduced their importance and their budget." The young Reagan, however, was unaware of this danger. As he described himself in his autobiography, *Where is the Rest of Me?* (1965), he was a "very emotional New Dealer" and a "near-hopeless hemophiliac liberal" who was "blinded" by the brilliance of the president and "blindly" joined any organization that "would guarantee to save the world." These two narratives, one of affectionate youthful remembrance and one of youthful indiscretion and conversion, formed part of a general generational ambivalence to the thirties which Reagan captured.

No events in Reagan's youth were evoked more positively than the American experience in World War II. In a 1981 interview he reminisced about FDR's 1937 "quarantine" speech. "I remember when Hitler was arming and had built himself up—no one has created quite the military that the Soviet Union has, but comparatively he was in that way," he told Walter Cronkite. "Franklin Delano Roosevelt made a speech in Chicago at the dedication of a bridge over the Chicago River. In that speech, he called on the free world to quarantine Nazi Germany, to stop all communications, all trade, all relations with them until they gave up that militaristic course and agreed to join with the free nations of the world in a search for peace." Reagan continued to remember that "the funny thing was he [FDR] was attacked so here in our own country for having said such a thing. Can we honestly look back now and say World War II would have taken place if we had done what he wanted us to do back in 1938?"

Conventional Republican assessments of New Deal foreign policy centered upon the "treason" at Yalta, but Reagan generally interpreted the conference as evidence of Soviet betrayal. To him, FDR was "a great war leader." Under his leadership, "there were less of the tragic blunders that have characterized many wars in the past. . . ." Reagan was especially generous in his accounts of the efficiency of the American war effort. FDR took a nation completely unprepared for war and, in forty-four months after Pearl Harbor, produced an awesome war machine. "We truly were an arsenal of democracy," he told one interviewer, as he noted that FDR was criticized for asking for 50,000 planes a year. The massive military budget increases in the 1980s were thus broadly justified by what Reagan regarded as FDR's own success in preparing to confront a hostile power despite the pessimism of his critics. Reagan's memories of the war also focused upon the battlefield valor and the autobiographical remembrances of those who participated in the war effort. The centerpiece of his remarks at the Omaha Beach commemoration was the narrative of a daughter of one of the participants in the invasion.

Reagan's memory of when he parted from New Deal politics varied. Still he remained a Democrat until 1962 when he finally registered as a Republican. Although Reagan's deep attachment to Whittaker Chambers, reiterated throughout many speeches, contains several meanings, one core significance involves Reagan's belief that he, like, Chambers, personally "witnessed" two great faiths of his time. In this case the two belief systems were liberalism and conservatism.

What exactly were the achievements of FDR that made him Reagan's idol? No New Deal program received Reagan's unqualified endorsement, and most were subject to severe criticism, including the TVA and social security. In his post-presidential autobiography, Reagan attempted an assessment. The appraisal consists of a series of positive and negative conclusions. After noting that Roosevelt brought hope to a despondent nation in 1932-33, Reagan offered another conclusion to FDR's legacy: "FDR in many ways set in motion the forces that later sought to create big government and bring a veiled form of socialism in America." He remembered, however, FDR's early pledge to cut government spending and speculates that "if he had not been distracted by war, I think he would have resisted the relentless expansion of the federal government that followed him." Quoting one of FDR's sons for support, Reagan concludes that FDR intended his programs to be only "emergency, stopgap measures to cope with a crisis, not the seeds of what others tried to turn into a permanent welfare state." On a final note, he expressed more doubts: "As smart as he was though, I suspect even FDR didn't realize that once you created a bureaucracy, it took on a life of its own."

Having praised and evaluated FDR in these series of autobiographical remembrances, Reagan engaged in a selective reinterpretation of Roosevelt's own policy swerves and turns. Reagan may have frequently identified with Al Smith's critique of the New Deal, but the central thrust of his own "revolution" rested on an identification with the populism of the second-term FDR that so infuriated Smith. Until 1936, FDR largely justified New Deal programs through a nationalized interpretation of Jefferson. After a brief period in which he seemed ideologically immobilized, FDR turned ferociously against American corporate capital. Expressly employing the symbols of Jackson and Jacksonian democracy, FDR attacked "economic royalists" who were trying to "gang up against the people's liberties." These were the same kind of men who had also once attacked Jackson, but the people "loved him for the enemies he made." Roosevelt, too, "welcome(d) their hatred." Roosevelt constructed the welfare state on Jackson's antipathy to finance capital.

The Great Depression, of course, highly magnified middle America's apprehensiveness over the power of large corporations. But in the post-New Deal era, what Tocqueville once described as "eagerness" (the desire to rise economically) re-emerged as a central desire of the mass of Americans, and Reagan's genius lies in re-reading Roosevelt's revision of Jacksonianism. As FDR had focused his attack on *economic* elites who would "gang up" against the people's liberties, Reagan focused his attack on *governmental* elites with the same ambitions. "Every businessman has his own tale of harassment," said Reagan in his 1964 speech. Roosevelt demanded that everyone be given "a chance to make a living," travel, obtain a better job and "a chance to get ahead." Reagan spoke of the "heroes" who "every day" go "in and out of factory gates" and their "right to heroic dreams." The theme of a hardworking, virtuous people whose aspirations and achievements are blocked by elites was a Jacksonian theme that Roosevelt applied and Reagan then applied from Roosevelt.

By breaking the object of FDR's populism from its subject (big capitalists) and substituting a new one (big government), Reagan was freed to repiece the remaining shards into his own "revolution." The decades of reluctant accommodation by Republicans with FDR and the New Deal were thus concluded as Reagan declared his own "rendezvous with destiny." One of the basic features of the New Deal was its use of a "brain trust" to implement FDR's ideological transformation, and Reagan too attracted a generation of experts from the academy. At a Conservative Political Action Conference in 1985, Reagan claimed that as FDR once had "ideas that were new" and "captured the imagination of the American people," now he (Reagan) led a movement that no longer was "diffuse and scattered" but had its own agenda. "We became the party of the most brilliant and dynamic of young minds; we are "not the defenders of the status quo but creators of the future."

Reagan simply ignored the divisions within the conservative movement. His economic programs broadly paralleled those of the libertarians (tax cuts, deregulation of industry). But he also spoke forcefully on policies recommended by the neo-conservatives (prayer in schools, opposition to abortion, criticism of affirmative action, crime issues) especially through the appointment of federal judges sympathetic to these viewpoints. One of the reasons both camps tolerated one another is that each largely accepted Reagan's analysis of the Cold War. While anti-communist views are standard for any American politician, Reagan's were noticeably more pronounced than any since the early days of the Cold War, especially after the policy of detente initiated in the Nixon administration. Both kinds of conservatives concluded that they had finally found a like-minded president. In his first term Reagan referred to the Soviet Union as the "focus of evil in the modern world," whose leaders felt they had the right to "lie, cheat and steal." He felt that Soviet conspiracy "underlies all the unrest that is going on." If it were not for them, "there wouldn't be any hot spots in the world."

A divisive issue among conservatives in the 1950s involved whether American policy should focus on containment only or on the liberation of nations from communist control. Reagan's policies shattered this disagreement. In addition to an arms build-up, the Reagan doctrine committed America's military and intelligence forces to supporting anti-communist guerilla forces worldwide; and the president announced his support for the Strategic Defense Initiative (SDI), which would in theory make nuclear weapons dropped on America "impotent and obsolete."

The abrupt end of the cold war, symbolically epitomized by the fall of the Berlin Wall in 1989, was greeted by conservatives as confirmation of Reagan's foreign policy and, indirectly, of his economic programs. In fact, Francis Fukuyama, a State Department official, wrote a widely discussed article in 1989 ("The End of History?"), asserting that the collapse of communism was evidence of the global superiority of both Western democracy and capitalism. He suggested that this form of government may represent the "end point of mankind's ideological evolution" and the "final form of human government" and thus constituted an "end to history." Unlike Kennan's "The Sources of Soviet Conduct," however, Fukuyama's essay did not produce a foreign policy consensus. While some conservatives acknowledged his analysis as proof of America's historic mission in the world, others demurred. Some argued that the linear view of history and the apparent optimism in Fukuyama's essay were not conservative ideas at all.

A split emerged between conservative "internationalists" who believed in continuing American commitments until a "new world order" was completely in place, and others who argued that a more cautious approach, even a version of isolationism, was more appropriate to conservatism now that communism was defeated. Christopher Layne, for example, who anticipated this debate in 1986 in his "The Real Conservative Agenda," charged that the Reagan administration was in "some Spielbergian time warp that has transported them back to the early 1950s." They forget, according to Layne, that the "real conservative agenda" lies in "rediscovering their intellectual antecedents" before the Cold War.

SUMMARY AND COMMENT

Daniel Bell described the generation that spanned the 1930s through the 1950s as "twice born" (*The End of Ideology*, 1960). Those who began their political lives in the 1930s were filled with faith and hope. World War II and the Cold War created a political thought that "finds its wisdom in pessimism, evil, tragedy and despair." A careful analysis of Cold War political theory does indeed reveal a sense of the limits of politics as well as an almost Augustinian perspective on the frailty of all human endeavor.

George Kennan was scrupulous in his attempt to outline a rational foreign policy in the face of a democracy's tendencies to react in terms of appeasement or war. James Burnham's ideological disappointments in the 1930s led him to conceive of all politics, domestic and international, in terms of brute power. Whittaker Chambers was a disillusioned man who expressed his weariness with the faiths of his time in his various conceptions of witness. Hannah Arendt was horrified by the crimes of her age. Sidney Hook's disillusionment with radicalism informed his position on freedom of speech.

But these cold warriors, despite their sense of tragedy and professed realism, wrote in an apocalyptic vein that was readily absorbable into American political culture. Kennan, Burnham, Chambers, Arendt, and Hook, even in their political second birth, spoke in a language of final victory of good over evil. It is difficult to judge the Cold War theorists on this point. The outcome of their radical hopes was so mangled and so horrific that one can hardly blame them for attempts to eradicate an evil for which many of them felt directly or indirectly responsible.

The failure of the cold warriors as political theorists, however, rests with their inability or unwillingness to convey their own sense of humility and tragedy to Americans at large. While American political debate has always been circumscribed by its own special history, the period between 1948 and the early 1960s was one in which political conversation was largely absent. When it did reemerge with the debate over the war in Vietnam, all the discussants seemed to suffer from a generation of relative silence. Discourse seemed to be as agitated and insensitive to criticism as that held during the height of the Cold War. There are, however, lessons from America's experience with empire that still need to be examined (ones that Mills and Marcuse raised in theoretical form): Can a republic undertake the responsibilities of world empire and still remain domestically a free and open society? Do worldwide commitments that involve treating others as subjects in important ways limit the moral significance of American citizenship? The end of the Cold War places these questions in even starker form, since the United States at the moment is the only superpower left standing. Rome dealt with such questions centuries ago, and Americans need to confront similar dilemmas today.

☆ *Bibliographic Essay*

Political theorists have expended great effort to assess the impact of various international systems on the internal actions of states. Perhaps the first and most impressive of these attempts is Thucydides' *Peloponnesian Wars*, which chronicles the changes in Athens' political culture as a result of international conflict. Also see Polybius's *Histories* as an interpretation of the Pax Romana. Both works are available in several translations. Contemporary theories of international systems include Richard N. Rosecrance, *Action and Reaction in World Politics* (Boston: Little, Brown, 1963); Hans J. Morganthau, *Politics among Nations* (New York: Alfred A. Knopf, 1985); and Morton S. Kaplan, *System and Process in International Relations,* 6th ed. (New York: John Wiley & Sons, 1957). Ernest Haas's *Tangle of Hopes* (Englewood Cliffs, NJ: Prentice-Hall, 1969) is recommended as an attempt to place American foreign policy in the context of an evolving bipolar system.

There are numerous narratives of the origin and progress of the Cold War. The following are especially helpful in their exploration of its theoretical aspects: Thomas G. Paterson, *On Every Front* (New York: W.W. Norton, 1979); John G. Stoessinger, *Crusaders and Pragmatics* (New York: W.W. Norton, 1979); John Lewis Gaddis, *Strategies of Containment* (New York: Oxford University Press, 1982); Ralph B. Levering, *The Cold War, 1945–1987* (Arlington Heights, IL: Harlan Davidson, 1988). For accounts that influenced or were influenced by the New Left, see Gar Alperovitz, *Atomic Diplomacy* (New York: Simon & Schuster, 1965); William Appleman Williams, *The Tragedy of American Diplomacy* (New York, 1962); Gabriel Kolko, *The Politics of War* (New York: Random House, 1968). Robert Tucker offers a rebuttal to revisionist histories of the Cold War in *The Radical Left and American Foreign Policy* (Baltimore: Johns Hopkins University Press, 1971). There are also several outstanding interpretations of American politics in the 1950s and 1960s with an emphasis on theoretical debates in the period. See William L. O'Neill, *American High* (New York: Free Press, 1986); John Patrick Diggins, *The Proud Decades* (New York: W.W. Norton, 1989); Richard H. Pells, *The Liberal Mind in a Conservative Age* (New York: Harper & Row, 1985).

George Kennan provides a background to his Mr. X article in his *Memoirs* (Boston: Little, Brown, 1967). David Mayer's interpretive biography, *George Kennan and the Dilemmas of Foreign Policy* (New York: Oxford University Press, 1988), is especially useful as an attempt to place Kennan's work in the American political tradition as well as for including a discussion of Kennan's unpublished response to Walter Lippmann's critique, *The Cold War* (New York: Harper & Brothers, 1947). Several writers have provided an assessment of the cold warriors and their radical past. Most notable is John Patrick Diggins, *Up from Communism* (New York: Harper & Row, 1975), which includes detailed analyses of Burnham as well as of Max Eastman, John Dos Passos, and Will Herberg. Also see George H. Nash, who celebrates the conservatism of former radicals in *The Conservative Intellectual Movement in America Since 1945* (New York: Basic Books, 1976), and William O'Neill, *A Better World* (New York: Simon & Schuster, 1982), who defends the centrality of anticommunism in their political thought. Alan M. Wald offers a Left critique in *The New York Intellectuals* (Chapel Hill: University of North Carolina Press, 1987). Chambers's *Witness* has had numerous critics, but perhaps the most acerbic analysis is Meyer A. Zelig's *Friendship and*

Fratricide (New York: Viking Press, 1967), which offers a psychoanalytic interpretation of Chambers's political thought. A recent, more sympathetic biography which includes evaluation of post-Cold War evidence is Sam Tannenhaus' *Whittaker Chambers* (New York: Random House, 1997). Crucial to an appreciation of Chambers is the collection of his letters to William F. Buckley, Jr., *Odyssey of a Friend* (Washington, DC: Regnery, 1987).

For criticisms and elaborations of Arendt and her treatment of totalitarianism, see Carl J. Friedrich et al., *Totalitarianism in Perspective: Three Views* (New York: Praeger, 1969), especially the essay by Benjamin Barber; Carl J. Friedrich, *Totalitarianism* (New York: Grosset & Dunlap, 1954); Margaret Canovan, *The Political Thought of Hannah Arendt* (New York: Harcourt Brace Jovanovich, 1974). Elizabeth Levy-Bruehl's biography, *For Love of the World* (New Haven: Yale University Press, 1982), attempts to alter Arendt's conservative American reputation by placing her thought in a European context. Arendt's interpretation of totalitarianism needs to be understood in terms of her larger political thought, which offers a unique perspective on modern politics. See especially her *The Human Condition* (Chicago: University of Chicago Press, 1958). Sidney Hook's political thought, developed as it was through two crises in American society (the Depression and the Cold War), badly needs a balanced general treatment. See Christopher Phelps' *Young Sidney Hook: Marxist and Pragmatist* (Ithaca, NY: Cornell University Press, 1997) for a biographical account of his early career. For examples of his attempts to justify the suppression of Communist party activity, see "Does the Smith Act Threaten Our Civil Liberties?," *Commentary* (1953); "Liberalism and the Law," *Commentary* (1957); "Academic Freedom and Communism," *New York Times Magazine*, February 27, 1949. Also see his retrospective on these positions in his memoirs, *Out of Step* (New York: Harper & Row, 1987). For a different view of the impact of limitations on freedom of speech and association, see David Caute, *The Great Fear* (New York: Simon & Schuster, 1978), and Ellen W. Schrecker, *No Ivory Tower* (Amherst: University of Massachusetts Press, 1986). Assessments of McCarthyism stressing its populist aspects include Leslie Fiedler, *An End to Innocence* (Boston: Beacon Press, 1955), and Daniel Bell, ed., *The New American Right* (New York: Criterion Books, 1955). Also see C. Vann Woodward's defense of populism in the face of its appropriation by anti-McCarthyites: "The Populist Heritage and the Intellectual," *American Scholar* 29 (Winter 1959–60).

C. W. Mills's political theory set off a major debate within American political science. See William E. Connolly, *Political Science and Ideology* (New York: Atherton, 1967), for a helpful review of the nature of the discussion within an academic discipline. Irving Louis Horowitz provides an assessment of Mills in *C. Wright Mills: An American Utopian* (New York: Free Press, 1983). Full understanding of Marcuse's own political project requires an appreciation of his attempt to synthesize Marx and Freud. See his *Eros and Civilization* (1950). Paul A. Robinson's *The Freudian Left* (New York: Harper & Row, 1969), pp. 147-244, is a useful review of Marcuse on this point. Also see Martin Jay's *The Dialectical Imagination* (Boston: Little, Brown, 1969). For analyses of the development of the New Left critique of the Cold War, Kirkpatrick Sales's *SDS* (New York: Vintage, 1973) is still unexcelled. For reprints of the New Left documents, see Mitchell Cohen and Dennis Hale, *The New Student Left* (Boston: Beacon Press, 1967), particularly the essays by Carl Oglesby and Paul Booth; and Priscilla Long, ed., *The New Left* (Boston: Beacon Press, 1969). *Weatherman* (Berkeley: Ramparts Press, 1970), edited by Harold Jacobs, contains important documents of a portion of SDS that formed into a terrorist organization. Irving Howe's collection, *Beyond the New Left* (New York: Horizon Press, 1970), contains important Old Left criticisms and evaluations. Two recent memoirs, Todd Gitlin's *The Sixties* (New York: Bantam Books, 1987) and Tom Hayden's *Reunion* (New York: Random House, 1988), contain background to the Port Huron Statement and reassessments of the Cold War critique by major New Left activists. Perhaps the most theoretically informed as well as the most balanced assessment of the New Left is James Miller's *"Democracy Is in the Streets": From Port Huron to the Siege of Chicago* (New York: Simon & Schuster, 1987). David Caute places student protest in international perspective in *The Year of the Barricades: A Journey through 1968* (New York: Harper & Row, 1988).

The nature and extent of the "Reagan Revolution" is much debated. Martin Anderson's *Revolution* (New York: Harcourt, Brace Jovanovich, 1988) is an able account by a former advisor. For a more critical assessment that attempts to measure the Reagan rhetoric to reality, see Michael Schaller, *Reckoning with Reagan* (New York: Oxford University Press, 1992). Eric J. Schmertz, Natalie Datlof and Alexej Ugrinsky present extensive evaluations by both academic and political actors based upon the Hofstra University Conference on the Reagan Presidency: *Ronald Reagan's America*, 2 vols. (Westport, CT: Greenwood Press, 1997). Especially useful are works that attempt to examine Reagan's role as "Great Communicator." See Gary Wills, *Reagan's America* (Baltimore: Penguin, 1988) and Paul D. Erickson, *Reagan Speaks* (New York: New York University Press, 1985). Reagan's unique background has inspired many to base their analysis of the Reagan revolution on the influence of Hollywood. Michael Paul Rogin, *Ronald Reagan, the Movie: And Other Episodes in Political Demonology* (Berkeley: University of California Press, 1987) considers the influence of the American cinema on Reagan's political outlook; Alan Nadel, *Flatlining on the Field of Dreams: Cultural Narratives in the Films of President Reagan's America* (New Brunswick, NJ: Rutgers University Press, 1997), argues that Hollywood confirmed the Reagan outlook in films ranging from *Wall Street* to *The Little Mermaid*.

Frank S. Meyer attempted to merge both forms of conservatism, which he called his "fusionist" project, throughout his life. His anthology, *What is Conservatism?* (New York: Holt, Rinehart, Winston, 1964) attempted to identify strains in the movement and locate points of agreement among conservatives. Mark Rozell and James F. Pontuso have edited a helpful volume which highlights the contributions of both traditional and libertarian political theorists including Friedman and Kristol. *American Conservative Opinion Leaders* (Boulder: Westview Press, 1990). David J. Hoeveler, *Watch on the Right: Conservative Intellectuals in the Reagan Era* (Madison: University of Wisconsin Press, 1991) is particularly astute in tracing the origins of conservative positions. Cecil V. Crabb, Jr. et. al., identify six post-Cold War foreign policy orientations and their premises in "Charting a New Diplomatic Course: Alternative Approaches to Post-Cold War Foreign Policy," *Miller Center Journal* IV (Spring, 1997), pp. 55–81. Francis Fukuyama presents a more nuanced version of his "end of history" thesis that highlights his conservative anchors in his *The End of History and the Last Man* (New York: Free Press, 1992). Timothy Burns collects conservative criticisms in *After History?* (Lanham, MD: Rowman Littlefield, 1994). The volume also includes an illuminating defense by Fukuyama.

☆ *Major Works*

1947	"The Sources of Soviet Power," George Kennan
1941	*The Managerial Revolution*, James Burnham
1943	*The Machiavellians*, James Burnham
1964	*The Suicide of the West*, James Burnham
1952	*Witness*, Whittaker Chambers
1951	*The Origins of Totalitarianism*, Hannah Arendt
1949	*Academic Freedom and Communism*, Sidney Hook
1951	*White Collar*, C. Wright Mills
1959	*The Power Elite*, C. Wright Mills
1960	*The End of Ideology*, Daniel Bell
1962	*"The Port Huron Statement," Tom Hayden
1962	*Capitalism and Freedom*, Milton Friedman
1964	*One Dimensional Man*, C. Wright Mills
1964	"Address on Behalf of Senator Goldwater," Ronald Reagan
1978	"When Virtue Loses All Her Loveliness," Irving Kristol
1989	"The End of History?," Francis Fukuyama

*A collaborative effort

Discrimination

INTRODUCTION

The persistence of systematic discrimination of groups of people does not, of course, constitute a single identifiable crisis in American political culture and thought, but rather a continuing problem that arises periodically as an emergency. For example, racial discrimination, the most egregious form of prejudice in this country, contributed to the outbreak of the Civil War. As we saw, efforts to remedy the status of African Americans led to another crisis in the 1870s as Congress attempted to "reconstruct" the South.

In the 1950s and 1960s protests against discrimination on the part of African Americans and resistance on the part of many white Americans formed the basis for another crisis that some writers called the *second reconstruction*. The spark that initiated the modern civil rights movement is generally traced to the refusal of Rosa Parks, a worker for the National Association for the Advancement of Colored People (NAACP), to move to the "colored" section of a Montgomery, Alabama bus in 1955. A boycott of public transportation was soon organized to protest the racial segregation of public municipal facilities. A leader in this project was the Reverend Martin Luther King, Jr., a young pastor of a Baptist church in the city. King formed a new organization, the Southern Christian Leadership Conference (SCLC), to protest segregation through the South. A year later a similar boycott was launched in Tallahassee, Florida. In 1960 a new strategy of protest was initiated by college students in North Carolina when they engaged in a sit-in in a restaurant when the owner refused to serve them. Sit-ins began in cities and towns throughout both the South and the North. The Supreme Court had declared segregated public school systems unconstitutional in 1954, but southern resistance to integrated education was so adamant that there were several national crises. In 1957, President Dwight D. Eisenhower reluctantly sent federal troops to Little Rock, Arkansas, when Governor Orville Faubus refused to obey a court order. (Subsequently Faubus closed all the high schools in the state rather than accept racial integration.) In 1962 President John F. Kennedy sent federal marshals to escort James Meredith, a black man who wished to register as a student at the University of Mississippi.

As the civil rights movement gained momentum throughout the South, white resistance became more and more violent. Protesters were beaten by angry mobs. Churches and schools were bombed. In Birmingham, Alabama, local police used fire hoses and dogs to disperse protesters. Medgar Evers, a black civil rights worker, was assassinated, as was Viola Luizzo, a white civil rights volunteer. The bodies of three missing northern civil rights workers (James Chancy, Michael Schwerner, and Andrew Goodman) were discovered by agents of the Federal Bureau of Investigation (FBI) after a massive search in Oxford, Mississippi. Civil rights leaders throughout the South, King preeminent among them, were committed to nonviolence both in principle and as a tactic. But as the conflict escalated other leaders began to evaluate this policy. Robert F. Williams, head of a local NAACP chapter in Monroe, North Carolina, organized members into rifle clubs and claimed the right of self-defense in the event of attack. New groups such as the Black Panthers and the Nation of Islam questioned the utility of nonviolence as well as the value of integration. Riots broke out in northern cities.

Despite the massive and embittered resistance of white Southerners, school integration proceeded; segregation of transportation, beaches, and restaurants was ended; and the Civil Rights Acts of 1964 and 1965 guaranteed voting rights for African Americans. The crisis subsided although many aspects of racial discrimination were left unresolved.

Another movement of protest indirectly related to the civil rights movement emerged in the 1960s. American women began to question their economic and political position in society. This protest against gender discrimination arose from two different sources. By the late 1960s New Left activists had spent nearly a generation protesting racial discrimination and the war in Vietnam. At several SDS conventions women members attempted to include issues of importance to women on the agenda only to be ignored (and sometimes ridiculed) by male radicals. Women began organizing in separate caucuses. In 1967 (the same year whites were expelled from many civil rights organizations), radical women began to form independent groups in cities throughout the country. This new generation of feminists had not only already been radicalized in general but had also attained considerable political and organizational skills from their activities in the student movement. The rise in membership in these women's groups paralleled the decline in New Left organizations. In 1970 there were reported to be about 300 members in women's groups; three years later the estimate was several thousand. In general, the primary early function of these small groups was to identify common problems facing all women, such as abortion, rape, limited economic opportunities, and child care.

Another group of activists emerged independent of the efforts of radical women to engage in what they called *consciousness-raising*. President Kennedy had established the President's Commission on the Status of Women in 1961. A 1963 report of the commission entitled *American Women* documented the limited rights of women both in law and informal practice. Politically active women, although more conventional in ideology than the SDS activists, supported the commission's recommendation that women's commissions be established in each state to examine patterns of gender discrimination with the goal of proposing remedial legislation. In 1964, largely because of the efforts of Michigan Representative Martha Griffiths, gender was added to Title VII of the Civil Rights Act prohibiting employment discrimination. The government agency responsible for enforcing this position, the Equal Employment Opportunity Commission (EEOC), was limited in its power and noticeably reluctant to treat this provision seriously. (The director insisted that "men were entitled to female secretaries.") Various newly organized feminist groups focused upon lobbying to expand the EEOC's authority.

By the early 1970s the various strands of the women's rights movement began to organize into national groups. The most successful in this regard was the National Organization for Women (NOW), which grew from 1,000 members in 1967 to over 40,000 in 1974. Numerous significant pieces of legislation were passed as a result of feminist protest, including Title IX of the Educational Amendments Act of 1972, which barred gender discrimination in federally aided education programs and the introduction of a tax credit for child care in the Revenue Act of 1972. Feminist groups, however, were unsuccessful in obtaining state ratification of an equal rights amendment to the Constitution that would have declared "equality of rights . . . on account of sex."

These two movements of protest against discrimination possess a number of common features in addition to overlapping personnel and chronological proximity. One way to assess the political thought that emerged from both movements is to examine similar problems any group confronts when it attempts to remove patterns of discrimination. Systematic discrimination has, of course, existed throughout history in many different societies. The structures of discrimination in general can be quite severe, as happens under slavery or in cases of genocide. Often these structures may exhibit more subtle permutations. Moreover, there are differences that arise when discrimination is based on ethnicity, religion, race, or gender. The kind of political system also influences the nature of discrimination. Under a dictatorship a group may be uniformly and rigorously oppressed. On the other hand, in a society like the United States, where political authority is decentralized and important distinctions are made between activities considered private and those regarded as public, private discrimination can be difficult to eradicate. The whole question becomes even more politically difficult to resolve when the discriminated group represents a minority of the population.

Keeping these variations in mind, we still find it possible to outline general structures of systematic discrimination that confront any protest ideology. First, a discriminated group is denied access to the decision-making structures of the political system. The most direct form of this aspect of repression involves the outright denial of citizenship. As congressional reconstructionists learned in the 1870s and civil rights activists learned in the 1960s, the denial of citizenship can take more indirect forms; these may include economic constraints (the poll tax) and eligibility standards for voting that are enforced in a discriminatory manner (literacy tests). Economic opportunity is also severely circumscribed in any discriminatory system. Generally, positions requiring skills that are not easily transferable and that carry higher status and compensation are not available to oppressed groups. For example, in 1950 in the American South there were fourteen medical schools open to whites, but none to African Americans; there were sixteen law schools for whites, but none for African Americans; there were fifteen engineering schools for whites, but none for African Americans; and there were five dentistry schools for whites, but none for African Americans.

In any discriminatory system, especially in a democratic society, discrimination must be "popular" in order to continue. One practice designed to ensure cultural support for repression involves the creation of *badges of inferiority* for discriminated groups. In the exemplary case of modern discrimination, the German Nazis required Jews to wear Stars of David on their clothing to visibly mark them off from the rest of the population. The Jim Crow system in the American South, with its daily humiliations, was another effort to attach a stigma to a discriminated group. In fact, the Supreme Court prominently featured this effect when it overturned the *separate but equal doctrine* in its 1954 decision. Finally, no discriminatory system is without a practice of terror, sometimes official but often unofficial, to ensure compliance. Violence and threats of violence are designed to prevent public protest. For most of American history, African-American activists and theorists have focused on this feature of oppression and attempted to gain legislative protection, such as anti-lynching laws. Feminist theorists have examined this aspect of gender discrimination; some of them have argued that both rape and the promotion of pornography are informal practices whose function is to keep women "in their place."

It becomes, then, a central task of political theorists protesting a discriminatory system to chronicle its four pillars: the denial of political rights, the denial of economic opportunity, stigmatic practices, and the use of terror. Then the theorists need to make a case that establishes the fact that the inferior position of the group under scrutiny is the result of these factors and not due to a lack of talent or initiative. Much of the efforts of the political theorists we shall review shortly have been devoted to this task.

But there are other even more difficult challenges to political theorists. One way to analyze these challenges is to study the strategic alternatives available to a discriminated group in terms of dichotomous pairs. One pair involves a decision as to whether the most productive avenue for change should be conciliatory and gradual or confrontational and militant. *Gradualist theorists* emphasize the need for a slow and systematic removal of discriminatory practices. This strategy seeks to gain the cooperation of the majority on which progress ultimately depends; it also seeks to ensure that the members of the discriminated group are capable of effectively utilizing their newly won freedoms. *Militant theorists*, on the other hand, argue that rapid change must be the central goal not only because justice demands it but because historical opportunities for change are rare and must be seized when they appear. Militants may advocate violence, including revolution; or they may promote less drastic means of confrontation such as civil disobedience.

Another alternative involves a decision as to whether the discriminated group should seek assimilation with its former oppressors or attempt to develop alternative practices that may lead to political, economic, or cultural independence. *Assimilationists* argue that the best protection against continued and future discrimination is to identify with the basic goals and political symbols of the majority and emphasize the essential similarities between discriminators and discriminated once the oppressive system has been dismantled. *Separatists*, on the other hand, argue that group autonomy is essential to removing discrimination because the solidarity of the oppressed group will disintegrate unless the differences between the two groups are cultivated.

These dichotomies contain many variations. Thus protest movements often lose their sense of cohesion once the discriminatory system has been identified and the critique is partially accepted by those who have supported the status quo, since these questions are so debatable. At a relatively simple level, theorists can be separatist-gradualists, separatist-militants, assimilationist-gradualists, or assimilationist-militants. Let us look at African-American and feminist political thought in terms of these differing positions. We will focus primarily on this period of our history for purposes of comparison. We will also present some analysis of earlier thinkers.

BLACK PROTEST

Systems of discrimination may produce periodic crises through society as a whole, but resistance is historically an ongoing process. Thus the alternatives of separatism and assimilation and of gradualism and militancy have been debated throughout American history. The debates are never exactly the same since history does not precisely repeat itself, but they do show remarkably similar patterns. A good example of an earlier debate that was influential among civil rights activists and theorists was the exchange between Booker T. Washington and W. E. B. Du Bois at the turn of the century. Although not always seen in this light, Washington was a separatist-gradualist; Du Bois was an assimilationist-gradualist.

Washington's career and political theory were forged in a period that represented a low point in terms of American willingness to evaluate racial discrimination. At the turn of the century, the Reconstruction was generally acknowledged to be a misguided and failed experiment. The grip of the Jim Crow system in the South grew tighter and tighter, and by 1895 the disenfranchisement of blacks in the South was complete. State legislatures spent two times more per pupil on white students than on African-American students. In 1892 the number of lynchings of African Americans in the South reached its peak at 162. Between 1893 and 1904 the number never went under 100. Moreover, the dominant ideology of social Darwinism was not a hospitable belief system for collective action on the part of discriminated groups.

Born a slave on a Virginia plantation, Washington graduated from Hampton Normal and Industrial Institute in 1875. Ten years later the first class was graduated from Tuskegee Normal School (later renamed Tuskegee Institute), an institution founded by Washington. In 1900 he published his autobiography, *Up from Slavery,* which summarized not only his own life but also his approach to racial discrimination in general. The autobiography is a deceptively complex work; in essence it outlined Washington's overall political thought, which he had expressed in countless speeches to his students as well as to white and black audiences around the country. One way to approach Washington's work is to analyze his position in two parts: the message delivered to white audiences and the one delivered to black audiences. To whites, Washington proposed in broad outlines a racial social contract. The address, in fact, became known as the "Atlanta Compromise." Blacks would abandon the struggle against segregation as well as delay demands for civil rights. "In all things social," he told the audience at his famous Atlanta Exposition Address in 1895, "we can be as separate as the fingers." In return, whites must adopt a laissez-faire, race-neutral approach to African-American economic aspirations. One-third of the southern population were African Americans; if southern whites gave blacks "a man's chance," both races would prosper in the region. Washington used the story of a ship lost at sea whose crew sighted a friendly vessel and cried, "Water! water; we die of thirst! " At which the captain of the other ship replied: "Cast down your bucket where you are!" To white southerners, the Tuskegee president repeated "what I say to my own race": "'Cast down your bucket where you are.' Cast it down among the eight millions of Negroes whose habits you know, whose fidelity and love you have tested. . . . Cast down your bucket among these people who have, without strikes and labour wars, tilled your fields, cleared your forests, builded your railroads and cities. . . ."

The message to whites in the Atlanta Exposition Address, which was reprinted verbatim in *Up from Slavery*, was as follows: Extend Algerism to black Americans! But black Americans could also read another message in the same text, for Washington was also challenging his white audience to a Darwinist competition on racial terms. Washington believed that one of the consequences of slavery was that work was denigrated by both races. The slave justly loathed work because he was robbed of its fruits. But the slave-owner and his sons "had mastered no special industry" because they were so reliant on the labor of others. Washington believed that if free blacks grasped the limited opportunities for economic independence they would outperform whites. At Tuskegee every student was required to learn a trade, preferably one that could be exercised independently. (In this respect Washington's rule is much like the conclusion reached by Jean Jacques Rousseau in *Émile* that the best occupation for an independent person is carpentry.) From Washington's perspective, at some point in the future whites would be forced to acknowledge the excellence of African-American labor; civil rights would then follow as a matter of course.

Booker T. Washington's general position was a separatist one. It was a separatism derived at least in part from prudence but also one that appealed to African-American pride and racial economic independence. W. E. B. Du Bois, a Harvard graduate, challenged Washington's position in a collection of essays, *The Souls of Black Folk*. Du Bois would change his viewpoints many times in his long life and later adopt his own version of separatism, but his debate with Washington in 1903 was based on a gradualist-integrationist position.

Du Bois gave Washington credit for the "enthusiasm, unlimited energy, and perfect faith" he put into his program. Du Bois contended, however, that what began as a "by-path" had become a "veritable Way of Life." The Atlanta Compromise had gained the sympathy of some white Southerners and the support of northern philanthropists and some politicians. But the success of the "Tuskegee machine" had also severely limited debate among African Americans. Washington's dominance has led "some of the best critics to unfortunate silence and paralysis of effort, and others to burst into speech so passionately and intemperately as to lose listeners."

Du Bois was intent upon reopening the debate. He argued that the popularity of the Atlanta Compromise rested in large part upon a conclusion reached by whites that "if that is all you and your race ask, take it." Reviewing the history of black protest in America from slave revolts to the activities of northern freemen to protests against the abandonment of Reconstruction, Du Bois concluded that the thought of men such as James Forten, Frederick Douglass, and others was characterized by a spirit of "self-assertion." They kept their eyes on the goal of "ultimate freedom and assimilation" despite the fact that "schemes of migration and colonization arose among them," and despite counsels of submission urging blacks to give up their voting rights. In fact, argued Du Bois, "in other periods of intensified prejudice all the Negroes' tendency to self-assertion had been called forth. . . . In the history of all other races and peoples the doctrine preached at such crises has been that manly self-respect is worth more than land and houses. . . ."

To Du Bois, Washington's political thought was riddled with paradoxes. While Washington called for African Americans to become artisans and property owners as a road to self-respect, it was "utterly impossible" for workingmen and property owners "to defend their rights and exist without the right of suffrage." Washington called for thrift and dedication to economic success but, according to Du Bois, Washington "counsels a silent submission to civic inferiority such as is bound to sap the manhood of any race in the long run." Washington called for common schools and industrial and craft training for blacks, but "neither the Negro common schools, nor Tuskegee itself, could remain open for a day were it not for teachers trained in Negro colleges, or trained by their graduates."

In place of Washington's program, Du Bois urged a comprehensive protest against discrimination. The Niagara Convention of 1905, of which Du Bois was a leading figure, committed itself to a struggle for full "manhood suffrage," "abolition of all caste distinctions based simply on race and color," "recognition of the highest and best human training as the monopoly of no class or race," and "recognition of the principle of human brotherhood as a practical present creed." While at this point in his life rejecting Washington's separatism, Du Bois largely accepted gradualism as a means for implementing assimilation. He also rejected the political thought and action of Denmark Vesey and Nat Turner as models because they represented "the attitude of revolt and revenge." He wrote that it was the "duty of black men to judge the South discriminately." "The present generation of

Southerners," Du Bois felt, "are not responsible for the past, and they should not be blindly hated or blamed." He asserted that African Americans "do not expect that the free right to vote, to enjoy civic rights, and to be educated, will come in a moment [and] disappear at the blast of a trumpet." Perhaps the proposal in this period with which Du Bois is more frequently associated was his emphasis on the *talented tenth*. In every race, argued Du Bois, there is a minority whose abilities and determination to excel outstrip others. A generation of college-educated African Americans could lead their brothers to full civil, social, and economic rights. According to psychiatrist and social theorist Alvin F. Poissaint, Du Bois believed many of the assumptions of social Darwinism that Washington did, but Du Bois interpreted them differently. Du Bois's education "set him at a great distance from the average black American of his time." He felt an exhilaration and freedom that was derived from his education. For example, Du Bois once wrote: "I sit with Shakespeare and he winces not. Across the color line I move arm and arm with Balzac and Dumas. . . . I summon Aristotle and Aurelius at will, and they come all graciously with no scorn nor condescension." The talented tenth would also share in this liberation. Poissaint added that Du Bois expected the talented tenth of whites to respond by righting the wrongs of discrimination.

In his analysis of Du Bois's early political thought, Poissaint concluded that the African-American people of the 1960s had learned that the basic assumptions espoused in *The Souls of Black Folk* were wrong:

> It was not simply a matter of presenting their misery in an objectively palatable fashion. The goodwill of the white man went so far as to partly acknowledge his guilt. It was therefore left again to the black people to go a step further and force him to act upon that guilt.

The debate over the racial discriminatory system in the 1960s reflects this rejection of gradualism. It articulated strategies of militancy derived in part from a belief that it was largely futile to chronicle the unfairness of racism and establish the existence and potential of African-American talent. The debate in this period between Martin Luther King, Jr., and Malcolm X— although usually interpreted as a debate in which the principles of nonviolence were attacked or defended—was foremost a debate over assimilation, separatism, and the most effective form of militancy.

King's extraordinary talents as an political leader have regrettably led to a failure to fully appreciate the depth and complexity of his political thought. As a student at Crozier Theological Seminary and Boston University, King had studied both Christian theology and political thought. In the summer of 1949 he divided his energies between preaching at his father's church and studying Marx and Hegel. King rejected Marxism but was impressed with the dialectical method and the emphasis Marx placed on the role of force and violence. If there is a single modern work that influenced King most, however, it was Reinhold Niebuhr's *Moral Man and Immoral Society* (1932). Niebuhr's book, written in the depths of the Depression, stressed "predatory self interest" as the basic cause of injustice in the world. For Niebuhr felt that both advocates of the Social Gospel and secular liberalism had ignored this point. Human beings, especially those in groups, would behave no more fairly because they were educated or socialized to express goodwill. Niebuhr rejected Marxism as a viable alternative; instead, he urged political action based upon standards of justice hardened by a militant confrontation with evil. According to Taylor Branch, a recent King biographer, when the young graduate student read the book in 1950, this position "pushed a number of buttons." Niebuhr wrote *Moral Man and Immoral Society* in response to his assessment of economic injustice in the 1930s. King, who also granted the influence of Mahatma Gandhi and Count Leo Tolstoy on nonviolence and of Henry David Thoreau on civil disobedience, proceeded to develop a political philosophy of protest against racial discrimination on the basis of Christian realism.

No single speech or book of King's better explains his attempt to find a morally acceptable form of protest that still recognized the role of predatory self-interest in the world than his "Letter from Birmingham Jail." Although the Letter has already become a classic of American political thought, the circumstances surrounding its writing were hardly auspicious. The civil rights campaign in Birmingham was faltering; moderate newspaper editors questioned the wisdom of protest; and President Kennedy had sent word that he would do little to help. What angered King most, however, was a statement by the white clergy of Birmingham urging the abandonment of the protest as "unwise and untimely" and arguing that the demonstrations incited "hatred and violence, however technically peaceful these actions may be. . . ." Just months earlier King had expressed his frustration with the reluctance of many churches to fully support the civil rights movement. He quoted St. Augustine's statement that "those who sit at rest while others take pains" are buying "their quiet with disgrace." King accused the churches of what Niebuhr called "the sin of triviality." The statement of the white clergy drove King to such anger that he began writing a reply on margins of the newspaper that carried the report. The scribbles were smuggled out of the jail and typed; copies were then smuggled back into the jail.

The essay is in the form of a letter to the Birmingham clergy. Each of the criticisms of the ministers—the wisdom of the tactics of direct action, their timeliness, and the question of "outside agitators"—is taken up by King and defended through application of the philosophy of Christian realism. Why did King come to this city? Why indeed, asks King, did St. Paul leave his village of Tarsus? King was in Birmingham because injustice was here and he had been asked to aid the oppressed. Moreover, "injustice any-where is a threat to justice everywhere." Christians were "caught in an ines-capable network of mutuality, tied to a single garment of destiny." King expands his argument by applying St. Augustine's distinction between the City of God and the City of Man to the crisis in Birmingham. For Augustine, the former represented the community of fellow Christians who had for-saken self-interest for love of God. But Augustine maintained that no matter how dedicated a Christian community was, the frailty of human nature required acceptance of the fact that the church would also contain charac-teristics of the City of Man. The "visible church" was destined to be a flawed community containing individuals who still pursued self-interest. True and false Christians would be sorted out at the Second Coming of Christ. King suggests that the organized churches today (the "visible church" in Augustine's terminology) had nearly abandoned the sense of selflessness and justice that characterized the City of God: "So often the contemporary church is a weak, ineffectual voice with an uncertain sound. So often it is an archdefender of the status quo." King argued that he must therefore direct his faith to the "inner spiritual church, the church within a church, as the true *ekklesia* and the hope of the world."

To the timeliness objection, King states his commitment to militancy: "[W]ait! It rings in the ear of every Negro with a piercing familiarity. This 'Wait' has almost always meant 'Never.'" To the question of the appropriate-ness of direct action to protest discrimination, even if such action breaks the law, King applies Niebuhr's formulation. "It is," he asserts,

> an historical fact that privileged groups seldom give up their privileges
> voluntarily. Individuals may see the moral light and voluntarily give
> up their unjust posture; but, as Reinhold Niebuhr has reminded us,
> groups tend to be more immoral than individuals.

King then proceeds to defend nonviolent civil disobedience as the most moral alternative possible in a situation in which force and violence are imminent. The African American, with so many pent-up resentments and latent frustrations, must have a "creative outlet" or else the anger will be released violently. Nonviolent direct action also forces the majority to con-front the issue of injustice. Simple remonstrances will not force those in power to respond, but a purposefully constructed crisis might. The larger purpose of direct action is to convert the tension brought to the surface in both communities, white and black, into a dialogue and a negotiation. For too long, concludes King, has "our beloved Southland been bogged down in a tragic effort to live in monologue rather than dialogue."

King's final point is an attempt to show that civil disobedience is not an anarchical doctrine that will disintegrate into a definition of justice as the interest of the strongest. Rather, it is a doctrine that has moral parameters which all Americans, indeed all participants in the Western political tradition, can readily recognize. There are just and unjust laws. Quoting St. Thomas Aquinas, King defines just laws as those which are rooted in natural law. "Any law," he continues, "that uplifts the human personality is just. Any law that degrades human personality is unjust." Segregation is a consummate example of an unjust law because it "gives the segregator a false sense of superiority and the segregated a false sense of inferiority." Segregation is not only politically, sociologically, and economically unsound, it is "morally wrong and sinful." Segregation in its separation of person from person actually mirrors sin itself, since the actions of the sinner represent an estrangement from God.

King lists example after example of the morality of refusing to obey unjust laws: the refusal of Shadrach, Meshach, and Abednego to obey the laws of Nebuchadnezzar; the refusal of the early Christians in Rome to forsake their religion; Socrates' refusal to stop teaching; and the Boston Tea Party. To assure that breaking laws does not lead to anarchy, King insists that the action must be undertaken "openly, lovingly, and with a willingness to accept the penalty." Thus King justifies restricted direct action— *civil disobedience* (a nonviolent protest in which participants accept legal penalties)—as an appropriate tactic both to force self-interested elites to negotiate and to assure that protesters recognize the seriousness of their actions.

King's militant assimilationist position was dependent upon both a Christian and a republican community of belief in America derived from the Western tradition of political thought. He argued that victory over segregation would be achieved in Birmingham and all over the nation because "the goal of America is freedom." Both "the sacred heritage of our nation" and the eternal will of God are embodied in our echoing demands. The "I Have a Dream" speech, delivered at the Lincoln Memorial during the 1963 March on Washington, combines a religious conception of liberation derived from the Hebrew prophets and Christian laments with a political understanding of America as the land of free citizens. But for many African-American protesters in the 1960s, King's approach was seen as utopian. What if there is no redeeming moral authority in the Judeo-Christian tradition? What if republican thought has no other function than to legitimatize the power of a white majority?

At various periods in American history a militant separatism has attracted some African Americans. Marcus Garvey's Universal Negro Improvement Association, Timothy Drew's Moorish Science movement, and Alfred Sims's Back to Africa movement represented versions of separatism that advocated racial cultural autonomy and/or migration to Africa. In the 1960s the Nation of Islam, a movement that had been in existence since the 1930s, enjoyed a rapid expansion of membership. Black Muslims faced a formidable recruitment obstacle through most of their history. Rejection of the goals of assimilation was not a new feature of African-American protest, but the Nation of Islam's rejection of Christianity in favor of Islam challenged the African American's historical religious commitments. In the turmoil of the 1960s, however, many African Americans were prepared to reexamine their entire cultural heritage. The Nation of Islam claimed that Christianity was a white man's religion, and they urged both cultural and economic separatism. In an address in 1960 Elijah Muhammad, the leader of the Nation of Islam, went further:

> The best thing the white man can do is give us justice and stop giving us hell. I'm asking for justice. If they won't give us justice, then let us separate ourselves from them and live in four or five states in America, or leave the country altogether.

The Nation of Islam had a highly visible but small membership, and it operated largely outside the civil rights movement. But various civil rights organizations also began to explore the alternative of militant separatism. The leadership of the Student Nonviolent Coordinating Committee (SNCC) and the Congress of Racial Equality (CORE) declared their sympathy for violent responses to racial discrimination and questioned the goal of racial integration. SNCC leaders Stokely Carmichael and H. Rap Brown explored the political implications of *black power*. Malcolm X, a leader in the Nation of Islam, undertook the difficult theoretical task of converting the religious nationalism of his organization into new political forms.

Once both Christian and republican thought had been rejected by these protest leaders, there existed a theoretical vacuum in terms of political expression. The concept of conversion to Islam, which is primarily a Third World religion, provided some support. Malcolm X and a number of thinkers who followed him searched for new philosophical exemplars to express their militant separatism. The leaders of newly independent African nations offered some assistance. For example, Kwame Nkrumah, the first president of Ghana, elucidated a conception of tribal democracy based upon African traditions. This view attracted a number of adherents in America. When SNCC leaders visited African nations, they found, in the words of James Forman, "no sheriffs to dread, no Klan breathing down your neck, no climate of constant repression." Pan-Africanism—that is, the cultural and political identification with the independent African nations—eventually led to the adoption of a new *back to Africa* migratory agenda on the part of such protesters as Carmichael.

Other activists, however, saw the successful political struggles in Africa in terms of a broader political theory. Frantz Fanon and C. L. R. James were two writers influential in developing this new version of militant separatism. Fanon, born in Martinique, was a French-educated psychiatrist active the National Liberation Front (FLN), an Algerian revolutionary independence movement. While dying of leukemia in a hospital, he wrote *The Wretched of the Earth* (1961), a passionate indictment of colonialism as a system that reduces human beings to objects. On this point Fanon's description of colonial rule is much like that of Hannah Arendt. Fanon argued that the Algerian middle class had been hopelessly coopted by Western culture. He then identified a social class Marx had dismissed as the *Lumpenproletariat* as the only agent of revolution. Only people made superfluous by imperialism, such as the displaced and unemployed former peasants living in urban centers, had the capacity to negate Western domination. Here Fanon's analysis departs from Arendt's. For Arendt had argued that the "masses" created by colonialism and the transformation of traditional society were the shock troops of totalitarian movements. Fanon, on the other hand, saw this grouping as a source for "positive and creative qualities." The most daring portion of Fanon's analysis was his justification of violence as a good in itself. Many revolutionaries excused violence as a necessary means to overthrow an entrenched order. Fanon contended, however, that violence was a "cleansing force" that "frees the native from his inferiority complex and his despair and inaction; it makes him fearless and restores his self-respect."

The Wretched of the Earth provided protesters with a model suggesting an integration of cultural and political separatism. Many separatist movements in American history had emphasized the need for racial pride independent of white approval. Both the Moorish Temple movement and the Nation of Islam instituted a practice of changing existing names for new ones in order to foster an independent black identity. Fanon applied this desire for racial dignity to the dilemma of the colonized African. As Allen J. Matusow argues in his history of the period (*The Unravelling of America*, 1984), "it was a simple . . . step for American nationalists to argue that ghettoes were analogous to colonies and could be liberated the same way. Thus did *The Wretched of the Earth* provide militants with an apologia for the ghetto riots."

C. L. R. James's writings were an important attempt to revise Marxist theory by taking into account the predominance of race in the politics of an advanced society. This was particularly the case in America. James was truly an international intellectual. Born in the West Indies, he resided at various times in London, New York, Detroit, and Trinidad. He was the author of the definitive book on cricket and of a provocative interpretation of Herman Melville's *Moby Dick*. Most of James's political work is inaccessible, since it is written in the hermetic intellectual language characteristic of radical sectarian conflicts among radical international leftists. But *The Black Jacobins* (1938), an account of the Haitian revolution in the late eighteenth century, is a classic work of historical narrative and political theory that spoke to a later generation of American militant separatists. The French colonial domination of Haiti had been particularly brutal. Nine out of ten inhabitants were slaves on plantations that produced indigo and sugar. James did not interpret the revolution as a minor incident that grew out of the ideology of the French Revolution or as a consequence of an overextended Napoleonic Empire. Instead, he viewed it as a new world historical event. Though admitting that the Haitian revolution had failed (Toussaint-Louverture, its leader, was captured by the French), James saw the conflict as the beginning of an international revolutionary struggle. Racial conflict would play a dominant role in this struggle, which would occur at the periphery of various European colonial empires. James's small group of radicals, which was centered in Detroit in the 1960s, encouraged the formation of revolutionary organizations among African-American workers in the auto industry. This activity was based on the belief that blacks possessed the potential to become a revolutionary vanguard in America.

Malcolm X explored these features of a new kind of political thought. According to this theory, African Americans were seen as a colony within America, and the world was thought to be on the brink of an international anticolonial revolt in which racial violence would play a central role. "Message to the Grass Roots," a speech Malcolm X delivered in Detroit in 1963, is an example of this effort. He ridiculed both the goals of integration and nonviolence: "There is no such thing as a nonviolent revolution," he told his audience. Advocates of integration missed the whole point of revolution: "Revolution is based on land. Land is the basis of all independence. Land is the basis of freedom, justice, and equality." The evocation of the symbols of the American Revolution is a common practice of protesters. Malcolm X cited the American Revolution, but he used it in order to establish the point that the use of organized violence in every great revolution has been to secure national independence:

> When you want a nation, that's called nationalism. When the white man became involved in a revolution in this country against England, what was it for? He wanted this land so he could set up another white nation. That's white nationalism.

Malcolm X's identification of the agent for change clearly owed much to Fanon. Although Malcolm X never advocated a therapeutic justification for violence (generally preferring to interpret violence in terms of self-defense), he offered as the basis of his analysis the distinction between the house slave and the field slave in terms of their respective militancy. The former, though oppressed, received enough benefits from the system to identify with his master and, according to Malcolm X, to remain on the plantation after the Civil War. In this analysis the modern equivalent to the house slave is the integrationist. The field slave, on the other hand, said only, "Let's separate. Let's run." For Malcolm X, the descendants of the field slaves represented the mass of American blacks.

Malcolm X was vague about the specific political objectives of his militant separatism. In the Grass Roots speech he seemed to accept James's conclusion. The black revolution was "world-wide in scope and nature"; hence, the revolutionary resistance of African Americans must be seen as part of an international movement, one in which presumably the American political system itself would be overthrown. Sometimes he spoke as if black power was a means by which African Americans could simply defend themselves both culturally and economically from definition by the white majority. In "The Ballot or the Bullet" (1964), he argued for the formation of a black nationalist political party as an alternative to revolution if circumstances permitted. In one of his last speeches before his assassination ("To Mississippi Youth"), Malcolm X seemed to be moving away from separationism, though not away from a militant position.

African-American political thinkers have continued to explore the liabilities and advantages of separatism and integration, although with a sense of pessimism that was largely absent in the civil rights movement. One prominent example is the work of Derrick Bell, a law professor. Bell employs hypothetical case studies, often derived from science fiction, to examine race relations in America. One such effort is "The Space Traders" (1990). Bell imagines America in the year 2000 beset by trade deficits and ecological disasters. A spaceship arrives and its crew proposes a business deal to the president of the United States. The aliens will solve all of America's debt and environmental problems with their advanced technologies if he delivers every single African American to their spaceship on January 17 (Martin Luther King's birthday). The space traders never disclose where the African Americans will be taken or what fate is in store for them. The president accepts the proposal without much hesitation and while there is a national debate, twenty million African Americans—men, women and children—are delivered to the space traders at the designated time. Bell offers no explicit commentary on his scenario, although his own opinion is reflected by the last lines of the essay:

> The inductees looked fearfully behind them. But, on the dunes above the beaches, guns at the ready, stood U.S. guards. There is no escape, no alternative. Heads bowed, arms now linked by slender chains, black people left the New World as their forebears had arrived.

The "Space Traders" is a powerful thought experiment that explores how welcome are African Americans in America, despite centuries of attempts to integrate. In "The Afrolantica Awakening" (1992), Bell examines a different kind of exodus. Here the fabled island of Atlantis arises from the Atlantic nine hundred miles from South Carolina. While exploration is attempted, it is soon discovered that only black people can live in the atmosphere over the island. There is an attempt to emigrate that creates a great national debate. Some African Americans point to leaders like Marcus Garvey for support, while others cite Frederick Douglass who said, "We are Americans. We are not aliens. We are a component part of the nation" in opposition. Just when an Afrolantica Armada of a thousand ships containing the first wave of settlers readies to leave on July 4, however, the island sinks back to the sea. Bell concludes this essay more optimistically. Despite the initial disappointment, the debate itself had been "a liberation—not of place, but of mind":

> Blacks held fast, like a talisman, the quiet conviction that Afrolantica had not been mere mirage—that somewhere in the word *America*, somewhere irrevocable and profound, there is as well the word *Afrolantica*.

In "The Afrolantica Awakening" black Americans do not give up on America and in the end reject separatism, at least in its most obvious form of emigration. Though it is not clear what is the position of other Americans on integration, this quest by African Americans for freedom is meant to parallel that of all Americans.

FEMINIST PROTEST

Feminist political thought has followed the same general patterns of assimilationism, separatism, gradualism, and militancy as African-American protest, but there are important historical differences. The political debate over African-American suffrage was formally resolved in 1870 with the passage of the Fifteenth Amendment. Of course, that closure was an extremely fragile one, because black electoral power only came into existence in the late 1960s. In contrast, women's suffrage and the theoretical debates it occasioned were not settled until 1920. Moreover, while the legal status of women was weak in several states in regard to the ownership of property and the right to independently enter into contracts, their status did not approach the formal rank of chattel slavery. These differences are reflected to some extent in the respective approaches to gradualism versus militancy. In African-American political thought, the selection of the methods to remove discrimination—whether the theorist is an assimilationist or a separatist—has tended to revolve around strategy and tactics: Must demands be met gradually or immediately, whether through nonviolence or revolution? While there have been important differences among feminists over the question of direct action and its nature, the theoretical cleavages have centered more upon the extent to which major institutions in society, such as the family, need to be changed in order to eliminate discrimination against women.

We can illustrate one historical version of this aspect of the debate by analyzing the agendas of two feminists in the Progressive Era: Jane Addams and Charlotte Perkins Gilman. Addams tended to espouse a moderate version of separatism, while Perkins was a militant assimilationist. Although their differences were not focused upon the tactics necessary to achieve female equality (both women were fundamentally committed to long-term electoral reform), Gilman's theories required a much more radical change in existing institutions than did those of Addams.

In an essay entitled "Why Women Should Vote" (1910), Jane Addams justifies the extension of the suffrage on the grounds that women's primary social role as mothers can no longer be adequately performed in the absence of political participation. According to Addams, a "woman's place is within the walls of her home," and it is "impossible to imagine the time when her duty there shall be ended or to forecast any social change which shall release her from that paramount obligation." But the most scrupulous housekeeping in an urban setting cannot guarantee a safe environment. The mother's

> basement will not be dry, her stairways will not be fireproof, her house will not be provided with sufficient windows to give light and air, nor will it be equipped with sanitary plumbing, unless the Public Works Department sends inspectors who constantly insist that these elementary deficiencies be provided.

Nor could women be responsible for securing untainted meat and milk for their children, for keeping their children from "vicious influences on the street," or for assuring their education, without legislation.

Nestled beneath Addams's analysis is the assumption that men cannot be trusted to provide for the defense of the family in the public sphere. But she did not raise the issue of what later feminists would call *patriarchal domination*. Instead, she advocated the right to vote for women as a means by which they could protect the home under modern conditions. In order to "bring cultural forces to bear upon a materialistic civilization" and to carry on "her memorial duties," each woman must have the ballot. Addams also did not dwell upon the question of whether women's responsibility for child rearing was the result of a political or a biological imperative. In general, she seemed to regard motherhood as a moral duty of her gender. For example, in *The Long Road of Woman's Memory* (1916), she defended women's historical acceptance of the responsibility for the protection of such social structures as the family. "Undoubtedly" in the past "women were told that the interest of the tribe, the diminishing food supply, the honor of the chieftain, demanded that they leave their particular caves and go out in the wind and weather without regard to the survival of their children." But, according to Addams,

> at the present moment the very names of the tribes and of the honors and the glories which they sought are forgotten, while the basic fact that mothers held the lives of their children above all else, insisted upon staying where the children had a chance to live, and cultivate the earth for food, laid the foundations for an ordered society.

While Charlotte Perkins Gilman was just as committed to securing the ballot as Addams, Gilman found a different lesson in the historical role of women. Her autobiographical short story, "The Yellow Wallpaper," has become a classic of American feminist protest. In this account Gilman describes a young woman so confined by the roles of wife and mother that her very personality disintegrates. In *Women and Economics* (1898) and *The Home* (1903), she traces the source of female personal discontent to the family itself. Addams regarded the ancient burden of motherhood as a moral obligation that must be combined with political participation in the new industrial society. Like many Progressive Era reformers, Gilman was taken with the theory of evolution if not with the social Darwinist interpretation. Nevertheless, she treated the family as a biological anachronism. The "sentimental" attachment to the home on the part of women was the result of an outmoded "sexual contract" (bodily submission to men in return for protection) and religion (placation of "household gods" as necessary for survival). The "modern" home must be socialized in much the same way as water and sewage treatment have become collective commodities. Gilman spoke of the irrationality of cooking for a few people when food could now be supplied by professional caterers and consumed in cafeterias. Children would be much better served if they were raised by "a good trained nurse" than by the happenstance of their biological mothers. It must be noted, however, that while Gilman argued for the socialization of individual family functions, she was no socialist. According to her theory, when freed from family responsibilities women would be able to reach the "higher plane" of evolution by entering the world of productive work and contributing to the "world's wealth."

Addams then seemed to accept a traditional role for women while arguing for their political rights. She justified both positions through the separatist argument that women were destined to represent "naturally cooperative forces" in society. Gilman not only advocated the ballot for women but also pursued an assimilationist position, contending that the family had to be drastically reorganized so that women could truly become "public persons." In the 1960s the Gilman position was redefined, and more radical interpretations of Addams's separatism were explored.

A newly stated version of Gilman's argument appeared in Betty Friedan's *The Feminine Mystique* (1963), which immediately became a work of popular political theory. Friedan, a frequent writer for *Redbook* and *Ladies Home Journal*, used the breezy writing style of a mass magazine to offer a critique of popular culture and its treatment and definition of women. The book is a product of popular culture that criticizes popular culture in order to create a new popular culture. The analysis falls into two basic parts: (1) a narration of the impact of the modern media, including advertising, upon women's consciousness and (2) an appeal for a new sense of individualism.

Friedan's essay is based in part upon her research on Smith College graduates. (The survey was rejected by both *McCalls* and *Redbook* magazines.) She begins by discussing the problem raised generations earlier by Gilman. Well-educated, economically secure American women are dissatisfied with their lives. This unhappiness is reflected in the sexual dysfunction, neuroses, ennui, and unfocused anger reported by American women. Friedan calls this "the problem that has no name" and traces the origin of this general frustration to the role of the housewife. Why then (and this is a central question that every reformer or radical asks) have the majority of women of all social classes chosen or acquiesced to such a stultifying role? Friedan replies that all the great socialization structures of modern society (the advertising, educational, and psychiatric establishments) have devoted their considerable powers of persuasion to convince women that housewifery is a natural and desirable role for all women.

Friedan's depiction of the persuasive powers of the organized agencies of public opinion in a modern democracy owes much to Cold War critics like C. Wright Mills and Herbert Marcuse. Yet she is noticeably vague as to the origins of the attempt to keep women in the home. She hints that corporate America concluded at the end of World War II that high levels of domestic consumption required the formation of a buying unit, the family, to purchase products. In one moment of theoretical discovery, Friedan suggests that "the subversion of women's lives in America to the ends of business" almost automatically has led to the "subversion of the sciences of human behavior to the business of deluding women about their real needs." In other words, the perceived demands of American business in modern society are almost automatically given legitimacy and definition by the academic community. As both Mill and Marcuse argued, the academy (despite its rhetoric of scientific objectivity and independence) has become subservient to the imperatives of a power elite whose authority depends on the Cold War. Friedan intimates that all the elite structures of modern society have limited alternatives for women.

The Feminine Mystique is, then, a call for opening a debate on the role of women in American society—a debate that had been closed for the postwar generation. Friedan is particularly adept at describing the ways in which the languages of advertising, marketing, and educational theory have closed that debate. For example, she cites an advertising memo that states that the purchase of new products in food preparation or house cleaning can be justified (that is, sold) on the basis that consumption is a creative act:

> Creativeness is the modern woman's dialectical answer to the problem of her changed position in the household. Thesis: I'm a housewife. Antithesis: I hate drudgery. Synthesis: I'm creative! . . .

"Every effort," the memo states, "should be made to sell X Mix, as a base upon which the woman's creative effort is used."

But despite providing impressive evidence of what could be called a totalitarian onslaught on the self-definition of women by modern corporate America, Friedan's theoretical explanations for this domination are slack. The failure to provide a systemic cause for the postwar focus of the mass media, however, is more than compensated for by Friedan's presentation of the second part of her critique. In essence, what she says is that whatever the source of women's oppression may be, the evidence is clear that American women are not happy. They can become happy, however, through their pursuit of what is the strongest symbol of American political culture: individualism.

Friedan contends that creative individualism can only be expressed naturally in the professional world of the marketplace—a world previously reserved for men. Family life has led to a "forfeited self" that produces passive and undirected children and spousal conflict. Only through the full pursuit of a career can a woman find release for her repressed energies. Friedan argues that the role of a "balanced homemaker" is inadequate; it is the result of a woman's reluctance to give up her identity as an "amateur" in the marketplace for the complete identity of the "professional." She calls upon women to reject the "feminine mystique" that women's destiny lies in child rearing and to formulate a "life plan" that will meet their "full human capacities," which can only be met outside the family.

The success of Friedan's analysis is the result of her ability to formulate her protest in the context of American political culture. Implicitly she argues that the American woman's role is the result of acquiescence to corporate definitions of women. Since she is vague about the causes of this massive public-relations effort to define women as wives and homemakers, her analysis seems to suggest that a simple act of will on the part of American women could redefine their identities. After all, the women Friedan interviewed (largely upper-middle-class Americans) were among the most educated and talented people in the nation. Why could they not redirect their potential?

Some feminists complained that the influence of *The Feminine Mystique* rested upon the power of Algerism in American political culture. Thus Jean Bethke Elshtain (*Public Man, Private Woman*, 1981) writes that "her [Friedan's] book is a paean of praise to what Americans themselves call the 'rat race'; she just wants to join it." Other critics questioned different aspects of her critique. Friedan herself rarely traced the source of the "problem that has no name" to men, nor did she attack the family itself as an obstacle to female self-fulfillment. Thus many feminist critics argued that *The Feminine Mystique*, for all its insight, failed to identify the real causes of female oppression and was insufficiently assimilationist in its conception.

Friedan came from the more traditional wing of the feminist movement. But an important basis of feminist theory originated in organizations of radical protest against the Cold War. When women in the war protest movement began to direct their attention to gender discrimination, they were not only theoretically adept as a result of their attempts to locate the ideological causes of the war in Vietnam, they were also politically radical. Anchoring the elimination of gender discrimination onto the tenets of American political culture had little attraction. Radical feminists sought more sweeping explanations for gender discrimination.

Shulamith Firestone, a Students for a Democratic Society (SDS) member in the 1960s and founder of one of the many feminist groups that emerged from the movement, wrote a book in 1970 that attempted to place gender discrimination in a wider perspective than Friedan had done and offered a much more radical solution. *The Dialectic of Sex* caustically reviews the commitment to gradualism in the history of the female protest thought and organization in America. According to Firestone, the National Organization of Women (NOW) concentrates only on the "more superficial symptoms of sexism—legal inequities, employment discrimination and the like." Firestone is sympathetic to the radical wing of the civil rights movement and frequently compares the structure of racial discrimination to gender discrimination. But she also argues that the revolutionary potential of radical feminism is far greater than any other protest movement:

> [U]nlike minority groups (a historical accident), or the proletariat (an economic development), women have always made up an oppressed majority class (51 percent), spread evenly throughout all other classes.

Moreover, the nature of women's oppression, reaching as it does into sexual relationships and child rearing, centers upon the very emotional and economic center of organized society. The feminist movement, according to Firestone, is the first protest movement to combine effectively the "personal" with the "political"; hence, it "will crack through the most basic structure of society."

Firestone attempts to show the unique potential of feminism by show-ing that even Marxist analysis, the most revolutionary political theory in modernity, is insufficiently radical in its concept of human liberation. Friedrich Engels, Marx's collaborator, outlined what became the standard Communist theory on the woman question in *The Origin of the Family, Pri-vate Property and the State* (1884). He argued that gender discrimination did not exist in human societies until new forms of economic organization, such as farming and the domestication of animals, created an economic surplus. Men might have been hunters and women berry gatherers, but food was communally shared. This rudimentary division of labor was therefore classless. Once subsistence became an obsolete economic goal, the question arose as to who would benefit from the additional wealth. Engels contended that since the transmission of property was determined through the female line, inheritance continued to remain the communal property of the tribe. But with the new accumulation of goods, men asserted their new economic power by establishing paternal inheritance. For Engels this change represented the "world historical defeat of the female sex":

> The man took command of the home also; the woman was degraded and reduced to servitude; she became the slave of lust and a mere in-strument for the production of children.

Although Engels's theory was based on doubtful anthropology, it served the larger Marxian project well, since the family was interpreted as an economic structure that changed form according to economic develop-ment. It would automatically disappear under communism when equality reigned. Thus, according to Engels, gender discrimination was a form of class discrimination, and the former would disappear when the latter was overcome. Firestone challenged this thesis. Gender discrimination did not begin with the domestication of animals, agriculture, and the formation of surplus wealth. It occurred, she maintained, in the very first division of labor, which was sexually based. Simply put, gender discrimination is the result of the fact that women bear children.

Firestone relentlessly pursues the implications of her thesis:

> So that just as to assure elimination of economic classes requires the revolt of the underclass (the proletariat) and, in a temporary dictator-ship, their seizure of the means of production, so to assure the elimi-nation of sexual classes requires the revolt of the underclass (women) and the seizure of control of the ownership of their own bodies.

She has much more in mind than the legalization of abortion. A minimal demand necessary for the end of gender discrimination is the "freeing of women from the tyranny of their biology." Only *in vitro* reproduction (test-tube babies) can liberate women from the "barbaric" nature of pregnancy. Firestone regards child-care centers as an "effort to buy women off." Instead, she recommends the replacement of biological families by contractual households consisting of ten adults and a regulated percentage of children, which would be voluntarily formed. Its residents would be legally bound for a period of seven to ten years.

The Dialectic of Sex has been criticized from many perspectives. Josephine Donovan (*Feminist Theory*, 1985) contends that its reliance upon technology is not part of the "humanist prospect" and questions whether children will not suffer from new forms of exploitation in Firestone's utopian households. Jean Bethke Elshtain (*Public Man, Private Woman*, 1981) sees in Firestone's attempt to overcome gender discrimination the advocation of a dehumanized humanity in which "abstract Man, Woman, and Child engage in a hard-edged pursuit of the best deal."

Firestone's approach is one of militant androgyny. Friedan argued for an androgynous marketplace. Firestone argues that discrimination can only be overcome when gender is removed from all psychological and cultural meaning. Other feminists, however, have devoted considerable theoretical energy to exploring the opposite approach. Just as African-American nationalism was presented as an alternative to integration, sexual autonomy was presented as an alternative to androgyny. Much like some African-American protest thinkers reviewing their history in search of a culture independent of white oppression, some women writers attempted to discover the existence of a feminine essence separate from male domination. Some feminist works in this vein exhibit a theoretical justification of hatred of men (as many of Malcolm X's earlier speeches espoused a hatred of whites). For example, Ti-Grace Atkinson, in "Theories of Radical Feminism" (1970), contended that patriarchy was a part of the nature of men. Males "must (they have no choice about it) alleviate their frustration through the oppression of others." Betsy Warrior ("Man as an Obsolete Life Form," 1969) described men as a pseudospecies that has reached an evolutionary cul-de-sac:

> He is an anachronism in this technological context. His muscles are no longer needed. The built-in obsolescence of his physical and emotional nature is now spent. The aggressive, destructive drives of man lack proper reasonable outlets. He is being phased out by technology. Sperm banks and test-tube babies can take over his last function, the only function that has positive effects for the human race.

Susan Brownmiller (*Against Our Will*, 1975) argued that the persistence of rape in human history can be explained in large part because men have the "biological capacity to rape" and a natural lust for power.

Some feminists defined separatism in terms of the creation of independent institutions for women (credit unions, women's shelters, rape counseling and self-defense centers). Others have pursued the separatist perspective to reevaluate various social practices. For example, it had become a standard position of modern liberalism to defend sexually explicit movies and reading matter as a question of free speech. By way of contrast, writers like Catharine A. MacKinnon, Andrea Dworkin, and Susan Griffin have argued that pornography represents a systematic assault on women's identity as human beings and is not deserving of legal protection. In this perspective, pornography is the theory, and rape and physical abuse are the practice of male domination. Other feminists came to the conclusion that a lesbian life-style is the only acceptable implementation of separatism. For instance, Mary Daly (*Gyn/Ecology*, 1979) reviews the designations men had assigned to independent women throughout history: *hags, spinsters, crones,* and *witches*. She contends then that the true meaning of being a woman is not yet clear and that her "Be-ing" only now is in the process of "becoming." In the meantime, any woman who does not become a lesbian halts this project since she is still a "heterosexualist" and "male defined."

One recent work which attempts both to assay the contemporary feminist movement as well as to defend an assimilationist position is Susan Faludi's *Backlash* (1991). She contends that just as "Reaganism shifted political discourse far to the right and demonized liberalism," so too has there been a *backlash* designed to convince the American public that "women's 'liberation' was the contemporary American scourge—the source of an endless laundry list of personal, social and economic problems." Drawing upon the works of feminist historians, Faludi contends that the backlash has been such a recurrent feature of American feminism that it can be characterized as a movement that proceeds historically with a "halting gait." After women won the right to vote, feminism was portrayed as outdated and mistakenly radical. Charlotte Perkins Gilman had difficulty getting her work published; Jane Addams was "labeled a Communist"; the media maligned suffragists as "career women" who were responsible for divorce and infertility; "'ex-feminists' began issuing confessions." The same pattern emerged again in the 1950s after women returned from the workforce during World War II.

Faludi, who is a reporter for the *Wall Street Journal*, criticizes a number of writers with close ties to the Reagan administration, such as George Gilder and Allan Bloom, whom she identifies as agents of the current backlash. But she also devotes her attention to other feminists whom she feels she also contribute to the climate of criticism. She is particularly concerned about the themes raised in Betty Friedan's 1981 book, *The Second Stage*. Friedan's reevaluation included a concern that the feminist movement had a "blind spot" about the family that produced a "female machismo" type that "undervalued feminine tasks and frills—stops baking cookies altogether, cuts her hair like a monk, decides not to have children, installs a computer in her bedroom." To Faludi, this is precisely the kind of confessional that has characterized other backlash periods. She is very suspicious of Friedan's recent exploration of "women's spheres" which she regards as "a call for a murkily defined new order that is heavy on old Victorian flourishes."

Faludi also is concerned about the impact of Carol Gilligan's *In a Different Voice* (1981), which she regards as "one of the most widely quoted and influential feminist works of the '80s" and "the famous emblem of scholarship on women's 'difference.'" Gilligan argues that men and women employ different styles of moral reasoning. She believes women tend to make moral choices more on the bases of particular situations and out of concern for other individuals than do men. Faludi is concerned not only with the size of Gilligan's sample (she studied twenty-five Harvard undergraduates) but also with the ease with which the scientific stamp of validation of gender differences can be used "on behalf of discriminatory arguments that could cause real harm to women." *Backlash* concludes with an appeal to women to resist the "infiltration" of their thoughts by critics both outside and within the feminist movement and to stand firm in their demands for equality.

SUMMARY AND COMMENT

Theorists of political protest against discrimination almost always are confronted with a difficult dilemma. On the one hand, their demands must be framed in symbols and in a language that is potentially capable of receiving support from the majority or from those holding political power. On the other hand, since the prevailing symbols have been partially responsible for the existence and maintenance of the discriminatory system, the protest theorist faces the prospect of a co-optation by those in power that leaves the system largely intact. Moreover, if a protester concludes that the risk of framing his or her theory in terms of the dominant culture is too great, the option of searching for independent languages and symbols derived from discriminated groups has its own hazards. A complete rejection of the existing political culture can effectively close off debate.

The theorists we have examined, who selected either militancy or moderation, assimilation or separatism, faced this dilemma. By accepting the symbols of Horatio Alger and social Darwinism, had Booker T. Washington shrewdly bidden for time for African Americans to recover a sense of pride and some measure of economic power after the defeat of Reconstruction? Or had he given in to a language that, by assigning success and failure to individual effort, was bound to be used as a justification for discrimination? In focusing upon the talented tenth in pursuit of the goal of assimilation, had Du Bois sacrificed the futures of the mass of African Americans? Or had he offered a strategy that identified a favorable point of convergence between African-American aspirations and Algerism? King combined a carefully circumscribed militancy (nonviolent direct action) with appeals to the Judeo-Christian and republican tenets in the American political tradition. While his protest theory met with general success in the South, were the same methods as useful in the North, where patterns of discrimination were more complex and subtle? Would King's methods work on issues in which there was more ambivalence in American culture, such as those involving economic rights? Without an international revolution by people of color, was Malcolm X's militant separatism a suicidal strategy for American blacks? Or was Malcolm X's formulation a model from which other conceptions of black power could be constructed?

In regard to feminist theory, was Addams's acceptance of the woman's primary role in the family a sensible strategy—one that quieted male fears about the suffrage and even represented a possible new synthesis of the relation between the public and the private roles? Or was Addams's position on the family one that made women's public role one of permanent second-class citizenship, since it was always to be subordinate to her more fundamental domestic obligations? Did Friedan's demand for the abolition of the feminine mystique through entry into the marketplace liberate women or add them to the American "rat race"? Were Gilman's and Firestone's attacks on the family an attempt to place the root cause of gender discrimination on the public agenda? Or were their proposals for collectivization so far from the American consensus on the centrality of family life as to place their efforts beyond effective discussion? Moreover, was there no aspect of womanhood—biological or cultural—that deserved preservation? Do the positions of the militant assimilationists play into the hands of antifeminists and/or contribute to gender discrimination through their stereotypes of men and insistence that there is a biological basis for male and female behavior? Or do the works of Dworkin, Daly, and others serve to focus upon aspects of a permanent antagonism between the sexes that needs to be recognized in public policy on issues such as abortion, rape, and pornography?

These and other difficult questions and debates became even more complex as the more egregious forms of discrimination were removed and, in the late 1970s and 1980s, efforts were made to resolve theoretical problems such as affirmative action and comparable worth in a bureaucratic, judicial, and legislative context. Affirmative action requires public and private institutions to provide goals and timetables for hiring and promoting more minorities and women. Comparable worth advocates the equalization of pay for people in similar positions across the broad spectrum of the professions and other kinds of employment. Are affirmative action and comparable worth justifiable ways to remove discrimination? Some theorists treat these policies as a form of reparations for past injustices; others see them as a realistic version of equality of opportunity for all. Critics, however, contend that both policies perpetuate racial and gender thinking; they are said to benefit individuals who least require the opportunities they provide, or to burden individuals who are least guilty of discrimination.

Whatever the outcome of these debates may be, it is worth noting that America—a society that has largely avoided extended argument over questions of class—has now been forced to confront the questions raised, sometimes in an aura of crisis, by both gender protest and race protest theorists.

☆ *Bibliographic Essay*

The features of discriminatory systems as structures of domination are explored at a basic philosophical level by G. W. F. Hegel in his discussion of *lordship and bondage* in *The Phenomenology of Mind* (1807) and by Friedrich Nietzsche in *On the Genealogy of Morals* (1887). Unlike Hegel, Nietzsche sees resistance to domination as fundamentally a negative theoretical enterprise. Albert Camus (*The Rebel*, 1956) joins the debate by siding with Hegel, but he also gives to resistance a strongly individual interpretation. Also see the works of Michael Foucault (*Madness and Civilization*, 1965, and *The Order of Things*, 1970). Foucault, like Nietzsche, emphasizes the latent irrationality in systems of power but identifies with the oppressed. American political scientists have generally focused upon the dynamics of political protest and its interaction within the restrictions imposed by American political culture. See, for example, William A. Gamson, *The Strategy of Protest* (Homewood, IL: Dorsey Press, 1975); Peter Bachrach and Morton Baratz, *Power and Poverty* (New York: Oxford University Press, 1970); Murray Edelman, *The Symbolic Uses of Politics* (Urbana: University of Illinois Press, 1964) and *Constructing the Political Spectacle* (Chicago: University of Chicago Press, 1988).

For a general account of the position of African Americans at the turn of the century, see J. Saunders Redding, *They Came in Chains* (Philadelphia: J. B. Lippincott, 1950). Booker T. Washington's *Up from Slavery* (1900), which contains the transcript of the Atlanta Exposition Address, is available in a number of editions. Houston A. Baker, Jr., provides an arresting defense of Washington as a master of both white and black discourse in *Modernism and the Harlem Renaissance* (Chicago: University of Chicago Press, 1987), chaps. 3 and 4. For other sympathetic accounts of Washington, see V. S. Naipul, "How the Land Lay," *New Yorker*, June 6, 1988, pp. 94–105; August Meier, *Negro Thought in America, 1880–1915* (Ann Arbor: University of Michigan Press, 1966), chap. 7; Herbert J. Storing, "The School of Slavery: A Reconsideration of Booker T. Washington," in Robert A. Goldwin, ed., *100 Years of Emancipation* (Chicago: Rand McNally, 1963). W. E. B. Du Bois, *The Souls of Black Folk* (New York: New American Library, 1969), contains his critique of Washington's position as well as Alvin F. Poissaint's essay, "The Souls of Black Folk: A Critique." For a full appreciation of Du Bois's contribution to American political thought, see Arnold Rampersad, *The Art and Imagination of W. E. B. Du Bois* (Cambridge: Harvard University Press, 1976), as well as *The Autobiography of W. E. B. Du Bois* (New York: International Publishers, 1968). Albert E. Stone offers an intriguing interpretation of Du Bois by comparing his autobiography to that of Henry Adams, an American who suffered from a very different kind of alienation. See *Autobiographical Occasions and Original Acts* (Philadelphia: University of Pennsylvania Press, 1982), chap. 2.

A complete analysis of the political philosophy of Martin Luther King, Jr., has yet to be written, but biographers have offered intimations. See David J. Garrow, *Bearing the Cross* (New York: Vintage, 1986), and Taylor Branch, *Parting the Waters: America and the King Years, 1951–1963* (New York: Simon & Schuster, 1988). King's own works include *Stride toward Freedom* (New York: Harper & Brothers, 1958), an account of the Montgomery boycott; *Why We Can't Wait* (New York: Harper & Row, 1963), a narrative of the Birmingham campaign; *Where Do We Go from Here?* (New York: Harper & Row, 1967), an evaluation of both black power and white backlash. Aldon D. Morris's *The Origin of the Civil Rights Movement* (New York: Free Press, 1984) is especially helpful in identifying the sources of protest. Also see for an overview of the movement Juan Williams, *Eyes on the Prize* (New York: Viking, 1987). Williams's account is especially recommended because it is a companion volume to a PBS television series; hence, it represents an effort at political education for later generations of Americans, black and white.

The most astute analysis of militant assimilation and separatism in the King years is Harold Cruse's masterpiece, *The Crisis of the Negro Intellectual* (New York: William Morrow, 1967). Cruse's presentation connects the protest ideology of the 1920s and 1930s to the dilemmas faced by radicals in the 1960s. For a forceful theoretical criticism of King's position from the Right, see Herbert J. Storing, "The Case against Civil Disobedience," in Robert A. Goldwin, ed., *On Civil Disobedience* (Chicago: Rand McNally, 1968). For a sympathetic early analysis of the Nation of Islam, see C. Eric Lincoln, *The Black Muslims of America* (Boston: Beacon Press, 1961). Malcolm X's autobiography was both a best seller and an exemplar for African-American radicals. For analyses of *The Autobiography of Malcolm X* (New York: Grove Press, 1965) see A. L. Elmesseri, "Islam as a Pastoral in the Life of Malcolm X," in *Malcolm X: The Man and His Times*, ed. J. H. Clark (New York: Macmillan, 1969); Larry Neal, "And Shine Swan On," in *Black Fire*, ed. Le Roi Jones and Roy Neal (New York: William Morrow, 1968). Philip Abbott, *States of Perfect Freedom* (Amherst: University of Massachusetts Press, 1987), chap. 1, compares the autobiography with Benjamin Franklin's and Abbie Hoffman's. Malcolm X's speeches are essential to an appreciation of his political theory: *Malcolm X Speaks* (New York: Grove Press, 1965) and *By Any Means Necessary* (New York: Pathfinder Press, 1970). For exemplars employed by African American separatists, see Frantz Fanon, *The Wretched of the Earth* (New York: Grove Press, 1961), and C. L. R. James, *The Black Jacobins* (London: Allison and Busby, 1938). Also see the interpretive biographies of both thinkers: David Caute, *Frantz Fanon* (New York: Viking, 1970), and Paul Buhle, *C.L.R. James: Artist as Revolutionary* (London: Verso, 1988). Derrick Bell's essays, "The Space Traders" and "The Afrolantica Awakening," are reprinted in his *Faces at the Bottom of the Well: The Permanence of Racism* (New York: Basic Books, 1992).

The origins of contemporary feminist thought are surveyed by Jo Freeman, *The Politics of Women's Liberation* (New York: David McKay, 1975), and Sara Evans, *Personal Politics* (New York: Vintage, 1980). For analyses of feminist thought on the suffrage question, see William L. O'Neill, *The Rise and Fall of Feminism in America* (Chicago: Quadrangle Books, 1969), and Aileen Kraditor, *The Ideas of the Suffrage Movement* (Garden City, NY: Doubleday, 1971). Also see Mary Jo Buhle's *Women and American Socialism, 1870–1920* (Urbana: University of Illinois Press, 1981). For models of Addams's moderate feminist separatism, see her *The Long Road of Women's Memory* (New York: Macmillan, 1916). Gilman's position is presented in her *The Home* (1903) (Urbana: University of Illinois Press, 1972), *Women and Economics* (1898) (New York: Harper Torchbooks, 1966), and her autobiography, *The Living of Charlotte Perkins Gilman* (New York: Appleton-Century, 1935). Also see Polly Wynn Allen, *Building Domestic Liberty* (Amherst: University of Massachusetts Press, 1988).

Jean Bethke Elshtain's *Public Man, Private Woman* (Princeton: Princeton University Press, 1981), and Josephine Donovan's *Feminist Theory* (New York: Frederick Ungar, 1985) are two important critical analyses of contemporary American feminism containing critiques of Friedan and of Firestone's *The Dialectics of Sex* (New York: William Morrow, 1970). Betty Friedan significantly revises *The Feminine Mystique* (New York: W.W. Norton, 1963) in *The Second Stage* (New York: Summit Books, 1981). Robin Morgan's *Sisterhood Is Powerful* as well as Betty Roszak and Theodore Roszak's *Masculine/Feminine* (New York: Harper & Row, 1969) are important anthologies, since they reprint the manifestos of radical feminist groups of the early 1970s such as SCUM, WITCH, BITCH, and the Redstockings. For contemporary feminist political thought that explores the separatist position, see Mary Daly, *Gyn/Ecology* (Boston: Beacon Press, 1979); Dorothy Dinnerstein, *The Mermaid and the Minotaur* (New York: Harper & Row, 1976); Susan Brownmiller, *Against Our Will* (New York: Simon & Schuster, 1975); Ti-Grace Atkinson, *Amazon Odyssey* (New York: Links, 1974). Andrea Dworkin presents the feminist case against pornography in *Pornography: Men Possessing Women* (New York: Perigan Books, 1981) and *Letters from a War Zone* (London: Secker & Warburg, 1988).

Also see Susan Griffin, *Pornography and Silence* (New York: Harper & Row, 1981).

For critiques of feminist thought, see Midge Decter, *The New Chastity and Other Arguments against Women's Liberation* (New York: Medallion Books, 1972), and Steven Goldberg, *The Inevitability of Patriarchy* (New York: William Morrow, 1974); Phyllis Schlafly, *The Power of the Positive Woman* (New Rochelle, NY: Arlington House, 1977); and Bryce J. Christenson, *Utopia against the Family* (San Francisco: Ignatius Press, 1990). Ironically, these analyses accept versions of the feminist separatist position. For important internal critiques of central aspects of feminism, see Jean Bethke Elshtain, "The Liberal Captivity of Feminism: A Critical Appraisal of (Some) Feminist Answers," in Philip Abbott and Michael Levy, eds., *The Liberal Future in America* (Westport, CT: Greenwood Press, 1985) and bell hooks, *Feminist Theory: From Margin to Center* (Boston: South End Press, 1984).

☆ *Major Works*

1895	"Atlanta Exposition Address," Booker T. Washington
1903	*The Souls of Black Folks*, W. E. B. Du Bois
1935	*Black Reconstruction*, W. E. B. Du Bois
1963	"Letter from Birmingham Jail," Martin Luther King, Jr.
1963	"I Have a Dream Speech," Martin Luther King, Jr.
1963	"Message to the Grass Roots," Malcolm X
1964	"The Ballot or the Bullet," Malcolm X
1910	"Why Women Should Vote," Jane Addams
1916	*The Long Road of Woman's Memory*, Jane Addams
1898	*Women and Economics*, Charlotte Perkins Gilman
1903	*The Home*, Charlotte Perkins Gilman
1963	*The Feminine Mystique*, Betty Friedan
1970	*The Dialectic of Sex*, Shulamith Firestone
1981	*The Second Stage*, Betty Friedan
1990	"The Space Traders," Derrick Bell
1991	*Backlash*, Susan Faludi
1992	"The Afrolantica Awakening," Derrick Bell

Index

"Man as an Obsolete Life Form" (Warrior), 326
Managerial Revolution, The (Burnham), 264–265
Marcuse, Herbert, 279, 284–286, 288, 322
Margin of Hope, A (Howe), 277
Marshall Plan, 274, 283
Marshall, John, 104, 107
Marx, Karl, 49
  Long on, 250
  Marcuse on, 284
  Mumford on, 234
  Russian Revolution and, 46
  Thomas and, 251
Marxism, 211, 238, 239
  agriculture and, 211
  Arendt on, 271, 273
  Burnham on, 264, 265
  Chambers and, 269
  Corey on, 239
  Debs on, 214–215
  feminism and, 324–325
  Firestone and, 325
  Hook and, 276
  James on, 316
  Kennan on Soviet Union, 261
  King on, 311
  Mills on, 280
  Niebuhr on, 238, 312
  Veblen and, 206
Mason, George, 60
Massachusetts Bay Colony, 16–29, 64
Massachusetts Constitution, 74, 78–80, 115
Mather, Increase, 23–24
Matthews, Richard K., 120
Matusow, Allen J., 316
Mayers, David, 263–264
McCarthy, Joseph, 263, 274–275, 278, 291
McCarthyism, 278
McCormick, Richard L., 105, 123, 202
McDonald, Forrest, 52, 74, 85
McKinley, William, 200–201, 217
Means, Gardiner, 233, 251
Meredith, James, 304

Meriwether, Elizabeth Mary, 158
"Message to the Grass Roots" (Malcolm X), 317
Meyers, Marvin, 124
Middletown (Lynd and Lynd), 235–236
Militant androgyny, 326
Militant assimilationism, 314, 320
Militant separatism, 314, 318
Militant theory of change, 307, 311
Mill, John Stuart, 322
Miller, James, 287
Miller, John C., 106
Miller, Perry, 23, 33
Miller, William, 183
Mills, C. Wright, 239, 265, 279–284, 286, 287, 288
Milton, John, 26, 50
Mind of the South, The (Cash), 166
Missouri Compromise of 1820, 162
Mitterand, François, 292
Modern Corporation and Private Property, The (Berle and Means), 233
"Modern Lear, A" (Addams), 204–205
Moley, Raymond, 241
Montesquieu, 50, 51, 90
Moorish Science movement, 314, 316
Moral communitarianism, 149
Moral Man and Immoral Society (Niebuhr), 236–238, 312
Morgan, A. E., 195, 248
Morgan, Edmund S., 24–25, 29
Morganthau, Hans, 286
Mosca, Gaetano, 266
Mugwumps, 201
Muhammad, Elijah, 315
Mumford, Lewis, 234, 235, 253

Narrative of the Life of Frederick Douglass (Douglass), 146
Nation of Islam, 304, 314–316
National Association for the Advancement of Colored People (NAACP), 303
National idea, 131–132
National Organization for Women (NOW), 305, 324

☆☆

About the Author

PHILIP ABBOTT, professor of Political Science at Wayne State University, is the author of *The Shotgun Behind the Door: Liberalism and the Problem of Political Obligation* (1976); *Furious Fancies: American Political Thought in the Post-Liberal Era* (1980); *The Family on Trial: Special Relationships in Modern Political Thought* (1981); *Seeking New Inventions: The Idea of Community in America* (1987); *States of Perfect Freedom: Autobiography and American Political Thought* (1987); *The Exemplary Presidency: FDR and the American Political Tradition* (1991); *Leftward Ho!: V. F. Calverton and American Radicalism* (1993) and *Strong Presidents: A Theory of Leadership* (1996). Professor Abbott is the author of two anthologies and has published articles in *Political Theory, Review of Politics, Journal of Politics, Political Research Quarterly, Studies in American Political Development , Presidential Studies Quarterly* and other journals. A graduate of American University, he earned his Ph.D. in Political Science at Rutgers University and has been awarded grants and fellowships from the National Endowment for the Humanities, the Ford Foundation, the Earhart Foundation, and the American Philosophical Society. At Wayne State University, where Abbott teaches courses in Political Theory and American Political Culture, he has received the President's Award for Excellence in Teaching, the Charles Gershenson Faculty Fellowship. the Distinguished Graduate Professor Award and the Michigan Association of Governing Boards' Higher Education Award. Professor Abbott held the Thomas Jefferson Chair in American Studies at the University of Amsterdam in 1997.